STRUCTURE AND STRUCTURAL CHANGE IN THE BRAZILIAN ECONOMY

T0347359

Structure and Structural Change in the Brazilian Economy

Edited by

JOAQUIM J.M. GUILHOTO
University of São Paulo and Iniversity of Illinois

GEOFFREY J.D. HEWINGS
University of Illinois

Routledge
Taylor & Francis Group

LONDON AND NEW YORK

First published 2001 by Ashgate Publishing

Reissued 2018 by Routledge
2 Park Square, Milton Park, Abingdon, Oxon OX14 4RN
711 Third Avenue, New York, NY 10017, USA

Routledge is an imprint of the Taylor & Francis Group, an informa business

Publisher's Note
The publisher has gone to great lengths to ensure the quality of this reprint but points out that some imperfections in the original copies may be apparent.

Disclaimer
The publisher has made every effort to trace copyright holders and welcomes correspondence from those they have been unable to contact.

A Library of Congress record exists under LC control number: 00134808

ISBN 13: 978-1-138-71279-9 (hbk)
ISBN 13: 978-1-138-71277-5 (pbk)
ISBN 13: 978-1-315-19907-8 (ebk)

Contents

List of Contributors

CLÓVIS OLIVEIRA DE ALMEIDA
EMBRAPA, Cassava and Tropical Fruit Crops, Rua Embrapa, s/n, CP.007
Cruz das Almas, BA 44380-000, BRAZIL
Phone: (+55 +75) 721-2120; Fax: (+55 +75) 721-2149
calmeida@cnpmf.embrapa.br

CARLOS R. AZZONI
FIPE, University of São Paulo, and Regional Economics Applications Laboratory, University of Illinois, Urbana, USA; FIPE – USP, Av. Prof. Luciano Gualberto, 908, Caixa Postal:11.474, São Paulo, SP 05508-900 BRAZIL
Phone: (+ 55 +11) 818-5870; Fax: (+55 +11) 813-4743
cazzoni@usp.br

CARLOS JOSÉ CAETANO BACHA
University of São Paul, DEAS – ESALQ – USP, Av. Pádua Dias, 11 – C.P. 9, Piracicaba, SP 13418-900, BRAZIL
Phone: (+55 +19) 429-4119; Fax: (+55 +19) 434-5186
cjcbacha@carpa.ciagri.usp.br

WERNER BAER
Department of Economics, University of Illinois, 218 David Kinley Hall, 1407 W. Gregory Drive, Urbana, IL 61801, U.S.A.
Phone: (+1 +217) 333-8388; Fax: (+1 +217) 244-8537
w-baer@uiuc.edu

FLÁVIA MARIA DE MELLO BLISKA
ITAL, CTC – Centro de Tecnologia de Carnes, Av. Brasil, 2880, Caixa Postal 139, Campinas, SP 13073-001, BRAZIL
Phone: (+55 +19) 241-5222 – Ext. 153; Fax: (+55 +19) 242-1246
bliska@ital.org.br

FRANCISCO C. CROCOMO
Universidade Metodista de Piracicaba, UNIMEP, Faculdade de Gestão e Negócios, Rodovia do Açúcar, km 156 - Campus Taquaral, Piracicaba, SP 13400-91, BRAZIL
Phone:(+55 +19) 430-1570
francisco.crocomo@merconet.com.br

JOAQUIM BENTO DE SOUZA FERREIRA FILHO
University of São Paulo, DEAS – ESALQ – USP, Av. Pádua Dias, 11 – C.P. 9, Piracicaba, SP 13418-900, BRAZIL
Phone: (+55 +19) 429-4119; Fax: (+55 +19) 434-5186
jbsferre@carpa.ciagri.usp.br

MANUEL A.R. DA FONSECA
Universidade Federal do Rio de Janeiro, Av. Pasteur, 250, Rio de Janeiro, SP 22290-240, BRAZIL
Phone: (+55 +21) 295-1447; Fax: (+55 +21) 541-8148
mfonseca@compuland.com.br

JOAQUIM J.M. GUILHOTO
University of São Paulo and Regional Economics Applications Laboratory, University of Illinois, Urbana, USA; University of São Paulo, DEAS – ESALQ – USP, Av. Pádua Dias, 11 – C.P. 9, Piracicaba, SP 13418-900, BRAZIL
Phone: (+55 +19) 429-4119; Fax: (+55 +19) 434-5186
guilhoto@usp.br

EDUARDO A. HADDAD
FIPE - USP and *Regional Economics Applications Laboratory, University of Illinois, Urbana, USA; FIPE – USP, Av. Prof. Luciano Gualberto, 908, Caixa Postal:11.474, São Paulo, SP 05508-900 BRAZIL*
Phone: (+ 55 +11) 813-1444 – Ext. 130; Fax: (+55 +11) 813-4743
ehaddad@usp.br

GEOFFREY J.D. HEWINGS
Regional Economics Applications Laboratory, University of Illinois, 607 S. Mathews, # 236, Urbana, IL 61801, U.S.A.
Phone:(+1 +217) 333-4740;   Fax:(+1 +217) 244-9339
hewings@uiuc.edu

RODOLFO HOFFMANN
University of Campinas and University of São Paulo; IE-UNICAMP, Caixa Postal 6135, Campinas, SP 13083-970, BRAZIL
Phone: (+55 +19) 788-5750; Fax: (+55 +19) 788-5752
rhoffman@carpa.ciagri.usp.br

DÉCIO K. KADOTA
FIPE – USP, Av. Prof. Luciano Gualberto, 908, Caixa Postal:11.474, São Paulo, SP 05508-900 BRAZIL
Phone: (+ 55 +11) 818-5876; Fax: (+55 +11) 210-8334
dkkadota@usp.br

ANA LÚCIA KASSOUF
DEAS – ESALQ – USP, Av. Pádua Dias, 11 – C.P. 9, Piracicaba, SP 13418-900, BRAZIL
Phone: (+55 +19) 429-4119; Fax: (+55 +19) 434-5186
alkassou@carpa.ciagri.usp.br

ANDRÉ MAGALHÃES
Federal University of Pernambuco, Departamento de Economia, Av. dos Economistas, S/N, Cidade Universitária, Recife, PE 50740-590, BRAZIL
Phone: (+55 +81) 271-8378 - Ext. 222; Fax: (+55 +81) 271-8378
magalhs@npd.ufpe.br

MARCO ANTONIO MONTOYA
University of Passo Fundo and Federal University of Rio Grande do Sul; Universidade de Passo Fundo, Departamento de Economia, Caixa Postal 611/631, Campus I - BR 285 - km 171 - Bairro São José, Passo Fundo, RS 99001-970, BRAZIL
Phone: (+55 +54) 316-8245; Fax: (+55 +54) 316-8125
montoya@upf.tche.br

ANTONIO CARLOS MORETTO
Universidade Estadual de Londrina, Campus Universitário, Departamento de Economia, Caixa Postal 6001, Londrina, PR 86051-990, BRAZIL
Phone: (+55 +43) 371-4255; Fax: (+55 +43) 371-4215
acmoretto@uel.br

FRANCISCO S. RAMOS
Federal University of Pernambuco, Departamento de Economia, Av. dos Economistas, S/N, Cidade Universitária, Recife, PE 50740-590, BRAZIL
Tel/Fax: (+55 +81) 453-9577
fsr@npd.ufpe.br

PAULO T.V. RESENDE
Rua Santa Rita Durão, 41 apto 503 Funcionários, Belo Horizonte, MG, Brazil
Phone: (+55+31) 3223-9122
paulo_resende@uol.com.br

ROSSANA LOTT RODRIGUES
Universidade Estadual de Londrina, Campus Universitário, Departamento de Economia, Caixa Postal 6001, Londrina, PR 86051-990, BRAZIL
Phone: (+55 +43) 371-4255; Fax: (+55 +43) 371-4215
rlott@uel.br

MICHAEL SONIS
Bar Ilan University, Israel and Regional Economics Applications Laboratory, University of Illinois, Urbana, USA; Department of Geography, Bar Ilan University, 52900 Ramat Gan, Tel Aviv, Israel
Phone: (+972 +3) 531-8222; Fax (+972 +3) 534-4430
sonism@mail.biu.ac.il

MARIA DA CONCEIÇÃO SAMPAIO DE SOUSA
Departamento de Economia UnB Campus Darci Ribeiro S/N, Asa Norte Brasília, DF 70910-900 BRAZIL
Phone: (+55 +61) 347-5304; Fax: (+55 +61) 347-5304
mcss@unb.br

Preface

WERNER BAER

Brazil's economy is large and complex. It poses enormous challenges to analysts who attempt to understand its functioning. From the second World War until the 1980s successive governments followed an import substitution industrialization (ISI) strategy. By closing the economy, they encouraged both foreign and domestic investors to establish new industries. This was complemented by a large participation of the state in various sectors - such as steel, petroleum, mining, and most public utilities. Although such policies resulted in many years of high growth rates and structural changes in the economy, they brought along many negative side-effects, which gradually forced the country's policy makers to change their orientation in the 1990s, opening up the economy and adopting neo-liberal policies.

The problems which ISI brought along were numerous: unorthodox government financing which resulted in decades of inflation; the neglect of agriculture and exports which brought along balance of payments problems; the continued and even accentuation in the concentration of income; the worsening of the country's regional distribution of income; low productivity and quality of many industrial sectors, due to lack of competition; etc. Although various governments have tried to deal with some of these problems prior to the 1990s, they were never completely successful.

It seems that some of these problems have been dealt with more effectively by the introduction of neo-liberal policies - such as bringing inflation under control with the *real* plan, improving productivity through an economy subject to world-wide competition, privatizing many government firms, etc - It remains to be seen, however, whether neo-liberalism will ultimately succeed in solving most of the country's structural problems.

This volume provides a wealth of information and insights into some of these questions. The articles were written by a group of very talented analysts, who combine a deep knowledge of Brazilian statistical and institutional information with highly sophisticated econometric and input-output techniques in dealing with some of the above-mentioned issues. This collection should become a standard reference volume for anyone dealing with such topics as: Brazil's inflation, investment trends, personal and regional distribution of income, productivity determinants, inter-regional economic relations, the impact of trade policies on various sectors and regions, etc.

Acknowledgements

The idea for this volume stemmed from a dearth of readily accessible analytical material on recent changes in the Brazilian economy. There is a strong Brazil-University of Illinois connection evident in the affiliation of many of the contributors; over the last two decades, there has been a veritable stream of high quality Brazilian students entering the economics' graduate program at the University of Illinois. Many have returned to Brazil to assume positions in academic and government institutions throughout the country; those in academia have already trained subsequent generations of Brazilian scholars (Illinois' intellectual grandchildren!) and several contributors to this volume fall into that category. However, all of this would not have occurred had the University of Illinois not been fortunate enough to attract Werner Baer to campus. He has been a passionate, committed Brazilianist whose influence extends well beyond the students with whom he has been involved. The editors of this volume would like to acknowledge Werner Baer's significant contributions to Brazilian economic analysis and to his advice and counsel over many years.

A grant from the Hewlett Foundation to the University of Illinois and the further support from the Regional Economics Applications Laboratory have provided significant funding at critical stages in the development of this monograph; Ms. Gerry Gallagher has been instrumental in facilitating the logistics of many visits between the two editors. Ms Barbara Bonnell assisted in the initial transformation of the manuscripts into the prescribed format and, at Ashgate Press, Ms Anne Keirby, Ms. Pauline Beavers and especially Ms. Frances Goldstone, have been helpful in seeing the project through to completion.

1 Introduction and Overview

JOAQUIM J.M. GUILHOTO and GEOFFREY J.D. HEWINGS

Brazil has become once again an economy that is being subject to considerable scrutiny by the world financial markets. The significant political and economic changes that have occurred therein in the last two decades have generated their own form of cyclical behavior with expectations that have risen and fallen with each new policy initiative. Whether the current initiative, based on the *Real* plan, will succeed in moving Brazil firmly into the league of economies with stable currencies is still unclear at the time this volume went to press.

What is very clear is the degree of change that has occurred in the economy at a variety of spatial scales. At the international level, Brazil is now a part of MERCOSUL/MERCOSUR with additional, strong trading relationships with Chile. Within the economy, decades of significant active policy intervention in the country appear not to have transformed the inherent core-periphery distinction in levels of regional development and welfare between the center-south and the northeast.

This volume attempts to explore some contemporary issues surrounding economic structure in Brazil from an explicitly analytical perspective. All of the contributions use some form of modeling to aid in the provision of insights; the models range in scope from econometric exercises, to econometric models, two forms of computable general equilibrium modeling and some recent innovations in nonlinear relative dynamics. However, the focus is not on the models per se but on the contributions they make to uncovering features of Brazil's economic structure that may have escaped attention to date.

Organization of the book

The book is organized into four sections reflecting the major source of focus of the chapters; however, there are significant spillover issues and thus the sections are not to be regarded as mutually exclusive. The first two chapters introduce the reader to current debates in macroeconomic policy and analysis. Fonseca has been working on these issues for well over a decade and his macroeconomic models have proven to provide valuable (and accurate) forecasts of the Brazilian economy. Fonseca examines in chapter 2 a history of recent policy initiatives that have attempted to marry growth with low(er) levels of inflations. As he notes, many of these policies were founded on faulty premises that almost guaranteed their ultimate failure. The most striking source for explanation of the current problems may be traced to a reversal in the sources of investment. Whereas once the public sector was a major provider of long-term credit to the private sector, the roles have essentially reversed at the same time that the financial requirements of the government have increased. The focus in chapter 3 is on inflation and Fonseca's analysis reveals the fragility of the current *Real* policy; while inflation has been reduced dramatically, Fonseca sees signs that suggest that the reduction is based on many other factors being controlled, some of which have proven to be enormously difficult to reign in (state and federal spending for example). Key to the analysis in his view is the role of total liquidity; with its strong link to fiscal and monetary policies of the Central Bank, only a major restructuring of the public sector will provide the necessary conditions for controlling monetary supply and offering some positive perspective for the success of the *Real* plan.

Brazil is a country in which it is difficult to ignore spatial implications of any macroeconomic policy; as a result, attention to regional equity concerns have long been a feature of central government development initiatives. Haddad and Azzoni provide a regional perspective on some recent federal trade policies – how have recent trade initiatives changed the macroeconomic structure and, importantly, the geographical location of production? Using a Walrasian-type computable general equilibrium (cge) model, they found that general decreases in tariffs increase economic activity in the Center-South at the expense of the Northeast. In large part the finding is new since prior analysis, accounting only for demand-driven considerations failed to identify the potential negative effect that trade liberalization might have on a peripheral region. While the inclusion of supply-side considerations yielded this insight, they also note another important factor, very much related to spatial, structural change; three or more decades ago, interregional linkages between the center-south and the northeast were relatively weak. Recent regional integration (albeit modest compared to other parts of the world - see chapter 7) has resulted '...in supply effects ... playing a more relevant role in the dynamics of regional interaction' (Haddad and Azzoni).

The next five chapters take an explicitly regional perspective, although the regional definitions vary from macro (e.g. the Northeast) to individual states. Regional income trends continue to be a source of intense debate in Brazil; are they converging or diverging? Are recent trends indicative of a turnaround or merely a statistical aberration? Hoffmann sets his analysis in the context of recent economic events to explore the degree to which economic crises, stagnation, inflation and its control and recent growth have had on income inequality. In his extensive sectoral and regional analysis, he also attempts to explore linkages with other demographic attributes. His findings suggest that the period between 1980-1993 was one in which absolute poverty increased; more recent data offer some hope for a movement in the right direction. His analysis reveals a very strong correlation between a lack of growth and increases in absolute poverty; one might conclude that few poverty policy measures are likely to be effective absent economic growth.

Azzoni's complementary chapter draws attention to regional competitiveness and industrial concentration. Exploring some early ideas of Kaldor and the so called Verdoorn Law, he attempts to examine regional competitiveness in Brazil. As Hoffmann noted early, the 1980s and early 1990s were a period in which prior trends abated; Azzoni points out that, for example, the dispersion of regional labor productivity rose during this period (having declined in the 1970s). He develops and an indicator of regional profitability and finds that the state of Rio de Janeiro lagged 32% behind the national average in 1997, below the levels for the Northeast. São Paulo was close to the national average while Minas Gerais and the South were slightly above and below, respectively. This focus on productivity/profitability is important because it provides a more comprehensive picture of a region's competitiveness than that afforded by wage rate information alone. One of the findings that should raise concern is the improvement in competitive indicators in the nation's core, industrialized areas; this will make it difficult to direct investment to other regions (such as the Northeast) where lower wage rates are not fully capitalized in gains in productivity.

Magalhães *et al.* place the structure of the Northeast economy is an international perspective by comparing it to a region of similar population size located in the US. Using some new developments in non-linear relative dynamics, they find that there are significant differences in the level of interaction between the Northeast states and those of the Midwest of the US. When they are few, demonstrable benefits from economic development in one state within a region spilling over to other states, it is not surprising that policy-makers view the competition for economic development initiatives as a zero-sum game.   In fact, the major beneficiaries from spillovers are the states of the Center-South.   In a sense, the Northeast finds itself in an untenable position wherein trade liberalization confers few benefits while increasing integration with the rest of Brazil continues along the same core-periphery path identified many decades ago.

Guilhoto *et al.* provide a more traditional perspective in the area of regional comparative analysis.   Operating at the level of five macro regions, they explore the degree to which production structures are similar across regions and how important changes in these structures have been over time.   Key sector analysis, using Hirschman-Rasmussen and pure linkage measures, reveals some important differences;   these differences are highlighted through visualization using a *electroeconomgram*, analogous to a electrocardiogram on an individual's vital systems, this procedure attempts to compare a regional economy with the nation or monitor its progress over time.   The results reveal considerable diversity in structure and change, with the South more closely aligned with Brazil as a whole.

Azzoni and Kadota then provide a case study using an econometric-input-output model built for the state of São Paulo.   They show just how important it is to have access to comprehensive models of this kind when state's are faced with making strategic investment decisions.   In their analysis, changes in the automobile and textile sectors are compared with a severe cutback in agriculture production.

The next three chapters examine infrastructure issues, broadly defined. The three contributions have different objectives- the efficiency of public sector spending, the role of education and problems with physical infrastructure in terms of transportation flows.   Sousa and Ramos examine the degree to which technical efficiency and returns to scale can be measured at the local level in Brazil under conditions of enormous heterogeneity in the size and structure of communities.   Using some recent advances in data envelopment analyses and similar techniques, they find that the diversity within the data set plays an important role in the determination of efficiency measures.   Their findings suggest that a variety of measures will have to be used since none of them is free of problems when faced with a variety of sizes and compositions in the structure of communities.

There is a clear link between a region's productivity and the skill endowment of the labor force; this set of characteristics, that might be referred to as occupational capital, will play an increasing role in the determination of a region's or a nation's competitiveness. Kassouf develops a multinomial logit model to explore the relationship between an individual's skill endowments (and other characteristics such as experience) and labor participation and earnings. One of her findings was that returns to education (in terms of earnings) ranged from 6 to 21%, while returns to experience ranged from 1.5% to 8%, much higher in the formal than in the informal sector. In a telling link with the previous chapter, she notes that resources allocated to education are not well managed, creating considerable inefficiency and low quality public schools.

Brazil's physical size present daunting problems for the allocation of investment funds for transportation infrastructure. Resende provides an overview of some of the current problems and then applies a model to consider the impact that trade liberalization brought on by MERCOSUR will have on highway capacities. One of the most striking findings is just how little commodity movement takes place by waterway (less than 1%), especially given the enormous potential that this offers in parts of the country. In contrast to many other more developed economies, there has also been little use of multi-modal systems in moving goods and services. All of these (and many other factors) combine to add significant costs to commodities, eroding their domestic and international competitiveness.

Three chapters focus on agriculture, still a major source for Brazilian export revenues as well as a contributor to employment and wealth generation within the country. Each successive chapter focuses on a smaller sub-set of agriculture. Ferreira provides some recent historical perspective and notes, in particular, the agriculture has outperformed the industrial sector (in terms of growth rates) during the 1980-1990 period. He is able to separate out some structural effects (decreases in demand for Brazilian industrial output) from some important technological advances in agricultural production that enhanced productivity and lowered costs, thereby enhancing demand. These findings are explored in a variety of scenarios using a CGE model under different external trade regimes. Almeida and Bacha concentrate on the trade balance for basic and processed agricultural products. They attempt to identify the most important variables in the foreign trade performance of these sectors for the period 1961-1995. While, in the long-run real, effective exchange devaluations have had statistically significant impacts on agricultural trade balance, domestic and foreign income and the terms of trade are more important in the short-run. Bliska and Guilhoto focus attention on the meat sector; Brazil occupies an important position in world production (second largest beef producer, third in poultry and seventh in pork) and a significant portion of this enters world markets. In concert with the other two agriculturally-related chapters, they explore the degree to which changes in foreign and domestic macroeconomic variables affect meat exports. However, their analysis stretches beyond the agricultural sector and traces the indirect impacts on other sectors of the economy. Hence, services and chemical sectors are strongly affected by changes in export demand.

The final chapter, by Montoya, offers some international perspective by exploring the impact of Brazil's joining MERCOSUL. An international input-output table for Argentina, Brazil, Chile, Uruguay is used to examine intersectoral and international interdependencies. The findings reveal some important differences in the current and expected impact of trade liberalization on the structure of production – Chile and Uruguay will increase their external dependence (and decrease domestic dependence) far more than either Brazil or Argentina. However, limited data prevent a complete, time-based picture from being drawn at the present time.

Final Remarks

No book focusing on structural change in a country as large, diversified and sophisticated as Brazil can claim to be comprehensive. The chapters represented here may be considered to be a sample of the type of analysis that is strongly rooted in an empirical, problem-solving tradition that will be much in demand as global competitive forces shape and re-shape economic structures over the next two decades. Brazil's hegemonic position in Latin America makes this a fascinating country to study and to monitor. Future analyses will focus even more strongly on external trade and foreign direct investment and the changing competitive position of MERCOSUL in the world economy; labor market and environmental issues are likely to occupy more attention while at the local level, indicators of welfare have become an increasing topic of analysis.

Trade and location – at all geographic levels – are now seen as important components of any economic development strategy. The chapters in this books offer another set of contributions to enhancing our understanding of the interplay between forces that cut across time, space and combinations of sectors and individuals.

PART I: MACROECONOMIC ANALYSIS

2 Analysis of Brazil's Macroeconomic Trends

MANUEL A.R. DA FONSECA

Introduction

Considering long-range data series – for a period of about a century – the Brazilian economy is very likely among those with the highest growth rates. Since the turn of the century, the average growth rate of the country's GDP has been 5%.[1] Since 1901, Brazil's GDP increased 121 times and in the period 1968-80 alone, the aggregate output doubled. Using the United States' economy for a comparative view, while the American GNP grew 367% from 1929 to 1980, the Brazilian GDP increased 2,192 % over the same period.[2]

This extraordinary performance can be attributed, in general terms, to high population growth – including major flows of immigration – extensive availability of natural resources, growing commercial and financial relations with other countries, and a strong government commitment to economic growth and development. The role of the State in this historical trend was especially important in the period from the 1950s to the first half of the 1970s, marked by a process of industrialization based on import substitution. Government's contribution was especially important in providing long-term capital otherwise unavailable in the country. Brazil's development bank – Banco Nacional de Desenvolvimento Econômico e Social (BNDES) – was created in 1952 with the goal of financing heavy industry and infrastructure. Moreover, government initiative was vital in the financing of housing construction, through the Banco Nacional da Habitação (BNH), created in 1965; in supplying credit to farmers, through the Banco do Brasil; and as an entrepreneur in intensive-capital segments, especially mining, steel, public utilities, chemicals and petrochemicals, and communications.[3]

Table 2.1 GDP growth (%), averages in the period*

1901-47	4.5
1948-62	7.6
1963-67	3.5
1968-80	9.0
1981-83	-2.1
1984-86	6.9
1987-98	2.0

Geometric averages.
Sources: *1901-47 – Abreu, op. cit.; 1948-70 – Conjuntura Econômica, v. 25, no. 9,*
              Sept. 1971 and v. 31, no. 7, July 1977; 1971-98 – Instituto Brasileiro de
              Geografia e Estatística (IBGE), Contas Nacionais, several issues

Nevertheless, as one can gauge from table 2.1, there was a dramatic change in the country's long-range economic performance. Since the beginning of the 1980s, and especially since 1987, the Brazilian economy has endured a long period of stagnation – at least, in comparison with the previous trend – which extends until today (beginning of 1999). The main goal of this chapter is to delve into the causes of this reversal. Also, by means of an analysis of long-trend series derived and estimated from primary data, several important macroeconomic changes that seem both to result from and contribute to the reduction of growth are investigated. Moreover, a macroeconometric model is used to investigate the dynamics of Brazil's economy, focusing especially on the role of investment.

Investment, economic performance and the role of government

Figure 2.1 illustrates the close relation between changes in aggregate output and the behavior of investment in Brazil. In this figure, data for GDP's real growth appear together with figures for the share of investment in GDP (both variables measured in real terms). It is clear that the periods of high growth rates are associated with increasing participation of investment in aggregate demand. This is especially true for the years of economic boom that lasted from 1967 until 1972, just before the first oil shock of the 1970s. On the other hand, the period of lower increase in activity, initiated in 1981, is undoubtedly related to a reduction in the investment share in GDP. This result is clearly in accordance with standard macroeconomic theory.[4]

The periods with sharp reductions in GDP growth are associated with major economic and political disturbances. These were, for example, the political crisis of 1963-64 that culminated in the overthrow of the Goulart government, the oil shock of 1973 which caused a sharp deterioration in the country's trade balance, the significant increase of interest rates in the United States in the beginning of the 1980s, which was followed by an interruption in the supply of foreign credit, and the period of the unorthodox stabilization plans that began in 1986. Since the middle of the 1970s, these developments have, as a rule, led to reductions in the share of investment in GDP.

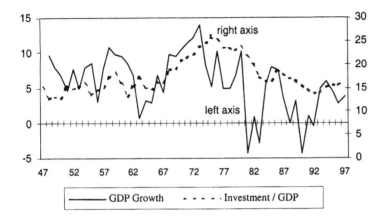

Figure 2.1   Growth rate of GDP and share of investment in GDP (%), 1947-97

Sources: *See Table 2.1*

Although in the oil crisis of the 1970s and the debt crisis of the 1980s the most important causes of the economic downturn were exogenous, that is not true in the case of the stagnation of the second half of the 1980s and in the 1990s; these events were undoubtedly caused by internal factors. The most important macroeconomic development in this period was a massive deterioration of government finances. Brazilian fiscal data – consolidating the federal, state and local administrations – appear in figure 2.2. One can see that the fiscal situation started to deteriorate in the middle of the 1970s, although government consumption did not show any significant increase until 1985, when a civilian government came to power after 21 years of military rule. In the 1970s, one verifies the beginning of a sharp increase in transfer payments, composed mainly of interest on the public debt and transfers to the social security system.

In the 1970s and 1980s, one important economic trend was the significant increase of the external debt of the public sector (including state-controlled companies). Brazil's external debt, which totaled $5.3 billion in 1970, reached $95.8 billion in 1985. The total share of the public sector debt increased from 52% in 1973 to 82% in 1985.[5] This increase in public sector indebtedness is partly explained by the fact that many private firms exchanged their foreign debt by depositing an equivalent amount in cruzeiros in the Central Bank, hence transferring to the government their liabilities in foreign currency. Although this may seem to be an undue form of subsidy for the private sector, one should bear in mind that this mechanism contributed to finance government expenditures at the time.[6]

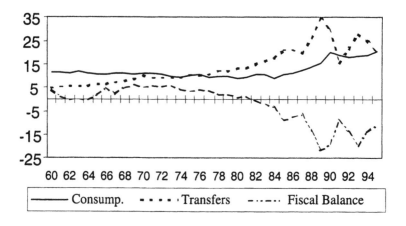

Figure 2.2   Government consumption and transfers, and fiscal balance (% of GDP), 1960-95

Sources: *See Table 2.1*

Growth in the (increasingly public) external debt is reflected in the interest payments to foreign creditors during that period. Balance of Payments data show that these payments rose from $359 million in 1972 to $9.65 billion in 1985 in liquid terms (deducting interest received from abroad). In the same period, the internal public debt outside the Central Bank also increased, climbing 283% in real terms.[7] These trends led to higher government deficits and, in 1985, the fiscal deficit reached 8.6% of GDP.

After 1985, government consumption increased significantly (see figure 2.2), due to both the creation of new working posts and to the rise in the average salary earned by civil servants. This latter trend (wage increases) was especially important in the Legislative branch of government and in the Judicial system. The presence of greater deficits led to even larger (internal) debt and interest payments that, in turn, contributed to worsen the financial position of the government. Data on public internal debt – outstanding government bonds outside the Central Bank – and interest rates paid by the government appear in table 2.2. The most important final effect of these developments was a substantial increase in inflation rates that eventually rose to hyperinflationary levels (for a fuller discussion of the Brazilian inflationary process, see Fonseca, 1988).

Table 2.2   Internal public debt in the market and interest paid by the government (% of GDP), averages in the period

	Debt	Interest
1947-62	2.0	-.-
1963-67	1.3	-.-
1968-80*	6.3	1.5
1981-84	10.7	4.3
1985-86	15.0	11.5
1987-97**	30.3	13.6

* Interest payments correspond to the period 1970-80
**The years 1990-91 (debt confiscation) were not included. Interest data correspond to the period 1987-95
Sources: Public debt – Boletim do Banco Central do Brasil, several issues; GDP and interest payments – see Table 2.1

One of the most important effects of the increasing government indebtedness, and the interest payments associated with it, is that increasing shares of tax revenues have been transferred to government creditors, both nationals and foreigners. Since a large part of tax revenues comes from indirect taxes charged on items of widespread consumption, such as basic food items, this trend constitutes a perverse form of income transfer from the poorest members of the population to the richest ones.[8] This process of income concentration, intensified by very high interest rates on public debt, is in part the result of government efforts to finance its growing expenses in a very limited internal capital market.[9]

The worsening of government finances affected private investment in two major ways. First, the extremely high inflation rates coupled with the harsh measures of the unorthodox stabilization programs of the 1980s and 1990s – especially price and wage freezes – led to a deterioration of business confidence. Secondly, the rise in interest rates increased the effective cost of new capital goods. Table 2.3 shows data on the real growth of private investment and real interest rates; with the exception of the 1984-86 period, the years of highest investment growth were also periods of very low or even negative average interest rates. The contrary, however, is not true, that is, from 1981 to 1983 real interest rates were close to zero and there was a dramatic fall in investment. These years were characterized by a major restructuring of the economy directed at reversing the increasing Current Accounts deficits following the Mexican crisis of 1982.[10] On the other hand, the very low growth rates of private investment after 1987 were accompanied by extremely high interest rates in real terms. Therefore, there is strong evidence that the pattern of interest rates has in fact contributed to determine the trends in investment verified in the last decades, although they are not the only cause. Further, internal savings were increasingly directed to the financing of government, leaving little room to maneuver for the funding of private firms. This latter trend is analyzed in the next section.

Table 2.3   Private investment growth and real interest rates (%), averages in the period*

	Investment	Interest**
1948-62	6.9	-.-
1963-67	5.0	-9.1
1968-80	13.5	0.7
1981-83	-12.3	0.9
1984-86	7.5	7.6
1987-97	1.1	15.0

* Geometric averages
**Average rates on short run public and private bonds deflated by the IGP-FGV
Sources: Interest rates – Conjuntura Econômica, several issues and Boletim do Banco Central do Brasil, Feb. 1994; private investment – see Table 2.1

Another important development in the 1990s, and one that contributed to diminish the manufacturing share in GDP, was the process of opening the economy to foreign competition, a period that lasted from 1990 to 1994.[11]   The average import tariff was reduced from 41.0% in 1989 to 13.2% in 1994. Furthermore, several import restrictions were eliminated (see Silber, 1997). Although the reduction of protectionism generally leads to desirable gains in efficiency, for this to have occurred without damaging the industrial sector it would have been necessary for the firms exposed to increased competition to be able to invest in new and improved technologies, and in order to do that, they would have needed financing. However, with the extremely high interest rates that have prevailed in Brazil in the 1990s, the cost of introducing improved technologies has become unbearably high.[12]

Aggregate saving and the capital market

By all accounts, long term financing has historically been deficient in Brazil. The country's capital market does not go beyond the stock exchange; there is no real market for long-term debt securities. Even the trading of stocks has been subject to severe distortions and limitations; trade has been concentrated on the equities of very few companies, usually state-owned, and many of the largest firms operating in the country, such as the automobile assembly companies, do not have stocks traded on the exchange. In the last few years, the equities of the large state (or formerly state-owned) companies have completely dominated overall trading. "Four companies [Telebras, Eletrobras, Petrobras and Vale do Rio Doce] correspond to more than 80% of the market and only 20% of the daily trade is left to more than 400 companies," (Carvalho, nd). By international standards, the Brazilian stock exchange is very limited, even in comparison to those of other developing economies (see table 2.4).

Table 2.4   Market value of stocks, % of aggregate output*

	1987	1996
Brazil	5.0	29.0
Argentina	1.7	16.9
Mexico	48.6	32.0
Malaysia	58.0	332.0
USA	49.0	115.5
England	98.0	152.0
Switzerland	66.0	137.0
France	15.5	38.0
Japan	98.0	67.0

*GDP or GNP
Source: Carvalho, (nd)

Although the amount of bonds and notes issued by the federal government and certain state and municipal governments has been relatively large, the average maturity of these securities is extremely short. The most traded government bond in the 1964-85 period, the *Obrigação Reajustável do Tesouro Nacional* (ORTN), showed a tendency of reducing average maturity. It went from around 59 months upon its creation in 1964 to 17 months in 1970, to around 38 months in 1975, to 34 months in 1980, and finally to 12 months in 1985.[13]

In historical perspective, the weakness of Brazil's capital market has been due in part to high and unpredictable inflation rates, which could inflict heavy losses on lenders in real terms. This deficiency was partly remedied by the creation of the ORTN in 1964, since this bond was automatically adjusted for previous inflation.[14] On the other hand, loss of confidence in the government, and especially in its capacity and disposition to honor its debt, also seems to have played a role, since in the periods immediately before the inauguration of a new administration the average maturity of the public debt was sharply reduced. In December 1989, for example, just before the commencement of the Collor administration, the average maturity of the *Letra Financeira do Tesouro* (LFT), that accounted for almost 98% of the federal debt at the time, was around four months. On this occasion, market distrust proved to be correct, since shortly afterwards two thirds of the government debt was confiscated: in February 1990, the total amount of federal bonds on the market was $60.1 billion; the following month this figure dwindled to $21.9 billion.[15]

Also, long-term credit is not generally available either to Brazilian private firms or to individuals. Actually, "short-term credit is the most important form of financing (in Brazil)," (Lima and Fonseca, 1996). In 1994, 65.6% of the total supply of credit by financial institutions was provided by commercial banks. In comparison, the share of the federal and regional development banks, that provide longer-term loans, was 5.9%.[16] Given this chronic deficiency in the country's credit market, Brazilian companies have been able to finance investment projects basically through retained profits (see next section). Also, since 1991 and particularly after the agreement reached in 1992 with international creditors of the country's foreign debt, Brazilian firms have increasingly obtained longer term financing abroad. The total amount raised by Brazilian companies through the selling of bonds on international markets climbed from $1.5 billion in 1991, to $7.6 billion in 1993, to $18.0 billion in 1996 and to $20.5 billion in 1997.[17] On the other hand, institutional investors, such as pension funds, insurance companies and investment funds, have gradually become more active in Brazil's financial system, following international trends, but this has not contributed to reducing the shortage of long term credit.

In the late 1970s and through the first half of the 1980s, aggregate saving declined sharply, in a trend similar to that of aggregate investment. Also, the deterioration of public finances observed since the early 1980s, and aggravated from 1985 onwards, led to increasing government deficits and, consequently, to the use of ever greater shares of private saving to finance government consumption in excess of its revenues.   Table 2.5 provides an overview of the effects of the greater financing requirements of the government in aggregate saving. Although data for the years after 1985 very likely carry some distortion due to the extremely high inflation rates, one can conclude that, in the second half of the 1980s and the first half of the 1990s, private firms were squeezed out of the credit market by the government.   This trend is also clearly reflected in the rise of public internal debt discussed in the previous section.

Table 2.5   Aggregate saving, % of GDP*

	Private	Govt.	Internal	External
1970-79	14.8	4.4	19.2	2.2
1980-84	18.1	-0.6	17.5	4.4
1985-90	34.7	-12.6	22.1	0.1
1991-95	32.3	-12.8	19.4	-0.03

*Changes of stocks are not taken into account, which affects the column for External Saving (it is underestimated). In the period 1985-95 (high inflation), Private Saving is probably overestimated due to interest payments (in real terms) on the public debt, which are part of government transfers
Sources: See Table 2.1

An important point to be made here is that the increasing financial requirements of the government are behind the systematic rise of interest rates analyzed above, since ever-greater amounts of government bonds have had to be sold to the public. This causality was made even stronger given the structural deficiencies in Brazil's capital market. Therefore, the cost of financing private investment has continuously increased, leading, as a rule, to investment reductions and to lower economic growth.

Changes in aggregate demand and income components

Considering the components of Brazil's aggregate demand in the last decades, one can observe certain distinct trends (see figure 2.3). One such trend extends from the 1960s until the first oil shock of 1973 and is characterized by a persistent increase in investment share and a parallel decrease in both private and government consumption. In the 1973-74 period, strong investment demand was sustained by large trade deficits, and this pattern was maintained throughout the rest of the decade since foreign credit was flowing in. During the 1970s, there was a major investment program in capital-goods industries, which was promoted and financed by the public sector.[18] From 1982 to 1985, there was virtually no change in the shares of either government or private consumption, but the investment share declined sharply as trade deficits turned into surplus, the debt crisis of the early 1980s had virtually eliminated the supply of foreign credit to Latin American countries. Trade surplus made possible the payment of financial obligations on foreign debt accumulated in the 1970s.

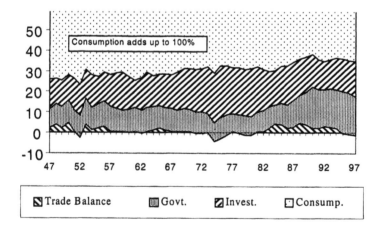

Figure 2.3   Components of aggregate demand (% of total), 1947-97
Sources: *See Table 2.1*

Since 1985, though, there was strong, persistent growth of government consumption at the expense of investment and, to a lesser extent, of private consumption that lasted until 1990. Also, a surplus in foreign trade was the rule until 1993 but, since the start of the *Real* plan in 1994, two simultaneous developments have occurred: relatively strong increases in private consumption and investment and, since government expenses have not been reduced, trade deficits have reappeared (see Fonseca, 1988). Hence, it seems fair to characterize the *Real* plan as a program in which external credit was used to finance an increased internal demand. In spite of the much-publicized commitment of the Cardoso administration to government reform, no real adjustment has been made, as can be judged from figure 2.3.[19]

The dramatic rise of the share of government in aggregate demand, verified in the second half of the 1980s, is also reflected in the patterns of aggregate income. Figure 2.4 shows data on wages in three sectors of the economy –agriculture, industry and services. From 1960 to 1980, one observes an increase in the share of services and a parallel decrease in the agricultural share, while the participation of industry remained virtually unchanged.[20] From 1980 to 1990, there was a significant growth in the share of wages in the services sector (that also includes government activities) mainly at the expense of wages in the industrial sector. After 1994, there was a further, but smaller, increase in the share of services and a reduction in industrial participation.

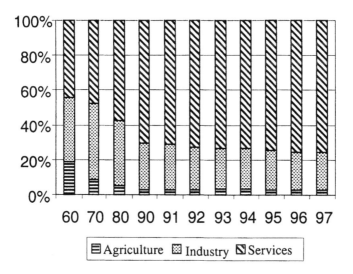

Figure 2.4   Share of wages in the economy (% of total), selected years

Sources: *1960-80 – estimates made by the author from data in IBGE, Estatísticas Históricas do Brasil, rev. ed., 1990 (census data); IBGE, Tabela de Relações Intersetoriais, 1970 and 1980; and Rijckeghem (1969); 1990-97 – IBGE, Contas Nacionais*

Changes in the pattern of aggregate income are also revealed by comparing total wages and profits. Such a comparison appears in figure 2.5, revealing that the transformations that occurred in the second half of the 1980s led to reductions in profits and to compensating rises in wages. In principle, this could be considered a most welcome change, since the extremely high share of profits in aggregate income verified in Brazil is undoubtedly linked to the extreme income inequality that prevails in the nation. However, two aspects should be considered. First, the significant wage increase observed since 1985 is most likely due to the rise in government spending noted earlier, that is, larger shares of income were simply transferred to government workers. Also, given the limitations of Brazil's capital market that were described in the previous section, retained profits are the most important source of investment financing. Therefore, one may conclude that the transformations depicted in figure 2.5 simply reflect other aspects of the causes of Brazilian stagnation analyzed previously: larger government spending, higher government debt, deteriorating public finances, falling investment, lower economic growth, and reduced share of the industrial sector.

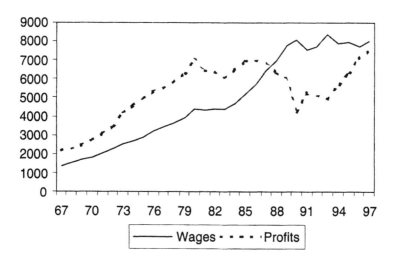

Figure 2.5   Real wages and profits (billions of 1980 cruzeiros), 1967-97

Sources: 1967-89 – estimates made by the author from data listed in Table 2.1 and in Figure 2.4; 1990-97 – IBGE, Contas Nacionais

Figure 2.5 also shows that, from 1994 to 1997, there was a significant increase in profits while wages decreased slightly. In the same period, as can be seen in figure 2.1, there was a recovery of investment.[21] Although more recent data were not available by the time this chapter was written, these trends have very likely been reversed since the financial crises in Asia and Russia started to affect the Brazilian economy.

Going beyond economic analysis, probably the worst aspect of these transformations is that, in spite of the major increase in government spending since 1985, there is strong evidence that public services have not improved and, in many cases, have greatly deteriorated. The dramatic deficiencies in basic education remain an unsolved problem and, in this area, Brazilian statistics are only rivaled by those of the poorest countries in Latin America, such as Guatemala and Haiti (see Chaffee, 1998, for an account of the state of education in Brazil). The deterioration of the public health system can be accessed by the increase in the health insurance business; health insurance, which was non-existent until the early 1980s, is now the second line of insurance in the country.[22] On the other hand, one can gauge the deficiencies in infrastructure by the recent drive to transfer public utilities companies, public transportation companies, and state and federal roads to private administration (see Mello, 1994; Almeida, 1997). Summing up, social reality in Brazil remains nothing but a dismal picture.[23]

A Macroeconometric model for the Brazilian economy

Synthesizing the main tendencies of the Brazilian economy in the last decades, one may say that, after the first half of the 1980s, the country was marked by long periods of stagnation, a strong reduction of investment's share in GDP, a sharp increase of government spending, extremely high inflation and real interest rates and, more recently, by a major increase in imports. Most economists would agree that these trends could be characterized as *demand-side* changes. Therefore a system of equations devised to model these developments as well as to forecast future tendencies must be demand based, and this is the case of the model to be described below.

In the model, production is divided into three sectors, agriculture, industry and services, and is determined by total demand. The most important demand equations are those for private consumption and private investment. To these two items, government spending and the trade balance are added. The model also has equations that determine employment and total income of three different income-groups: entrepreneurs, wage earners and autonomous workers. In the employment equations, the coefficients are not estimated; instead, they are labor coefficients of the input-output type. The model's equations are presented in table 2.6.

Table 2.6   Model equations

Equations	Endogenous Variables	Exogenous Variables
1. $Ygdp = Yagr + Yind + Yserv + Ind\_tax/P - Subsidies/P$	GDP, real values	Agr. GDP, Subsidies, GDP deflator
2. $Yind = f_1 (Ygdp\text{-}1, \Delta Ydem)$	Industry GDP	
3. $Yserv = f_2 (Ygdp\text{-}1, \Delta Ydem)$	Services GDP	
4. $Ydem = C + I + G + (X - M)e$	Aggregate demand	Govt. cons., Trade balance, Exchange rate
5. $Ipriv = f_3 (Ygdp\text{-}1, \Delta Ygdp\text{-}1, \Delta Profits/P, Interest\_real, Igov)$	Private investment	Real interest, Govt. invst., GDP deflator
6. $C = f_4 (Ygdp\text{-}1, \Delta Profits^*/P, \Delta Wages\_1^*/P, \Delta Wages\_2^*/P, Interest\_real)$	Private consumption	Real interest, GDP deflator
7. $I = Ipriv + Igov$	Total investment	Government investment
8. $Stocks\_change = Ygdp - Ydem$	Change of stocks	
9. $Wages\_1 = Wage\_rate\_1.Emp\_1$	Wages	Wage rate
10. $Wages\_2 = Wage\_rate\_2.Emp\_2$	Avg. income of autonomous workers	Average rate
11. $Emp\_1 = c_{11}.Yagr + c_{12}.Yind + c_{13}.Yserv$	No. of wage earners	Agriculture GDP
12. $Emp\_2 = c_{21}.Yagr + c_{22}.Yind + c_{23}.Yserv$	No. of autonomous workers	Agriculture GDP
13. $Profits = Ynom - Ind\_tax + Subsidies - Wages\_1 - Wages\_2$	Profits	Subsidies
14. $Wages\_1^* = (1\text{-}t_{21}).Wages\_1$	Wages liquid of taxes	
15. $Wages\_2^* = (1\text{-}t_{22}).Wages\_2$	Income aut. workers liquid of taxes	
16. $Profits^* = (1\text{-}t_{31}).Profits$	Profits liquid of taxes	
17. $Ynom = Ygdp.P$	Nominal GDP	GDP deflator
18. $Ind\_tax = (Yagr + Yind + Yserv). P.t_1$	Indirect taxes	GDP deflator
19. $Dir\_tax = t_{21}.Wages\_1 + t_{22}.Wages\_2 + t_{23}.Profits$	Direct taxes	

The main factors behind the macroeconomic changes analyzed in sections above are treated as *exogenous* variables – that is, general price changes, government spending, interest rates and trade balance are exogenous. In this way, one can effectively model the consequences of changes in these variables that indeed occurred in the past, or that are assumed to happen in the future. Another purely exogenous variable of the model – that is, not including the endogenous variables with a one period lag – is agricultural GDP. In addition, considering the variables defined in real terms, most equations can be treated as linear functions, thus considerably simplifying the estimation of the model. In particular, linearity is a necessary condition for the use of simultaneous equations estimation methods – like two-stage least squares (2SLS). As will be shown below, model performance can be considered quite satisfactory when compared with historical data.

Table 2.7   Estimation of equations 5 and 6
(Data in Cr$ billions of 1980; regression from 1968 to 1996)

Private consumption
OLS

Independent Variables	Estimated Coefficients	Standard Error
Const.	504.18598	203.19408
Ygdp-1	0.1203917	0.0174318
ΔProfits*/P	0.2341884	0.1184740
ΔWages_1*/P	0.3775288	0.2272764
ΔWages_2*/P	-0.335417	0.8839177
Interest_real +	-13.20501	4.7543473

$R^2 = 0.7001195$

F statistic = 10.739442
Durbin-Watson statistic = 0.6641237
Number of observations = 29
Residual sum of squares = 2245310.3
Standard error of the regression = 312.4455

Private investment
OLS

Independent Variables	Estimated Coefficients	Standard Error
Const.	572.07061	224.64391
Ygdp-1	0.1442490	0.0236296
ΔYgdp-1	0.3294007	0.1313089
ΔProfits/P	0.1732147	0.1035662
Interest_real +	-9.726364	4.1590221
Igov	-1.268631	0.9178099

$R^2 = 0.7417443$

F statistic = 13.211802
Durbin-Watson statistic = 1.2305350
Number of observations = 29
Residual sum of squares = 1933650.0
Standard error of the regression = 289.95134

Private consumption
2SLS

Independent Variables	Estimated Coefficients	Standard Error
Const.	432.75273	249.07124
Ygdp-1	0.1255374	0.0194832
ΔProfits*/P	0.3047959	0.2214631
ΔWages_1*/P	0.5773800	0.3311273
ΔWages_2*/P	-1.003018	1.1316949
Interest_real +	-14.55762	5.0338392
+ Percentage		

Private investment
2SLS

Independent Variables	Estimated Coefficients	Standard Error
Const.	614.82604	246.47886
Ygdp-1	0.1424405	0.0237062
ΔYgdp-1	0.3243074	0.1298699
ΔProfits/P	0.1222487	0.1651325
Interest_real +	-9.507340	4.1307441
Igov	-1.313787	0.9105098
+ Percentage		

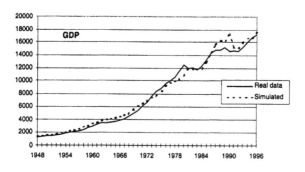
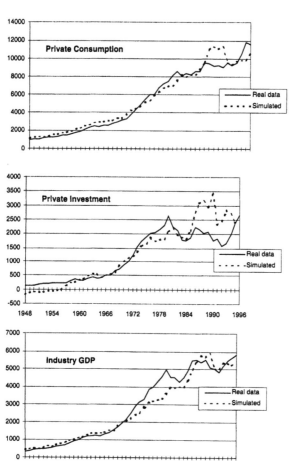

Figure 2.6   Simulations one-period ahead, 1948-96
(1980 Cr$ billions)

Note: *Historical data were used for the lagged endogenous variables*

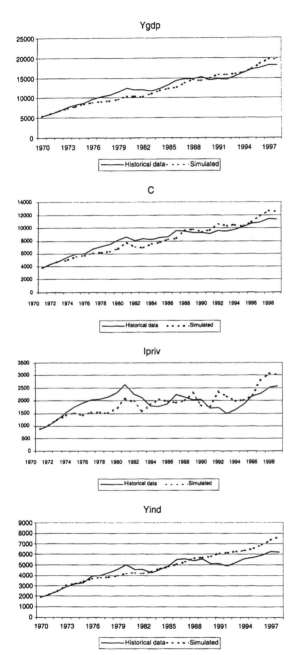

Figure 2.7 Simulations with 1973 as the base period, 1973-98
(1980 Cr$ billions)

Historical simulations

The most important equations regarding the dynamic behavior of the model are the ones for private investment and private consumption. For these equations, two methods of estimation were used: single equation estimation methods (ordinary least squares – OLS) and a simultaneous equations estimator (2SLS). All estimations were performed using data for the period 1968-1996. These estimates are presented in table 2.7. The estimation results from the two methods did not vary much, especially in the case of private investment. The coefficients estimated using the 2SLS method were used, since they generally have better properties.[24]

Although the model described above is relatively simple, it is *nonlinear* due to the presence of both real and nominal variables. Therefore, a numerical method for the solution of nonlinear, dynamic systems of equations is necessary for its solution. The procedure that was actually used is generally known as the Gauss-Seidel method, and the computer codes that implement the method were written in a standard programming language (*Excel's Visual Basic*).[25]

The model was used to generate two sets of solutions that can be compared with historical data in order to gauge the model's overall performance. In the first set, one-period-ahead solutions were computed. That is, for each year, historical values for the endogenous lagged variables were used together with the purely exogenous variables. Results were generated for the period from 1948 to 1996. In the second set, starting with data from 1970 to 1972, values for the endogenous variables generated by the model were used to determine next-year solutions. Thus, only the truly exogenous data were fed into the model. Results were generated for the period from 1973 to 1998. These results, together with historical data, appear in figures 2.6 and 2.7.

The overall results, as can be judged from the figures, can be considered quite satisfactory. As it might be expected, the simulations for investment, a less regular variable, were further distant from historical data. However, it is somewhat surprising that, considering the differences from historical data, the solutions with 1973 as the base year (figure 2.7) were not generally worse than the one-period-ahead simulations (figure 2.6), especially for the 1986-1995 period.

Focusing on the one-period-ahead solutions for private investment, one is led to say that after 1986, a period that marks the beginning of the unorthodox stabilization programs, the observed levels were much lower than what might be expected only from macroeconomic variables.

Apparently, the artificial and inconsistent economic measures that characterized the programs of that period and the climate of deep uncertainty that predominated, had strong negative effects on aggregate investment and, consequently, on overall economic activity.

Concluding comments: an assessment of macroeconomic trends in Brazil

From the 1950s until the early 1970s, the important and positive role of the Brazilian public sector in the significant economic growth and development that characterized that period is indisputable.   Public initiative was especially important in supplying long term credit to the private sector and, either directly or through state firms, in achieving a strong investment surge in capital-intensive sectors and in infrastructure. This government-led development surge has resisted even major foreign upheavals, represented by the oil crises of the 1970s and the debt crisis of the early 1980s. From 1968 to 1980, the Brazilian economy grew at an annual rate of 9.0% and, after a deep adjustment to the debt crisis in the three following years, the average growth from 1984 to 1986 was close to 7% (see table 2.1). Yet, since the second half of the 1980s, this entire framework seemed to have changed drastically, and from 1987 to 1998 average growth plunged to 2%.

The main conclusion that can be derived from this analysis is that the major factor behind this change of pattern is the reversal in the investment trend.   The explanation for this reversal seems to lie in the structural deficiencies of Brazil's capital market and in the extremely high real interest rates observed since the second half of the 1980s. It seems clear that the rise of interest rates is due to the increasing financial requirements of the government.

In order to reverse the chronic stagnation of the last decades it would be necessary to induce a new investment surge. Since, in the long run, economic growth has been the rule rather than the exception in Brazil, it might suffice to reduce the cost of financing new capital goods. That is, all efforts should be made to extend the availability of long-term credit and to develop the country's capital markets. In addition, it is certainly necessary that a major restructuring of the country's public sector be implemented, so that a fiscal balance may be achieved.

Notes

[1] Geometric average.

[2] The Brazilian data were gathered from the country's *National Accounts* and from Abreu (1990). American data appear in W. J. Baumol and A. S. Blinder, *Economics, Principles and Policy* (San Diego, H. B. Jovanovich, 1985).

[3] For an analysis of this period, see Baer (1995), especially ch. 11; Suzigan et al. (1974); and Suzigan (1975).

[4] The role of investment in economic growth is emphasised, for example, in ch. 22 of Keynes' *General Theory*.

[5] These figures appear in Abreu (1990) pp. 409-10. The causes and consequences of foreign indebtedness during this period are analysed in Batista, Jr. (1987) and Martone (1987).

[6] This point has been overlooked in the analysis of that period. One reason may be that, with the exchange rate devaluations of the early 1980s, the increase of government obligations due to the external debt led to a strong increase of the *internal* debt. Therefore, there was no gain for the government in the long run. For an analysis of the worsening of public finances during this period, see Werneck (1986).

[7] This figure was obtained using the *Índice Geral de Preços* of Fundação Getúlio Vargas.

[8] In 1997, 52.6% of the total tax revenue corresponded to indirect taxes.

[9] Brazil's capital market is analysed in the next Section. For a discussion of the effects of inflation on income distribution, see Fonseca (1995).

[10] For an account of this period, see Baer (1995), ch. 6, and Carneiro and Modiano (1990).

[11] The share of industry in GDP, which was 39.9% in 1980 and 36.4% in 1989, decreased to 34.9% in 1990 and reached 33,1% in 1992. It has remained around this level since then.

[12] One alternative that many firms used was to get financing in foreign markets. By so doing they became exposed to the risk of exchange rate devaluation. The effects of the major devaluation that occurred in January 1999, affecting Brazilian firms that carried liabilities in foreign currencies, had not yet been determined at the time this paper was written (February 1999).

[13] Figures correspond to December of each year. See ANDIMA (year of publication unknown).

[14] This inflation correction mechanism gradually spread to the wage market and to the markets of most goods and services, becoming an important cause of price increases. See Fonseca (1998).

[15] In national currency, though, this loss was less dramatic: from CR$ 1,843 million to CR$ 934 million. See ANDIMA, op. cit. The confiscated bonds, and the bank deposits that backed them, were returned 18 months later, in 12 monthly instalments.

[16] Data for December, see *Boletim do Banco Central do Brasil – Suplemento Estatístico*, September 1995. Commercial banks include the "multiple banks" – that, is the ones that operate more than one line of business –, and the state-owned Banco do Brasil.

[17] *Boletim do Banco Central do Brasil*, Jan. 1999.

[18] Such a program is known as the 2nd PND – *Plano Nacional de Desenvolvimento*. An account appears in Carneiro (1990).

[19] The difficulties in accomplishing changes in Brazil's public sector derive, in great part, from the deficiencies of the country's political system. See, on this subject, Chaffee (1998).

[20] The share of industrial wages actually increased in the 1960s, and diminished in the 1970s.

[21] One is led to conclude that these data support Kalecki's conclusion that, everything else constant, increased investment causes greater profits. See specially ch. 3 of his *Theory of Economic Dynamics*.

[22] In Brazil, automobile, health and life insurance account for two thirds of the total premiums. See Lima and Fonseca (1996).

[23] For deeper analyses of this picture, see Rocha (1992), and Camargo and Barros (1992).

[24] See Judge *et. al.* (1985) and Maddala (1987). The coefficient for the variable Δ Wages_2*/P in the consumption equation has the wrong sign and was set equal to zero.

[25] For a description of the method using simple econometric models, see Klein and Young (1982). A more standard mathematical approach appears in Franklin (1980) and Sydsaeter (1981).

References

Abreu, M. P. (ed.) (1990) *A Ordem do Progresso*. Rio de Janeiro, Campus.

Almeida, F. G. de. (1997) "A privatização na era do Real," *Conjuntura Econômica*, 51, 16-20.

Baer, W. (1995) *The Brazilian Economy*. Westport-Connecticut, Praeger.

Batista, Jr., P. N. (1987) "International Financial Flows to Brazil Since the Late 1960s," *Discussion Papers*, 7, World Bank, Washington, D.C.

Camargo, J. M. and R. P. Barros, (1992) "As Causas da Pobreza no Brasil" in IPEA – Ministério do Planejamento, *Perspectivas da Economia Brasileira,* (Rio de Janeiro).

Carneiro, D. D. (1990) "Crise e Esperança." In M.P. Abreu, (ed.) *A Ordem do Progresso*. Rio de Janeiro, Campus, pp.295-322.

Carneiro, D. D. and E. Modiano, (1990) "Ajuste externo e desequilíbrio interno: 1980-1984." In M.P. Abreu, (ed.) *A Ordem do Progresso*. Rio de Janeiro, Campus, pp. 323-46.

Carvalho, E. R. de. (nd) "O mercado de capitais, a globalização e o comportamento das multidões", in Conselho de Economia do Rio de Janeiro, *Cadernos de Política Monetária e Mercado Financeiro.*

Chaffee, W. A. (1998) *Desenvolvimento: Politics and Economy in Brazil.* Boulder-Colorado, Lynne Rienner.

Desai, M. (1976) *Applied Econometrics.* Oxford, Philip Allan.

Fonseca, M. A. da. (1991) "Um modelo macroeconométrico de simulação e previsão," *Annals of the XII Meeting of the Brazilian Econometric Society.* Curitiba-Paraná, pp. 191-214.

Fonseca, M. A. da. (1995) *O Processo Inflacionário: Análise da Experiência Brasileira.* Petrópolis-Rio de Janeiro, Vozes.

Fonseca, M. A. da. (1998) "Brazil's *Real* Plan," *Journal of Latin American Studies*, 30, 619-39.

Franklin, J. (1980) *Methods of Mathematical Economics.* New York, Springer-Verlag.

Judge, G. et. al. (1985) *The Theory and Practice of Econometrics*, 2nd ed. New York, John Wiley.

Kenkel, J. (1974) *Dynamic Linear Economic Models.* New York, Gordon and Breach.

Klein, L. and R. Young. (1982) *An Introduction to Econometric Forecasting and Forecasting Models.* Toronto, Lexington.

Lima, F. C. and M. A. da Fonseca (1996) "The Role of the Insurance Market in the Development of the Capital Markets in the Long Run: The Case of Brazil," unpublished working paper, Universidade Federal do Rio de Janeiro.

Maddala, G. (1987) *Econometrics.* Singapore, McGraw-Hill.

Martone, C. L. (1987) "Macroeconomic Policies, Debt Accumulation, and Adjustment in Brazil, 1965-84," *Discussion Papers*, 8, World Bank, Washington, D.C.

Mello, M. F. de. (1994) "Privatização e ajuste fiscal no Brasil," *Pesquisa e Planejamento Econômico*, 24, 445-518.

Rijckeghem, W. van. (1969) "An intersectoral consistency model for economic planning in Brazil." In H. S. Ellis (ed.), *The Economy of Brazil.* Berkeley, University of California Press.

Rocha, S. (1992) "Pobreza metropolitana: balanço de uma década" in IPEA – Ministério do Planejamento, *Perspectivas da Economia Brasileira* Rio de Janeiro.

Silber, S. D. (1997) "The External Sector of the Brazilian Economy." In M. J. F. Willumsen and E. G. da Fonseca (eds.), *The Brazilian Economy: Structure and Performance in Recent Decades.* Miami, University of Miami.

Suzigan, W. (1975) "Industrialização e política econômica: uma interpretação em perspectiva histórica," *Pesquisa e Planejamento Econômico*, 5, 433-74.

Suzigan, W. et. al. (1974) *Financiamento de Projetos Industriais no Brasil.* Rio de Janeiro, IPEA-Ministério do Planejamento.

Sydsaeter, K. (1981) *Topics in Mathematical Analysis for Economists.* London, Academic Press.

Wallis, K. (1979) *Topics in Applied Econometrics*, 2nd ed. Oxford, Basil Blackwell.

Werneck, R. L. (1986) "Poupança estatal, dívida externa e crise financeira do setor público," *Pesquisa e Planejamento Econômico*, 16, 551-74.

Sources of Data

Associação Nacional das Instituições do Mercado Aberto (ANDIMA), *Séries Históricas: Dívida Pública* (year of publication unknown).

Boletim do Banco Central do Brasil, several issues.

Conjuntura Econômica, several issues.

Instituto Brasileiro de Geografia e Estatística (IBGE), *Contas Nacionais*, several issues.

Instituto Brasileiro de Geografia e Estatística (IBGE), *Estatísticas Históricas do Brasil*, rev. ed., 1990.

Instituto Brasileiro de Geografia e Estatística (IBGE), *Tabela de Relações Intersetoriais*, 1970 and 1980.

3   Analysis of Brazilian Inflation[1]

MANUEL A.R. DA FONSECA

Introduction

In the last decades, the Brazilian economy has certainly been one of the most affected by a chronic inflationary process. Moreover, this process was sharply accentuated in the period from 1986 to 1994. On two occasions, the country was at the brink of a fully-fledged hyperinflation.[2] In this chapter, the background of this period of accelerating price changes is analyzed. The unorthodox stabilization plans adopted since 1986, and especially the first one, the so-called *Cruzado* plan, are discussed and the reasons for their failure investigated. Also, the stabilization program introduced in 1994, the *Real* plan, will be discussed. Additionally, a model of inflation will be used to take into account the major components of an inflationary process – that is, demand factors (monetary expansion) and cost factors (inertial inflation).[3] Based on this analysis, future perspectives for inflation in Brazil will be assessed.

Structural Causes of Brazilian Inflation: The Pre-1986 Period

The Brazilian economy, as is the case of some other Latin American countries, has been chronically affected by high inflation rates. In the five decades from the end of the Second World War up to 1995, annual inflation was below 10% on only two occasions: in 1948 and 1957. Therefore, it is clear that inflation has been the rule rather than the exception in Brazil. Also, a similar tendency was present in neighboring Argentina. This historical trend is depicted in table 3.1 and in figures 3.1 and 3.2, covering the last 50 years.

The major cause of this chronic inflation is that there has been historically very little concern in the Brazilian society about the basic elements of price stability, that is, fiscal and monetary policy.[4] Government projects and state-sponsored investment programs were devised through the years without virtually any concern about their financing, ultimately leading to government deficits and sharp increases in money supply. In the Brazilian case, the most ambitious among these projects was the building of a new capital in the country's heartland in the 1950s and 1960s. Further, an extremely expensive program was designed and implemented after the oil crisis of the 1970s aiming at replacing part of gasoline consumption by alcohol made from sugar cane.

Table 3.1   Annual Inflation in Brazil and Argentina: 1948-95
(Averages in the period, %)

	1948-57	1958-67	1968-77	1978-87	1988-95
Brazil	14.6	44.9	26.0	138.2	893.4
Argentina	20.2	32.9	75.2	211.2	229.1

Sources: *For Brazil: Fundação Getúlio Vargas, Conjuntura Econômica, several issues*
For Argentina: A. Krieger and E. Szewach, "Inflation and indexation in Argentina" in J. Williamson (ed.), Inflation and Indexation. Washington, MIT Press, 1985 (period 1948-72); Brazil – Ministry of Planning, Indicadores da Economia Mundial, several issues (period 1973-95)

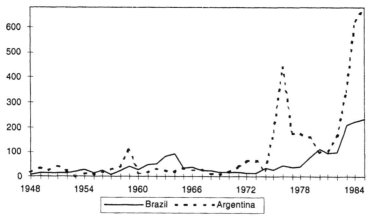

Figure 3.1   Inflation in Brazil and Argentina: 1948-85 (%)
Source: Same as Table 3.1

In Brazil, the most striking feature regarding monetary policy is the lack of a Central Bank until 1964. Furthermore, even after its creation it remained closely tied to the government and, up to now, the president of the Central Bank has been one of the aides of the Finance Minister. Another unusual feature of Brazils monetary system is that, until 1986, the largest state commercial bank, the Banco do Brasil, was entirely free to provide loans beyond its deposits since any shortage of currency was automatically covered by the Central Bank.   In addition, most public financial institutions at the federal and state levels were able, until recently, to create credit in a relatively free way since their losses were ultimately covered by the Central Bank.   Moreover, deficit financing through money and credit expansion has been the rule in Brazil, since the Central Bank is the financial agent of the Treasury: it supplies credits to the federal government whenever needed and, afterwards, sells bonds to the public to reduce the monetary expansion of government financing.

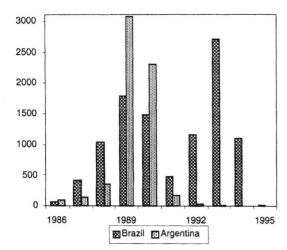

Figure 3.2   Inflation in Brazil and Argentina: 1986-95 (%)
Source: *Same as Table 3.1*

These chronic inflationary pressures were aggravated in the second half of the 1970s and first half of the 1980s due to the oil shocks of 1973 and 1979, and the increase of international interest rates, culminating in Mexico's default of 1982.   These developments caused major increases in Brazil's trade and current account deficits and one of the main policies adopted to restore equilibrium was to introduce significant exchange rate devaluations that contributed to the elevation of inflation.   By the mid

1980s, loose monetary and fiscal policies, coupled with the measures adopted to eliminate the trade deficits, had pushed inflation to above 200% a year. Both the external and internal government debts were increasing and interest rates were high in real terms, which was due mainly to the government's financial needs that needed to be met by a limited credit supply in the country's capital market, since external financial markets were closed to Latin American countries.[5]

Another important cause of Brazil's inflation, at that time, was a fully developed indexation mechanism that led to regular revisions of most prices of goods and services based on the inflation of previous periods. Among these prices were the exchange rate, wages and salaries, public utilities' prices, including oil and gasoline, rents and monthly payments in private schools.[6]

The Unorthodox Stabilization Programs: 1986-1991

In the second half of the 1980s, two ideas were dominant among Brazilian politicians. First, economic growth was viewed as a necessity in order to reduce poverty and promote development in a country plagued by social inequalities. Secondly, there was strong opposition to any proposal perceived as conservative, especially those viewed as originating from international financial institutions, particularly the IMF. Therefore, any initiative in the direction of reducing the deficit and promoting monetary discipline met strong opposition. With this background, a new line of economic thinking emerged that became very popular among Brazilian economists. It argued that fiscal and monetary policies were useless in promoting stability and that, in order to curb inflation, it was necessary only to eliminate its so-called *inertial component* – that is, the indexation of wages and prices.[7] Based on ideas of this sort, several unorthodox stabilization programs were attempted from 1986 to 1991, that centered on wage and price freezes (see table 3.2). Their final result was to push price increases to hyperinflationary levels.[8]

All these unorthodox programs had the same basic elements, introduced first in the *Cruzado* plan. Therefore, in the description that follows, emphasis will be given to this first experience with unorthodox economic policies in the country. The final result of these plans was, however, in total contradiction with their initial aim: as a rule, at the end of each plan, inflation rates were significantly higher than at the start (see figure 3.3).

Table 3.2   Unorthodox Stabilization Plans in Brazil

	Month when Plan Initiated
Cruzado	Mar. 1986
Bresser	June 1987
Verão	Jan. 1989
Collor	Mar. 1990
Collor II	Feb. 1991

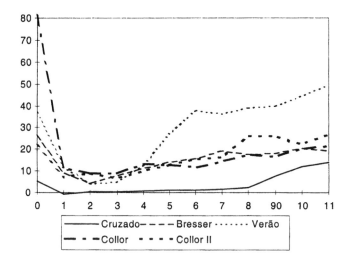

Figure 3.3   Inflation in the First 11 Months of the Unorthodox Plans
(Monthly data, %)
Source: *Same as Table 3.1*

The *Cruzado* plan was initiated on 28 February 1986 with the introduction, on that day, of several presidential decrees containing its main measures.[9]   There was no previous debate about these measures and, moreover, no previous discussion in Congress. Secrecy was an important aspect of the *Cruzado* and later unorthodox plans in order to avoid major disruptions in the economy and, particularly, in financial markets.   The main instruments of the plan were:

1. A new currency was introduced – the *cruzado* – with the elimination of three zeros from the old one – the *cruzeiro*;
2. All prices were legally fixed at the levels prevailing on 27 February 1986. The freeze also applied to the exchange rate;

3. All contracts and payments due in the old currency were subject to rules of conversion to the new currency.[10] The justification was that these contracts contained an expectation of very high inflation that was no longer valid. Therefore, all payments due after the start of the plan were converted to the new currency with a discount. The discounting factors, varying according to the length of time until the due date, were fixed by the government;

4. Wages were converted to *cruzados* based on their averaged real value for the previous 6 months. All the rules were fixed by the government that also imposed an 8% increase for all workers on top of the real wage averages. House rents were also fixed in *cruzados* using this real average method;

5. The government also tried to eliminate all indexation in prices and contracts. After the start of the plan, contracts could only be revised after a one-year period. Before the plan, this revision usually occurred on a monthly basis.

The *Cruzado* plan was, initially, very successful in keeping inflation under control (figure 3.3). However, with the exchange rate freeze and the increase in activity that occurred at the beginning of the plan, exports stagnated and imports rose sharply, leading to trade deficits by the end of 1986. The government was eventually forced to devaluate the *cruzado* and this movement was an important factor behind the acceleration of inflation that happened afterwards. By April 1987, monthly inflation was again above 20%. In May, a new economic team replaced the group that had designed the *Cruzado* plan and, one month later, another unorthodox shock was tried. This new stabilization attempt came to be known as the Bresser plan, after the Finance Minister at the time. The plan introduced a three-month wage and price freeze and several measures were devised to reduce the fiscal deficit. However, those measures were not implemented and, at the same time, the *cruzado* was devalued by 10%. As a result, prices rose sharply after the freeze period. By the end of 1987, it was clear that the Bresser plan had failed and the Finance Minister resigned.

The economic team that took office in December 1987 initially refused to introduce further wage and price controls but, since inflation kept accelerating, getting close to 30% by the end of 1988, the government announced another unorthodox shock on 15 January 1989 – the so-called *Plano Verão* (Summer Plan). Its main measures were another currency change – the *cruzado novo*, equivalent to 1000 *cruzados*, was introduced – and a new price and wage freeze. The basic goal of these measures was to avoid price increases reaching hyperinflationary levels but, again, government initiatives backfired; inflation declined at the beginning of the plan, but started to accelerate afterwards, rising to 38% in July, 49% in December, and 81% in March 1990.

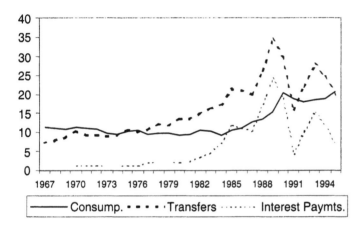

Figure 3.4   Main Government's Spending Items: 1967-95 (% of GDP)

Note: *Transfers include interest payments on the public debt, subsidies and*
                 payments to the social security system
Source: *IBGE, Brazil's National Accounts*

The major flaw of the *Cruzado* and the other unorthodox plans was that virtually no measure was taken to reduce government deficits and to control money supply. At the time of the plans, government spending was increasing considerably and the fiscal deficit mounted (see figure 3.4). Greater spending was partially due to the payment of interest on ever-increasing internal public debt. This situation led, as part of the Collor plan, which was introduced in March 1990, to the confiscation of the major part of government bonds sold to the private sector, and the bank deposits that backed these bonds. These deposits were eventually returned 18 months later, in 12 monthly instalments. Essentially, the Collor plan contained the same elements of the previous unorthodox stabilization attempts and its achievements match those of the former plans: after an initial decline, inflation soon accelerated. In February 1991, yet another wage and price freeze was adopted unsuccessfully – this came to be known as the Collor II plan.

The *Real* Plan

After a long series of failed stabilisation attempts, all of them based on ideas proposed by Brazil's so-called *economistas heterodoxos*, monthly inflation reached almost 50% in June 1994, immediately before the *Real* plan was launched. The plan implemented one of the ideas suggested a decade earlier by two exponents of the unorthodox school: the introduction of an indexed currency to curb high inflation rates.[11] This proposal was not really original since it had been applied in Hungary immediately after World War II, with disastrous consequences.[12]   What was somewhat original was to use an indexed currency as the basis of a stabilization program 50 years after the Hungarians had tried it.   The fact that this proposal was indeed adopted in Brazil, after so many failed unorthodox stabilisation programs, is somewhat puzzling.

The backbone of the plan was the elimination of indexation in the exchange market, the labour market, public utilities' prices, including oil and gasoline, and some generally used contracts – especially those applying to rents, private schools and medical insurance. After July 1994,[13] wages, public utilities' prices, and prices settled by legal contracts could no longer be raised according to previous inflation; any increase occurring before a one-year interval was prohibited. Another fundamental aspect of the plan was that the new currency that was created in July 1994, the *real*, was initially pegged to the dollar; there was a fixed maximum exchange rate to which the Central Bank was committed.

There were some initiatives in the direction of reducing the government deficit, but those were very limited and basically aimed at increasing government revenues. The rates of the main federal taxes were raised, especially income tax rates. Another measure that augmented the revenues at the federal level was the reduction, approved by Congress, of the funds transferred by the federal government to states and municipalities by 15%.

A few months before the start of the *Real* plan, an official price index was introduced, the *Unidade Real de Valor*, or URV for short, that was used compulsorily to adjust prices in government controlled markets, especially the labor market. This index was, in reality, the official *cruzeiro real*-dollar exchange rate and was fixed daily by the Central Bank. The practical effect of this measure was to make prices that followed the URV change according to the dollar exchange rate.   The strategy of the government was to make most internal prices vary according to the exchange rate, using the URV device. Once most prices were following the

URV, they would be transformed into a new currency – the *real* – and it was hoped that the latter would keep a constant rate in relation to the dollar. Consequently, inflation in the new currency would be reduced to near zero. The essence of this idea was that, although the old currency – the *cruzeiro real* – was depreciating very fast due to high inflation rates, the new currency that was going to be created could remain stable, at least for some time. The challenge, as had happened in Hungary in the 1940s, was to keep the new currency free from inflationary pressures. To accomplish that, a major fiscal and monetary restructuring was needed, but this did not happen.

Contrary to government expectations, the use of the URV in the private sector as a basis for determining price changes remained very limited. Nevertheless, the plan was set in motion and on 1 July 1994 the new currency was introduced and it was determined that the conversion rate between the *real* and the former currency would be R$ 1 = CR$ 2,750.[14] The URV and the dollar were rated at CR$ 2,750 on 30 June 1994 (table 3.3). Therefore, the initial exchange rate of the new currency in relation to the dollar was 1 to 1.

Table 3.3   Dollar-*cruzeiro real* exchange rate and URV
(Figures for the last day of the month, CR$ per dollar)

	Jan. 94	Feb. 94	Mar. 94	Apr. 94	May 94	June 94
Buying rate*	458.65	637.27	913.34	1302.26	1875.25	2612.50
Selling rate*	458.66	637.28	913.35	1302.28	1875.27	2750.00
URV**	458.16	637.64	931.05	1323.92	1875.82	2750.00

Note:	* Average of the day's trade; ** Fixed by the Central Bank
Source:	Data Analysis Consultores Associados, Síntese Econômica, vol. 3, no. 6 (1994)

This currency change created a complex logistical problem since all the bills and coins used in a very large country like Brazil were exchanged in a few days. In comparison, in all of the many currency changes that had previously occurred in the country, the old bills did not disappear immediately. They only received a stamp to indicate that it was in fact a new currency. The main purpose of changing the bills immediately was to make a major psychological impact that, it was hoped, would help to convince Brazilians that inflation had indeed been wiped out together with the old bills. Also, in another initiative aimed at improving expectations about the new currency, government officials declared that the *real* would be exchanged freely for dollars. This statement, however, proved to be false. The emphasis on changing expectations about inflation was clearly justified since, by the time the *real* was introduced, annual inflation was above 9,000% a year.

Table 3.4   Dollar-*real* exchange rate
(Figures for the last day of the month, R$ per dollar)

	June 94	July 94	Aug. 94	Sep. 94	Oct. 94	Nov. 94	Dec. 94
Selling rate*	1.000	0.940	0.889	0.854	0.846	0.845	0.846
	Jan. 95	Feb. 95	Mar. 95	Apr. 95	May 95	June 95	July 95
Selling rate*	0.842	0.852	0.896	0.913	0.906	0.922	0.936

Note: * Average of the day's trade
Source: Data Analysis Consultores Associados, Síntese Econômica, vol. 4, no. 7 (1995)

The new currency was initially pegged to the dollar, which helped to convince Brazilians that it was actually a strong currency, in contrast to the long series of currencies that had been previously introduced and that were rapidly eroded by inflation. Actually, in the first months of the plan, the Central Bank allowed the real to float and it appreciated in relation to the dollar due to the large influx of foreign capital (table 3.4). This tendency was mainly the result of the very high levels of internal interest rates, as compared to rates in the international market. By the end of September 1994, the dollar exchange rate had fallen 15% in relation to the 1 July rate. In the same period, the country's most followed price index increased by 31%, given that inflation did not fall instantaneously. The new currency thus became strongly overvalued.

After the start of the *Real* plan, inflation fell mainly due to the stability imposed on the labor market, the exchange market, on government controlled prices and on prices determined by contracts. Prices in these markets were varying according to the URV and they were no longer allowed to rise once the URV was converted to the real. This was, in fact, a subtle form of price freeze, although one that applied only to some segments of the economy, but they were some of the more vital ones.

Another factor that contributed to the reduction of inflation was the process of opening the Brazilian economy, the so-called *abertura*, that started in 1990. Import tariffs were reduced considerably and virtually all industrial sectors were exposed to foreign competition.[15]   Also, a major agreement was reached in 1992 with international creditors on the country's external debt, an agreement that made it possible for large

Brazilian companies to raise money in international financial markets. Until 1992, the country was in default on its debt payments and this made it practically impossible to raise money abroad.   Another factor that contributed to the inflow of foreign capital, that was vital to the success of the plan, was the large availability of credit in the international market that existed since the end of the 1980s.

During the first months of the plan, money supply increased considerably, even taking into account that money demand would necessarily be greater due to the fall of inflation rates. By September 1994, the monetary base had expanded by 303% in relation to June of that year. In the same period, M1 increased 113%. It was clear that the Central Bank did not have a firm control of money supply, despite some harsh measures that were adopted to avoid credit expansion and that pushed interest rates to even higher levels.[16] This happened mainly because government bonds had a very short maturity period – less than three months, on average – and when part of these bonds were not renewed, which often happened after the start of the plan since money demand had increased, the Central Bank was forced to finance the government by putting more money into the economy.

Modeling Brazilian Inflation

Inflation is usually attributed to two basic elements: excess demand and cost or inertial factors. Tobin (1981), for example, lists four basic elements behind any persistent price increase: purely monetary, excess demand, inertial and important changes in the price of a specific product (like the oil shocks of the 1970s).[17]   Clearly, the first two of these elements can be classified as excess demand factors and the last two as cost determined factors. Most economists would agree that, in the inflationary process that Brazil has endured, both excess demand and cost factors are present. Therefore, in order to model Brazilian inflation, one has to develop a set of relations in which both elements are included.[18] [Definitions are provided in table 3.5]

Define:

$$\left(\frac{\dot{P}}{P}\right) = \frac{d}{dt}(\ln P) = \frac{1}{P}\frac{dP}{dt}$$ as the rate of inflation when prices are assumed to

vary continuously. Assuming, for simplicity, that two factors contribute to determine the inflation rate in a *linear* relation, we have:

$$\frac{\dot{P}}{P} = \beta \left(\frac{\dot{P}}{P}\right)_m + \gamma \left(\frac{\dot{P}}{P}\right)_i \tag{3.1}$$

where $\left(\dot{P}/P\right)_m$ represents inflation caused purely by demand and monetary factors and $\left(\dot{P}/P\right)_i$ represents inertial or cost inflation. Using the equation of exchange $MV=PY$, demand inflation can be represented by:

$$\left(\frac{\dot{P}}{P}\right)_m = \frac{\dot{M}}{M} + \frac{\dot{V}}{V} - \frac{\dot{Y}}{Y} \tag{3.2}$$

Inertial inflation, on the other hand, can be considered as being determined by some fundamental cost items that, directly and indirectly, are present in the cost structure of most products:

$$\left(\frac{\dot{P}}{P}\right)_i = a_1 \frac{\dot{D}}{D} + a_2 \frac{\dot{A}}{A} + a_3 \frac{\dot{T}}{T} + a_4 \frac{\dot{W}}{W} \tag{3.3}$$

where D: dollar exchange rate; A: average price of commodities; T: average price of public utilities; and W: average wage. Introducing equations (3.2) and (3.3) in (3.1), we have:

$$\frac{\dot{P}}{P} = \beta \left(\frac{\dot{M}}{M} + \frac{\dot{V}}{V} - \frac{\dot{Y}}{Y}\right) + \alpha_1 \frac{\dot{D}}{D} + \alpha_2 \frac{\dot{A}}{A} + \alpha_3 \frac{\dot{T}}{T} + \alpha_4 \frac{\dot{W}}{W} \tag{3.4}$$

were $\alpha_i = \gamma a_i$. Further, in a fully indexed economy, the cost components of the inflationary process are determined by the inflation rate of the previous period, such as the previous month, quarter or semester. This dynamic behavior can be represented as:

$$\left(\frac{\dot{D}}{D}\right)_t = c_1 \left(\frac{\dot{P}}{P}\right)_{t-1} \tag{3.5}$$

$$\left(\frac{\dot{A}}{A}\right)_t = c_2 \left(\frac{\dot{P}}{P}\right)_{t-1} \tag{3.6}$$

$$\left(\frac{\dot{T}}{T}\right)_t = c_3 \left(\frac{\dot{P}}{P}\right)_{t-1} \tag{3.7}$$

$$\left(\frac{\dot{W}}{W}\right)_t = c_4 \left(\frac{\dot{P}}{P}\right)_{t-1} \tag{3.8}$$

Table 3.5   Estimation of Equation 3.4

Variables (All data in logarithmic differences)

P	General Price Index (IGD-DI) - Fundação Getúlio Vargas.
M	M1 stock, end of period - Brazil's Central Bank (12-month moving average).
V	Income velocity of M1 - Brazil's Central Bank (12-month moving average).
Y	Index of industrial output - Brazil's Statistical Bureau, IBGE (12-month moving average).
A	Price index of agricultural products - Fundação Getúlio Vargas.
D	Dollar exchange rate, selling rate, end of period.
T	Price index of public services - Fundação Getúlio Vargas.
W	Average nominal industrial wages in the state of São Paulo - Federation of Industries, FIESP (6-month moving average).

OLS Regression from Jan. 1981 to Dec. 1985
Dependent variable: P

Independent Variables		Estimated Coefficient	T-statistic
$M+V-Y$		0.32169	2.05326
D		0.08455	1.48997
A		0.26851	6.04387
T		0.05993	0.91731
W		0.26857	2.56979
$R^2 =$	0.7133	Corrected $R^2 =$	0.6925

F-statistic $(5,55) = 27.3708$; Durbin-Watson statistic $= 1.4938$; Number of observations $= 60$

Equations (3.4) to (3.8) represent a model of inflation incorporating both excess demand and cost or inertial factors. The coefficient, c_1, reflects the exchange rate policy prevailing in the country. On the other hand, if the public utility companies are mainly state-controlled, the coefficient, c_3, reflects basically government decisions.[19]

The coefficients of equation (3.4) were estimated using monthly data from January 1981 to December 1985. The regression period was chosen so that it did not include the unorthodox plans. All data are in logarithmic differences, thus generating an approximation for the rate of change. The estimation results are presented in table 3.5. Although the R^2 and F statistics as well as the Durbin-Watson are also presented, they do not have a straightforward meaning since the regression is restricted to a zero intercept.

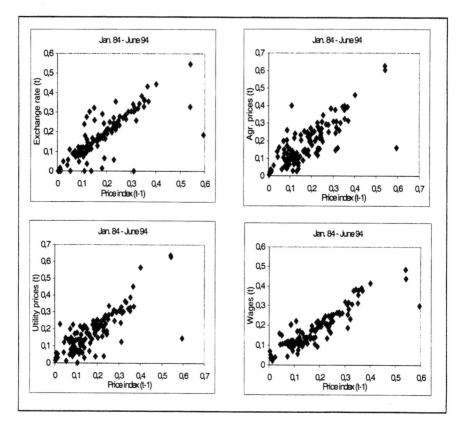

Figure 3.5   Cost components of inflation, Jan. 1984 – June 1994
(Logarithmic differences)

For most part of the period before the Real plan, it is reasonable to assume that the coefficients c_i $(i = 1,...,4)$ were close to one, representing a perfectly indexed economy on a monthly basis. Figure 3.5 illustrates this characteristic of the Brazilian economy; for the pre-Real period, the model above was used to simulate different phases of the Brazilian inflationary process. In the simulations, the exogenous variables are M, V and Y. All other variables were generated by the model, that is, to determine inflation in period t, the inflation rate obtained from the model in t-1 was used. All the c_i coefficients were set equal to one. The simulation results, together with historical data, appear in figures 3.6 and 3.7.

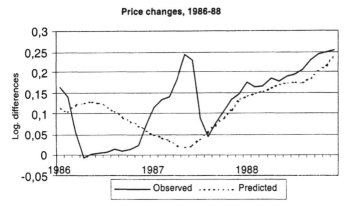

Figure 3.6   Monthly Inflation in Brazil: Jan. 1986 – Dec. 1988

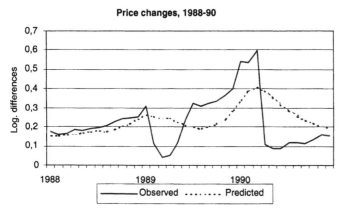

Figure 3.7   Monthly Inflation in Brazil: Jan. 1988 – Dec. 1990

From the simulations, one can deduce that, with the exception of the periods of wage and price freezes, the model reproduces the historical data reasonably well.   The comparison between observed and simulated data also illustrates the artificial component that was introduced in the Brazilian economy by the unorthodox plans; after the start of each plan, inflation falls more than that predicted by the model. Later on, though, it shows a sharper increase than rates that might be expected from the simulation. This trend is especially clear during the *Cruzado* plan (introduced in March of 1986) and in the months following its end, when price controls were eliminated (first half of 1987).

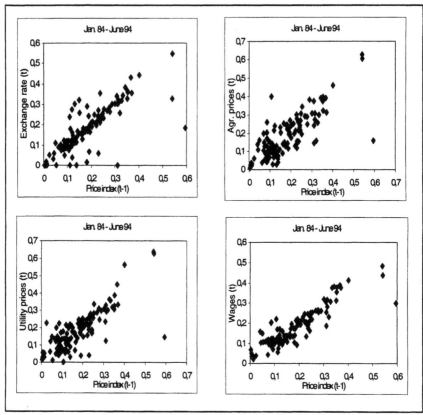

Figure 3.8   Cost components of inflation, July 1994 – Dec. 1998
    (Logarithmic differences)

Table 3.6   Velocity of Circulation of M1
    (Annual averages)

1983	1984	1985	1986	1987	1988	1989	1990	1991	1992	1993	1994	1995	1996	1997	1998
16.3	21.0	20.9	13.0	14.2	29.8	49.5	41.6	38.9	59.5	80.1	61.8	33.8	30.9	22.7	20.8

Source: *Brazil's Central Bank*

The previous analysis also helps to explain how the *Real* plan achieved the dramatic reductions in inflation rates. Basically, two developments occurred since July of 1994: indexation was virtually eliminated – that is, the c_i coefficients were reduced to near zero – and the velocity of circulation of M1 also declined sharply. These developments are illustrated in figure 3.8, that shows that the earlier pattern of indexation was virtually eliminated, and in table 3.6, showing that M1 income velocity, that had reached unprecedented levels during the period of extremely high inflation, returned to the pattern that prevailed before the years of accelerating price increases.

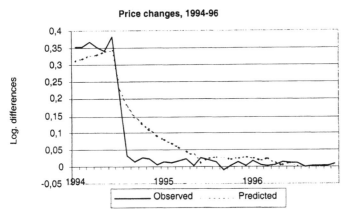

Figure 3.9   Monthly Inflation in Brazil: Jan. 1994 – Dec. 1996

Figure 3.9 presents historical and simulated data for the period immediately before and after the *Real* plan.   In the simulations, the c_i coefficients were set equal to zero after July of 1994.   The analysis based on the model does seem to show that the major accomplishment of the Plan was indeed the effective elimination of indexation – something that, in the earlier stabilization attempts, lasted for only brief periods.

An Assessment of Inflation in Brazil

The crucial variables in the model developed above are the money supply and the money velocity.   In effect, what distinguishes a regime of low inflation rates from one of high rates, in terms of the model's variables, is the behavior of what we may call *total liquidity*, that is *MV*, although other variables would be affected by and, at the same time, contribute to the inflationary process.   Therefore, according to the model, the future trend of inflation in Brazil, or in any other country, is generated by the behavior of total liquidity.

This last statement, though, is a tautology, since there is a strong circularity involving inflation and money supply.   One can say that inflation is determined by the behavior of the money supply multiplied by its velocity as much as that these variables are determined by the current inflation rate.[20] In the end, inflation depends crucially on the fiscal and monetary policies pursued by the government and the Central Bank in the long run and on how the private sector anticipates that this might change in the future. In terms of the model's dynamics, it can be demonstrated that the long run path of the rate of inflation is given by the $\left(\dfrac{\dot{M}}{M} + \dfrac{\dot{V}}{V} - \dfrac{\dot{Y}}{Y} \right)$ term in equation (3.4), whereas the other terms determine the *transient*, or short run dynamics of the inflationary process.[21]

Table 3.7   M4 and its Components
(Millions of Reais)

	June 94	Dec. 94	June 95	Dec. 95	Dec. 96	Dec. 97	Nov. 98
M1	7,466	23,081	18,269	29,078	30,636	47,363	46,091
Federal Govt. Securities	32,680	29,935	32,359	57,738	102,855	140,068	177,853
State & Municipal Sects.	14,861	7,040	7,048	7,828	11,193	8,739	9,358
Private Securities	41,552	57,654	70,272	79,799	83,429	92,894	95,952
Savings Accounts	29,593	44,945	55,489	63,635	72,024	97,062	106,205
Investment Funds	7,923	9,446	14,203	13,200	22,832	6,262	7,768
Other	2,575	3,345	2,697	0	0	0	0
M4	136,661	175,445	200,356	251,278	322,968	392,389	443,228

Source: *Brazil's Central Bank*

However, given a hypothesis about the future trend of the exogenous variables *M*, *V* and *Y*, one can derive reasonably reliable projections of the future trend of inflation, as can be gauged from the historical simulations. The crucial stage in this modeling process is to assess, from the current and anticipated fiscal and monetary policies, the future trend of those exogenous variables. The analysis based on the model helps to understand the mechanism through which the *Real* plan accomplished the reduction of inflation rates in Brazil and it helps to evaluate the important challenges that remain in order to keep inflation permanently under control. Due to the initial impact in the economy of the introduction of the new currency and to the freezing of wages, the exchange rate and government controlled prices accomplished by the URV device, the government managed to affect, simultaneously, the inertial components of equation (3.4) and the money velocity. Therefore, both the demand and the cost component of inflation were sharply reduced.

As long as the exchange rate remains under relative control and the public believes that the Plan will continue to work, thus contributing decisively to keep the money velocity at a low level, there should not be any major change in the trend of inflation. However, money supply has shown significant increases since the start of the plan (see table 3.7) and this might lead to stronger inflationary pressures in the long run.[22] In order to maintain prices under control in Brazil, it is necessary to promote a major restructuring of the public sector that would help to control money supply, and this remains as the major challenge facing the country in the near future.

Notes

[1] The first three sections are based on Fonseca (1998).

[2] Annualized inflation reached 126,174% in March 1990, and 9,735% in June 1994.

[3] This model is based on the analysis developed in Zottman (1989).

[4] The analysis that follows also seems to apply, in general terms, to some other Latin American countries and, in particular, to Argentina.

[5] At that time, the external debt was growing due to the accumulation of interest.

[6] With the growing inflation, the intervals between price revisions were ever shortened. Originally the revisions occurred annually or biannually, then quarterly and, in the later stages of the Brazilian inflationary process, monthly.

[7] These ideas are developed in F. Lopes, "Inflação inercial, hiperinflação e desinflação", *Revista da ANPEC*, vol. 7, no. 8 (1984) and in L. Pereira and Y. Nakano, *Inflação e Recessão* (São Paulo, Brasiliense, 1984).

[8] A thorough assessment of inflation in Brazil can be found in Baer (1995). See also Beckerman (1991) and Fonseca (1995).

[9] Brazil was, in fact, following the lead of Argentina, which had adopted a stabilization program based on wage and price freezes in June 1985.

[10] These conversion rules had also been previously introduced in Argentina.

[11] P. Arida and A. Resende. "Inflação inercial e reforma monetária." In P. Arida (ed.) *Inflação Zero*. Rio de Janeiro, Paz e Terra, 1986.

[12] At the beginning of 1946, the Hungarian government, trying to curb a hyperinflation, introduced a financial asset that was adjusted daily according to the previous day's inflation rate. Soon afterwards, these bonds started to be used as currency. The experience was by no means successful since, in July 1946 – after this indexed currency had been introduced – that country had the highest monthly inflation of all times: 4×10^{16} %. This number corresponds to a daily inflation rate of 258%. See, on this subject, Nogaro (1948).

[13] The *Real* plan was launched on 1 July 1994.

[14] One *real* was equaled to 2,750 *cruzeiros reais*.

[15] The average import tariff in Brazil was reduced from 32.2% in 1990 to 14.2% in 1993. This trend was more significant in the case of consumer durable goods: from 50.6% to 17.4%.

[16] In July 1994, the Central Bank created a compulsory reserve of 100% on new bank check deposits. In October of that year, it created a compulsory reserve of 30% on all time

deposits and a compulsory reserve of 15% on any credit provided by banks. See A. C. Pastore, "Porque a Política Monetária Perde a Eficácia?", *Revista Brasileira de Economia*, vol. 50, no. 3 (1996), p. 309 n.; and F. C. Lima, 'A Política Monetária e o Plano Real', unpub. working paper, Universidade Federal do Rio de Janeiro, 1995, p. 2.

[17] Tobin (1981).

[18] One such model is developed in Fonseca (1995), who elaborates on an earlier work by Zottman (1989). This approach is followed here.

[19] This was certainly the case in Brazil until 1996 but, since then, many public utility companies have gradually been sold to the private sector.

[20] Friedman (1987) develops on this point.

[21] See Fonseca (1995), chapter 5.

[22] If the money supply shows a continued tendency of sharp growth, the velocity component in equation (3.4) could also increase due to a loss of confidence in the plan.

References

Baer, Werner (1995) *The Brazilian Economy* (4th ed.). Westport-Connecticut, Praeger.

Beckerman, Paul (1991) "Recent 'heterodox' stabilization experience: Argentina, Israel, and Brazil, 1985-1989". In W. Baer, J. Petry and M. Simpson (eds.), *Latin America: the Crisis of the Eighties and the Opportunities of the Nineties*. Champaign-Illinois, Bureau of Economic and Business Research-University of Illinois.

Fonseca, Manuel A.R. da (1995) *O Processo Inflacionário: Análise da Experiência Brasileira*. Petrópolis-Rio de Janeiro, Vozes.

Fonseca, Manuel A.R. da (1998) "Brazil's *Real* plan". *Journal of Latin American Studies*, 30, 619-639.

Friedman, Milton (1987) "Quantity theory of money". In J. Eatwell, M. Milgate and P. Newman (eds.), *The New Palgrave: Money*. London, Macmillan.

Nogaro, Bertrand (1948) "Hungary's recent monetary crisis and its theoretical meaning". *American Economic Review*, 38, 526-542.

Tobin, James (1981) "Diagnosing inflation: a taxonomy". In M. Flandes and M. Razin (eds.) *Development in an Inflationary World*. New York, Academic Press.

Zottman, Luis (1989) "Inflação, processo decisório governamental e a modelagem: um comentário metodológico." Fortaleza-Ceará, *Annals of the XI Meeting of the Brazilian Econometric Society*.

4 Trade Liberalization and Location: Geographical Shifts in the Brazilian Economic Structure

EDUARDO A. HADDAD and CARLOS R. AZZONI

Introduction

Recent research on trade and location has proposed different approaches to analyze the effects of globalization on industrial location.[1] Considering the two main driving forces – trade liberalization and technical progress – the globalization process is responsible for important shifts in the economic centers of gravity not only in the world economy but also within the national economies. In the latter case, the question one poses addresses equity concerns: are regional inequalities likely to widen or narrow?

Although it is agreed that there is inherent unpredictability created by some of the forces involved, the research agenda seeks to use new techniques to illuminate at least some of the forces at work reshaping the economic geography of the world and provide an empirical assessment to quantify these forces (Venables, 1998). In this chapter, we focus on the regional impacts of one of these driving forces in a national economy.

A cost-competitiveness approach, based on relative changes in the sectoral and regional cost and demand structures, is adopted to isolate the likely state effects of the tariff reduction verified in Brazil in the early 1990s. It tackles three bases for the analytical framework proposed in the literature: comparative advantage is grasped through the use of differential regional production technologies; geographical advantage is verified through the explicit modeling of the transportation services and the costs of moving products based on origin-destination pairs; and cumulative causation appears through the operation of internal and external multipliers and interregional spillover effects in comparative-static experiments, such as those proposed here.

Brazil was late in its efforts towards the integration of the country in the global network, as was the case for most Latin American countries until the 1990s. Among the measures adopted in the trade reform initiated in 1990, the restructuring of the tariff schedule played an important role. Between 1990 and 1995, the average tariff was reduced from 32.2% to around 14%.

The discussion of regional (sub-national) impacts on the Brazilian economy of unilateral liberalization and the Mercosul trade agreement has often lacked a formal analytical framework. The debate has often focused on sectoral implications considering economy-wide effects (Flores Jr., 1997; Campos-Filho, 1998; Gonzaga *et al.*, 1999). The few incursions on sub-national issues have not gone further than exercises of well-educated speculation (Pacheco, 1998), nor presented an integrated interregional framework, treating the regions as isolated entities in aspatial dimensions (Barros, 1998). To close this gap, this study uses an interregional CGE model (Haddad and Hewings, 1997; Haddad, 1999) to analyze the short-run and long run regional effects of unilateral trade liberalization policies, represented by tariff cut simulations, on the Brazilian economy. The model produces estimates for three Brazilian macro-regions, using a bottom-up approach (national results are obtained from the aggregation of regional results). Further, top-down disaggregation of the macro-regional results to the state level is proposed and implemented; estimates for 26 sectors in 27 states are reported. By using the results to evaluate changes in the sectoral production gravity center, it is shown that the more open policies of the 1990s generated geographical shifts towards the Center-South, increasing regional inequality in the country.

Modeling Issue

The specification of linkages between the national and regional economy represents an interesting theoretical issue in regional modeling. Two basic approaches are prevalent – top-down and bottom-up – and the choice between them usually reflects a trade-off between theoretical sophistication and data requirements.

The top-down approach consists of the disaggregation of national results to regional levels, on an *ad hoc* basis. The disaggregation can proceed in different steps (e.g. country-state $\rightarrow$ state-municipality), enhancing a very fine level of regional divisions.[2] The desired adding-up property in a multi-step procedure is that, at each stage, the disaggregated projections have to be consistent with the results at the immediately higher level. The starting point of top-down models is economy-wide projections. The mapping to regional dimensions occurs without feedback from the region; in this sense, effects of policies originating in the regions are precluded. In accordance with the lack of theoretical refinement in terms of modeling the behavior of regional agents, most top-down models are not as data demanding as bottom-up models.

In the bottom-up approach, agents' behavior is explicitly modeled at the regional level. A fully interdependent system is specified in which national-regional feedback may occur in both directions. Thus, analysis of policies originating at the regional level is facilitated. The adding-up property is fully recognized, since national results are obtained from the aggregation of regional results. In order to make such highly sophisticated theoretical models operational, data requirements are very demanding. To start with, an interregional input-output database is usually required, with full specification of interregional flows. Data also include interregional trade elasticities and other regional parameters, for which econometric estimates are rarely available in the literature.

The strategy adopted in this chapter utilizes an interregional computable general equilibrium model to evaluate shifts in the economic center of gravity and regional specialization in the Brazilian economy due to liberal tariff policies undertaken in the early 1990s. Previous work by Haddad and Hewings (1998a) has analyzed the short-run and long run regional effects of these unilateral trade liberalization policies, represented by tariff cut simulations. A further disaggregation of the macro-regional results to the state level is proposed and implemented in a later Section. The states results are then used to estimate geographical shifts in the Brazilian economic structure. Before that, a summary of the results reported in the study by Haddad and Hewings (1998a) follows. A brief description of the interregional CGE model is presented in the Appendix, which follows concluding remarks.

The Big Picture: Macro-Regional Results[3]

The Brazilian Multisectoral And Regional/Interregional Analysis Model (B-MARIA) is the first fully operational interregional CGE model for Brazil.[4] The model is based on the MONASH-MRF Model, which is the latest development in the ORANI suite of CGE models of the Australian economy. B-MARIA contains over 200,000 equations, and it is designed for forecasting and policy analysis. Agents' behavior is modeled at the regional level, accommodating variations in the structure of regional economies. The model recognizes the economies of three Brazilian regions: North, Northeast, and Center-South (Rest of Brazil). Results are based on a bottom-up approach – national results are obtained from the aggregation of regional results. The model identifies 40 sectors in each region producing 40 commodities, a single household in each region, regional governments and one federal government, and a single foreign consumer who trades with each region. Special groups of equations define government finances, accumulation relations, and regional labor markets. The model is calibrated for 1985, representing the economic structure before the trade reform that was initiated in 1990; a rather complete data set is available for 1985, which is the year of the last economic censuses for the country, facilitating the choice of the base year.

B-MARIA has been widely used for policy analysis (Haddad and Hewings, 1998ab, 1999; Haddad 1999). The model was applied in Haddad and Hewings (1998a) to analyze the effects on the Brazilian economy of a uniform 25% decrease in all tariff rates; the analysis concentrated on the effects on industrial activity levels, and on some general macro and regional variables. The results suggest that the interplay of market forces in the Brazilian economy favors the more developed region of the country (Center-South): all the regions were positively affected in the short-run, and, in the long-run, only the less developed region (Northeast) presented negative results; in both cases, however, the tariff reduction worsened the Northeast's relative position in the country.

At the sectoral level,[5] the B-MARIA industry activity results implied that, in the short-run, export sectors benefited most from the tariff cut, through reductions in the cost of production, while import-competing sectors were the main losers, as they face stronger competition from imported goods. Figures 4.1-4.3 show the short-run percentage changes in activity level, for each sector in each region. With a few exceptions, the changes are similar in sign across the three regions although the percentage changes do vary, with negative changes of greater intensity in the North and Northeast and somewhat greater positive changes in the Center-South.

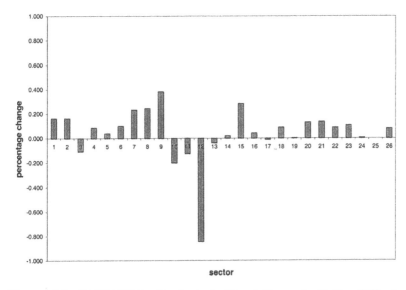

Figure 4.1 **B-MARIA Projected Short-Run Activity Effects of a Uniform 25% Tariff Reduction: North**

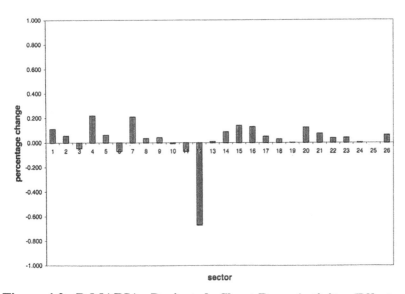

Figure 4.2 **B-MARIA Projected Short-Run Activity Effects of a Uniform 25% Tariff Reduction: Northeast**

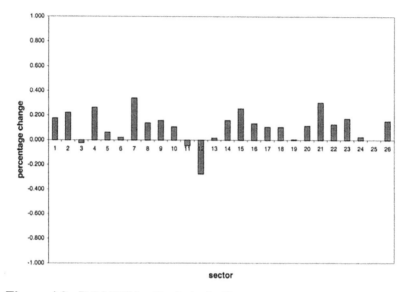

Figure 4.3   B-MARIA Projected Short-Run Activity Effects of a Uniform 25% Tariff Reduction: Center-South

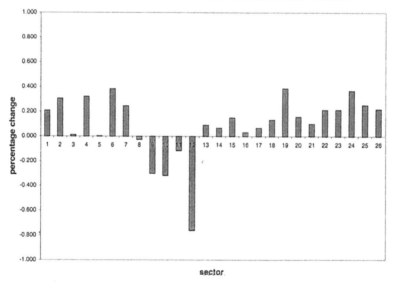

Figure 4.4   B-MARIA Projected Long-Run Activity Effects of a Uniform 25% Tariff Reduction: North

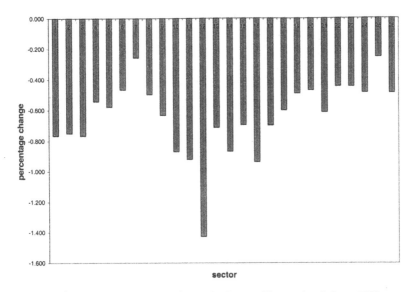

Figure 4.5 B-MARIA Projected Long-Run Activity Effects of a Uniform 25% Tariff Reduction: Northeast

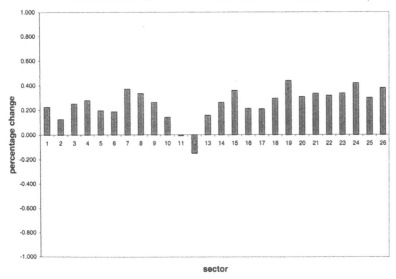

Figure 4.6 B-MARIA Projected Long-Run Activity Effects of a Uniform 25% Tariff Reduction: Center-South

Long-run sectoral results revealed the weak performance of industries in the Northeast (figure 4.5).   In the North (figure 4.4), capital-good industries led growth in the region, with sectors producing consumer goods and services also achieving positive outcomes.   The expansion of the mining sector was mainly induced by the increase in its exports, the only regional sector with a favorable record in the international arena.   Finally, the Center-South (figure 4.6) presented the best performance overall.   With the exception of the chemical complex, all the sectors were positively affected.   Because of the higher internal multipliers in the region, the relative performance of the non-capital-good-producing sectors was better than in the North.   Moreover, the region also benefited from increased international competitiveness, as suggested by the rise in its exports.

In the next section we set out a method for disaggregating B-MARIA results to the state level.   The method is then applied to results from the tariff experiment reported in Haddad and Hewings (1998a) and summarized here.   For each of the 26 Brazilian states and the Federal District we provide short-run and long-run projections of the effects of a 25% across-the-board tariff decrease on the level of economic activity.

Kaleidoscope Analysis: State-Level Disaggregation

The results described in the previous section are very relevant for the understanding of an integrated interregional system.   The model produces results only at the national and macro-regional levels, fully recognizing the general equilibrium nature of economic interdependence and the fact that the policy impacts in various regional markets differ.   However, in the Brazilian federalism, states play an important role, and thus, for many policy purposes, state disaggregation may be required.   In order to meet such needs, under conditions of limited information at the state level, a top-down disaggregation scheme has been adapted from Dixon *et al.* (1982) and implemented.   It takes B-MARIA regional results as an input and produces results for each of the states that constitute a specific region.[6]

The method proposed here can be summarized in four different steps: 1) use B-MARIA to project economy-wide and macro-regional effects of the exogenous shock; 2) allocate each commodity to one of two groups, regional and local; 3) determine gross effects for each sector; 4) scale gross projections to ensure that the adding-up restriction holds.

Data requirements for the implementation of this top-down methodology include a minimal amount of data.   Estimates of sectoral value added generated across states are the main piece of information needed. After estimating state input-output tables from the respective regional tables using the location quotient approach (Miller and Blair, 1985), one can proceed with the task of disaggregating B-MARIA results.

The allocation of state commodities into regional or local relies on the ability of each state industry to supply the demands placed upon it by other industries in the state and by state final demand. If an industry is less concentrated in the state than in the region, its demand in the state is satisfied mainly from production in that state; on the other hand, if an industry is more concentrated in the state than in the region, it is assumed that the commodity it produces is traded extensively across state borders.

In the case of regional commodities, the gross effects are set exogenously; it is assumed that the growth rate estimated for the sector in the region applies to the state. For local commodities, production in state r is set equal to demand in state r (plus exports); it is assumed that there is no inter-state trade in local commodities.[7] Thus, we can determine the gross effects on economic activity of sectors producing local commodities as follows.

$$x_L^r = B_R^r z_R^r + B_L^r z_L^r + B_{FD}^r x_{FD}^r \tag{4.1}$$

where x_L^r is the vector of percentage changes in activity level of local industry L in region r; z_R^r is the vector of percentage changes in the demand for regional commodity R in region r to be used as an input to production; z_L^r is the vector of percentage changes in the demand for local commodity L in region r to be used as an input to production; x_{FD}^r is the vector of percentage changes in total final demand for local commodity L in region r; B_R^r is the matrix of sales shares of local commodity L to regional industry R in region r; B_L^r is the matrix of sales shares of local commodity L to local industry L in region r; and B_{FD}^r is the vector of sale shares of local commodity L to final demand in region r.

Equation (4.1) tells us that the aggregate output of any local commodity in a state is equal to the aggregate demand for the commodity in the state (plus exports, included in the final demand vector). Since $x_L^r = z_L^r$ in equilibrium, we have a system of L equations and L unknowns, which can be easily solved. After we obtain estimates for all z_R^r and all z_L^r, we might need to scale these gross effects so that the adding-up property holds, i.e., we want to ensure that state sectoral results add up to regional sectoral results, and, therefore, the aggregate state results must be consistent with the aggregate regional results.

This method takes into account the industrial composition of activity in each state and the internal multiplier effects. State disaggregations of the results from the 25% tariff decrease simulation are presented in tables 4.1-4.3; each table reports the short-run and long-run percentage changes in sectoral activity in the constituent states of each region. Regarding the distribution of gross output among states, different patterns appear (figures 4.7-4.8).

In the short run, two groups of state performance can be distinguished: first, the states belonging to the Center-South, that achieve overall better results in comparison with the states in the less developed regions, that form the second group. In the Center-south, São Paulo does not accompany the higher level of growth in the region, securing the lowest ranking; the poor results of the chemical, and pharmaceutical and veterinary sectors, that correspond to 10% of the state economy, dictate the less favorable aggregated results. The states in the South region (PR, SC, RS) present a more uniform positive performance, with above-average results; above-average projections are also verified in the states of Minas Gerais, Espírito Santo and Rio de Janeiro.

In the group of states located in the poorer regions, which present lower levels of growth in the simulations, the state of Bahia is projected to be adversely affected because its economy is relatively concentrated in chemical-based sectors, which achieve negative results. In the Northeast, the state of Alagoas is also hampered by the weak prospect in the chemical industry, which is responsible for 8.1% of the state gross output; the state economy is also adversely affected by the poor results of some service sectors.

In the North, Amapá and Roraima worsen their relative position in the region, heavily influenced by the neutral role of the government sector in the short-run, imposed by our assumptions. Pará and Tocantins, states where agriculture play a prominent role, benefit from strong sectoral performance; in the case of Pará, the prospects of the mining sector also helped to foster growth in the short-run.

	Short-Run									Long-Run								
	RO	AC	AM	RR	PA	AP	TO	MT	N	RO	AC	AM	RR	PA	AP	TO	MT	N
1 Agriculture	0.179	0.179	0.127	0.155	0.179	0.150	0.179	0.129	0.162	0.216	0.216	0.205	0.236	0.216	0.238	0.216	0.173	0.208
2 Mining	0.089	–	0.089	–	0.289	0.089	0.322	0.315	0.162	0.577	–	0.577	–	-0.167	0.577	-0.236	-0.211	0.306
3 Nonmetallic Minerals	0.011	0.011	0.045	0.012	-0.171	0.011	0.050	0.008	-0.108	0.034	0.034	0.033	0.033	0.001	0.035	0.029	0.034	0.012
4 Metal Products	0.048	0.033	0.102	0.031	0.040	0.034	0.097	0.035	0.086	0.317	0.327	0.319	0.323	0.339	0.361	0.246	0.325	0.322
5 Machinery	0.076	–	0.021	–	0.121	0.066	–	0.094	0.039	0.030	–	0.000	–	0.006	0.043	–	0.023	0.003
6 Electrical and Electronic	0.026	0.026	0.100	–	0.026	–	–	0.026	0.099	0.333	0.333	0.384	–	0.333	–	–	0.333	0.383
7 Transportation Equipment	0.069	–	0.250	–	0.069	0.067	0.070	0.076	0.232	0.266	–	0.243	–	0.265	0.269	0.267	0.250	0.245
8 Wood Products and	0.225	0.266	0.295	0.269	0.225	0.218	0.325	0.265	0.243	-0.126	0.142	0.178	0.137	-0.126	0.208	0.068	0.143	-0.026
9 Paper Products and	0.258	0.256	0.267	0.248	0.462	0.255	0.260	0.255	0.382	0.358	0.364	0.401	0.376	-0.760	0.378	0.366	0.349	-0.301
10 Rubber	-0.341	-0.341	-0.341	–	0.087	0.053	0.047	0.088	-0.201	-0.815	-0.815	-0.815	–	0.705	0.733	0.704	0.634	-0.317
11 Chemicals	0.158	0.152	0.056	–	0.167	–	0.175	-0.190	-0.126	0.409	0.419	-0.221	–	0.354	–	0.446	-0.221	-0.115
12 Pharmaceuticals and	0.059	–	0.056	–	-0.887	–	0.073	0.057	-0.845	0.276	–	0.276	–	-0.810	–	0.269	0.273	-0.762
13 Plastics	–	–	-0.043	–	0.043	–	–	–	-0.037	–	–	0.077	–	0.275	–	–	–	0.090
14 Textiles	–	–	0.008	–	0.042	–	–	0.031	0.020	–	–	0.037	–	0.123	–	–	0.129	0.067
15 Clothing and Footwear	0.072	0.073	0.329	0.070	0.329	0.069	0.084	0.069	0.283	0.226	0.226	0.134	0.227	0.134	0.228	0.222	0.225	0.150
16 Food Products	0.068	0.068	0.067	0.067	0.066	0.066	0.075	0.030	0.041	0.080	0.081	0.081	0.081	0.011	0.082	0.079	0.011	0.032
17 Other Manufacturing	0.121	–	-0.020	0.110	0.134	–	–	0.117	-0.011	0.224	–	0.059	0.222	0.178	–	–	0.219	0.067
18 Electric, Gas and Sanitary	0.048	0.037	0.097	0.097	0.097	0.097	–	0.050	0.089	0.210	0.209	0.117	0.117	0.117	0.117	–	0.216	0.134
19 Construction	0.001	0.004	0.003	0.004	0.002	0.002	–	0.002	0.002	0.380	0.372	0.386	0.365	0.390	0.390	–	0.385	0.387
20 Trade	0.134	0.134	0.122	0.064	0.134	0.064	0.098	0.134	0.129	0.133	0.133	0.227	0.241	0.133	0.250	0.219	0.133	0.158
21 Transportation	0.122	0.109	0.157	–	0.106	–	0.110	0.157	0.135	0.135	0.151	0.065	–	0.140	–	0.162	0.065	0.100
22 Communication	0.090	0.090	0.080	0.090	0.087	–	–	0.093	0.087	0.198	0.198	0.248	0.198	0.206	–	–	0.191	0.213
23 Financial Institutions	0.071	0.073	0.065	0.067	0.073	0.061	0.146	0.146	0.105	0.244	0.242	0.248	0.241	0.240	0.249	0.180	0.180	0.214
24 Real Estate	0.001	0.008	0.007	0.007	0.008	0.001	–	0.001	0.005	0.453	0.315	0.319	0.318	0.316	0.453	–	0.453	0.368
25 Public Administration	0.000	0.000	0.000	0.000	0.000	0.000	0.000	0.000	0.000	0.236	0.236	0.272	0.236	0.272	0.236	0.236	0.236	0.252
26 Other Services	0.079	0.057	0.087	0.079	0.079	0.058	0.062	0.079	0.079	0.209	0.240	0.245	0.209	0.209	0.254	0.243	0.209	0.219
TOTAL	0.090	0.075	0.083	0.072	0.105	0.067	0.137	0.090	0.093	0.222	0.172	0.270	0.232	0.158	0.356	0.207	0.179	0.209

Table 4.1   **State Effects on Industry Activity Level of a 25% Across-the-Board Tariff Cut: North**

	Short-Run										Long-Run									
	MA	PI	CE	RN	PB	PE	AL	SE	BA	NE	MA	PI	CE	RN	PB	PE	AL	SE	BA	NE
1	0.105	0.105	0.115	0.154	0.105	0.118	0.105	0.147	0.105	0.111	-0.743	-0.743	-0.845	-0.612	-0.743	-0.892	-0.743	-0.622	-0.743	-0.765
2	0.123	0.112	0.134	0.049	0.118	0.143	-0.046	0.097	0.049	0.056	-0.634	-0.670	-0.673	-0.755	-0.696	-0.712	-0.896	-0.625	-0.755	-0.749
3	0.001	-0.109	0.040	-0.109	-0.109	-0.109	0.038	-0.109	0.033	-0.044	-0.585	-0.906	-0.623	-0.906	-0.906	-0.906	-0.620	-0.906	-0.589	-0.765
4	0.217	0.315	0.293	0.220	0.333	0.176	0.300	0.203	0.217	0.219	-0.497	-0.724	-0.694	-0.650	-0.743	-0.621	-0.740	-0.627	-0.497	-0.543
5	0.077	0.074	0.086	0.061	0.081	0.060	0.056	0.058	0.060	0.062	-0.510	-0.545	-0.606	-0.638	-0.599	-0.571	-0.640	-0.558	-0.571	-0.578
6	0.149	0.137	0.156	0.114	0.145	-0.185	—	0.104	0.132	-0.069	-0.467	-0.465	-0.471	-0.477	-0.469	-0.455	—	-0.473	-0.491	-0.466
7	0.065	0.062	0.262	0.073	0.076	0.262	0.056	0.054	0.055	0.210	-0.387	-0.389	-0.209	-0.425	-0.422	-0.209	-0.391	-0.390	-0.396	-0.257
8	0.035	0.035	0.049	0.023	0.048	0.035	0.040	0.015	0.032	0.035	-0.499	-0.499	-0.484	-0.492	-0.486	-0.499	-0.492	-0.490	-0.500	-0.497
9	0.056	0.032	0.051	0.053	0.037	0.037	0.045	0.047	0.042	0.042	-0.530	-0.536	-0.618	-0.537	-0.689	-0.689	-0.609	-0.560	-0.586	-0.632
10	0.025	0.063	0.087	0.070	-0.019	-0.019	0.039	0.031	-0.019	-0.006	-0.469	-0.568	-0.591	-0.614	-0.919	-0.919	-0.526	-0.514	-0.919	-0.870
11	0.364	0.522	0.545	0.536	0.470	0.476	-0.170	0.533	-0.170	-0.070	-0.650	-0.725	-0.748	-0.721	-0.727	-0.744	-0.956	-0.723	-0.956	-0.921
12	-1.056	-1.056	-1.056	0.076	0.077	-1.056	0.076	0.077	0.076	-0.668	-1.850	-1.850	-1.850	-0.604	-0.607	-1.850	-0.612	-0.607	-0.613	-1.426
13	0.026	0.021	0.026	0.011	0.003	0.003	0.025	0.006	0.018	0.010	-0.575	-0.610	-0.657	-0.567	-0.777	-0.777	-0.662	-0.549	-0.606	-0.711
14	0.172	0.146	0.068	0.068	0.068	0.068	0.163	0.068	0.167	0.088	-0.702	-0.700	-0.910	-0.910	-0.910	-0.910	-0.736	-0.910	-0.699	-0.867
15	0.084	0.151	0.151	0.151	0.083	0.151	0.082	0.082	0.082	0.139	-0.535	-0.731	-0.731	-0.731	-0.527	-0.731	-0.526	-0.525	-0.527	-0.695
16	0.164	0.157	0.098	0.171	0.167	0.098	0.098	0.173	0.166	0.129	-0.778	-0.777	-1.073	-0.759	-0.762	-1.073	-1.073	-0.761	-0.768	-0.937
17	0.074	0.099	0.131	0.059	0.059	0.059	-0.021	0.080	0.019	0.051	-0.498	-0.537	-0.585	-0.698	-0.698	-0.698	-0.796	-0.534	-0.747	-0.697
18	0.029	0.036	0.045	0.028	0.039	0.050	0.019	0.028	0.022	0.029	-0.467	-0.502	-0.551	-0.529	-0.534	-0.587	-0.603	-0.541	-0.625	-0.599
19	0.001	0.002	0.002	0.001	0.001	0.001	0.002	0.001	0.001	0.001	-0.490	-0.491	-0.491	-0.490	-0.491	-0.492	-0.491	-0.490	-0.490	-0.490
20	0.166	0.166	0.166	0.068	0.166	0.166	0.166	0.059	0.060	0.123	-0.445	-0.445	-0.445	-0.488	-0.445	-0.445	-0.445	-0.484	-0.509	-0.469
21	0.052	0.048	0.098	0.024	0.098	0.098	0.048	0.040	0.044	0.074	-0.532	-0.547	-0.658	-0.658	-0.658	-0.658	-0.575	-0.546	-0.557	-0.612
22	0.077	0.044	0.044	0.024	0.044	0.044	0.029	0.023	0.026	0.038	-0.468	-0.439	-0.439	-0.414	-0.439	-0.439	-0.396	-0.436	-0.456	-0.443
23	0.031	0.026	0.093	0.024	0.027	0.028	0.093	0.022	0.024	0.041	-0.460	-0.444	-0.415	-0.447	-0.445	-0.450	-0.415	-0.451	-0.455	-0.444
24	0.001	0.011	0.011	0.001	0.001	0.001	0.010	0.010	0.001	0.003	-0.484	-0.483	-0.483	-0.484	-0.484	-0.484	-0.483	-0.478	-0.484	-0.484
25	0.000	0.000	0.000	0.000	0.000	0.000	0.000	0.000	0.000	0.000	0.000	-0.402	-0.402	-0.402	-0.402	-0.402	-0.402	0.000	0.000	-0.252
26	0.058	0.074	0.074	0.053	0.074	0.074	0.051	0.051	0.051	0.062	-0.479	-0.489	-0.489	-0.475	-0.489	-0.489	-0.478	-0.474	-0.488	-0.486
	0.070	0.066	0.085	0.062	0.083	0.084	0.039	0.058	0.014	0.050	-0.534	-0.573	-0.645	-0.596	-0.606	-0.672	-0.686	-0.524	-0.638	-0.630

See page 63 for sector definitions

Table 4.2   State Effects on Industry Activity Level of a 25% Across-the-Board Tariff Cut: Northeast

	MG	ES	RJ	SP	Short-Run PR	SC	RS	MS	GO	DF	CS
1 Agriculture	0.163	0.163	0.201	0.215	0.163	0.163	0.163	0.163	0.163	0.143	0.176
2 Mining	0.223	0.223	0.223	0.015	0.264	0.223	0.332	0.356	0.223	0.570	0.222
3 Nonmetallic Minerals	-0.165	-0.165	0.349	-0.165	0.380	-0.165	0.945	0.377	-0.165	0.819	-0.022
4 Metal Products	0.248	0.248	0.220	0.248	0.477	0.458	0.418	0.448	0.368	0.641	0.263
5 Machinery	0.194	0.194	0.179	0.023	0.245	0.217	0.023	0.279	0.246	0.329	0.061
6 Electrical and Electronic Equipment	0.079	0.071	0.051	0.007	0.070	0.082	0.079	0.056	0.051	0.079	0.021
7 Transportation Equipment	0.406	0.407	0.383	0.319	0.410	0.418	0.403	0.408	0.402	0.397	0.339
8 Wood Products and Furniture	0.159	0.123	0.080	0.162	0.123	0.123	0.123	0.082	0.071	0.160	0.137
9 Paper Products and Printing	0.196	0.154	0.139	0.154	0.173	0.154	0.178	0.194	0.180	0.116	0.157
10 Rubber	0.343	0.337	0.256	0.085	0.359	0.311	0.085	0.380	0.333	0.438	0.106
11 Chemicals	0.259	0.253	0.249	-0.232	0.240	0.227	0.268	0.241	0.241	0.362	-0.044
12 Pharmaceuticals and Veterinary	0.163	0.164	-0.307	-0.307	0.163	0.161	0.161	0.161	0.163	0.134	-0.274
13 Plastics	0.071	0.059	0.032	0.006	0.052	0.006	0.062	0.040	0.031	0.062	0.017
14 Textiles	0.135	0.284	0.268	0.135	0.279	0.135	0.206	0.304	0.292	0.000	0.158
15 Clothing and Footwear	0.254	0.254	0.253	0.252	0.254	0.254	0.254	0.253	0.253	0.253	0.253
16 Food Products	0.174	0.174	0.172	0.169	0.070	0.070	0.070	0.169	0.070	0.175	0.133
17 Other Manufacturing	0.173	0.162	0.147	0.083	0.160	0.167	0.172	0.150	0.151	0.120	0.105
18 Electric, Gas and Sanitary Services	0.106	0.126	0.110	0.101	0.106	0.116	0.111	0.079	0.084	0.052	0.104
19 Construction	0.011	0.002	0.002	0.010	0.002	0.011	0.010	0.002	0.002	0.009	0.005
20 Trade	0.125	0.125	0.100	0.105	0.125	0.125	0.125	0.125	0.125	0.083	0.113
21 Transportation	0.351	0.351	0.274	0.260	0.351	0.351	0.351	0.284	0.255	0.328	0.302
22 Communication	0.127	0.127	0.125	0.125	0.120	0.128	0.126	0.125	0.125	0.125	0.125
23 Financial Institutions	0.163	0.164	0.159	0.155	0.160	0.160	0.220	0.220	0.220	0.220	0.172
24 Real Estate	0.031	0.033	0.011	0.028	0.031	0.032	0.032	0.011	0.011	0.011	0.024
25 Public Administration	0.000	0.000	0.000	0.000	0.000	0.000	0.000	0.000	0.000	0.000	0.000
26 Other Services	0.151	0.150	0.177	0.137	0.144	0.148	0.149	0.177	0.177	0.177	0.152
TOTAL	0.169	0.159	0.129	0.084	0.149	0.141	0.170	0.133	0.115	0.111	0.119

Table 4.3   State Effects on Industry Activity Level of a 25% Across-the-board Tariff Cut: Center-South

	MG	ES	RJ	SP	PR	SC	RS	MS	GO	DF	CS
						Long-Run					
1 Agriculture	0.195	0.195	0.349	0.303	0.195	0.195	0.195	0.195	0.195	0.346	0.224
2 Mining	0.116	0.116	0.116	0.066	0.329	0.116	0.342	0.377	0.116	0.447	0.124
3 Nonmetallic Minerals	0.221	0.221	0.368	0.221	0.367	0.221	0.354	0.381	0.221	0.373	0.252
4 Metal Products	0.251	0.251	0.373	0.251	0.399	0.376	0.354	0.414	0.399	0.428	0.279
5 Machinery	0.300	0.295	0.322	0.161	0.362	0.326	0.161	0.389	0.360	0.404	0.195
6 Electrical and Electronic Equipment	0.312	0.317	0.324	0.146	0.317	0.317	0.310	0.324	0.325	0.316	0.187
7 Transportation Equipment	0.404	0.403	0.409	0.359	0.407	0.408	0.403	0.414	0.412	0.411	0.371
8 Wood Products and Furniture	0.370	0.312	0.390	0.352	0.312	0.312	0.312	0.387	0.389	0.373	0.335
9 Paper Products and Printing	0.335	0.235	0.317	0.235	0.323	0.235	0.316	0.348	0.333	0.315	0.264
10 Rubber	0.332	0.328	0.341	0.118	0.348	0.323	0.118	0.372	0.357	0.379	0.141
11 Chemicals	1.059	1.057	1.265	-0.737	1.077	1.015	1.103	1.097	1.126	1.369	-0.007
12 Pharmaceuticals and Veterinary	0.505	0.506	-0.200	-0.200	0.503	0.502	0.501	0.505	0.506	0.488	-0.150
13 Plastics	0.270	0.267	0.279	0.114	0.257	0.114	0.244	0.288	0.279	0.290	0.157
14 Textiles	0.240	0.368	0.373	0.240	0.363	0.240	0.319	0.377	0.372	0.000	0.262
15 Clothing and Footwear	0.372	0.372	0.373	0.371	0.373	0.337	0.337	0.373	0.373	0.373	0.358
16 Food Products	0.257	0.256	0.262	0.254	0.138	0.138	0.138	0.253	0.138	0.266	0.212
17 Other Manufacturing	0.280	0.276	0.302	0.173	0.306	0.289	0.298	0.317	0.311	0.300	0.209
18 Electric, Gas and Sanitary Services	0.266	0.307	0.335	0.296	0.266	0.313	0.333	0.351	0.335	0.332	0.295
19 Construction	0.442	0.436	0.436	0.442	0.436	0.443	0.443	0.436	0.436	0.443	0.438
20 Trade	0.273	0.273	0.355	0.329	0.273	0.273	0.273	0.273	0.273	0.363	0.308
21 Transportation	0.321	0.321	0.379	0.329	0.321	0.321	0.321	0.373	0.355	0.402	0.334
22 Communication	0.353	0.348	0.304	0.304	0.357	0.344	0.344	0.304	0.304	0.304	0.317
23 Financial Institutions	0.345	0.344	0.350	0.344	0.347	0.345	0.305	0.305	0.305	0.305	0.336
24 Real Estate	0.411	0.406	0.432	0.414	0.412	0.406	0.407	0.432	0.432	0.432	0.418
25 Public Administration	0.308	0.308	0.287	0.308	0.308	0.308	0.308	0.287	0.308	0.287	0.300
26 Other Services	0.369	0.365	0.399	0.374	0.378	0.371	0.370	0.399	0.399	0.399	0.380
TOTAL	0.336	0.310	0.423	0.149	0.363	0.284	0.339	0.340	0.329	0.323	0.264

Table 4.3   (Continued)

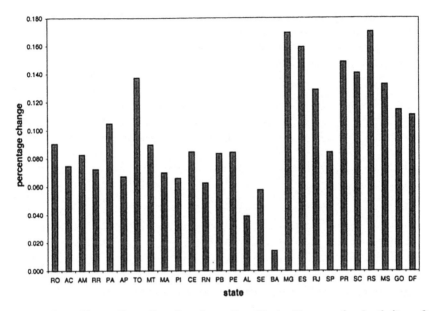

Figure 4.7 Short-Run Implications for State Economic Activity of a Uniform 25% Tariff Reduction

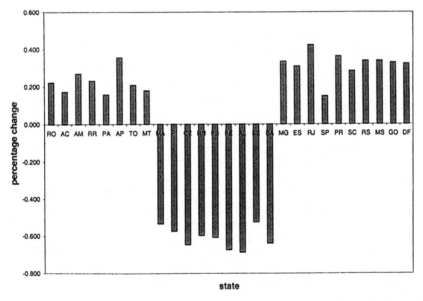

Figure 4.8 Long-Run Implications for State Economic Activity of a Uniform 25% Tariff Reduction

The long-run results reveal a more striking picture, where states in the Northeast are all adversely affected. Again, the Center-South states achieve a higher level of growth, while the Northern states remain in an intermediate level. It is worth mentioning the poor performance of chemical-based industries in the Center-South, reflected in the low outcomes of the state of São Paulo. The other states comprising the Southeast (MG, ES, RJ) perform more consistently, especially Rio de Janeiro; the Center-West states (MS, GO, DF) present a more uniform pattern while in the South, Santa Catarina exhibits slower growth due to adverse effects in agriculture and agricultural-based industries, which form the economic base of the state.

The overall poor results verified in the Northeast are driven by the regional performance. However, Alagoas, Bahia, Ceará and Pernambuco worsen their relative position in the region due to even stronger negative effects in key sectors. Ceará and Pernambuco suffer from competition in traditional industries, such as textiles, clothing and footwear, and food products, which play an important role in the respective state economies. Poor sectoral performance of agriculture, chemicals and food products, that are responsible for around 40% of the economy in Alagoas, hinder state economic growth, while Bahia is again hampered by the impacts on the chemical industry.

Finally, in the North, Amapá and Amazonas particularly benefit from spillovers from capital creation and the good results in the mining sector; at the other end of the distribution, Pará is shown to be strongly affected by the relative retraction of important sectors (e.g. wood products and furniture, and paper products and printing).

The Moving Picture: Locational Implications

The Brazilian economy is highly concentrated in geographical terms. The state of São Paulo, with only 2.9% of the territory, hosts 36% of national GDP and 22% of the population; the Northeast region, with one third of national population, produces only 16% of national GDP (1996 figures). Starting in 1939, when state GDP statistics started being calculated, there was a clear trend towards regional concentration in the Southeast until the mid-1970s. From then on, some signs of polarization reversal were present, leading some analysts to predict the future deconcentration of the national production (Diniz, 1994; Zini, 1998; Azzoni, 2001). Since financial problems affecting the data collection agencies precluded the production of updated regional GDP figures, this belief remained in all analysis of regional concentration in Brazil until recently. However, new data released indicate that reconcentration took place after the mid-1980s, relating to production restructuring, the liberalization of the national economy, the weakening of the public sector (downgrading all kinds of regional policies), the creation of a free trade area with Argentina, Uruguay and Paraguay, etc. (see Azzoni, chapter 6 in this volume).

Although some sectors presented higher than average growth in the Northeast, mainly non-durable consumption goods, the traditional industrial area was able to keep and even increase its share in national GDP. The expected deconcentration is taking place mainly among the neighboring states of São Paulo, the richest state in the country, despite the development of resource-oriented activities (agriculture, agribusiness, mining) in the West and North areas of the country. The neighboring states of São Paulo, Paraná and Minas Gerais, in the South and Southeast, together sum up to over 50% of total GDP; in manufacturing, their share sums up to over 67%, and it does not seem to be falling (data for 1997).

Although explicit regional policies were almost absent in the last two decades, macroeconomic (five stabilization plans after 1986; undervalued exchange rate between 1994 and 1998) and sectoral policies (a large scale incentive program for the production of alcohol as fuel, for example) were very active, producing regional consequences. It is of interest of this section to focus on the spatial implications of trade liberalization, considering the results described above. In order to do that, the concept of economic gravity center will be utilized.

The economic gravity center can be defined as the weighted location of a specific economic activity in a given geographical area. One is usually interested in production estimates; in cases where output data are not consistently available, other measures of relative size may also be used as weights – employment, personal income earned, value added, and so on. Given a geographical area R, constituted by r sub-areas, in each of which an economic activity i takes place in a specific location, defined by geographical coordinates $(latitude, longitude)^r$, generating an output X_i^r, one can formally define the economic gravity center of activity i, Φ_i, as

$$\Phi_i = \sum_{r \in R} \frac{X_i^r}{\sum_{r \in R} X_i^r} (latitude, longitude)^r \qquad (4.2)$$

Figure 4.9 shows the national economic gravity center, located somewhere in the Southern part of the state of Minas Gerais, as well as the economic gravity centers of the North, Northeast, and Center-South.   In figure 4.10, we present the sectoral economic gravity centers, corresponding to observations in the benchmark year.

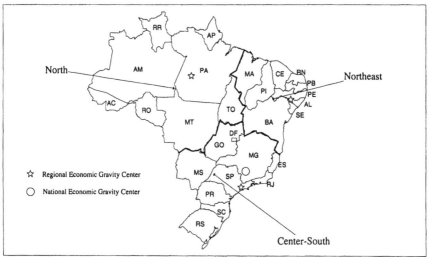

Figure 4.9   Regional and National Economic Gravity Centers: Brazil, 1985

The concentration of most manufacturing and services around the national economic gravity center is very noticeable, reflecting the more intense economic activity encountered in the Center-South. Some sectors, such as mining, wood products and furniture, and rubber, that are heavily dependent on specific inputs, or electrical and electronic equipment, that receives strong fiscal incentives in a specific location, have their gravity center attracted to those regions where these "comparative advantages" appear. In order to evaluate the impact of the tariff component of trade liberalization on the locational patterns of economic activity in Brazil, we used the sectoral results reported in the previous section to determine the geographical shifts in the *loci* of economic activity in the country. Estimates for short-run and long-run regional and sectoral economic gravity centers were computed and plotted against the estimates for the benchmark year. Figure 4.11 shows the results for the shifts in the regional gravity centers; figures 4.12abc present the sectoral results for the country.

The regional influence of the top-ranking states is clearly revealed in figure 4.11. In the North, in the short-run, there is a shift towards the east, due to the better performance of Tocantins and Pará; in the long-run, however, a shift to the northwest occurs, towards Manaus. The resultant long-run change in the Northeast is less intense, and in the South, a movement away from São Paulo metropolitan region is also perceived, first in the direction of the Southern states, with the long-run effects promoting a northward reversal towards the southern part of Minas Gerais.

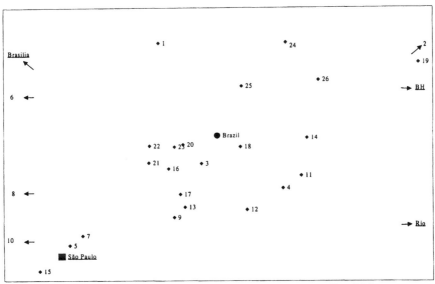

Figure 4.10 Sectoral Economic Gravity Centers: Brazil, 1985
Note: For sector definitions, see table 4.1

As for the national results (figures 4.12abc), a general trend implying a southwest shift, both in the short-run and in the long-run, is a striking result. Protection has historically been claimed to harm the Northeast in favor of the Center-South.   The argument considers only demand constraints: by facing protection walls, the region was constrained to the consumption of the more expensive manufactures produced in the South, whose regional specialization in manufacturing goods, protected by tariff barriers, created a deterioration of the terms of trade unfavorable to the peripheral area, generating recurrent interregional trade deficits. However, when both demand and supply considerations are taken into account, the relative position of the Center-South is likely to worsen with protection, as the region is more open and dependent upon imported inputs. Thus, as it has been shown, the supply side effects, in 1985, were more likely to offset the demand effects, and trade liberalization became a force that enhanced regional inequality in the country.

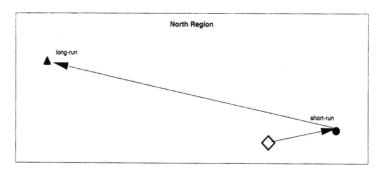

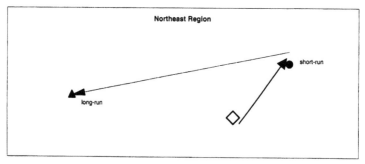

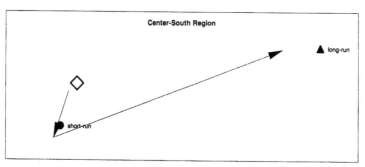

**Figure 4.11 Geographical Shift in the Regional Economic Gravity
Center Induced by a Tariff Decrease**

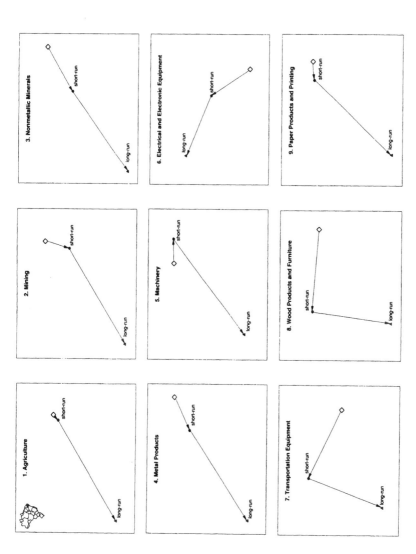

Figure 4.12a   Geographical Shift in the Sectoral Economic Gravity Center Induced by a Tariff Decrease

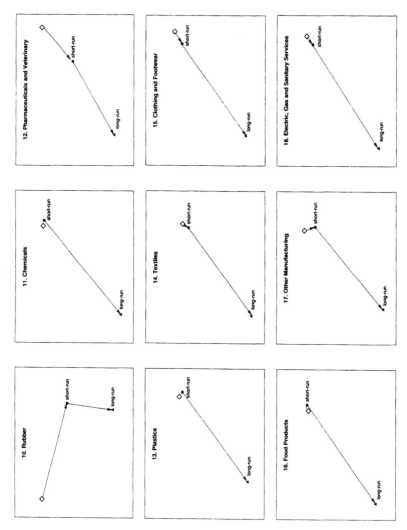

Figure 4.12b   Geographical Shift in the Sectoral Economic Gravity Center Induced by a Tariff Decrease

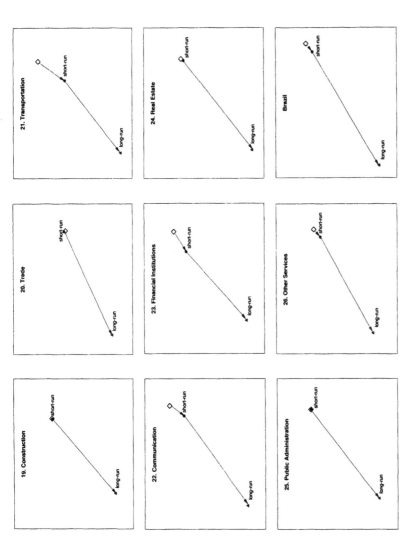

Figure 4.12c   Geographical Shift in the Sectoral Economic Gravity Center Induced by a Tariff Decrease

Final Remarks

The results described above provide important insights to the debate on regional inequality in the country. B-MARIA simulations have supported the argument that general decreases in protection increase economic activity in the Center-South at the expense of the Northeast. Contrary to general beliefs, that have often taken into account only demand-driven considerations, trade liberalization is likely to harm the peripheral region.

It is important to situate this claim in time. When the core-periphery theory of regional development was first framed to the Brazilian case (Furtado, 1963), interregional linkages were very weak in the economy. However, what may have been true in the import substitution era, perpetuated as a strong and recurrent argument in regional analysis in Brazil up to the present time. As the economy became more and more diversified and integrated, in the 1970s and 1980s, supply effects started playing a more relevant role in the dynamics of regional interaction. As has been shown, Furtado's argument was not valid anymore, already in the mid-1980s, as tariff protection was more likely to bring about adverse welfare implications in the more developed region of the country.

Finally, as a methodological note, the extension of the B-MARIA model, proposed and implemented here, has proved worthwhile under conditions of very limited information. Despite its obvious limitations, it has produced seemingly consistent results, which provided interesting insights into regional inequality in a federative system. Although a less add-hoc disaggregation of the model results needs to be explored, this very first attempt to generate state-level results for policy analysis in Brazil in a general equilibrium framework represents a first step into more sophisticated methods, as data availability permits.

Notes

[1] For a survey, see the *Oxford Review of Economic Policy*, Summer 1998, vol. 14, no. 2, "Trade and Location".
[2] Adams and Dixon (1995) report regionally disaggregated projections for 56 statistical divisions in Australia derived from national forecasts of the MONASH Model.
[3] This section draws on Haddad and Hewings (1998a).
[4] The complete specification of the model is available in Haddad and Hewings (1997).
[5] In this chapter, the results were aggregated into 26 sectors rather than 40 sectors in order to be consistent with the state data base.

[6] Results for the North region generate projections for eight states (Rondônia, Acre, Amazonas, Roraima, Pará, Amapá, Tocantins, and Mato Grosso); results for the Northeast region generate projections for nine states (Maranhão, Piauí, Ceará, Rio Grande do Norte, Paraíba, Pernambuco, Alagoas, Sergipe, and Bahia); and those for the Center-South region generate projections for nine states and the Federal District (Minas Gerais, Espírito Santo, Rio de Janeiro, São Paulo, Paraná, Santa Catarina, Rio Grande do Sul, Mato Grosso do Sul, Goiás, and Distrito Federal).

[7] Inter-state trade is taken care of in the fourth step, when the gross effects are scaled to accommodate the adding-up property. Although the problem is tackled mechanically, lack of inter-state trade estimates precludes a more rigorous procedure to be implemented.

References

Adams, P. D. and Dixon, P. B. (1995) "Prospects For Australian Industries, States And Regions: 1993-94 To 2001-02," *Australian Bulletin of Labour*, 21, 57-73.

Azzoni, C.R. (2001) "Economic growth and regional income inequality in Brazil," *Annals of Regional Science*, 35, 133-152.

Barros, A. R. (1998). "Os Impactos do Mercosul no Nordeste do Brasil," *Revista ANPEC*, 4, 221-238.

Campos-Filho, L. (1998) "Unilateral Liberalisation and Mercosul: Implications for Resource Allocation," *Revista Brasileira de Economia*, 52, 601-636.

Diniz, C.C. (1994) "Polygonized development in Brazil: Neither decentralization nor continued polarization," *International Journal of Urban and Regional Research,* 18, 293-314.

Dinsmoor, J. and Haddad, E. A. (1996) "Brazil: The Use of State Fiscal Data Bases for Financial Projections," *Region I Technical Note*, Inter-American Development Bank, August.

Dixon, P. B., Parmenter, B. R., Sutton, J. and Vincent, D. P. (1982) *ORANI: A Multisectoral Model Of The Australian Economy.* Amsterdam, North-Holland.

Flores Jr., R. G. (1997) "The Gains from Mercosul: A General Equilibrium, Imperfect Competition Evaluation," *Journal of Policy Modeling*, 19, 1-18.

Furtado, C. (1963) *The Economic Growth of Brazil.* Berkeley and Los Angeles, University of California Press.

Gonzaga, G. M., Terra, M. C. T. and Cavalcante, J. (1999) "O Impacto do Mercosul sobre o Emprego setorial no Brasil," *mimeo*, Catholic University, Rio de Janeiro.

Haddad, E. A. (1999) *Regional Inequality and Structural Changes: Lessons from the Brazilian Experience.* Aldershot, Ashgate.

Haddad, E. A. and Hewings, G. J. D. (1997) "The Theoretical Specification of B-MARIA," *Discussion Paper REAL 97-T-5*, Regional Economics Applications Laboratory, University of Illinois at Urbana-Champaign.

Haddad E. A. and Hewings, G. J. D. (1998a) "Trade and Regional Development: International and Interregional Competitiveness in Brazil," paper presented at the international workshop on *Theories of Regional Development – Lessons for Policies of Regional Economic Renewal and Growth*, Uddevalla, Sweden, 14-16 June.

Haddad E. A. and Hewings, G. J. D. (1998b) "Transportation Costs and Regional Development: An Interregional CGE Analysis," paper presented at the 38th European Congress of the Regional Science Association, Vienna, Austria, 28 August - 1 September.

Haddad E. A. and Hewings, G. J. D. (1999) "The Short-Run Regional Effects of New Investments and Technological Upgrade in the Brazilian Automobile Industry: An Interregional CGE Approach," *Oxford Development Studies*, 27, 359-83.

Horridge, J. M., Parmenter, B. R. and Pearson, K. R. (1993) "ORANI-F: A General Equilibrium Model of the Australian Economy," *Economic and Financial Computing*, 3, 71-140.

Miller, R. E. and Blair, P. D. (1985) *Input-Output Analysis: Foundations and Extensions*. Englewood Cliffs, N.J., Prentice Hall.

Pacheco, C.A. (1998) *Fragmentação da Nação*. Campinas, SP, Unicamp, IE.

Peter, M. W., Horridge, M., Meagher, G. A., Naqvi, F. and Parmenter, B. R. (1996) "The Theoretical Structure Of MONASH-MRF," *Preliminary Working Paper no. OP-85*, IMPACT Project, Monash University.

Savedoff, W. D. (1990) "Os Diferenciais Regionais de Salários no Brasil: Segmentação Versus Dinamismo da Demanda," *Pesquisa e Planejamento Econômico*, 20, 28-36.

Venables, A. J. (1998). "The Assessment: Trade and Location," *Oxford Review of Economic Policy*, 14, 1-6.

Zini, A. (1998) "Regional income convergence in Brazil and its socio-economic determinants," *Economia Aplicada*, 2, 383-411.

Appendix A: General Features of B-MARIA

CGE Core Module

The basic structure of the CGE core module comprises three main blocks of equations determining demand and supply relations, and market clearing conditions. In addition, various regional and national aggregates, such as aggregate employment, aggregate price level, and balance of trade, are defined here. Nested production functions and household demand functions are employed; for production, firms are assumed to use fixed proportion combinations of intermediate inputs and primary factors are assumed in the first level while, in the second level, substitution is possible between domestically produced and imported intermediate inputs, on the one hand, and between capital, labor and land, on the other. At the third level, bundles of domestically produced inputs are formed as combinations of inputs from different regional sources. The modeling procedure adopted in B-MARIA uses a constant elasticity of substitution (CES) specification in the lower levels to combine goods from different sources.

The treatment of the household demand structure is based on a nested CES/linear expenditure system (LES) preference function. Demand equations are derived from a utility maximization problem, whose solution follows hierarchical steps. The structure of household demand follows a nesting pattern that enables different elasticities of substitution to be used. At the bottom level, substitution occurs across different domestic sources of supply. Utility derived from the consumption of domestic composite goods is maximized. In the subsequent upper-level, substitution occurs between domestic composite and imported goods.

Equations for other final demand for commodities include the specification of export demand and government demand. Exports are divided into two groups: traditional exports (agriculture, mining, coffee, and sugar), and non-traditional exports. The former faces downward sloping demand curves, indicating that traditional exports are a negative function of their prices in the world market. Non-traditional exports form a composite tradable bundle, in which commodity shares are fixed. Demand is related to the average price of this bundle.

One new feature presented in B-MARIA refers to the government demand for public goods. The nature of the input-output data enables the isolation of the consumption of *public goods* by both the federal and regional governments. However, productive activities carried out by the public sector cannot be isolated from those by the private sector. Thus, government entrepreneurial behavior is dictated by the same cost minimization assumptions adopted by the private sector. This may be a very strong assumption for the Brazilian case but the liberalization process of the 1990s offers some enhanced credibility for this assumption. Public good consumption is set to maintain a (constant) proportion with regional private consumption, in the case of regional governments, and with national private consumption, in the case of the federal government.

A unique feature of B-MARIA is the explicit modeling of the transportation services and the costs of moving products based on origin-destination pairs. The model is calibrated taking into account the specific transportation structure cost of *each* commodity flow, providing spatial price differentiation, which indirectly addresses the issue related to regional transportation infrastructure efficiency. Other definitions in the CGE core module include: tax rates, basic and purchase prices of commodities, tax revenues, margins, components of real and nominal GRP/GDP, regional and national price indices, money wage settings, factor prices, and employment aggregates.

Government Finance Module

The government finance module (drawing on data assembled by Dinsmoor and Haddad, 1996) incorporates equations determining the gross regional product (GRP), expenditure and income side, for each region, through the decomposition and modeling of its components. The budget deficits of regional governments and the federal government are also determined here. Another important definition in this block of equations refers to the specification of the regional aggregate household consumption functions. They are defined as a function of household disposable income, which is disaggregated into its main sources of income, and the respective tax duties.

Capital Accumulation and Investment Module

Capital stock and investment relationships are defined in this module; however, only the comparative-static version of the model produces reliable results, restricting the use of the model to short-run and long-run policy analysis. When running the model in the comparative-static mode, there is no fixed relationship between capital and investment. The user decides the required relationship on the basis of the requirements of the specific simulation. For example, it is typical in long-run comparative-static simulations to assume that the growth in capital and investment are equal (see Peter *et al.*, 1996).

Foreign Debt Accumulation Module

This module is based on the specification proposed in ORANI-F (Horridge *et al.*, 1993), in which the nation's foreign debt is linearly related to accumulated balance-of-trade deficits. In summary, trade deficits are financed by increases in the external debt.

Labor Market and Regional Migration Module

In this module, regional population is defined through the interaction of demographic variables, including interregional migration. Links between regional population and regional labor supply are provided. Demographic variables are usually defined exogenously, and together with the specification of some of the labor market settings, labor supply can be determined together with either interregional wage differentials or regional unemployment rates. In summary, either labor supply and wage differentials determine unemployment rates, or labor supply and unemployment rates determine wage differentials.

Closures

B-MARIA can be configured to reflect short-run and long-run comparative-static, as well as forecasting simulations. At this stage, two basic closures for alternative time frames of analysis in single-period simulations are available. A distinction between the two closures relates to the treatment of capital stocks encountered in the standard microeconomic approach to policy adjustments. In the short-run closure, capital stocks are held fixed, while, in the long-run, policy changes are allowed to affect capital stocks.

Short-run   In addition to the assumption of interindustry and interregional immobility of capital, the short-run closure would include fixed regional population and labor supply, fixed regional wage differentials, and fixed national real wage. Regional employment is driven by the assumptions on wage rates, which indirectly determine regional unemployment rates. These assumptions describe the functioning of the regional labor markets as close as possible to the Brazilian reality. First, changes in the demand for labor are met by changes in the unemployment rate, rather than by changes in the real wage. This seems to be the case in Brazil, given the high level of disguised unemployment in most of the areas of the country; excess supply of labor has been a distinctive feature of the Brazilian economy. Secondly, labor's interregional immobility in the short-run suggests that migration is not a short-term decision. Finally, nominal wage differentials in Brazil are persistent, reflecting the geographical segmentation of the workforce (Savedoff, 1990). On the demand side, investment expenditures are fixed exogenously – firms cannot reevaluate their investment decisions in the short-run. Household consumption follows household disposable income, and government consumption, at both regional and federal levels, is fixed (alternatively, the government deficit can be set exogenously, allowing government expenditures to change). Finally, since the model does not present any endogenous-growth-theory-type specification, technology variables are exogenous.

Long-run   A long-run (steady-state) equilibrium closure is also available in which capital and labor are mobile across regions and industries. The main differences from the short-run are encountered in the labor market and the capital formation settings. In the first case, aggregate employment is determined by population growth, labor force participation rates, and the natural rate of unemployment. The distribution of the labor force across regions and sectors is fully determined endogenously. Labor is attracted to more competitive industries in more favored geographical areas. While in the same way, capital is oriented towards more attractive industries. This movement keeps rates of return at their initial levels.

PART II: REGIONAL ECONOMIC ANALYSIS

5 Income Distribution in Brazil and the Regional and Sectoral Contrasts

RODOLFO HOFFMANN

Introduction

The general objective of this chapter is to analyze the income distribution in Brazil from 1960 to 1996. The next section discusses the main limitations of income data. The third section summarizes the evolution of income distribution in Brazil from 1960 to 1980. The following section analyzes the income distribution among economically active persons from 1979 to 1996, showing the effects of economic crisis, stagnation, inflation and its control and resumption of growth on inequality and poverty. The fifth section shows the regional and sectoral contrasts using data on earnings of occupied persons in 1995. The same data are used in the following section to estimate earnings equations for Brazil and the three economic sectors, evaluating the influence of education, gender, position on occupation and other factors on personal earnings. The seventh section concludes the chapter.

Main limitations of income data

Income data analyzed in this chapter come from Census or PNAD (Pesquisa Nacional por Amostra de Domicílios), a sample survey carried out annually by IBGE, the Brazilian national statistical office. The information about the income of persons at least 10 years old is obtained through a questionnaire that considers money income and income in kind. The production for own consumption, however, is not considered. The main limitation of these data is the tendency of people, especially richer ones, not to fully declare their income, leading to an underestimation of total income and of the inequality of the distribution.[1]

Lluch (1982) compares the value of net domestic product per capita and the income declared in the 1970 Demographic Census in 87 areas of Brazil. He shows that the income per capita obtained from Census is, in general, smaller than the income per capita estimated from National Accounts and observed that the degree of underestimation increased with the income level of the area. Hoffmann (1988) makes a similar analysis comparing the average income for 26 Federation Units obtained from 1980 Demographic Census and the corresponding gross domestic product (GDP) per capita, showing that the degree of underreporting in Census income increases for the richer units.

Table 5.1   Income per capita from PNAD and gross domestic product per capita for 21 Brazilian federation units in 1995

State or Federation Unit	Income per capita* (Y)	GDP per capita** (P)	Y/P
Piauí	947	974	0.972
Tocantins	1227	1117	1.098
Maranhão	871	1180	0.738
Paraíba	1392	1289	1.080
Ceará	1230	1565	0.786
Alagoas	1418	1652	0.858
Pernambuco	1318	1915	0.688
Bahia	1211	2057	0.589
Rio Grande do Norte	1435	2064	0.695
Sergipe	1210	2527	0.479
Mato Grosso	1919	2590	0.741
Goiás	1859	2976	0.625
Minas Gerais	2090	3213	0.650
Espírito Santo	2157	3314	0.651
Mato Grosso do Sul	2087	3901	0.535
Santa Catarina	2734	3988	0.686
Paraná	2418	4308	0.561
Rio Grande do Sul	2805	4350	0.645
Rio de Janeiro	3152	4474	0.705
São Paulo	3457	6055	0.571
Distrito Federal	4332	7582	0.571

Notes: *Value in 1995 reais, obtained multiplying the average monthly income of persons at least 10 years old by their number, dividing by the state population and multiplying by 12 and by a correction factor for inflation.
**From "Atlas Regional de Desigualdades", IPEA/DIPES (in CD-ROM)

To evaluate the degree of underestimation, let us compare the income declared in the 1995 PNAD and gross domestic product for 21 Brazilian states.[2] The monthly income declared in PNAD is transformed in an annual income per capita, including a correction for inflation (because PNAD refers to September's income). In table 5.1, the Federation Units are ordered according to the value of their gross domestic product (GDP) per capita. The relation between income declared in PNAD and GDP is near one for the poorest states and decreases to below 0.6 for the richest units.

A linear regression of income per capita (Y) against GDP per capita (P) was fitted, weighting each observation by the unit's population. The result (t test in parentheses) is

$$\hat{Y} = 383.8 - 0.523P \qquad (5.1)$$
$$\quad\ (3.48) \quad (19.47)$$

with coefficient of determination equal to 0.952. Since the regression coefficient is near 0.5 and is statistically greater than zero, it is also statistically lower than 1, showing that the increase in Y is relatively smaller than the increase in P. These results indicate that the underestimation of declared income tends to increase with the level of GDP per capita.

The period 1960-1980

Before analyzing the 1980s, some basic facts should be established about what happened with income distribution and with absolute poverty in the period 1960-1980. From 1950 to 1980, the economic growth of Latin America was strong, with per capita GDP increasing 3% a year. Brazil, in particular, showed a higher growth rate of per capita GDP: 4.2% a year (Cardoso and Fishlow, 1990). Brazilian economic growth during the period 1960-1970 was moderate, with per capita GDP increasing around 36% (IBGE, 1990a). The effect of this growth on absolute poverty was, to a large extent, cancelled out by a strong increase in inequality of the income distribution.

Economic growth was more intense in the period 1970-1980, with per capita GDP increasing 81%, and the increase in inequality was much less intense than in the previous decade. Therefore, a substantial reduction in absolute poverty took place.

Table 5.2 shows the main indicators of inequality and absolute poverty for the distribution of income among economically active persons with some income, according to data from the Demographic Censuses of 1960, 1970 and 1980. It is possible that the reduction of absolute poverty in the 1960s is greater than what is indicated in table 5.2, since the average income per economically active person increased 23% while per capita GDP increased 36% from 1960 to 1970. The reason for the difference in these numbers can be the use of an inappropriate deflator and/or problems of comparability of the data from the 1960 and 1970 Censuses.

Table 5.2   Average income, inequality and absolute poverty in the distribution of income among economically active persons with some income, in Brazil, in 1960, 1970 and 1980

Statistic	1960	1970	1980
Average income*	1.349	1.665	2.926
Median income*	0.870	0.920	1.399
Gini index	0.504	0.561	0.592
Share of income of 50% poorest	18.0	15.6	13.8
Share of income of 10% richest	40.5	46.7	49.6
Proportion of poor (%)**	58	55	34

Notes: * *In units equal to the real value of the minimum wage of August 1980, using the implicit deflator of national accounts for the period 1960-70 and the cost of living index of DIEESE (Departamento Intersindical de Estatística e Estudos Sócios-Econômicos) for the period 1970-80*
** *The interpolated poverty line is equal to the real value of one minimum wage of August 1980*

Source: *Basic data from the Demographic Censuses of 1960, 1970 and 1980*

Table 5.2 shows that there was a substantial reduction in absolute poverty from 1960 to 1980. The proportion of economically active persons with real income lower than the minimum wage of August 1980 decreased from 58% in 1960 to 34% in 1980. It should be stressed that the reduction in absolute poverty would have been substantially larger if the inequality of the income distribution had not increased as it did. If everybody's income had increased as much as the average income, without any change in the form of the income distribution, the proportion of persons with income lower than the minimum wage would have been only 26% in 1980.

During the period 1970-1980, economic inequality increases when income distribution among economically active persons is considered, but is practically constant when the distribution of income among families is considered. The main reason is an increase in the number of economically active persons per family in the same period, due to the increasing participation of women in the labor force.

It can be verified that, during the 1970s, economic inequality increased substantially in the rural sector and was stable in the urban sector. At the same time, the inequality between these two sectors decreased, due to a greater increase in the rural sector's average income (Hoffmann and Kageyama 1986).

The substantial increase of inequality in the rural sector in the period 1960-1970 is related to the process of agricultural modernization, supported by policies such as subsidized rural credit, that benefited mostly a restricted group of farmers.

The period 1980-1996

The outstanding growth of the Brazilian economy was interrupted at the beginning of the 1980s, with per capita GDP *decreasing* 13% from 1980 to 1983. In 1989 per capita GDP was practically equal to its value nine years before and in 1990 it decreased substantially (*Conjuntura Econômica* 45(7):36, July 1991). In order to evaluate the changes in income distribution in Brazil after 1980, we will analyze, in this section, the distribution of economically active persons according to their monthly income, in the period 1979-1996. For 1980 the data are from the Demographic Census and for the other years they come from PNAD. Comparisons between 1980 and the other years should be made with caution since questions about income in the Census questionnaire are different from the questions in the PNAD questionnaire. There was also a change of the structure of PNAD questionnaire after 1990.

The PNAD data used in this section are the number of economically active persons and also the average income for eight income classes whose lower limits are 0, .5, 1, 2, 3, 5, 10 and 20 times the current minimum wage. IBGE publications present also the number of economically active persons with zero income and the number that did not declare income.

In order to estimate the inequality within classes and interpolate percentiles and poverty lines, we assume that the distribution within classes has a linear density function or is the Pareto distribution with two parameters (see Hoffmann 1979 and 1984). Although the income classes in the 1980 Census and in the yearly PNAD sample surveys are established as multiples of the minimum wage, they are not directly comparable because of the changes in the real value of the minimum wage. The use of a unit with a constant real value is essential to evaluate the evolution of the average and median incomes and the computation of absolute poverty measures. The basic real income unit used in this chapter is the value of the highest minimum wage of August 1980 (equal to 4,149.60 cruzeiros[3]).

The 1980 Demographic Census registers, in the case of stable income, the amount received in August and, for variable incomes, the average of the amounts received in the twelve months before the Census reference data (August 31). Since most incomes are considered as stable, August 1980 is adopted as the basis for the computation of real values. The reference months for the PNAD are: October for 1979 and 1981 and September for 1983 through 1996. It is important to keep in mind that the PNAD data reflect the economic situation in the reference month, and not a yearly average.

The deflator used is the national consumer price index (the so called "INPC *restrito*"), with the reference period adjusted to the civil month before March 1986. It must be noted that results related to the evolution of average income, median income and absolute poverty measures are very much affected by the choice of deflator. The INPC was chosen because it is a cost of living index with a broad geographic coverage and also because the changes in real average income obtained using this index are in general coherent with the changes in per capita GDP.

Tables 5.3 and 5.4 show the evolution of the main characteristics of the distribution of income among economically active persons who received some income, from 1979 to 1996. Table 5.3 shows the variations of average and median income; the unit is the minimum wage of August 1980. The effect of the economic crisis can be clearly observed, with the average income per economically active person assuming its lowest values in 1983 and 1984. The exceptionally high income of September 1986 corresponds to a short lived boom associated with the Cruzado Plan and the campaign for the elections that took place in November of that year (see chapter 3 in this volume). It should be remembered that September 1989 is also within an electoral campaign period, which helps to explain the almost 19% increase in average income per economically active person from September 1988 to September 1989, while per capita GDP increased only 1.2% from 1988 to 1989. Notice that the average and median incomes per economically active person in 1992 and 1993 are lower than the corresponding values in 1979-1981. Worse than a "lost decade", Brazil had a "lost 14 year period" in terms of economic growth.

A substantial increase in average and median incomes is observed from 1993 to 1995. However, it must be stressed that this result depends crucially on the deflator used; in this two-year period, Brazilian per capita GDP increased 7.6%. From 1995 to 1996, the average income increased a little more, so that the increase between 1993 and 1996 was greater than 30%. In this period the median income increased even more, by 36%, but national accounts indicate that during these three years, GDP per capita increased only 9.2%.

Table 5.4 shows the variation of several inequality measures of the income distribution among economically active persons who received some income, from 1979 to 1995. All indicators show a sharp increase in inequality from 1987 to 1989, probably related to the increasing speed of inflation. In September of 1985, 1986, 1987, 1988 and 1989 the average price increase in the month (INPC index) was, respectively, 10.1%, 1.2%, 7.2%, 26.9% and 36.3%.

It is possible to distinguish two effects of high inflation on inequality measures computed from PNAD data. One is the real increase in inequality due to the delay in the adjustment of the incomes of certain groups of people. Wages and salaries, in general, tend to loose real value, in contrast with interest and profit, with wage earners of weakly organized sectors particularly penalized. Secondly, there is also an effect that corresponds to statistical "noise." With high inflation, the nominal incomes change drastically from one month to the next. Two workers with the same real income in 1988 (or 1989) could have very different wages in September of that year if, for example, one pertains to a category that has their wages adjusted in September and the other pertains to a category that received adjustment in October. When inflation is very high, the meaning of monetary values becomes less clear to people, and income declaration errors increase. With monthly inflation reaching 40% and wage adjustments around 100%, the simple confusion between incomes earned or received in August or September introduces "noise" in the data, increasing the dispersion and the inequality of the distribution. One challenge to researchers is to devise ways to separate the real and "noise" effects of inflation on income distribution data.

From a peak in 1989, the measures of inequality decrease substantially in 1990 and 1992, reaching a relatively low value in this last year. They increase in 1993 and decrease, again, in 1995. Notice that the measure of inequality that decreases most from 1993 to 1995 is the Theil-*L*, which is particularly sensitive to changes in the lower part of the distribution (among the poor). The decrease in inequality from 1993 to 1995 can be interpreted as a beneficial consequence of *Plano Real* and the control of inflation. Notice, however, that the inequality level in 1995 cannot be considered very low.[4] The value of the Gini index in 1995 is similar to its average value from 1979 to 1986. The same is true for the percentage of total income received by the richest tenth (10[+]). In 1996, the inequality is only slightly lower than in 1995.

Table 5.3   Distribution of income among economically active persons who received some income, in Brazil, from 1979 to 1996

(average income (m), median income (D), proportion of poor (H), Sen's poverty index (P) and FGT (Foster, Greer and Thorbecke) index for a poverty line equal to one minimum wage of August 1980)

Year	m^*	D^*	H^{**}	P^{**}	FGT^{**}
1979	2.68	1.33	0.376	0.210	0.0891
1980	2.93	1.40	0.342	0.178	0.0703
1981	2.59	1.36	0.370	0.213	0.0924
1983	2.21	1.06	0.476	0.280	0.1240
1984	2.19	1.06	0.477	0.282	0.1253
1985	2.54	1.20	0.427	0.251	0.1113
1986	3.55	1.72	0.301	0.142	0.0525
1987	2.73	1.34	0.393	0.227	0.0991
1988	2.69	1.20	0.425	0.257	0.1168
1989	3.19	1.34	0.399	0.227	0.0975
1990	2.60	1.21	0.436	0.256	0.1135
1992	2.29	1.17	0.435	0.252	0.1107
1993	2.47	1.18	0.438	0.255	0.1127
1995	3.17	1.51	0.315	0.163	0.0652
1996	3.26	1.61	0.307	0.154	0.0593

Notes: **In minimum wages of August 1980. The deflator is the national consumer price index (INPC restrito) with reference period adjusted to the civil month in the years before 1986 (IBGE 1988: 497, IBGE 1990b: 493 and Conjuntura Econômica)*
** Interpolating a poverty line with real value equal to the minimum wage of August 1980
1979 data excluded the rural area of Region VII (North and Midwest), except the Federal District. 1981-1996 data excluded the rural area of Rondonia, Acre, Amazonas, Roraima, Pará and Amapá

Source: *Basic data from PNAD and, only for 1980, from Demographic Census. For 1979, 1981 and 1983 the data are from IBGE 1984: 142-143 and IBGE 1985: 612, 668. It should be recalled that the questions about income in PNAD and Census questionnaires are different. For the 1980 Census data it was necessary to establish the mean income of the classes (see Hoffmann and Kageyama 1986). Figures for 1982 are excluded due to lower reliability.*

Table 5.3 shows the evolution of three absolute poverty measures: the proportion of the poor in total population (H), Sen's poverty index (P) and the measure proposed by Foster, Greer and Thorbecke (FGT), with a poverty line equal to the minimum wage of August 1980 and using the INPC as deflator.

A graphical analysis shows that the lines illustrating the variation of absolute poverty measures in Brazil from 1979 to 1996 are similar to images, in a horizontal mirror, of the lines illustrating the variation of average and median incomes. The coefficients of correlation between median income and H, P or FGT are -0.972, -0.974 and -0.969, respectively.

Table 5.4 **Distribution of income among economically active persons who received some income, in Brazil, from 1979 to 1996**

(Gini index (G), Theil's inequality measures, percentage of income corresponding to the 50% poorest (50⁻), to the 10% richest (10⁺) and to the 5% richest (5⁺)

Year	G	Theil-T	Theil-L	50^-	10^+	5^+
1979	0.585	0.722	0.648	13.7	47.6	34.4
1980	0.592	0.810	0.640	13.8	49.6	37.0
1981	0.572	0.666	0.613	14.1	45.9	32.7
1983	0.591	0.719	0.652	13.1	47.4	33.8
1984	0.586	0.696	0.658	13.2	46.9	33.4
1985	0.599	0.745	0.695	12.6	48.0	34.5
1986	0.589	0.751	0.638	13.3	47.8	34.6
1987	0.595	0.740	0.675	12.7	47.8	34.1
1988	0.617	0.805	0.755	11.8	50.2	36.2
1989	0.636	0.897	0.792	10.9	52.5	38.5
1990	0.607	0.789	0.697	11.9	48.7	34.9
1992	0.574	0.691	0.636	14.0	45.8	32.7
1993	0.604	0.805	0.711	12.7	49.5	36.5
1995	0.589	0.749	0.637	13.1	47.6	34.0
1996	0.585	0.725	0.627	13.4	47.3	33.6

Notes: *1979 data excluded the rural area of Region VII (North and Midwest), except the Federal District*
1981-1996 data excluded the rural area of Rondonia, Acre, Amazonas, Roraima, Pará and Amapá

Source: *See Table 5.3*

Using the 15 values of average income (m) per economically active person, Gini index (G) and Sen's poverty index (P) presented in tables 5.3 and 5.4, and introducing a binary variable (B) equal to 1 in 1980 and equal to zero in the other years (to capture the effect of the difference between Census and PNAD questionnaires), the following regression is obtained (t values between parenthesis):

$$P = -0.0135 - 0.2656m + 0.0277m^2 + 1.2664G - 0.0180B$$
$$\quad (-0.18) \quad (-5.19) \quad (3.10) \quad\quad (14.28) \quad (-3.25)$$

(5.2)

with $R^2 = 0.991$. The minimum of the parabolic relation between P and m occurs with $m = 4.79$, which is a value greater than any of the observed values of this variable (see table 5.3). Thus, the fitted equation shows that poverty is a decreasing function of the average income and an increasing function of the inequality of the distribution, as could be expected.

It can be verified that the changes in absolute poverty in Brazil during the 1979-1996 period are much more related to changes in average income than to changes in inequality. A regression of P against m, m^2, G, G^2 and B (the binary variable for Census data) has a coefficient of determination equal to 0.992. Excluding m and m^2, the coefficient of determination reduces to 0.127, but if we keep m and m^2 and exclude G and G^2 the coefficient of determination is 0.812.

Notice, in table 5.3, that the three absolute poverty measures have similar values in 1988, 1990 and 1992. Notice, also, that these values are substantially higher than the corresponding values in 1981, at the beginning of the economic crisis.

The evolution of absolute poverty in Brazil during the 1980s is not so bad when one considers all persons classified according to their per capita family income, because family size is decreasing, especially among low income groups (IBGE, 1989). With a per capita poverty line with real value equal to one quarter of the October 1981 minimum wage, the proportion of poor is 0.225 in 1981, 0.224 in 1988 and 0.228 in 1990. With a per capita poverty line twice that value, the proportion of poor in those years is 0.461, 0.440 and 0.438, respectively (Hoffmann, 1995). Using poverty lines for each metropolitan area based on local consumption baskets and data on per capita family income, Rocha (1995) concludes that, for a set of eight metropolitan areas, the absolute poverty measures in 1981 and 1990 are practically the same. Table 5.3 shows that there was a large decrease in the absolute poverty measures from 1993 to 1995, associated with the increase in average and median incomes. In contrast to what happened in 1986, when the beneficial effects of the Cruzado Plan were very short lived, the poverty measures decrease a little more in 1996.

Regional and sectoral contrasts

In this section, the regional and sectoral contrasts of the Brazilian economy will be analyzed using data on earnings (income from occupation) of occupied persons from the 1995 PNAD file. For each person in the sample, the file provides an expansion factor or weight. The sum of these weights for a set of persons in the sample is the corresponding estimated population.

Considering the analysis that will be developed in this section and in the next one, only persons with complete information for the relevant variables are included. These variables are earnings, age, gender, education, position in occupation, color, region, sector of activity and weekly working time. Persons with no earnings are excluded. The remaining sample has 124,365 observations, corresponding to a population of 56,566,132 occupied persons with positive earnings.

The earnings from the principal occupation correspond to 95.7% of earnings from all activities, which correspond to 93.9% of all declared income (including retirement income, rent and interest). Notice that all employer's income that is considered a result of his activities is registered as earnings. It should be kept in mind that the PNAD survey does not collect data in the rural areas of almost all the states of the North region (only in Tocantins, which was formerly part of the Midwest region, does the survey collect data from the rural area).

Tables 5.5 through 5.7 show several characteristics of the distribution of earnings among occupied persons, considering the division of Brazil in six regions. The southeast region is divided in two parts, one including the states of Minas Gerais, Espírito Santo and Rio de Janeiro, and the other including only the state of São Paulo. Table 5.5 shows that the employed persons in the Northeast region account for a little more than one fourth of the total, but receive less than 15% of total earnings. Average earnings in the state of São Paulo are 2.45 times greater than the average earnings in Northeast. The ratio between the corresponding medians is almost 3.

The strong positive asymmetry of the income distribution among employed persons in Brazil is characterized by the fact that its average (R$ 441) is 2.13 times greater than its median (R$ 207). The second decile of the distribution is R$ 100, equal to the official minimum wage in September 1995. The inequality of the distribution can be characterized in different ways: the Gini index is greater than 0.58, the poorest 50% receive only 13.5% of total earnings, the richest tenth receives 46.8% and the richest 5% receive one third of total earnings.

The ratio between the average earnings of the richest tenth and the average earnings of the poorest 40% is equal to 20.6. Trying to explain why Brazil has one of the most unequal income distributions of the world, Barros and Mendonça (1995) show that one outstanding characteristic of this distribution is the large ratio between the average income of the richest 10% and other groups of the population.

Table 5.5   Employed persons with positive earnings in six Brazilian regions in 1995

Region	Employed persons (1000)	%	Earnings %	Average[a]	Median[a]
North[b]	2465	4.4	4.0	402	200
Northeast	14329	25.3	14.6	255	120
MG+ES+RJ[c]	12738	22.5	22.1	434	200
SP[d]	13807	24.4	34.6	625	350
South	9201	16.3	17.5	475	250
Midwest	4026	7.1	7.2	444	200
Brazil[b]	56566	100.0	100.0	441	207

Notes: [a] *In Reais of September, 1995*
               [b] *Excluding the rural area of Rondônia, Acre, Amazonas, Roraima, Pará and Amapá*
               [c] *States of Minas Gerais, Espírito Santo and Rio de Janeiro*
               [d] *State of São Paulo*
Source: *Basic data from 1995 PNAD file*

Table 5.6   Earnings inequality among occupied persons (with positive earnings) in six Brazilian regions in 1995

Region	Gini index (G)	Theil-T	Theil-L	50[-]	10[+]	5[+]
North[a]	0.569	0.673	0.574	14.6	46.7	33.5
Northeast	0.592	0.777	0.634	14.1	50.2	37.5
MG+ES+RJ[b]	0.572	0.677	0.581	14.4	46.8	33.3
SP[c]	0.532	0.565	0.496	16.3	42.7	29.7
South	0.553	0.621	0.542	15.2	44.4	31.4
Midwest	0.577	0.672	0.590	14.1	47.0	33.2
Brazil[a]	0.581	0.688	0.617	13.5	46.8	33.3

Notes: [a] *Excluding the rural area of Rondônia, Acre, Amazonas, Roraima, Pará and Amapá*
               [b] *States of Minas Gerais, Espírito Santo and Rio de Janeiro*
               [c] *State of São Paulo*
Source: *Basic data from 1995 PNAD file*

It is interesting to remember that Kuznets (1963) pointed out that the *shape* of the income distribution curve is different in underdeveloped and developed countries. He associated the wider inequality in the income distribution in the underdeveloped countries to the fact that their upper income groups receive a larger share of total income.

Table 5.6 shows that Northeast is the region with greatest inequality. It is the only region where the Gini index, Theil-*T* and Theil-*L* are greater than for Brazil. The State of São Paulo and the South are the regions with lower measures of inequality.   It was already shown that there are important differences between the six regions' average earnings. However, inequality between regions is a small part of total inequality. The value of Theil-T for inequality between the six regions is 0.046, corresponding to only 6.7% of total inequality among occupied persons in Brazil. The value of Theil-L between regions is 0.049, corresponding to only 8.0% of total inequality. The Gini index for inequality between the six regions is equal to 0.163.

Table 5.7   Absolute poverty among occupied persons with positive earnings in six Brazilian regions in 1995, with a poverty line of R$ 143.151

Region	Poor persons		Proportion of poor	Sen's index	FGT [a]	
	Number ('000)	%	(H)	(P)	Index	% contribution
North [b]	808	4.5	0.328	0.156	0.0580	3.9
Northeast	8155	45.9	0.569	0.331	0.1460	57.0
MG+ES+RJ[c]	3797	21.4	0.298	0.138	0.0501	17.4
SP[d]	1684	9.5	0.122	0.050	0.0165	6.2
South	2138	12.0	0.232	0.110	0.0403	10.1
Midwest	1186	6.7	0.295	0.135	0.0487	5.3
Brazil [b]	17768	100.0	0.314	0.163	0.0648	100.0

Notes: *This poverty line is the same used in table 3 for 1995, with real value equal to the minimum wage of August 1980, using INPC as deflator*
[a] *Absolute poverty index proposed by Foster, Greer and Thorbecke (1984)*
[b] *Excluding the rural area of Rondônia, Acre, Amazonas, Roraima, Pará and Amapá*
[c] *States of Minas Gerais, Espírito Santo and Rio de Janeiro*
[d] *State of São Paulo*
Source: *Basic data from 1995 PNAD file*

Analyzing the distribution of income among economically active persons with positive income in 22 Brazilian Federation Units in 1995, Hoffmann (1997) verified that inequality between these units corresponds to only 7.4% of total inequality for Theil-T and to 9.3% when Theil-L is used.

Table 5.8   Employed persons with positive earnings in three sectors of six Brazilian regions in 1995: average and median earnings and measures of inequality

Sector and Region	Earnings		Gini index (G)	Theil-T	Theil-L	50⁻	10⁺	5⁺
	Average[a]	Median						
1-North [b]	268	150	0.559	0.705	0.554	16.4	48.2	36.2
1-Northeast	131	90	0.485	0.651	0.430	20.2	40.6	31.0
1-MG+ES+RJ [c]	271	130	0.584	0.903	0.602	15.7	52.7	41.5
1-SP [d]	331	200	0.510	0.591	0.443	19.3	45.3	33.0
1-South	286	150	0.540	0.656	0.511	16.7	45.0	33.3
1-Midwest	306	150	0.549	0.715	0.521	17.3	49.0	37.6
1-Total	220	120	0.560	0.780	0.563	16.3	48.4	37.6
2-North [b]	370	230	0.486	0.478	0.400	19.2	40.1	28.2
2-Northeast	280	150	0.533	0.613	0.505	17.2	45.2	33.3
2-MG+ES+RJ [c]	422	250	0.509	0.546	0.441	18.2	42.2	30.1
2-SP [d]	657	400	0.485	0.466	0.398	19.2	39.4	27.0
2-South	456	280	0.495	0.506	0.417	19.0	41.0	28.8
2-Midwest	383	222	0.502	0.541	0.431	18.6	42.0	30.2
2-Total	473	280	0.522	0.551	0.476	17.1	42.3	29.8
3-North [b]	432	200	0.585	0.705	0.612	13.5	47.6	34.0
3-Notheast	313	150	0.603	0.766	0.662	12.9	50.1	36.5
3-MG+ES+RJ [c]	472	230	0.579	0.672	0.602	13.6	46.5	32.7
3-SP [d]	640	350	0.546	0.595	0.528	15.4	43.7	30.5
3-South	541	300	0.562	0.627	0.568	14.3	44.4	31.0
3-Midwest	500	240	0.586	0.667	0.623	12.9	46.4	31.9
3-Total	489	250	0.584	0.683	0.625	13.1	46.6	32.9
Brazil [b]	441	207	0.581	0.688	0.617	13.5	46.8	33.3

Notes: [a] *In Reais of September, 1995*
[b] *Excluding the rural area of Rondônia, Acre, Amazonas, Roraima, Pará and Amapá*
[c] *States of Minas Gerais, Espírito Santo and Rio de Janeiro*
[d] *State of São Paulo*

Measures of absolute poverty among employed persons are presented in table 5.7, for Brazil and the six regions. The poverty line adopted is R$ 143.15, with real value equivalent to the poverty lines used in tables 5.2 and 5.3. In September 1995, when the PNAD data were collected, the exchange rate was R$ 0.96 *per* US dollar. With this poverty line, the proportion of poor (H) among Brazilian occupied persons with positive earnings is 0.314, Sen's poverty index (P) is 0.163 and the *FGT* index is 0.0648. The poorest region is, indeed, the Northeast; the values of P and *FGT* for the Northeast are more than twice the value of the same poverty measure in any other region. Almost 46% of all poor are in the Northeast and approximately 57% of the value of FGT for Brazil is due to poverty in the Northeast. Considering a fixed poverty line, the region with the lowest absolute poverty measures is São Paulo.

Table 5.9   Absolute poverty among employed persons with positive earnings in three sectors of six Brazilian regions in 1995, with a poverty line of R$ 143.15[a]

Section and Region	Employed persons (1000)	Poor persons (1000)	Proportion of poor (H)	Sen's index (P)	FGT [b] Index	FGT [b] % contribution
1-North [c]	258	119	0.464	0.256	0.1067	0.7
1-Northeast	4151	3242	0.781	0.485	0.2276	25.8
1-MG+ES+RJ [d]	1694	894	0.527	0.264	0.1011	4.7
1-SP [e]	899	263	0.293	0.114	0.0348	0.8
1-South	1567	670	0.428	0.221	0.0868	3.7
1-Midwest	749	292	0.389	0.175	0.0614	1.3
1-Total	9319	5480	0.588	0.336	0.1456	37.0
2-North [c]	487	112	0.230	0.091	0.0287	0.4
2-Northeast	2289	1014	0.443	0.221	0.0853	5.3
2-MG+ES+RJ [d]	2887	578	0.200	0.077	0.0235	1.8
2-SP [e]	4054	224	0.055	0.021	0.0060	0.7
2-South	2421	355	0.147	0.059	0.0186	1.2
2-Midwest	682	155	0.227	0.094	0.0308	0.6
2-Total	12821	2438	0.190	0.083	0.0287	10.0
3-North [c]	1720	576	0.335	0.159	0.0589	2.8
3-Northeast	7889	3898	0.494	0.279	0.1206	25.9
3-MG+ES+RJ [d]	8156	2325	0.285	0.133	0.0490	10.9
3-SP [e]	8854	1197	0.135	0.057	0.0194	4.7
3-South	5213	1113	0.214	0.100	0.0364	5.2
3-Midwest	2594	740	0.285	0.134	0.0497	3.5
3-Total	34427	9849	0.286	0.144	0.0564	53.0
Brazil	56566	17768	0.314	0.163	0.0648	100.0

Notes: [a] *In Reais of September, 1995*
[b] *Absolute poverty index proposed by Foster, Greer and Thorbecke (1984)*
[c] *Excluding the rural area of Rondônia, Acre, Amazonas, Roraima, Pará and Amapá*
[d] *States of Minas Gerais, Espírito Santo and Rio de Janeiro*
[e] *State of São Paulo*

Using poverty lines based on local consumption baskets and data on per capita family income in 1990, Rocha (1995) shows that the proportion of poor in Brazil is 30.3%. The distribution of the poor among the Regions is similar to the one presented in table 5.7: 5.3% in the North, 45.0% in Northeast, 21.2% in MG+ES+RJ, 12.2% in the State of São Paulo, 10.4% in the South and 5.9% in the Midwest.

Tables 5.8 and 5.9 present the main characteristics of income distribution among employed persons for a more detailed division of the economy, considering six regions and three sectors. Sector 1 includes the occupations in agriculture, sector 2 corresponds to industry and sector 3 includes commerce, transportation, communication, public administration and other services. In Brazil, the average earnings in industry are more than twice the average in agriculture. Average earnings in sector 3 are higher than in sector 2 for Brazil and most regions; the only exception is São Paulo, where average earnings in industry are a little higher than in sector 3.

Industry is the sector with less internal inequality. The result of the comparison between sectors 1 and 3 depends upon the inequality measure that is chosen: considering Theil-*T*, which is more sensitive to changes in the upper tail of the distribution, inequality is substantially higher in sector 1 than in sector 3, but if one uses Theil-*L*, which is more sensitive to changes among the poor, inequality is higher in sector 3 than in sector 1. Notice, also, that the value of Theil-*T* in the Northeast is substantially higher for sector 3 than for sector 1. The Northeast is also the only region where the Gini index for sector 1 is lower than for sector 2.

Using the decomposition properties of Theil-*T* and Theil-*L*, it can be verified that the inequality between the three sectors corresponds to only 4.3% and 5.8%, respectively, of total inequality. Subdividing the population of occupied persons into 18 groups (6 regions and 3 sectors), inequality between groups corresponds to 9.5% and 12.5% of total inequality, for Theil-*T* and Theil-*L*, respectively.

Table 5.9 shows the distribution of poor occupied persons with positive earnings in the 18 groups (3 sectors and 6 regions), using, again, a poverty line equal to R$ 143.15. Most of the poor (55.4%) are in sector 3 simply because 60.9% of the population is in this sector. Sector 2 has 22.7% of the population and 13.7% of the poor. Sector 1, with only 16.5% of the population, has 30.8% of the poor. In all 6 regions, the measures of absolute poverty are higher in sector 1 (agriculture) and lower in sector 2 (industry), with sector 3 in an intermediate position.

The last column of table 5.9 shows the contribution of each group to total poverty, according to the *FGT* measure. This measure, as well as Sen's index, takes into account the extension of poverty, measured by the number of poor, and also the intensity of poverty, measured by the income gap of each poor person (the distance of the poor person's income and the poverty line). According to this measure, 53% of total poverty is in sector 3, with 25.9% of that in sector 3 of the Northeast. Sector 1 contributes

37%, with 25.8% coming from sector 1 of the Northeast; sector 2 contributes only 10%.

Determinants of personal earnings

An earnings equation is adjusted to the data in order to evaluate the influence of gender, age, education, position in occupation, color, region, weekly working time and sector of activity. The dependent variable (y) is the logarithm of income from all activities (earnings) for each occupied person.[5]

All the explanatory variables are dummies whose coefficients are the increase in the expected value of y when the person pertains to a category, in comparison with a "reference" category, which is a male 10 to 14 years old with less than 1 year of formal education, employee, white, resident in Northeast and working 15 to 39 hours per week in sector 2 (industry). The other categories for each factor are presented in table 5.11. The regression equation was estimated by weighted least squares, considering the expansion factor for each person in the sample.

The regression equation was estimated for Brazil and also for each of the three sectors. Table 5.10 shows the sample size, the coefficient of determination and the factor's marginal contribution to regression sum of squares for each equation. In all cases the factor's contributions are significant at 1%. The explanatory power of the regression is somewhat lower for sector 1, with R^2 equal to 0.409; for the other equations, this coefficient is above 0.57. The marginal contribution of education (12 dummies) is 24.4% in the equation for Brazil and is near 30% in the equations for sectors 2 and 3, but is only 7.9% in the equation for agriculture. The factor with the largest contribution in sector 1 is position in occupation, with 14.8%. The typical employer, in Brazilian agriculture, is a landowner, and the typical employee is a landless person. Hence, the importance of position in occupation in the equation for sector 1 indicates the importance of access to land in the determination of the income of persons occupied in Brazilian agriculture.

Since the work of Langoni (1973), all earnings equations fitted to Brazilian data, particularly when limited to urban areas or sectors, show the importance of education. It is possible that position in occupation in urban activities is a very bad proxy for capital ownership. In this case, the coefficients for education may be biased, capturing the influence of this omitted variable.

Table 5.10   Earnings equations for Brazil and for three sectors in 1995

Statistic	Brazil	Sector 1	Sector 2	Sector 3
N	124,365	17,959	27,641	78,765
R^2	0.593	0.409	0.572	0.595
Marginal contribution of (%)				
Gender	4.8	3.6	5.7	5.6
Age	9.5	5.8	15.3	10.7
Education	24.4	7.9	30.6	28.9
Position in occupation	4.3	14.8	3.6	4.1
Color	0.4	1.7	0.7	0.3
Region	5.6	7.4	9.5	5.3
Work time	3.4	7.0	2.5	4.1
Sector	3.0	-	-	-

Education is, indeed, an important determinant of personal earnings. Note that it is the second most important factor in the equations for sector 1. It is probable that the influence of education is overestimated in the earnings equations, due to the omission of capital ownership and family status. The unsolved question is the quantification of that overestimation.

Table 5.11 shows, for each factor and for each equation, index numbers indicating the percentage increase of expected earnings for a person pertaining to a category, in comparison with the reference category. If β is an estimated coefficient of the earnings equation, the correspondent index number is [100 exp (β)]. Keeping constant the other factors listed in table 5.11, the expected earnings of a female is 35.2% lower than for a male. The relative difference is a little smaller in sector 1. Earnings tend to increase with age up to the 40-49 years range. This increase is steeper in sectors 2 and 3 than in sector 1.

More education is always associated with higher income. Notice that the increase in expected earnings shows higher steps for 4 and 8 years of education, corresponding to the completion of the former "primary" and today's "first degree", respectively. This is the "diploma effect" discussed by Ramos and Vieira (1996).

For up to four years of education, the average increase in earnings is 7.5% per year in sector 1 and is around 8.8% per year for Brazil and in sectors 2 and 3. Considering the 12 to 14 years of education category, the average yearly increase in earnings is 9.4% for sector 1 and is around 10.6% for Brazil and in sectors 2 and 3.

The index numbers in table 5.11 show that the expected earnings of a self-employed person, *ceteris paribus*, are very similar to the average earnings of an employee. Employers, however, have much higher expected earnings, the relative difference being greater in sector 1.

Table 5.11   Earnings equations for Brazil and for three sectors in 1995

(index numbers of the expected level of earnings for each level of the factors; the index for the reference category of each factor is 100)

Factor	Category	Brazil	Sector 1	Sector 2	Sector 3
Gender	Male	100	100	100	100
	Female	64.8	68.7	64.2	64.5
Age	10 to 14	100	100	100	100
(years)	15 to 17	135.0	129.8	135.4	138.2
	18 to 19	161.1	147.4	168.4	167.1
	20 to 24	196.5	161.9	206.9	209.0
	25 to 29	236.0	171.4	253.0	255.3
	30 to 39	279.9	191.5	306.0	304.3
	40 to 49	320.2	209.0	352.9	351.8
	50 to 59	308.4	206.1	344.5	339.4
	60 or more	270.2	192.3	280.7	293.7
Education	Less than 1	100	100	100	100
(years)	1	110.1	108.4	112.2	107.9
	2	118.9	116.6	122.7	115.7
	3	125.5	119.2	125.2	127.0
	4	140.1	133.6	139.9	140.8
	5	148.2	136.7	148.8	151.1
	6	158.0	143.7	159.4	161.3
	7	164.7	146.1	164.2	169.4
	8	186.3	153.0	185.5	190.5
	9 or 10	198.9	168.0	197.6	205.9
	11	270.7	226.3	269.1	276.6
	12 to 14	367.0	323.2	370.8	374.3
	15 or more	622.0	406.4	661.9	626.1
Position	Employee	100	100	100	100
in occupation	House workr.	79.1	-		81.3
	Self-employ.	103.3	102.4	99.9	107.9
	Employer	219.0	301.7	190.5	214.8
Color	White	100	100	100	100
	Indian	84.5	72.9	79.1	99.9
	Black	88.4	84.9	88.0	89.2
	Asian	113.0	154.4	121.1	106.2
	"Parda"	88.8	84.9	88.2	90.3
Region	Northeast	100	100	100	100
	North	135.8	149.4	132.4	135.4
	MG+ES+RJ	130.8	133.2	129.6	130.6
	SP	182.0	172.6	192.8	178.6
	South	140.3	130.0	141.8	143.9
	Midwest	143.1	152.0	131.1	144.3
Work Time	15 to 39	100	100	100	100
	40 to 44	138.4	131.8	153.5	137.7
	45 to 48	140.1	145.0	155.9	137.0
	49 or more	161.9	168.6	167.1	162.8
Sector	1	63.2	-	-	-
	2	100	-	-	-
	3	96.4	-	-	-

The expected earnings of a black or a "pardo" is 10 to 15% lower than for a white. This can be associated with discrimination against these groups in Brazilian labor market. However, the fact that the expected earnings are higher for an Asian indicates than the explanations can be more complex, involving unmeasured variables such as ambition, cultural characteristics of the group, etc.

The expected earnings of a person living in São Paulo is 82% higher than for a person living in the Northeast, *ceteris paribus*. However, table 5.5 shows that the average earnings in São Paulo are 145% higher than in Northeast. These results are found because other factors are not constant; education, for example, is much lower in Northeast, where 60.7% of occupied persons have 4 or less years of education and only 5.6% have 12 or more years of education. In São Paulo these percentages are 36.8% and 14.0%, respectively.

We saw, in table 5.8, that the average earnings in sector 1 are less than half the average in sector 2. However, the index numbers in table 5.11 indicate that the expected earnings in sector 1 are only 36.8% lower than in sector 2, *ceteris paribus*. The level of education is clearly lower in sector 1, where 85.0% of occupied persons have 4 years of education or less, and only 0.9% have 12 or more years of education. In sector 2, these percentages are 46.0% and 6.8%, respectively, and in sector 3, they are 34.1% and 13.8%.

Conclusion

The previous analysis shows that in the 1970s there was a substantial reduction in absolute poverty in Brazil, due to a sizeable increase in per capita income, with relative stability in the inequality of the income distribution. The period 1980-1993, however, can be characterized as a "lost period" in terms of economic growth. Absolute poverty among economically active persons in 1993 is greater than 13 years before.

The data indicate a substantial reduction in absolute poverty in 1995 and 1996, but Brazilian people hope that this will be only a first step in a new period of economic development. The conjunction of factors responsible for the lack of economic growth is, to a large extent, also responsible for the increase in poverty. This is not to deny that some poverty alleviation measures are feasible even in the absence of growth, but the constraints are, of course, far greater than in a growth period.

It does not seem probable that a reduction of absolute poverty in Brazil, in the next years, can be obtained without economic growth, and through a substantial redistribution of income. Therefore, hopes are directed to the resumption of steady growth. It is important, however, that the poor should be the principal beneficiaries of economic growth, through a reduction in income inequality, contrary to what happened during the 1960s. Even if it cannot be considered the only instrument for income redistribution, education must be supported in order to prepare persons for economic changes.

Notes

[1] On data limitations see Médici (1984 and 1988), Hoffmann (1988) and Hoffmann and Kageyama (1986).

[2] Six states of the North Region are excluded because there the survey (PNAD) does not cover the rural area.

[3] In August 1980 the official exchange rate was 54.645 cruzeiros per dollar (*Conjuntura Econômica* 35(12):3), making the minimum wage equal to U$ 75.94.

[4] Part of the decrease in inequality is due to the elimination of the statistical "noise" effect of high inflation, as shows Neri (1997).

[5] This is the reason to consider only persons with positive earnings in the analysis developed in sections 5 and 6.

References

Barros, R.P. de, Mendonça, R.S.P. de (1995) Os determinantes da desigualdade no Brasil, *Texto para Discussão* n° 377, IPEA, Rio de Janeiro.

Cardoso, E.A. and Fishlow, A. (1990) "Desenvolvimento econômico na América Latina: 1950-80," *Revista de Economia* 44, 311-335.

Foster, J., Greer, J. and Thorbecke, E. (1984) "A class of decomposable poverty measures," *Econometrica*, 52, 761-766.

Hoffmann, R. (1979) "Estimação da desigualdade dentro de estratos no cálculo do índice de Gini e da redundância," *Pesquisa e Planejamento Econômico*, 9, 719-738.

Hoffmann, R. (1984) "Estimation of inequality and concentration measures from grouped observations," *Revista de Econometria*, 4, 5-21.

Hoffmann, R. (1988) "A subdeclaração dos rendimentos," *São Paulo em Perspectiva* 2, 50-54. São Paulo: SEADE.

Hoffmann, R. (1995) "Pobreza, insegurança alimentar e desnutrição no Brasil," *Estudos Avançados* 9, 159-172.

Hoffmann, R. (1997) "Desigualdade entre estados na distribuição da renda no Brasil," *Economia Aplicada* 1, 281-296.

Hoffmann, R. and Kageyama, A.A. (1986) "Distribuição da renda no Brasil, entre famílias e entre pessoas, em 1970 e 1980," *Estudos Econômicos* 16, 25-51.

IBGE (1984) *Indicadores Sociais* - Tabelas Selecionadas. Vol 2-1984. Rio de Janeiro.

IBGE (1985) *Anúario Estatístico do Brasil 1985*. Rio de Janeiro.

IBGE (1988) *Anúario Estatístico do Brasil 1987-88*. Rio de Janeiro.

IBGE (1989) *Família - Indicadores sociais*. Rio de Janeiro, vol.1.

IBGE (1990a) *Estatísticas Históricas do Brasil*. Séries Econômicas, Demográficas e Sociais de 1550 a 1988. 2nd ed., reviewed and updated. Rio de Janeiro.

IBGE (1990b) *Anúario Estatístico do Brasil 1990*. Rio de Janeiro.

Kuznets, S. (1963) "Quantitative aspects of the economic growth of nations: VIII - Distribution of income by size," *Economic Development and Cultural Change*, 11, 1-80.

Langoni, C.G. (1973) *Distribução da Renda e desenvolvimento Econômico do Brasil*. Rio de Janeiro, Expresião e Cultura.

Lluch, C. (1982) "Sobre medições de renda a partir dos Censos e das contas nacionais no Brasil," *Pesquisa e Planejamento Econômico* 12, 133-148.

Médici, A.C. (1984) "Notas interpretativas sobre a variável 'renda' nos Censos Demográficos." *In* ABEP, *Censos, Consensos, Contra-sensos*. III Seminário Metodológico dos Censos Demográficos, Ouro Preto.

Médici, A.C. (1988) "A mensuração da subjetividade: notas sobre a variável renda nas PNADs." In D.O. Sawyer. (ed.) *PNADs em foco - anos 80*. Belo Horizonte: ABEP (Associação Brasileira de Estudos Populacionais).

Neri, M. (1997) "Dynamics of income distribution in Brazil," *XXV Encontro Nacional de Economia*, Anais, 2, 1141-1156.

Ramos, L. and Vieira, M.L. (1996) "A relação entre educação e salários no Brasil." In *A Economia Brasileira em Perspectiva - 1996*. IPEA, 2, 493-510.

Rocha, S. (1995) "Governabilidade e pobreza: o desafio dos números," *Texto para Discussão* n° 368, IPEA, Rio de Janeiro.

6 Recent Trends in Regional Competitiveness and Industrial Concentration

CARLOS R. AZZONI

Introduction

The problem of regional inequalities in Brazil has gained new interest recently, partly due to the release of new statistical information on Brazilian states and regions, such as the national survey of households (PNAD), as well as the 1996 population census, and GDP estimates for individual states made by the Applied Economic Research Institute (IPEA). At the same time, there has been a reawakening of theoretical interest in regional inequalities within the mainstream of economic thought, in association with the so-called 'convergence controversy' within growth theory. Thus, there has been a large volume of academic papers on the subject, both within Brazil and at international level.[1]

In the case of Brazil, a large number of studies have pointed to a reduction in regional inequalities from 1970 onwards. More recent papers covering the early 1990s have nevertheless revealed that this trend is showing clear signs of stagnation or even reversal. This chapter aims to offer new empirical evidence on the subject in the specific case of manufacturing, and thereby to clarify the situation. The industrial sector has been the principal target of regional development programs, due to the fact that it is more footloose than natural resources oriented activities (agriculture, agroindustry, mining and mineral processing industries, etc.), and activities oriented by the spatial distribution of population and income (retail and wholesale activities, services, etc.). Although manufacturing is less location specific, it usually presents the highest degree of regional concentration, and is one of the main contributors to regional income inequalities at the level of both individual countries and international regions. It is therefore important to study the trends observed in this sector in so far as these provide significant pointers to future regional inequalities within Brazil.

In the next section a brief theoretical discussion of regional competitiveness in attracting new industrial investment, using the model developed by Kaldor and explored in Azzoni (1986), is developed; the indicators to be calculated to measure regional competitiveness are also presented in this section. The results derived from the calculations of the regional competitiveness indicators are presented next. Thereafter, attempts are made to develop explanations for these results, as well as to explore their implications for regional inequalities within Brazil in the future. Finally, some concluding remarks are offered.

Regional competitiveness in attracting industrial investments

The choice of an optimal location is based on the expected return at each feasible location within any given territory, based on both current conditions at the time of decision, and expected future conditions. In conceptual terms, therefore, entrepreneurs attempt to choose a location for their businesses that will allow them to achieve their objectives, at least with regard to their expectations. In microeconomic models, this objective is normally assumed to be profitability, and this study adopts the same perspective (see Azzoni, 1982). Since, different locations are expected to deliver different returns, firms will tend to concentrate in the more profitable locations.

It is well known that the process of choosing a location for an establishment is complex, requiring detailed information on different options, as well as constituting a task that falls outside day-to-day decision making by companies. Indeed, location studies are normally highly detailed and expensive to compile. An alternative method is to observe the operating results of similar establishments located in different areas. Since variations in operating results are at least partially due to differing location conditions, a precise location study will reveal the advantages of different locations to the decision maker, to the degree that these are reflected in the operations of existing establishments. That is to say, by one means or the other, geographical variations in profitability will both determine location decisions by new entrepreneurs, and condition the growth potential of established firms.

Hence, it is important to identify regional trends in industrial profitability, in order to identify regional industrial location trends. This is the stance adopted in Kaldor's (1970) model, in his analysis of the regional concentration of industry in Great Britain.[2] The model uses the concept of an efficiency wage, defined as the ratio between nominal wage and labor productivity. In essence, firms may seek locations in which the efficiency wage is low, even if the nominal wage is high, since in such cases, high wage levels are offset by higher productivity.

Variations in productivity between regions arise from economies of scale and of agglomeration, while regional variations in wages are determined by the supply of and demand for labor, and tend to be narrower than variations in productivity. One of the reasons for this, according to Kaldor, is labor union activity, which tends to homogenize wage levels. It may be added that for less developed countries, in addition to legislation that is probably more restrictive, generally low wage levels are in themselves an obstacle to the further reduction of wages, since they are already close to minimum subsistence levels. Summarizing Kaldor's argument, regional variations in productivity levels are larger than regional variations in wage levels.

In order to explain the growth of regional inequalities, Kaldor makes use of the so called Verdoorn Law, which states that productivity grows in proportion to the volume of production in a given region. Thus, (a) economies of scale and agglomeration determine that the level of productivity in the regional manufacturing center of a country is greater than at its industrial periphery, (b) since wage levels vary less than productivity levels, the efficiency wage will be lower, and thus the level of profitability higher in the regional manufacturing center, (c) this higher profitability will attract further production, with the result that (d) by Verdoorn's Law, productivity will grow even more in this region. This closes a virtual circle for the regional manufacturing center, and a vicious circle for the industrial periphery of a country.

While it is not the aim of this study to apply Kaldor's model to the recent experience of Brazil, the efficiency wage concept will be used to indicate the competitiveness of different Brazilian regions. Let P_{irt}, W_{irt} and N_{irt}, be, respectively, the level of output, the aggregate payroll and the number of employees of sector i of region r at time t. Labor productivity is given by $p_{irt} = P_{irt} / N_{irt}$ and the average wage by $w_{irt} = W_{irt} / N_{irt}$.

The comparative regional productivity indicator is constructed by comparing the observed production level in a region with the one that would occur if the regional level of labor productivity were equal to the national level, for each sector. If observed production is higher than estimated production, then we may conclude that regional productivity is higher than the national average. Specifically, for each sector we calculate:

$$IP_{i,r,t} = \frac{P_{i,r,t}}{N_{i,r,t} \cdot p_{i,t}} \qquad (6.1)$$

If $IP_{irt} > 1$, region r is more 'productive' in sector i than the national average level, and less 'productive' if $IP_{irt} < 1$. The general indicator for all sectors is given by:

$$IP_{r,t} = \frac{\sum_i P_{i,r,t}}{\sum_i \left(N_{i,r,t} \cdot p_{i,t} \right)} \qquad (6.2)$$

It is important to note that this indicator takes into consideration differences in industrial structure between regions; the production observed in a given region for each of its sectors is compared with the expected production in the same sectors. The indicator for manufacturing as a whole is based on the sum of sectoral values, both observed and expected, and thus considers the different sectorial structures of regions. The same observation may be made with respect to the wage and 'surplus' indicators that are presented below.

The comparative regional wage indicator follows the same mechanism. We calculate the aggregate payroll expected for a given region as though its wage levels were equal to the national average; this is then compared with the observed aggregate payroll for the same region,

$$IW_{i,r,t} = \frac{W_{i,r,t}}{N_{i,r,t} \cdot w_{i,t}}, \text{ for each sector} \qquad (6.3)$$

$$IW_{r,t} = \frac{\sum_i W_{i,r,t}}{\sum_i \left(N_{i,r,t} \cdot w_{i,t} \right)}, \text{ for the aggregate of all sectors} \qquad (6.4)$$

These wage level indicators are interpreted in the same way as the productivity indicators described above.

Finally, the profitability indicator utilizes the idea of 'surplus,' which is defined as the difference between value added and payroll. Two surplus values, observed and estimated, are obtained for each region by the above procedure. The regional surplus indicator is the ratio between the two, namely:

$$IE_{i,r,t} = \frac{P_{i,r,t} - W_{i,r,t}}{\left(N_{i,r,t} \cdot p_{i,t}\right) - \left(N_{i,r,t} \cdot w_{i,t}\right)} , \text{ for each sector } i \tag{6.5}$$

$$IE_{r,t} = \frac{\sum_i \left(P_{i,r,t} - W_{i,r,t}\right)}{\sum_i \left[\left(N_{i,r,t} \cdot p_{i,t}\right) - \left(N_{i,r,t} \cdot w_{i,t}\right)\right]} , \text{ for the aggregate of all sectors} \tag{6.6}$$

A region with a surplus indicator greater than one will have a level of profitability that is higher than the national average, and is thus qualified to compete for future industrial investments. On the other hand, regions with a surplus indicator <1 will face difficulties in competing.

Regional industrial competitiveness indicators for Brazil

In order to calculate the indicators presented in the previous section, data from the industrial census of 1985 were updated by the author using regional production and employment indicators produced by the Brazilian Statistics Institute (IBGE). Table 6.1 presents the general results for production by region; it includes census data for the years 1970, 1975 and 1980.

Table 6.1   Share of regions in national manufacturing production

	70	75	80	85	86	87	88	89	90	91	92	93	94	95	96
Northeast Region	0.06	0.07	0.08	0.09	0.08	0.08	0.08	0.08	0.08	0.08	0.09	0.07	0.08	0.07	0.08
South Region	0.12	0.15	0.16	0.17	0.16	0.16	0.15	0.16	0.16	0.16	0.17	0.16	0.18	0.17	0.17
Minas Gerais State	0.06	0.06	0.08	0.08	0.08	0.08	0.09	0.10	0.09	0.09	0.10	0.09	0.09	0.09	0.09
Rio de Janeiro State	0.16	0.13	0.11	0.09	0.10	0.10	0.09	0.08	0.08	0.08	0.08	0.08	0.07	0.07	0.07
São Paulo State	0.58	0.56	0.53	0.52	0.53	0.54	0.54	0.54	0.54	0.54	0.53	0.52	0.53	0.55	0.53

Source: *For 1970, 1975, 1980 and 1985, FIBGE, Industrial Censuses; for 1986 onwards, updating of 1985 Industrial Census data by the monthly indices published by FIBGE in its 'Pesquisa Industrial Mensal'*

The table highlights regional manufacturing concentration in the country: the state of São Paulo still accounts for 53.2% of production, in spite of having had 58.1% in 1970. A clear declining trend from 1970 through 1985 is observed; however, from this year on a stagnation or even reversal is noticeable. If the neighboring states of Minas Gerais and Rio de

Janeiro are added to São Paulo, this macroregion's share in 1997 goes up to 69.2% of total manufacturing production in Brazil; in 1985 the same macroregion's share was 69.7%, almost the same, indicating that the declining trend observed in the 1970s and early 1980s is no longer present.

Before presenting results for the period 1985-97, it should be noted that the calculations referring to 1970, 1975 and 1980 are marginally different from those for 1985 and on. For the first three censuses, we considered both the sectorial structure of each state and the distribution by size of enterprises for each state. This approach allowed us to present the differences between states in a more reliable way, although it was not possible to extend this procedure to more recent years due to the lack of relevant information, an obstacle that also applied to the 1985 Census. For the Northeastern states, the indices for 1985 were calculated only for the states of Pernambuco, Ceará and Bahia. In order to overcome the problem, we calculated averages of state indicators for the first three years, weighting these by the contribution of each individual state to the total of the three states. For example, the wage indices for Bahia, Pernambuco and Ceará for 1970 were taken and an average value calculated, weighting by the contribution of each state's payroll to the total payroll for those three states. The same calculation was made for productivity and surplus indicators, in such a way as to generate approximations to the regional indicators. In the same manner, a weighted average was calculated for the three Southern states for those years, in order to allow comparisons over the 28-year period under consideration. This problem does not arise in the case of the states of São Paulo, Rio de Janeiro and Minas Gerais, since comparative data are available for all years of the period in question.

Table 6.2   Comparative indicators of wages, labor productivity and surplus

WAGES	70	75	80	85	86	87	88	89	90	91	92	93	94	95	96	97
Northeast Region	0.79	0.74	0.86	0.72	0.67	0.66	0.63	0.63	0.61	0.60	0.59	0.57	0.56	0.56	0.56	0.59
South Region	0.84	0.86	0.85	0.81	0.83	0.84	0.83	0.88	0.88	0.89	0.90	0.91	0.90	0.93	0.95	1.00
Minas Gerais State	0.85	0.89	0.90	0.81	0.80	0.80	0.79	0.84	0.81	0.77	0.80	0.84	0.85	0.86	0.91	1.00
Rio de Janeiro State	1.08	0.97	0.95	0.97	0.92	0.94	0.93	0.93	0.90	0.90	0.92	0.88	0.82	0.83	0.86	0.83
São Paulo State	1.11	1.12	1.05	1.11	1.12	1.12	1.13	1.11	1.12	1.14	1.14	1.14	1.16	1.15	1.15	1.13

Table 6.2 (continued)

LABOR PRODUCTIVITY

	70	75	80	85	86	87	88	89	90	91	92	93	94	95	96	97
Northeast Region	0.72	0.78	1.03	0.70	0.65	0.59	0.49	0.48	0.41	0.52	0.49	0.50	0.56	0.61	0.67	0.71
South Region	0.89	0.93	0.95	0.96	0.91	0.94	0.91	0.93	0.93	0.93	0.92	0.89	0.98	0.93	0.94	0.94
Minas Gerais State	1.05	0.95	0.99	0.99	0.99	0.98	1.02	1.14	1.10	1.09	1.16	1.09	1.08	1.05	1.03	1.06
Rio de Janeiro State	1.09	1.02	1.01	0.88	0.90	0.84	0.79	0.71	0.74	0.74	0.74	0.77	0.70	0.69	0.71	0.73
São Paulo State	1.12	1.08	1.05	1.02	1.02	1.03	1.04	1.04	1.04	1.04	1.04	1.00	1.00	1.03	1.02	1.02

PROFITABILITY (SURPLUS)

	70	75	80	85	86	87	88	89	90	91	92	93	94	95	96	97
Northeast Region	0.71	0.79	1.05	0.81	0.82	0.85	0.83	0.80	0.79	0.86	0.83	0.74	0.87	0.86	0.84	0.84
South Region	0.91	0.95	0.97	1.00	0.94	0.96	0.93	0.95	0.95	0.94	0.92	0.88	1.00	0.93	0.94	0.93
Minas Gerais State	1.11	0.97	1.03	1.03	1.05	1.03	1.10	1.23	1.19	1.15	1.25	1.15	1.14	1.10	1.06	1.07
Rio de Janeiro State	1.09	1.03	1.02	0.86	0.89	0.81	0.75	0.64	0.69	0.71	0.70	0.74	0.67	0.66	0.69	0.72
São Paulo State	1.12	1.07	1.05	1.00	0.99	1.01	1.01	1.02	1.02	1.01	1.01	0.97	0.97	1.00	0.99	1.00

Table 6.2 and figures 6.1 - 6.3 show production, wage and surplus indicators for the five regions under consideration; the national average in each variable is set equal to 1. Due to the different procedures applied to the first three years, these are highlighted on the graph with a different type of line. Even considering these differences, however, the joint presentation of the series allows the overall longer-term trends to be observed.

It may be seen from the figures that the regional dispersion of labor productivity indicators fell sharply in the 1970s, rose significantly in the 1980s and early 1990s and has diminished since then. The same phenomenon may be observed with wage indicators, but with no reduction in the dispersion in recent years. As a consequence, the surplus indicators show a similar pattern of behavior to the productivity indicator, albeit with a degree of magnification. That is to say, in the 1970s, there was a relative convergence of industrial profitability levels in the regions considered; from 1985 onwards, however, this trend was reversed.

As far as labor productivity in manufacturing (figure 6.1), it may be seen that there was a consistent fall in this indicator in Rio de Janeiro over the period 1985-97, from a level 10% below the national average to a level in the final years of the series some 30% below the national average, with a noticeable improvement from 1995 onwards. The Northeast region has oscillated over the 13 years of the series around a level some 20% below the national average, with no apparent tendency to shift from this level, excepting for some sporadic movements. The South region also produced indicators that were below the national average throughout the period under consideration, registering a declining trend until 1993, and a slight improvement since then. These three areas thus exhibit productivity levels below the national average, with Rio de Janeiro showing a declining trend, the Northeast, a stable trend, and the South, a slight increase over the last few years. The states of São Paulo and Minas Gerais present above average indicators. While the latter state began the period with indicators slightly below the national average, it demonstrated a strong growth trend until 1992, reaching a level 16% above the national average in that year, before falling sharply from then onwards to a level 6% above the national average in 1997.[3] The neighboring state, São Paulo, which contains most of the national industrial base, showed indicators above the national average in all 13 years (excepting 1993, when it coincided with the national average), registering a level over the last three years of some 2% above the national average.

In summarizing productivity data, we find a large gap between the less productive areas analyzed (Rio de Janeiro and the Northeast) and the most productive areas (Minas Gerais and São Paulo), with the South below the national average, but closer to it. Moreover, there is no clear evidence to suggest that these levels are changing, with the exception of the sustained fall in Rio de Janeiro, although even in this case, the level has stabilized in recent years. In addition, the oscillations recorded do not seem to be of sufficient strength to alter the established levels.

Productivity indicates the value of product per worker that an entrepreneur may obtain, and may be considered as an indicator of competitiveness in each area. It is now appropriate to analyze the unit labor costs, which indicates the cost of generating the corresponding output (figure 6.2). It may be observed that wage levels in São Paulo are the highest in the country and are systematically more than 10% above the national average, having moved to a premium of 15% over the last three years, and showing a rising trend since 1989, having increased by some 4 percentage points. At the other extreme is the Northeast, with levels 40% or more below the national average, showing a sharp declining trend until 1995, and a moderate recovery in 1996 and 1997. Rio de Janeiro shows a

similar pattern of decline, starting at a level 1% below the national average
to reach a level 17% below the corresponding national average figure in
1997. Minas Gerais had the second-lowest level at the start of the period
under consideration, lying some 20% below the national average;
nevertheless, this state showed a systematic pattern of growth throughout
the whole period, reaching the national average level in the last year of the
period. Finally, the South, which had the third lowest level of wages in
1985, after São Paulo and Rio de Janeiro, demonstrated a stable pattern of
wage behavior until 1991, when wages began to recover at a vigorous pace,
almost reaching the national average level by the end of 1997.

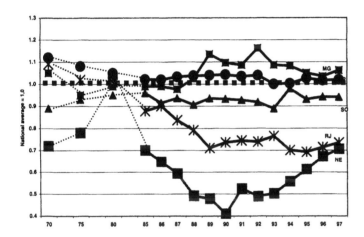

Figure 6.1   Labor productivity in manufacturing

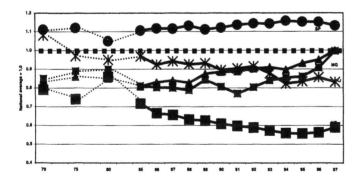

Figure 6.2   Regional wage indicators

The wage indicators show that there are two areas with levels far below the national average (Northeast and Rio de Janeiro), two areas rapidly approaching the national average (South and Minas Gerais) and the state of São Paulo, with levels remaining above and even diverging from the national average. This information is highly relevant to an analysis of regional competitiveness over time. As mentioned above, entrepreneurs are interested not only in the cost of labor, but also the level of output per unit of wage, the efficiency wage. The indicators in figure 6.3 refer to the 'surplus' (the difference between value added and total payroll), which approximates to the net final return to the entrepreneur.

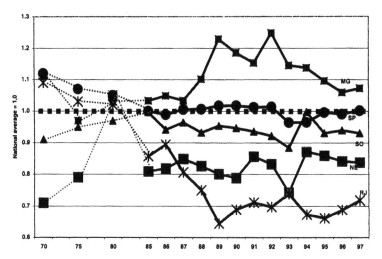

Figure 6.3 Regional indicators of profitability

As may be observed from in table 6.2 and figure 6.3, Rio de Janeiro, which is associated with relatively high wage levels (even if these are in moderate decline) and low productivity, has an extremely low level of profitability, standing some 32% below the national average. More than this figure, the worst indicator for this state is its declining trend at the start of the period under consideration, which then stabilizes, but then shows only a modest recovery in the last two years of the survey. The Northeast has the second lowest level of profitability, which is due to wage levels well below the national average, and productivity only moderately better than that of Rio de Janeiro; there is no clear trend towards an improvement in this area. In the South region, where wages are rapidly approaching and productivity is slightly below the national average, profitability has also been below the national average level, albeit close to it in recent years. This region also lacks a clear trend, registering a notable decline until 1993, followed by growth from then onwards, reaching the national average in 1994.

The indicator for the state of Minas Gerais, on the other hand, is well above the national average, and has shown a consistent improvement in its position until 1992, when, as a result of high productivity and low salaries, it stood some 25% above the national average. After this year, however, there is a clear declining trend, although the levels for the last two years, while the lowest since 1992, are still 6-7% above the national average level of profitability. Finally, the state of São Paulo has maintained a level close to the national average throughout the entire period under consideration, without any clear trend.

The above indicators reveal that higher wage levels in the industrial core of Brazil have been more than offset by higher levels of productivity (with the exception of Rio de Janeiro), with the consequence that the less industrialized areas have failed to attract private investment. More importantly, it should be noted that the indicators point to a reversal of the contrary trend registered between 1970 and 1985. For example, in 1970, the state of São Paulo had a level of industrial profitability 12% above the national average, falling to 5% above it in 1980, and to the national average in 1985; from then onwards, this trend was interrupted. On the other hand, Minas Gerais, which showed strong growth during the 1970s and early 1980s, continued to grow from then onwards, despite the fall registered after 1992, which left the indicator for the state only 7% above the national average. The state of Paraná, which is not highlighted in this analysis, is also worthy of mention. In the 1970s, this state had the highest level of industrial profitability in Brazil. While there are still no comparable figures for the 1980s and 1990s, it should be noted that its share of total national industrial GDP has grown from 5.2% in 1985 to around 5.8% in 1996-97), suggesting that its profitability levels continue to attract companies.

These indicators are relevant as pointers to the future regional industrial concentration in the country. In order to receive new industrial investments to the degree that the existing pattern of concentration is reversed, a given area must show profitability levels that are above the average, or entrepreneurs are likely to decide against investing there. As a consequence, its future growth possibilities are likely to be limited. An analysis of data for existing industries indicates that the country's principal industrial nucleus is still competitive with regard to the other areas. This holds for the state of São Paulo, but is even more the case for its neighboring states, Minas Gerais and Paraná, with Rio de Janeiro forming the exception. Therefore, both in terms of observed levels and in terms of the trends that may be identified from the indicators presented, there is no basis for affirming that the degree of industrial concentration of Brazil is likely to diminish in the near future.

Analysis of results

The results presented in this study provide important elements for a discussion of the future of regional inequalities within Brazil. As discussed earlier, the role of the industrial sector is fundamental for its potential for mobility. The first aspect to be considered is the increase in the relative share of traditional industrial areas within the country, most notably in the states of São Paulo and Minas Gerais. In the former case, from 1985 onwards, there was a sharp reversal in the trend of relative decline that began in 1970, with the state's share for 1997 almost reaching the same level as in 1980, namely, the significant figure of no less than 53%. At the same time, Minas Gerais increased its share by 50%, from 6.5% in 1970 to 9.4% in 1997, with no decline at any point in the period.

An analysis of the components of growth developed in Azzoni and Ferreira (1998) shows that the higher rate of relative growth of the state of São Paulo is associated with positive differential effects that include competitive advantages for the area relative to the other areas, since the growth of the state was greater than would have been expected on the basis of its sectoral structure. To a lesser degree, the same may be said of Minas Gerais. At the same time, these differential effects have shown themselves to be negative for the other areas, accentuating the relative fall for the Northeast over the period 1985-90. In the following period, however, the effects became positive, but were still unable to offset the negative impact of the industrial structure of the region. In the case of Rio de Janeiro, the impact of differential effects is immense, causing the state to suffer successive losses of its relative share, and revealing competitive disadvantages that resulted in growth rates for the industrial sectors within the state that fell below the national average.

Regional competitiveness indicators confirm the results described above, and reveal that profitability in traditional industrial areas rose from 1985 onwards. The state of Minas Gerais enjoys a highly competitive position, with levels of profitability well above the national average; the state of São Paulo reverted a declining trend that had been in place since 1970, and maintained levels that were always close to or above the national average.

This is basically due to improvements in the relative productivity of these areas, with São Paulo producing indicators for recent years that were always above the national average, and Minas Gerais even higher values. Even considering that wage levels are higher in São Paulo, this differential is more than offset by a positive productivity differential, giving this region a competitive advantage. In the case of Minas Gerais, its favorable position with regard to productivity is combined with low wage level indicators, resulting in the highest level of regional competitiveness of all the regions considered.

Unfortunately, the lack of data prevented us from highlighting the case of the state of Paraná, which is included in this analysis together with the states of Santa Catarina and Rio Grande do Sul. A previous study revealed that at the end of the 1970s Paraná was the most competitive state in the country (Azzoni, 1986). In addition, this state has enjoyed substantial GDP growth in recent years, with its share rising from 6.1% in 1990 to 6.6% in 1995, its highest level of any year since 1970, with the industrial sector contributing half of this growth. Judging by these data, we might speculate that this state would have competitiveness indicators similar to those of Minas Gerais. This would strengthen the case for affirming that the principal industrial area of Brazil is increasing its competitiveness, with an expanding nucleus that is spilling over from São Paulo into the neighboring states (with the exception of Rio de Janeiro).

In the case of the Northeast, its wage levels, that are the lowest in the country, do not compensate for its low level of productivity, leading to profitability indicators that are some 20% below the national average, ahead of Rio de Janeiro alone. The latter state is in competition with the Northeast to achieve the worst productivity levels, and with the South for the second highest wage levels. That is to say, Rio de Janeiro combines low productivity with high wage levels, and thus produces the worst competitiveness indicators of any area considered in this study.

The results of this analysis thus raise concerns with regard to the future of regional inequalities within Brazil. The competitiveness indicators point to an improvement in the traditional industrial center, and a relative decline in the less industrialized areas of the country. This greater competitiveness has already led to an increase in industrial concentration, as was revealed in the previous section. Given that new investments are likely to be directed by this competitiveness, it appears that the trend in the future towards greater industrial concentration is a well-defined one. It is interesting to note the reversal from the mid-1980s onwards, when changes in the majority of the previously observed trends began to take effect.

The same scenario may also be observed by analyzing announcements of new investments (Araújo, 1997; Guimarães Neto, 1995). Of investments that can be assigned to a given region and whose potential investors may be identified, no less than 64.3% of the total (until the year 2000) were allocated to the Southeast, with 17.6% going to the Northeast, 9.4% to the South, 7.5% to the North and 1.2% to the Center West. According to the data, three states are notable recipients of investment: São Paulo, with 28.2% of the total, Rio de Janeiro, with 19.4%, and Minas Gerais, with 14%. Outside the Southeast region, notable cases are Pará, with 4.2% of the total, Bahia, with 9.4% and Rio Grande do Sul, with 4.6%. Rodrigues (1998), who also analyzed announcements of investments made in 1996 and 1997, arrived at the following percentages:[4] Southeast – 58.2%, South – 22.7%, Northeast – 12.3%, North – 4.2% and Center-West – 2.6%. As may be observed, there is nothing to suggest from these preferences among new investors that the current pattern of concentration is likely to change in the near future.

It is evident that information on investment intentions is subject to a series of limitations. Firstly, they are mere declarations of intent that are subject to the ups and downs of the economic cycle, political interests, etc. before they become concrete realities. In addition, they only include those investments that are announced, and thus exclude others that are made without publicity. This problem is particularly significant in areas where there are already high levels of production prior to the new investment, since in such cases additions to existing plants are more likely, leading us to expect that data based on announcements will be biased against such cases. Finally, it must be considered that even in the absence of the problems mentioned above, it is not possible to draw a direct comparison between such information and data on regional shares, since there are no data on the output from these new investments. Even with this necessary caution, new investment information is of relevance in indicating future trends in the regional distribution of production.

Concluding remarks

This study has attempted to analyze the competitiveness of the Brazilian manufacturing by region, and has aimed to evaluate trends in this competitiveness over the last 28 years, as well as to identify information that is relevant for predicting its future over the next few years. The results of the 1985 Industrial Census were updated using indicators for the evolution of production, wage levels and employment produced by the IBGE. The results obtained point to an increase in industrial concentration in the Southeast over the last ten years, with a considerable increase in the share of Minas Gerais, and with a loss of relative share by the other regions considered (the Northeast and South regions and the state of Rio de Janeiro).

The competitiveness indicators developed illustrate a revival in the competitiveness of the traditional industrial center, with São Paulo halting a declining trend observed during the 1970s and the first half of the 1980s, and Minas Gerais distinguishing itself with the best indicators of any region considered in the study. To judge by this competitiveness, both in terms of levels and trends, the traditional industrial center has regained potential for attracting new industrial investments, both in new plants, and in the expansion of production in existing plants. This state of affairs may be observed in announcements of new investments by the private sector over the next few years. The results of competitiveness indicators thus explain not only the reconcentration that occurred between 1985 and 1997, but also point to a continuation of this concentration trend in the future.

Notes

[1] See Barro and Sala-i-Martin (1995) for a theoretical discussion. The following Brazilian studies are worthy of mention: Affonso and Silva, 1995; Azzoni, 1985, 1993, 1994, 1996a, 1996b, 1997; Cano, 1985; Diniz, 1994; Ellery and Ferreira, 1994; Ferreira and Diniz, 1995; Lavinas, Henrique and Amaral, 1996; Lemos and Cunha, 1996; Souza, 1993; Schwartsman, 1996; Vergolino and Monteiro Neto 1996; Zini, 1998.

[2] For a more detailed analysis see Azzoni (1986), Chapter II. Teles Da Rosa (1996) develops an analysis similar to the one presented in this chapter, although it is restricted to the case of the Northeast of Brazil.

[3] It should be added that since this index is a relative indicator, the fact that a given state stands 6% above (below) the national average implies that it is even further ahead (behind) of other states with indicators below (above) the national average, since the average value for the indicator includes the value for the state itself.

[4] The percentages refer to investments with a defined location, excluding 'simultaneous' or 'undefined' investments.

References

Affonso, R. B. A. e Silva, P. L. B., organizadores (1995) *Desigualdades regionais e desenvolvimento*, São Paulo, FUNDAP - Editora da Unesp.

Araujo, T. B. (1997) "Dinâmica regional brasileira: rumo à desintegração competitiva?", Fundação João Pinheiro, Belo Horizonte, mimeo.

Azzoni, C. R. (1982) *Teoria da localização: uma análise crítica*, IPE/USP, Série Ensaios Econômicos.

Azzoni, C. R. (1986) *Indústria e reversão da polarização no Brasil*, IPE/USP, Série Ensaios Econômicos.

Azzoni, C. R. (1993) "Equilíbrio, progresso técnico e desigualdades regionais no processo de desenvolvimento econômico" *Análise Econômica*, UFRGS, 11, No. 19, 5-28.

Azzoni, C. R. (1994) "Crescimento econômico e convergência das rendas regionais: o caso brasileiro à luz da Nova Teoria do Crescimento" *Anais do XXII Encontro Nacional de Economia*, ANPEC, Florianópolis.

Azzoni, C. R. (1996a) "Economic growth and regional income inequalities in Brazil: 1939-92" FEA/USP, Programa de Seminários Acadêmicos, *Texto para Discussão Interna* No. 06/96.

Azzoni, C. R. (1996b) "Distribuição pessoal de renda interna aos estados e desigualdade de renda entre estados no Brasil: 1960, 70, 80 e 91" FEA/USP, Programa de Seminários Acadêmicos, Texto para Discussão Interna No. 14/9.

Azzoni, C. R. (1997) "Concentração regional e dispersão das rendas per capita estaduais: análise a partir de séries históricas estaduais de PIB, 1939-1995," mimeo.

Azzoni, C. R. and Ferreira, D. A. (1998) "Competitividad regional y reconcentración industrial: el futuro de las desigualdades regionales en Brasil," *Revista Eure*, Santiago, Chile, No. 73, 81-111.

Barro, R. and X. Sala-i-Martin. (1995) *Economic Growth*, McGraw-Hill.

Barros, A. R. (1998) "Os impactos do Mercosul no Nordeste do Brasil", Revista ANPEC No. 4.

Cano (1985) *Desequilíbrios regionais e concentração industrial no Brasil: 1930-1970*, São Paulo, Ed. Global.

Diniz, C. C. (1994) "Polygonized development in Brazil: neither decentralization nor continued polarization" *International Journal of Urban and Regional Research*, 18, 293-314.

Ellery, Jr. R. R. E Ferreira, P. C. G. (1994) "Crescimento econômico e convergência entre as rendas dos estados brasileiros" *Anais do XVI Encontro Brasileiro de Econometria*, 264-286.

Ferreira, A. H. B. e Diniz, C. C. (1995) "Convergência entre las rentas per capita estaduales en Brasil" EURE - *Revista Latinoamericana de Estudios Urbano Regionales*, 21.

Guimarães Neto, L. (1995) "Desigualdades regionais e federalismo." In R. Affonso, and P.L.B. Silva. (eds.) *Desigualdades regionais e desenvolvimento*, Fundap/Editora Unesp.

Haddad, P. R., Ferreira, C. M. C., Boisier, S. e Andrade, T. A. (1989) *Economia Regional: Teorias e Métodos de Análise*, BNB, Fortaleza.

Lavinas, L., Henrique, E. E Amaral, M. R. (1996) "Desigualdades regionais: indicadores socio-econômicos nos anos 90" *Revista Econômica do Nordeste*, 27, 857-921.

Lemos, M. B. and A.R.A.A. Cunha. (1996) "Novas aglomerações industriais e desenvolvimento regional recente no Brasil" *Revista Econômica do Nordeste*, 27, 752-762.

Rodrigues, D.A. (1998) "Os Novos investimentos no Brasil: aspectos sectoriais e regionais" *Revista do BNDES*, 5 Junho.

Schwartsman, A. (1996) "Convergence accross Brazilian states" FEA/USP, Programa de Seminários Acadêmicos, *Texto para Discussão Interna* No. 02/96.

Teles Da Rosa, A. L. (1996) "Produtividade, competitividade e estrutura da indústria nordestina a partir de 1980" *Revista Econômica do Nordeste*, 27, 277-298.

Vergolino, J. R. O. and A. Monteiro Neto. (1996) "A hipótese da convergência da renda: um teste para o Nordeste do Brasil com dados microrregionais," *Revista Econômica do Nordeste*, 27, 701-724.

Zini, A. A. (1998) "Regional income convergence in Brazil and its socio-economic determinants" *Economia Aplicada*, 2, 383-41.

7 Regional Competition and Complementarity reflected in Relative Regional Dynamics and Growth of GSP: a Comparative Analysis of the Northeast of Brazil and the Midwest States of the U.S.

ANDRÉ MAGALHÃES, MICHAEL SONIS and GEOFFREY J.D. HEWINGS

Introduction

Economic changes can have their origin in a specific state of a region. Examples of such events are droughts, installation of new factories or economic booms of locally concentrated industries. The initial effects of these changes will most likely be concentrated in the income and employment of the state in which they originated; it is also likely, however, that such effects will, at some point, spillover to other states.

These spillover effects are the result of what is called "spatial dependence", or spatial correlation, and they can arise for various reasons. It could be the case, for instance, that trade among states could generate interdependence that would be reflected in changes of income and employment. If such spatial dependence exists, how can it be characterized? In other words, how do regions and states relate to each other? Does this spatial dependence take the form of some sort of competition among states or is it the case that their growth can be characterized as being complementary? Answering these questions can be of fundamental importance in determining the application and impact of regional policies or even significant economic events occurring in one state. Knowing the magnitude that the spatial spillover effects of any

125

policy will have over all the states of a region can help policymakers to better predict the results of their actions, to enhance the allocation of available resources, and to assess the consequences of growth originating outside their state. This paper intends to approach these questions using the model proposed by Dendrinos and Sonis (D-S) (1987). Their model is designed to capture the time-interaction of a single statistical population over multiple locations. In the present paper, the statistical population will be gross state product. Hewings *et al.* (1996) used the same model to study the role of regional interaction in the growth of U.S. regions. In their paper, they tried to classify the U.S. regions as complements or competitive with each other. Here, the model will be applied to very distinct regions: the Brazilian's Northeast, and the Midwest of the U.S.

The chapter is divided into five sections. Following this introduction, the second section will provide a brief economic historical background on the two regions, focusing on a general economic performance of the two regions and the participation of the states in the regional product. The third section presents the Dendrinos-Sonis model. The fourth section will provide the estimations of the model for the two regions together with their respective summary statistics, so that their results can be compared. This section also includes an analysis of the relation between the states' share and the interregional trade flows for the Midwest. The final section will summarize the main conclusions of the analysis.

Historic Background

The Brazilian Northeast

The Brazilian Northeast is composted of nine states, displayed in figure 7.1. They are very different with respect to economic characteristics. The Northeastern economy achieved, in 1996, a GDP of approximately US$117 billion (at 1996 prices). This represented approximately 15.6% of the Brazilian GDP. In 1994 the Northeast population was approximately 45 million, corresponding to 29% of the Brazilian population; however, GDP per capita (US$ 2.567) amounted to only 55.1% of the national average (US$ 4.742). Thus, the Northeast GDP is equivalent to the GDP of countries like Venezuela or Greece, while its population is larger than Argentina's population (see Ministério do Planejamento e Orçamento, 1995).

Figure 7.1   Map of Brazil – Northeast States in Gray

In the last 35 years, the Northeast has experimented with a variety of policy initiatives to attempt to transform its economy. During this period, the growth rate of the region was around 4.7%, only 0.3% smaller than the Brazilian rate for the same period. An intense industrialization process was coordinated by the Superintendência do Desenvolvimento do Nordeste[1] (SUDENE), created especially to guide the development of this region. As a result of these efforts, 30% of the Northeastern GDP in 1990 was generated by industry, in contrast to 22% in 1960.[2]

Table 7.1 presents the share of each gross state product of the Northeast gross regional product for some selected years between 1970 and 1995. As can be observed from the table, Bahia is the state with the largest share, and even though this has been decreasing over the years, the state still accounts for more the 30% of the gross regional product in 1995. The second largest state is Pernambuco, followed very closely by Ceará. These latter two states have managed to keep their shares between 10 and 20%, with the distinction that while Ceará's share has increased over the years (from 10% in 1970 to 15.9% in 1995), while Pernambuco's share has exhibited the opposite behavior (declining from 18.0% in 1970 to 17.2% in 1995). All the other states present shares below 10%.

Table 7.1   Share of Each State in Gross Regional Product (%) *

	1970	1975	1980	1985	1990	1995
MA	6.0	4.9	6.2	6.7	8.7	8.8
PI	3.8	3.4	3.8	4.0	4.7	4.4
CE	11.8	11.9	14.0	16.1	14.0	16.0
RN	4.1	4.1	4.7	5.1	6.0	6.5
PB	8.1	7.9	6.4	7.0	6.9	6.9
PE	21.4	20.2	20.6	17.3	18.3	17.3
AL	5.1	5.3	5.2	6.3	5.4	5.4
SE	3.7	3.7	4.1	4.1	4.0	3.6
BA	35.9	38.5	35.1	33.4	32.1	31.2
Total	100.0	100.0	100.0	100.0	100.0	100.0

* The abbreviations for the states used in the first column are as follow: Maranhão (MA), Piauí (PI), Ceará (CE), Rio Grande do Norte (RN), Paraíba (PB), Pernambuco (PE), Alagoas (AL), Sergipe (SE), Bahia (BA)

Source: SUDENE – Contas Nacionais (1997)

Midwest

The Midwest region, as defined by the Bureau of Economic Analysis, comprises five states: Illinois (IL), Indiana (IN), Michigan (MI), Ohio (OH), and Wisconsin (WI), presented in figure 7.2.   As a whole, the Midwest economy achieved, in 1996, a GDP around US$ 1,145 billion (at 1992 prices). This represented approximately 16.2% of the US GDP (see table 2.2). The regional population was approximately 44 million (1996), corresponding to 16% of the American population; GDP per capita (US$ 24,521) was slightly above the national average (US$ 24,436). Thus, while the two regions, Midwest and Brazilian Northeast, are very close in terms of population size, the per capita income in the former is approximately 10 times larger than the per capita income of the latter.

Figure 7.2   Midwest States

Table 7.2   Share Each State in the Midwest Region GSP

	1963	1972	1975	1980	1985	1990	1996
Illinois	29.5	30.1	31.0	30.4	29.9	30.4	30.2
Indiana	12.2	12.2	12.3	11.9	11.7	12.1	12.5
Michigan	23.6	22.8	21.4	21.6	22.1	21.2	21.1
Ohio	25.2	25.2	25.1	25.2	25.5	25.3	24.7
Wisconsin	9.5	9.7	10.2	10.6	10.8	11.0	11.4
Total	100.0	100.0	100.0	100.0	100.0	100.0	100.0

Source: Calculated based on data from United States Department of Commerce/Bureau of Economic Analysis

Table 7.2 provides the GSP shares of the individual states in the gross regional product (GRP) for selected years. It can be observed that there has been little change in the share participation. Throughout the period, Illinois has maintained its share at around 30% of the GRP. The other two important states in term of shares are Michigan and Ohio, both with shares above 20% for any year in the series. However, both seem to be experiencing a downward trend, especially in the last 10 years. The last two states, Indiana and Wisconsin, participate with approximately 10% of the regions' GRP. While Indiana's share has not varied significantly, Wisconsin's share has increased steadily over time (from 9.53% in 1963 to 11.45% in 1996).

Expectations: interdependencies among States and levels of development

The Heckscher-Ohlin-Samuelson (HOS) theorem, which dominated international trade theory for more the 25 years, states that countries will export goods that are intensive in the relatively abundant factor or factors. The theorem is still able to explain part of the trade, especially that between developing and developed countries. However, a different form of trade, intraindustry trade, became apparent when economists started to investigate the process of economic integration in Europe by the middle of this century (see for instance, Verdoorn 1960, and Balassa 1966). The HOS theorem was unable to explain this significant fraction of the trade;[3] hence, a new theory was developed in the late 1970s and early 1980s (Krugman 1979, and Helpman and Krugman 1985). The main driving force of this new theory was the existence of economies of scale. Large markets allowed firms to concentrate in specific products, generating returns to scale, and consequently reduced cost per unit. Another explanation for the existence of the intra-industry trade was based on the regional characteristics, such as income levels;[4] the theory was able to explain the high levels of trade of similar products, intra-industry trade, among the industrialized countries.

It is important to try to understand how these two theories are linked to the problem at hand. Countries at early stages of economic development tend to behave according to the HOS theorem, i.e., by exporting the goods in which they have comparative advantage. Hence, it should be expected that the trade between two developing countries would be largely concentrated in some specific goods. At the other end of the spectrum, developed countries would tend to export and import from each other a greater volume of a wider variety of industrialized goods. That is to say, the volume of trade between two countries at early stages of development tends to be rather small, while the volume of trade between two developed economies tends to be large.

At the regional level, Thompson (1965) approached the development of urban areas from an evolutionary point of view. He examined the relationship between the level of development and degree of interaction between sectors within an economy, and argues that the greater the level of development the more intense would be the interactions. At the other end of the development spectrum, Okazaki (1989) observed a decline in the degree of integration within the Japanese economy. He termed this phenomenon as a hollowing out effect, and attributed it mainly to the competition from Korea, China and Indonesia.

Hewings *et al.* (1998) put together the ideas of Thompson and Okazaki in trying to answer the question of what happens to the degree of internal interaction within an economy as it continues to grow. They argue that Thompson's idea implies a logistic evolutionary path, i.e. internal interdependence increasing with degree of development. However, as the economy reaches an advanced level of development a hollowing out effect dominates with decreasing internal interdependence and increasing interactions with other economies. Thus, one could expect that the trade volume among states of a poor region, or in the early stages of development, would be small. When the level of development increases so will the volume of trade within the region, thus increasing the interdependence inside the region. At advanced stages of development, one would expect the state economies to experience hollowing out effects with a concomitant increase in the economic interactions with other states. At the same time, the new trade theory would indicate a large volume trade among the matured economies, with a large flow of similar industrialized goods.

Figure 7.3 displays the trade relationship among states at the same level of development. The y-axis at the left measures the volume of trade, while the y-axis at the right hand side measures the percentage of interindustry trade in the total volume. Thus higher levels of development imply larger volumes of trade with a lower percentage of interindustry trade. The solid line in the figure 7.3 represents the logistic curve implied by Thompson's idea, while the doted line would correspond to the ideas of the new trade theory. The Northeast of Brazil would be closer to the origin along the x-coordinate than the Midwest, given the gap in the level of development based on the level of GSP and GSP per capita of the two regions. Therefore, the volume of trade within the Northeast of Brazil would be considerably smaller than within the Midwest, and highly concentrated in interindustry trade. If one believes in the relationship between level of trade and interdependence, this implies that the level of interaction among the Midwest states would be larger that the level of interaction among the Northeast ones.

Moreover, a variety of factors in the Brazilian Northeast economy, such as the deficient internal transportation system within the region, give rise to a relatively small internal flow of trade and services. Also, the strong dependence of the Northeast on the Southeast economy accentuates this problem, making those flows especially small when compared to the flow of trade and services of the Northeast with other regions of Brazil and with the other countries. The Midwest region of the United States, on the other hand, presents a very significant level of internal trade, with volumes approaching those for the whole of NAFTA (see Hewings, *et al.*, 1997).

The Dendrinos-Sonis (D-S) model, presented in the next section, is capable of capturing the regional dynamics of interaction using only the shares of each state in the gross regional product. Furthermore, the coefficients of the D-S model will explicitly indicate the existence of competitive (negative sign) or complementary (positive sign) relationships between the states for their participation in the gross regional product.

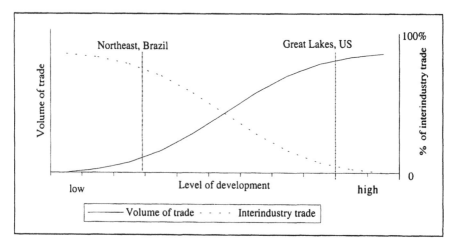

Figure 8.3   Level and Type of Trade among States at Similar Levels of Development

The next section will contain a detailed explanation of the structure and tools of the model as well as the estimation procedure that will be adopted.

The Dendrinos-Sonis model

To capture the possible spatial interaction effects, one usually makes use of a weight matrix. The assumption behind the use of a weight matrix is that greater correlation should be expected between regions that are spatially closer together. The drawback in the application of this matrix is that the weights in the matrix have to be arbitrarily defined or specified according to some *a priori* expectation about the nature of spatial interaction. In order to minimize any possible bias associated with a particular specification of a weight matrix, different matrix specifications are often used.

As an alternative, instead of imposing a given matrix form, it might be preferable to estimate a model where spatial interaction would not depend on any prior specification of the spatial relations. Such an approach was adopted by White and Hewings (1982) where they tried to capture the effects of spatial iteration using Seemingly Unrelated Regression (SUR) methods. Another attempt to avoid the weight matrix was made by Hewings *et al.* (1996). They claimed that the Dendrinos-Sonis model captures the spatial effects without making use of any *a priori* weight matrix. In addition, this model is capable of generating results for the structure of the spatial correlation among the states within a given region; it is also possible to look at the effects of any individual state on the others. From the policy makers' point of view, these results can be very helpful, in the sense that the analysis of regional policies can now take into account the spatial effects that an investment in any given state will have on the rest of the region.

Growth in regional output is traditionally viewed in regional growth theory as either (i) a zero-sum game or (ii) generative (see Richardson, 1973). In the first approach, growth in one region can only happen at the expense of another region, so that regional interaction plays an important role in the process. In the second case, some endogenous process within a region can also generate regional growth. In the Dendrinos-Sonis model, the first approach is taken, so that the model presented in the next sub-section represents a zero-sum game. The important point here is that *relative* growth is modeled, not absolute growth, so that by definition, it is zero-sum. However, a state can have a decrease in its share of gross regional product yet still experience some growth in its absolute GSP.

The discrete relative nonlinear dynamic model

The iterative mapping of relative discrete dynamics used here was introduced in Sonis and Dendrinos (1987), where they dealt with the problem of two locations and one stock.[5] Dendrinos and Sonis (1987) extended the initial results by using numerical computations and Dendrinos and Sonis (1988) provided the first empirical application for the model with multiple locations and one stock. They estimated the model for the population of the U.S. regions using data from 1850 to 1983, and they also undertook a forecast exercise for the shares of population by region for a 70 year-period. The results were statistically significant, and robust in response to random fluctuations in the systems.

Hewings *et al.* (1996) were the first to adopt this model for economic variables. Following their notation, let Γ_{ST} be an economy defined over space and time and define S to be a finite number of regions in the economy and T to be the time horizon. Define $Y_t' = (Y_{1t}, Y_{2t}, ..., Y_{st})$ as an S-dimensional vector represents state economy activity within a region: $[0 < Y_{st} < 1;\ s = 1,...S;\ t = 1,...,T]$. In their application, Gross State Products (GSP), at constant prices of 1980, were used. In order to observe the pattern of interaction among states, the analysis focused on the relative values of GSP.[6]

Now consider a set of arbitrary positive real-valued functions, $F_{jt} = (F_{1t}, F_{2t}, ..., F_{St})$, such that each F_{jt} is defined at each time period t by a subset of Y_{st}. The general discrete nonlinear process can then be defined as:

$$Y_{st+1} = \frac{F_{st}}{\sum\limits_{j} F_{jt}} \qquad j = 1, 2, 3, ..., S \tag{7.1}$$

If the first state is taken to be the numéraire (reference) state, i.e., if the following relation is used:

$$F_{ojt} = \frac{F_{jt}}{F_1} \qquad j = 1, 2, 3, ..., S \tag{7.2}$$

Then, the process defined in (7.1) can also be represented by:

$$Y_{1t+1} = \frac{1}{1 + \sum\limits_{j} F_{ojt}} \qquad j = 1, 2, 3, ..., S \tag{7.3}$$

$$Y_{st+1} = \frac{F_{ost}}{1 + \sum\limits_{j} F_{ojt}} \qquad j = 1, 2, 3, ..., S \tag{7.4}$$

where $\sum\limits_{s} Y_{st} = 1 \qquad s = 1, 2, ..., S$

and $\dfrac{Y_{st+1}}{Y_{1t+1}} = F_{ost} \qquad s = 1, 2, ..., S$ \hfill (7.5)

This makes it possible to generate the results in relative terms, i.e., the function F_{ojt} represents the temporal "comparative advantages" enjoyed by location s in reference to a *numéraire* location (Dendrinos and Sonis, 1990).

A log-linear specification of the function F_{ost} suggested by Dendrinos and Sonis (1988) is adopted, and given by:

$$F_{ost} = A_S \prod_k Y_{kt}^{a_{sk}} \qquad F_{st} > 0; s = 2,...,S; k = 1,...,S \qquad (7.6)$$

where $A_s > 0$ represents the locational advantages of all states $s \in S$, and

$$a_{sk} = \frac{\partial \ln F_{ost}}{\partial \ln Y_{kt}} \qquad s = 2,3,...,S; k = 1,2,...S \qquad (7.7)$$

are the state growth elasticities, with $-\infty < a_{sk} < \infty$. Using the log-linear form we can rewrite the process as:

$$\ln Y_{st+1} - \ln Y_{1t+1} = \ln A_s + \sum_{k=1}^{s} a_{sk} \ln Y_{kt} \qquad s = 2,...,S; t = 1,...,T \qquad (7.8)$$

Regional interaction at this level of aggregation is assumed to involve a competition whereby each region attempts to increase its share of gross regional product, which is attained by improving their comparative advantages. However, this improvement will depend upon the behavior of the rest of states, behavior that is reflected in the sign and magnitude of the elasticities (a_{sk}). A negative sign for a_{sk} means the existence of competitive relation between the states s and k, i.e., if the GSP share of state s increases the share of state k will decrease and vice-versa. On the other hand, a positive coefficient means a complementary relationship between s and k.

Maximum likelihood estimation

In previous work (Hewings *et al.* 1996), the models have been estimated by maximum likelihood method; this approach will be followed here. The model can be expressed in matrix form as follows:

$$y_j = X\beta_j + \varepsilon_j \qquad j = 2,3,...,S \qquad (7.9)$$

where:

$$
y_j = \begin{bmatrix} \ln Y_{j2} - \ln Y_{12} \\ \vdots \\ \ln Y_{jt} - \ln Y_{1t} \\ \vdots \\ \ln Y_{jT} - \ln Y_{1T} \end{bmatrix} ; \quad X = \begin{bmatrix} 1 & \ln Y_{11} & \ln Y_{21} & \cdots & \ln Y_{s1} \\ \vdots & \vdots & \vdots & \vdots & \vdots \\ 1 & \ln Y_{1t} & \ln Y_{2t} & \cdots & \ln Y_{st} \\ \vdots & \vdots & \vdots & \vdots & \vdots \\ 1 & \ln Y_{1T-1} & \ln Y_{2T-1} & \cdots & \ln Y_{ST-1} \end{bmatrix} ; \quad \beta_j = \begin{bmatrix} \ln A_j \\ a_{j1} \\ \vdots \\ ajs \end{bmatrix}_{(S+1)\times 1}
$$

Assuming that the Y's have a log-normal distribution, $\ln Y$ is normally distributed and the log-likelihood function is then given by:

$$
l(\theta) = -\frac{T-1}{2}\ln(2\pi) - \frac{T-1}{2}\ln(\sigma_j^2) - \frac{(y_j - X\beta_j)'(y_j - X\beta_j)}{2\sigma_j^2} \tag{7.10}
$$

where, $l(.)$ denotes $\ln L$ and $\theta = (\beta, \sigma^2)'$.

Maximizing $l(.)$ with respect to β yields

$$
\hat{\beta}_j = (X'X)^{-1} X' y_j \tag{7.11}
$$

which is an unbiased and efficient estimator for β_j

Maximizing $l(.)$ with respect to σ^2 yields:

$$
\sigma_j^2 = \frac{(y_j - X\hat{\beta}_j)'(y_j - X\hat{\beta}_j)}{T-1} \tag{7.12}
$$

where

$E[\sigma_j^2] = \sigma_j^2 \dfrac{(T-1)-(S+1)}{T-1}$ i.e., the MLE is a biased estimator for the variance. The unbiased estimator for the variance can be found by multiplying the ML estimator by $(T-1)/[(T-1)-(S+1)]$.

Results for the Dendrinos-Sonis model

This section presents the estimation of the D-S model for the states of the two regions. First, some considerations are made about the expected signs of the coefficients; thereafter, the estimations are presented, and the relationships are analyzed based on the signs of the coefficients.

Results for the Northeast of Brazil

With respect to the significance and signs of the coefficients, one should expect to find a significant relationship among the largest states; in particular, one would expect to find a negative relationship between Ceará and Pernambuco, and Ceará and Bahia. The reason for this can be attributed to the fact that while Ceará has been enjoying continuous increases in its share, the other two states have seen their shares decrease throughout the years (see table 7.1 for a summary of the data). Again for the same reason, a similar relationship can be expected to appear between Maranhão and Pernambuco, and Maranhão and Bahia. A positive and significant coefficient for the own lag of the dependent variable should also be anticipated. In order to make a choice of the numéraire, the regions were ranked by their shares of gross regional product (GRP); for the application to the Northeast of Brazil, the state with lowest share was picked, in this case, the state of Piauí.

Table 7.3   **Results of the D-S model for the Northeast states** [*]

	BA(-1)	SE(-1)	AL(-1)	PE(-1)	PB(-1)	RN(-1)	CE(-1)	PI(-1)	MA(-1)
BA	-1.035	-0.131	0.449	0.334	0.142	-0.544	0.140	-0.465	-0.057
	(0.654)	(0.468)	(0.316)	(0.455)	(0.277)	(0.334)	(0.312)	(0.394)	(0.277)
	(-1.583)	(-0.281)	(1.420)	(0.734)	(0.512)	(-1.629)	(0.449)	(-1.179)	(-0.207)
SE	-0.409	0.306	0.304	0.183	**-0.280**[c]	-0.395	**0.452**[b]	-0.037	-0.285
	(0.286)	(0.301)	(0.199)	(0.202)	(0.158)	(0.302)	(0.221)	(0.202)	(0.201)
	(-1.429)	(1.013)	(1.532)	(0.906)	(-1.774)	(-1.308)	(2.048)	(-0.183)	(-1.422)
AL	-0.676	-0.354	**0.735**[b]	0.809	**-0.549**[b]	-0.505	**0.769**[b]	-0.121	-0.162
	(0.615)	(0.429)	(0.306)	(1.707)	(0.228)	(0.373)	(0.319)	(1.707)	(0.271)
	(-1.101)	(-0.826)	(2.402)	(0.474)	(-2.407)	(-1.354)	(2.408)	(-0.071)	(-0.599)
PE	-0.314	-0.291	0.169	0.425	0.045	**-0.462**[b]	0.245	-0.085	-0.213
	(0.594)	(0.485)	(0.183)	(0.315)	(0.207)	(0.187)	(0.326)	(0.301)	(0.134)
	(-0.528)	(-0.600)	(0.923)	(1.347)	(0.217)	(-2.463)	(0.750)	(-0.283)	(-1.592)
PB	0.458	**-1.074**[b]	0.247	**0.648**[a]	**0.547**[b]	-0.615	0.443	-0.232	0.150
	(0.510)	(0.477)	(0.307)	(0.187)	(0.196)	(0.430)	(0.337)	(0.187)	(0.307)
	(0.897)	(-2.252)	(0.804)	(3.465)	(2.793)	(-1.433)	(1.312)	(-1.239)	(0.487)
RN	0.067	**-0.814**[b]	**0.540**[b]	-0.209	-0.011	-0.015	0.231	-0.079	0.233
	(0.275)	(0.404)	(0.257)	(0.138)	(0.145)	(0.277)	(0.247)	(0.138)	(0.203)
	(0.243)	(-2.012)	(2.100)	(-1.512)	(-0.078)	(-0.053)	(0.937)	(-0.573)	(1.146)
CE	0.637	**-0.965**[b]	0.490	0.340	-0.161	-0.262	**0.593**[c]	-0.440	-0.042
	(0.616)	(0.361)	(0.297)	(0.606)	(0.253)	(0.369)	(0.314)	(0.606)	(0.252)
	(1.034)	(-2.673)	(1.648)	(0.562)	(-0.635)	(-0.709)	(1.888)	(-0.726)	(-0.167)
MA	-0.343	-0.017	0.169	-0.534	**-0.464**[b]	0.380	-0.020	0.076	0.099
	(0.612)	(0.277)	(0.251)	(0.416)	(0.209)	(0.272)	(0.273)	(0.416)	(0.188)
	(-0.561)	(-0.061)	(0.675)	(-1.2820)	(-2.221)	(1.394)	(-0.071)	(0.183)	(0.525)

*Numéraire: Piauí. The equations are represented across the rows. Standard deviation and t-statistics in parentheses (adjusted by $(T-1)/[(T-1)-(S+1)]$).
[a] significant at 1% level; [b] significant at 5% level; [c] significant at 10% level.

The maximum likelihood estimates of the D-S model are shown in table 7.3. The coefficients for the lag of the dependent variable have the expected sign, with the exception of Bahia.[7] Few coefficients turned out to be significant, and most of those were significant at the 5% level; however, some degree of interaction is confirmed. For instance, Paraíba responds negatively to changes in Sergipe. In terms of the model, this means that those two states present a competitive relationship. Also, the coefficient for Ceará in the equation of Sergipe is positive and significant, which indicates that Ceará complements Sergipe, i.e., a positive shock on Ceará's share would increase the share of Sergipe relative to the share of Piauí.

Table 7.4   Qualitative Analysis of the Competitive and Complementary Relationships

(a) Qualitative Relationships

	BA	SE	AL	PE	PB	RN	CE	PI	MA	+	-
BA	-	-	+	+	+	-	+	-	-	4	5
SE	-	+	+	+	-	-	+	-	-	4	5
AL	-	-	+	+	-	-	+	-	-	3	6
PE	-	-	+	+	+	-	+	-	-	4	5
PB	+	-	+	+	+	-	+	-	+	6	3
RN	+	-	+	-	-	-	+	-	+	4	5
CE	+	-	+	+	-	-	+	-	-	4	5
MA	-	-	+	-	-	+	-	+	+	4	5

(b) Qualitative ordering

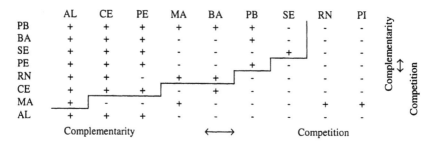

Some qualitative results of the model are presented table 7.4(a) where the number of positive and negative signs for each state's elasticity are shown. Table 7.4(b) orders the states by their level of complementarity and competitiveness in an attempt to develop a qualitative spatial dependence hierarchy. Looking across the rows of table 7.4, what is revealed is the existence of a balanced number of complementary and competitive relationships in the region. Paraíba is the state with the highest degree of complementarity among the Northeast states (six out nine coefficient were positive), while Alagoas is the one with the smallest level (six out nine coefficient were negative). The interpretation is as follows: for Paraíba, a positive shock in the GSP of any state, at time t would have a positive impact on the GSP of Paraíba and would increase its GSP's share in time $t+1$. For Alagoas, the story would be exactly the opposite. However, it is important to notice that very few coefficients are significant; those that are, affect mainly the small states. For instance, shocks in Pernambuco are only significant to Paraíba, which represents less than 7% of the gross regional product (see table 1).

By observing the columns of the same table, one can see that a positive shock in the GSP of Alagoas would cause increases in the shares of all the states. On the other hand, a positive shock in Piauí or Rio Grande do Norte's GSP would decrease all shares but that for Maranhão, and shocks in Sergipe would be strongly self concentrated, tending to reduce the shares of all the other states.

The results of the model indicate a week degree of interaction in the region. The dynamics are mainly present among the small states (Paraíba, Rio Grande do Norte, and Sergipe), which are struggling to increase their shares in the regional product. Among the three largest states (Bahia, Pernambuco, and Ceará), Ceará is the one that displays the greatest number of significant coefficients in the equations of the other states (looking down the columns). This could be explained by the recent dynamic behavior of Ceará's GSP in the last few years, suggesting that its strong growing economy is positively associated with growth in the other states in the region. Similarly, one would expect that Bahia would have some impact on the other states. However, this does not seem to be the case according to the results of the model. One reason for this could be the fact that, although it is one of the largest economies in the region, it is strongly oriented towards other parts of the country, especially the Southeast (São Paulo, Rio de Janeiro, and Minas Gerais).

Figure 7.3 provides the forecast for the shares of the states of the Northeast of Brazil, from 1998 to 2030. The shares are forecast using equations (7.4) and (7.5), substituting the estimated value of equation (7.6) for F in (7.4) and (7.5). The figure indicates a strong fluctuation in the economy for the first six years of forecast (1998-2003). Large movements between Pernambuco and Ceará are revealed, even indicating the possibility that the latter would become larger than the former. This could be attributed to the recent strong dynamic of Ceará's economy, and the slow grow rate presented by Pernambuco in the last few years. The trend is, however, reversed and Ceará falls below Pernambuco's share in 2001. Other fluctuations also occur at the small states level, with the model predicting the Paraíba economy growing faster than Alagoas. All the dynamic exchanges stop, however, after 2007. The economy tends to a steady state, with the shares being constant from there on.

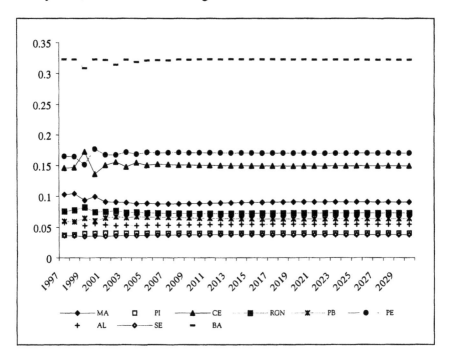

Figure 7.4   Steady State Attractors of Shares of the Northeast's States

Results for the Midwest

This section presents the results of the Dendrinos-Sonis model for the Midwest states. The numéraire state is Wisconsin, which was chosen because, as the case of Piauí for the Northeast, since it has the smallest share in the region, although this share is still larger than 10%. It should be expected that the coefficient for the own lag of the dependent variable would be positive. Also, it is expected that the largest states would have a significant effect upon the others.

The results of the maximum likelihood estimation are displayed in table 7.5. A quick look at the table reveals that the coefficients of the dependent's variable lag have the expected positive sign (looking across each row). Ohio is the only state for which the lag is not significant. The table also shows that the shares are affected by both contiguous and non-contiguous states. For instance, the share of Illinois responds to changes in all the other states (the coefficients are all significant at the one percent level) while Indiana responds to Michigan, and Michigan to Indiana. Finally Ohio's share is significantly affected by all states in the region.

Table 7.5   Results of the D-S model for the Midwest *

Dependent Variable	IL(-1)	IN(-1)	MI(-1)	OH(-1)	WI(-1)
IL	**0.590**[b]	**-0.308**[a]	**0.245**[a]	-0.215[c]	**-0.520**[a]
	(0.222)	(0.035)	(0.032)	(0.109)	(0.070)
	(2.663)	(-8.849)	(7.764)	(-1.966)	(-7.374)
IN	-0.305	**0.405**[b]	**0.214**[c]	-0.238	-0.267
	(0.356)	(0.162)	(0.115)	(0.249)	(0.195)
	(-0.856)	(2.505)	(1.859)	(-0.954)	(-1.372)
MI	0.005	**-0.917**[a]	**1.265**[a]	-0.573	0.049
	(0.551)	(0.285)	(0.212)	(0.414)	(0.336)
	(0.010)	(-3.216)	(5.977)	(-1.384)	(0.145)
OH	**0.227**[a]	-0.674	**0.484**[a]	0.098	**-0.251**[a]
	(0.055)	(0.068)	(0.040)	(0.071)	(0.032)
	(4.171)	(-9.889)	(11.955)	(1.377)	(-7.957)

* Numéraire: Wisconsin; standard deviation and t-statistics in parentheses. [a] significant at 1% level;
[b] significant at 5% level; [c] significant at 10% level

Table 7.6 provides an overview of the qualitative relationships among the states. Looking across each row, the signs in the table indicate that Michigan is the most complementary state, in the sense that it tends to benefit from changes in all the states (with exception of Indiana). This implies that when Illinois' share increases, Michigan's share tends to increase with respect to the numéraire state (Wisconsin). At the same time, Michigan also is the most complementary state in the sense that it generates a positive impact on the shares of the other states (looking by column). Thus, a shock in Michigan's gross product tends to increase the shares of the other states with respect to Wisconsin. A similar analysis can be extended to the competitive states, in this case, Illinois and Indiana.

Table 7.6   **Qualitative   Analysis   of   the   Competitive   and Complementary Relationships**

(a) Qualitative Relationships

	IL	IN	MI	OH	WI	+	-
IL	+	-	+	-	-	2	3
IN	-	+	+	-	-	2	3
MI	+	-	+	+	+	4	1
OH	+	-	+	+	-	3	2

(b) Qualitative Ordering

	MI	IL	OH	IN	WI
MI	+	+	+	-	+
OH	+	+	+	-	-
IL	+	+	-	-	-
IN	+	-	-	+	-

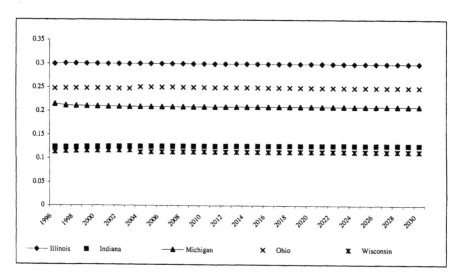

Figure 7.5   **Steady State Attractor for the Shares of the States of the Midwest**

The estimation results indicate a strong presence of spatial interaction among the Midwest states. Michigan and Indiana are the states that have great effect on the others. Both states present significant coefficients at the 1% level in all the equations. Michigan has the most complementary (positive) relationship, while Indiana has the least complementary (most competitive). The interactions occur between neighbors (Ohio and Michigan) and non-neighbors (between Illinois and Michigan, and the negative one between Ohio and Illinois) states. However, as the magnitudes of the elasticities demonstrate, the spatial interaction is stronger among the neighbor states.[8]

Figure 7.5 presents the forecast for the share of the Midwest states between 1997 and 2030. As in the case of the Northeast, the model predicts fluctuations in the initial few years (from 1997 to 2007). The changes are relatively small compared to the Northeast case; Wisconsin and Ohio tend to increase their participation in the region, while the opposite seems to be happening to Michigan and Indiana. After 2007 the economy achieves a steady state, where no future fluctuations take place.

Participation in intra-regional trade and GSP share

This sub-section presents a comparison involving the trade flow and the share of gross state product used in the model estimations.[9] Table 7.7 presents the share of each state in the intra-regional trade and the share of the each state in the gross regional product for 1992. The trade share was calculate as the percentage of each state in the total trade flow (exports + imports) among the Midwest states. The shares in the GRP were calculated as defined in section 7.2. It can be observed from the table that the distribution of the trade shares is similar to the GSP shares. In particular, the "rank" is the same both cases. For instance, Illinois, the largest economy in the region, is also the one with the largest percentage in the intra-regional trade.

The results of figure 7.5 indicate the existence of steady state attractors for the gross product of the states in the regions. This fact, together with the information of table 7, indicates that the steady state attractors would also be present in the intra-regional trade flow, i.e., the shares of the states in interstate trade would follow a long-run trend. This could mean the existence of some sort of agreement, among the industries in the different states, which would be reflected in a stable level of trade flow. Unfortunately, similar data were not available to enable analysis of these relationships for the Northeast states.

Table 7.7   Comparison between the States' shares in Trade and States' Share in GRP (1992) (%)

	Trade share[a]	GRP share[b]
Illinois	29.0%	30.5%
Ohio	26.7%	25.1%
Michigan	22.5%	20.6%
Indiana	13.2%	12.5%
Wisconsin	8.7%	11.3%

[a] Share of each state in the Imports + Export in the Midwest
[b] Share of each state in the gross regional product of Midwest

Interpretations

The analysis in the work showed a significant difference in the level of spatial interaction within the two regions considered. It was argued that the higher degree of interconnection within the Midwest was related to the level of development in that region (higher levels of development would be related to larger volumes of trade, with greater percentage of intra-industry trade). However, it should be noticed that, although causality can be inferred from the relationship (i.e., the fact that high level of development implies high interaction), it could be argued that by increasing the degree of interaction within a region one would also tend to induce development. That is to say that by creating conditions for the states economically interact with each other would induce regional growth.[10]

It is important to perceive that if the Northeast of Brazil were to become an economy as integrated as the Midwest, the spatial interaction, or so far the lack of it, should be taken into consideration when formulating and evaluating regional policies. The regional policies for the Northeast so far adopted in Brazil did not take into account the spatial and economic regional interconnections. By failing to recognize these aspects, these policies ended up creating a few economics poles that are strongly, economically linked to centers outside the region, more specifically the Southeast, but that generate very little backward and forward effects within the Northeast. Moreover, the discussion on section 2 pointed out that the development of the Northeast of Brazil during the 1970s and 1980s was strongly based on tax incentives and direct investment programs from the Federal Government that are no longer available in the 1990s. What is seen today is the existence of few isolated subsidies, which lack any global strategy. Besides that, the states have engaged in predatory tax wars in seeking new private investments, which tends only to relocate industry within the region, and worsen the economic condition of the states in the long run.

What would be the solution? It should be clear that the economic growth of the Northeast is dependent on the performance of the national economy. However, this should not preclude any attempt to increase the pace of regional economic growth. With respect to the problem of the Northeast, it seems evident that one of the important factors missing is an efficient transportation system. Most of the transport of goods in Brazil is by land, with most of this being done by trucks. This modal concentration is even more pronounced in the Northeast where the use of railroads is practically nonexistent (see Resende *et al.*, 1997). However, the poor conditions of the roads in the region increase the cost of the products, making them less competitive. Improving the road conditions would with no doubt contribute to an increase in the flow of trade in the region. Finding alternative ways to transport the good would also help (for example, the use of waterways). There has been some investment in this direction, for instance, in modernizing ports, or even the construction of new ones, in an attempt to increase flow of good by sea. However, such efforts, such as SUAPE in Pernambuco, have faced high cost problems that have preclude a more extensive use. Furthermore, this investment must be accompanied by the already mentioned road improvement, so that the products could arrive and leave the port by land.

Finally, the regional policies should be coordinated in such way to make the best use of the existing economic interactions, and at the same time try to enhance them. The region should be thought of as a whole, so that the spillover effects of the investment made in one specific state would be considered. Although the zero-sum game was applied to the Dendrinos-Sonis model when modeling relative growth, the same is not true for absolute growth. Competitive and complementary relationships exist at the relative level, however, all states would grow in absolute terms. In this sense, policies should focus on exploring the complementary relationships revealed by the model and reduce the competitive (negative) effects, thus increasing the spatial interaction and growth.

Conclusions

At this point it is important to add some remarks about the relationship between the elasticities, a_{sk}, and the w from the weight matrix. As mentioned before, one of the disadvantages of the space-time autoregressive (STARMA) models is the fact that W matrix has to be defined *a priori*. The results of the model are likely to depend on the specification of the matrix. In the D-S model, the coefficients are in some sense capturing the same type of spatial relationship. The main difference here is that no *a priori* expectations are imposed on the model. The absence of restrictions provides for the possibility that non-neighbors states may present significant coefficients. The elasticities will reflect the degree of spatial correlation among the states; significant coefficients will indicate the existence of interaction, while non-significant coefficients will indicate no interaction.

The results of the model indicated that the level of interaction among the states of the Midwest is higher than the level of interaction among the states of the Northeast of Brazil. This is not surprising, given the difference in the level of development of these two regions. In the Midwest, Michigan and Indiana presented the strongest level of interaction with the other states. The results do show a difference between the influence of neighbors and non-neighbors, showing that neighbors do have a stronger influence. For the Northeast, the results indicate some degree of interaction among the smallest states; however, very few coefficients were significant.

The forecast exercises indicate that both economies tend quickly to a steady state solution. The process takes approximately seven years for the Northeast of Brazil and, ten years for the Midwest states. The results do indicate one change in the regional product distribution for the Northeast, with Paraíba becoming largest the Alagoas. No changes are predicted for the Midwest.

Another interesting finding is the qualitative similarities between the distributions of the state share in the interstate trade flow and the gross state product share in the GRP. This similarity would indicate the existence of steady state attractors for the intra-regional trade flows. Whether such steady states exist or not, is a question for future work.

It was argued here that the higher the developed level of the states the greater would be the percentage of intra-industry trade among then, which would lead to greater interaction. While this issue was not explored in this paper, recent work by Munroe and Hewings (1999) found a dominating presence of intra-industry trade among the Midwest states. More interesting, their analysis indicates that most of this trade is direct to other states in the Midwest, which shows the importance of intra-industry trade for the degree of interaction among those economies.

From a policy perspective, it would be important to the governments (at state and federal level) to consider the current lack of interaction among the Brazilian Northeast states in the formulation of their policies. Assuming that at least some qualitative interpretation can be made from the data, the Northeast Brazil experience would appear to be very different from the US case. The search for explanation need not look much beyond the levels of per capita income and the density of the transportation network. The exploitation of the complementarity between states in the US has provided an important explanatory mechanism for the growth over the post-war period. Development strategy in Northeast Brazil remains a much more comprehensive challenge than one that is narrowly focused on specific sectors or activities. Exploitation of potential complementarities between the states may serve as an important component of this broader strategy.

Notes

[1] Further details about SUDENE and industrialization in the Northeast may be found in Guimarães Neto (1989).
[2] From 1970 to 1980, the industry in the Northeast grew at an average annual rate of 9.1%, and during the 80's the rate was 1.0%. The growth rates for the industry of the whole country were 9.3% and 0.2%, according to the SUDENE.
[3] More specifically, the inability to explain the high levels of intra-industry trade among industrialized countries.
[4] The higher the income level of the countries the lager in the proportion of the intra-industry trade (see Stone, 1997).
[5] The stock would be, for instance, population.
[6] See Dendrinos and Sonis (1990) for further discussion about relative dynamic models.
[7] This coefficient is not, however, significant.
[8] All the significant coefficients for the neighbor states are larger than those for the non-neighbors ones.
[9] Unfortunately, comparable data were not available for the Northeast of Brazil.
[10] That seems to be the idea behind the creation of the European Union and the South Common Market (MERCOSUR) in South America. That is, the reduction of economic barriers would induce regional economic growth.

References

Balassa, B. (1961) *The Theory of Economic Integration*, Homewood: Irwin.
Dendrinos, D. and Sonis, M. (1987) "The onset of turbulence in discrete relative multiple spatial dynamics," *Applied Mathematics and computation*, 22, 25-44.

Dendrinos, D. and Sonis, M. (1988) "Nonlinear discrete relative population dynamics of the U.S. Regions," *Applied Mathematics and Computation*, 25, 265-285.

Dendrinos, D. and Sonis, M. (1990) *Chaos and Socio-Spatial Dynamics*. Spring-Verlag: New York.

Guimarães Neto, L. (1989) "Introduction to northeastern economic formation," (*Introdução à Formação Econômica do Nordeste*), Recife, Massangana.

Helpman, E., and Krugman, P. (1985) *Market Structure and Foreign Trade: Increasing Returns, Imperfect Competition, and the International Economy*, Cambridge: MIT Press.

Hewings, G., Sonis, M., Cuello, F., Mansouri, F. (1996) "The role of regional interaction in regional growth: competition and complementarity in the U.S. regional system," *Australian Journal of Regional Studies* 2(2).

Hewings G.J.D., P.R. Israilevich, Y. Okuyama, D.K. Anderson, G.R. Schindler, M. Foulkes, and M. Sonis (1997). "Returns to Scope, Returns to Trade and the Structure of Spatial Interaction in the US Midwest," *Discussion Paper* 97-P-3, Regional Economics Applications Laboratory, University of Illinois, Urbana.

Hewings, G., Sonis, M., Guo, J., Israilevich, P., Schindler, G. (1998) "The hollowing-out process in the Chicago economy, 1975-2011," *Geographical Analysis* 30, 217-33.

Krugman, P. (1979) "Increasing returns, monopolistic competition, and international trade," *Journal of International Economics* 9, 469-79.

Ministério do Planejamento e Orçamento - MPO (1995) Northeastern: a strategy of sustainable development (*Nordeste: uma estratégia de desenvolvimento sustentável*), Oct.

Munroe, D., and Hewings, G. (1999) "The role of intraindustry trade in interregional trade in the Midwest of the US," *Discussion Paper REAL-99-T-7* Regional Economics Applications Laboratory, University of Illinois, Urbana.

Okazaki, F. (1989) "The hollowing-out phenomenon in economic development," Paper presented at the Pacific Regional Science Conference, Singapore.

Resende, P.T., J.J.M. Guilhoto, and G.J.D. Hewings, (1997) "Free Trade and Transportation Infrastructure in Brazil: Towards an Integrated Approach," *Discussion Paper* 97-P-4, Regional Economics Applications Laboratory, University of Illinois, Urbana.

Richardson, H.W. 1973. *Regional Growth Theory*. New York, Wiley.

Sonis, M., and Dendrinos, D. (1987) A discrete relative growth model: switching, role reversal and turbulence. In Eichborn, P., and Friedrich, P. (ed.), *International Perspectives on Regional Decentralization*.

Stone, L.L. (1997) *The Growth of Intra-Industry Trade*. Garland Publishing: New York.

Superintendência do Desenvolvimento do Nordeste - SUDENE (1997) "*Boletin conjuntural: Nordeste do Brasil*," Nov.

Thompson, W. (1965) *A Preface to UrbanEeconomics*. Baltimore: Johns Hopkins Press.

Verdoorn, P. (1960) The intra-block trade of Benelux. In Robinson, E. (ed.), *Economic Consequences of the Size of Nations*, London: Macmillan.

White, E. and Hewings, G. (1982) "Space-time employment modeling: some results using seemingly unrelated regression estimates," *Journal of Regional Science*, 22, 283-302.

8 Comparative Analysis of Brazil's National and Regional Economic Structure, 1985, 1990, 1995

JOAQUIM J. M. GUILHOTO, FRANCISCO C. CROCOMO, ANTONIO CARLOS MORETTO, and ROSSANA LOTT RODRIGUES

Introduction

The goal of this chapter is to provide some recent historical perspectives on structural changes to analyze the differences in the productive structure in the Brazilian economy and five macro regions for the years of 1985, 1990, and 1995, using some established and recent contributions to linkage analysis applied to input-output tables. The issue derives from a sense that the Brazilian economy is one characterized by striking differences in regional performance and structure; while chapters in this collection have focused on income distribution and changes in the location of industry, this chapter will explore differences in economic structure and structural change from an interindustry perspective. The main sources of data are interregional and intersectoral input-output matrices constructed by the authors for the years of 1985, 1990, and 1995 for the five Brazilian macro regions (North, Northeast, Central West, Southeast, and South).

The next section will present an overview of the Brazilian economy in the 1980s and 1990s; in the third section, a brief discussion about the regional differences in Brazil will be made, while the methodology will be presented in the fourth section. The results follow in the fifth section and some concluding comments complete the chapter.

A Brief Overview of the Brazilian Economy in the 1980s and 1990s

In the 1980s, the Brazilian economy experienced a very low growth rate especially when compared to its long run history. In the 1980s, the national

GDP grew at a yearly average rate of only 1.56% (Bonelli and Gonçalves, 1998). The 1990s can be divided into two periods; from 1990 to 1993, the economy went through a period of recession, with the GDP growing at a yearly average rate of 1.6%; industry and the agriculture grew at yearly rates of 0.3% and 2.3%. In the second period, from 1993 to 1997, the yearly average GDP growth rate was of 4.4%, while industry, agriculture, and services grew, respectively, 3.8%, 6%, and 3.1% (Bonelli and Gonçalves, 1998).

In 1994, investment accounted for 16.3% of Brazilian GDP; in 1995 this share grew to 19.2% (Baer, 1996 and Conjuntura Econômica, 1997). The quality of the investment also improved and at the same time there was a growth in the share of imported capital goods. Together, these changes contributed to an increase in productivity; with a consequent increase in wages (5.7% in 1993, and 6.2% in 1995) there was also a decrease in the unemployment rates from 5.3% in 1993 to 4.6% in 1995 (IBGE, 1997a and Conjuntura Econômica, 1997).

The strong performance of the industrial sector in the 1990s was followed by the growth in importance of the service sector, mainly due to increased subcontracting by the industrial sector after the economy was opened up, a process that began in 1990 (Bonelli and Gonçalves, 1998). While the 1980s are characterized by a closed economy, the 1990s can be said to be a decade of openness and modernization in Brazil.

Finally, we should stress the tendencies and the sectoral composition in the Brazilian economy in the last decade. The share of the industrial sector in the economy declined from 48% in 1985 to 42% in 1990 and to 34% in 1995, while the service sector's shares grew respectively from 40%, to 47% and to 54%. The shares of the agricultural sector were maintained, 12% for 1985, 11% for 1990, and 12% for 1995 (Melo *et al.*, 1998).

The Brazilian Macro Regions

Using the IBGE classification, the Brazilian Economy can be divided into 5 macro regions (figure 8.1) North (7 States); Northeast (9 States); Central West (3 States and the Federal District); Southeast (4 States); and South (3 States). The overall size of the Brazilian territory is 8.5m km^2 of which 45.3% belongs to the North region, 18.3% to the Northeast, 18.9% to the Central West, 10.9% to the Southeast, and 6.8% to the South. However, the economic and population distribution do not follow the geographical distribution, as can be seen in table 8.1.

Having 45.3% of the Brazilian territory, the North region has only 7.2% of the Brazilian population, the lowest density, the smallest share of population living in cities (62.4%) and the smallest share in the Brazilian GDP (4.6% in 1995). The most developed regions in Brazil are the Southeast and the South region. The Southeast region had a share of 58.7% (1995) of the Brazilian GDP with 42.7% (1996) of its population and 10.9% of the territory, while the South region had a share of 17.9% (1995) in the Brazilian GDP with 6.8% of the territory and 15.0% (1996) of the population. The Southeast region is the most industrialized region in Brazil, while the South region, the closest to the MERCOSUL countries, is, potentially, the region that stands to gain most from MERCOSUL integration.

Figure 8.1 Map of Brazil and Its Five Macro Regions

The Central West region has been an important region for Brazil in terms of agriculture, mainly because of the favorable type of land in this region, and this is reflected in its share in the population, 6.69% in 1996, and GDP, 5.98% in 1995, of Brazil. Currently, the Northeast region has serious drought problems whereas at the time of the formation of the Brazilian State it used to be its most important region. This region has 18.3% of the Brazilian territory, 28.5% (1996) of its population and 12.8% (1995) of its GDP; recently, oil extraction and processing have been one of the most rapidly growing sectors in the region and with the openness of the Brazilian economy, a number of industries have been installing their production units in the region (in part due to the fiscal incentives provided by the various levels of state government).

Table 8.1   Main Economical and Geographical Indicators of the Brazilian Macro Regions

Regions	Size		Population (1996)			GDP Shares		
	km²	Share	Number	Share	Urban Share	1985	1990	1995
		%	1,000	%	%	%	%	%
North	3,851,560	45.25	11,288	7.19	62.36	3.84	4.94	4.64
Northeast	1,556,001	18.28	44,767	28.50	65.21	14.10	12.86	12.78
Central West	1,604,852	18.85	10,501	6.69	84.42	4.81	5.16	5.98
Southeast	924,266	10.85	67,001	42.66	89.29	60.15	58.83	58.72
South	575,316	6.76	23,514	14.97	77.22	17.10	18.21	17.89
Brazil	8,511,996	100.00	157,070	100.00	78.36	100.00	100.00	100.00

Source: IBGE (1997a, 1997b, and 1999)

Theoretical Background

In this section, the theory and methods used to analyze the differences in productive structure of the Brazilian macro regions will be described. They are based on some well-known indices associated with the work of Hirschman and Rasmussen and some recent modifications that are referred to as pure linkages approaches.

The Hirschman/Rasmussen Approach

The work of Rasmussen (1956) and Hirschman (1958) established the development of indices of linkages that have now become part of the generally accepted procedures for identifying key sectors in an economy. Define b_{ij} as a typical element of the Leontief inverse matrix, B; B^* as the average value of all elements of B, and if $B_{\bullet j}$ and $B_{i \bullet}$ are the associated typical column and row sums, the indices may be developed as follows:

Backward linkage index (power of dispersion):

$$U_j = \left[B_{\bullet j} / n \right] / B^* \tag{8.1}$$

Forward linkage index (sensitivity of dispersion):

$$U_i = \left[B_{i \bullet} / n \right] / B^* \tag{8.2}$$

One of the criticisms of the above indices is that they do not take into consideration the different levels of production in each sector of the economy; this is accommodated in the pure linkage approach presented in the next section.

The Pure Linkage Approach

As presented by Guilhoto *et al.* (1996, 1997), the pure linkage approach can be used to measure the importance of the sectors in terms of production generation in the economy. Consider a two-region input-output system represented by the following block matrix, A, of direct inputs:

$$A = \begin{pmatrix} A_{jj} & A_{jr} \\ A_{rj} & A_{rr} \end{pmatrix} \tag{8.3}$$

where A_{jj} and A_{rr} are the quadrat matrices of direct inputs within the first and second region, A_{rj} and A_{jr} are the rectangular matrices showing the direct inputs purchased by the first region from the second region and vice versa.

From (8.3), one can generate the following expression:

$$B = (I - A)^{-1} = \begin{pmatrix} B_{jj} & B_{jr} \\ B_{rj} & B_{rr} \end{pmatrix} = \begin{pmatrix} \Delta_{jj} & 0 \\ 0 & \Delta_{rr} \end{pmatrix} \begin{pmatrix} \Delta_j & 0 \\ 0 & \Delta_r \end{pmatrix} \begin{pmatrix} I & A_{jr}\Delta_r \\ A_{rj}\Delta_j & I \end{pmatrix} \tag{8.4}$$

where:

$$\Delta_j = \left(I - A_{jj} \right)^{-1} \tag{8.5}$$

$$\Delta_r = \left(I - A_{rr} \right)^{-1} \tag{8.6}$$

$$\Delta_{jj} = \left(I - \Delta_j A_{jr} \Delta_r A_{rj} \right)^{-1} \tag{8.7}$$

$$\Delta_{rr} = \left(I - \Delta_r A_{rj} \Delta_j A_{jr} \right)^{-1} \tag{8.8}$$

By utilizing the decomposition in (8.4), it is possible to reveal the process of production in an economy as well as derive a set of multipliers/linkages. From the Leontief formulation:

$$X = \left(I - A \right)^{-1} Y \tag{8.9}$$

and using the information contained in equations (8.4) through (8.8), one can derive a set of indexes that can be used to rank the regions in terms of its importance in the economy, and to explore how the production process varies across these regional economies.

From equations (8.4) and (8.9), one obtains:

$$\begin{pmatrix} X_j \\ X_r \end{pmatrix} = \begin{pmatrix} \Delta_{jj} & 0 \\ 0 & \Delta_{rr} \end{pmatrix} \begin{pmatrix} \Delta_j & 0 \\ 0 & \Delta_r \end{pmatrix} \begin{pmatrix} I & A_{jr}\Delta_r \\ A_{rj}\Delta_j & I \end{pmatrix} \begin{pmatrix} Y_j \\ Y_r \end{pmatrix} \tag{8.10}$$

which leads to the definitions for the pure backward linkage (PBL) and for the pure forward linkage (PFL), i.e.,

$$\begin{aligned} PBL &= \Delta_r A_{rj} \Delta_j Y_j \\ PFL &= \Delta_j A_{jr} \Delta_r Y_r \end{aligned} \tag{8.11}$$

where the PBL will yield the pure impact on the rest of the economy of the value of the total production in region j, $(\Delta_j Y_j)$: i.e., the impact that is free from the demand inputs that region j makes from region j, and the feedbacks from the rest of the economy to region j and vice-versa. The PFL will give the pure impact on region j of the total production in the rest of the economy $(\Delta_r Y_r)$.

As the PBL and PFL are shown in current values, the pure total linkage (PTL) can be obtained by adding the two previous indices, i.e.,

$$PTL = PBL + PFL \tag{8.12}$$

The pure linkage indices can also be normalized by the average value of the sectors in the economy such that the normalized indices show how many times a sector is larger or smaller than the average sector in the economy. In such a way, it is possible to use these indices for a direct comparison of the productive structure of economies of different sizes and even with different currencies. In the same way, the methods allow for a temporal comparison in economies that have experienced significant inflation or that have changed their currency.

The Productive Structure of Brazil and Its 5 Macro Regions

In analyzing the productive structure of Brazil and its five regions, through the lens of the Hirschman/Rasmussen and pure linkage approaches, this section is divided into three parts. First, an analysis is provided to reveal the set of key sectors. Secondly, a cross-section analysis is made, comparing the productive structure of the national economy with those of the macro regions. Finally, a temporal comparison is made using the productive structure of 1985 as the base year.

Key-Sectors

The determination of key sectors in a economy is not an easy task, since not every sector will be able to fulfill all the desirable characteristics, namely, having strong backward and forward linkages, generating a high level of production, employment and income, a better distribution of income, a low level of pollution, and so forth (see McGilvray (1977). In this section, we will use two measures to determine which sector is a key sector; first one is based on the Hirschman/Rasmussen backward and forward linkages that take into consideration only how the sectors relate with each other based on their technical coefficients, and the second measure that is based in the pure linkage approach. In addition to considering the productive structure, it also accounts for the importance of a sector in generating production value in the economy.

For the Hirschman/Rasmussen approach, we define key sectors, following McGilvray (1977), as those whose backward and forward linkages are greater than one. For the pure linkage approach, if a sector presents a value greater than one for the normalized pure total linkage it is considered a key sector for the economy. (It should be noted that key sector identification is not insensitive to the level of aggregation). The complete set of results for these two approaches are shown in summary form in tables 8.2 and 8.3. For the Brazilian economy as a whole (table 8.2), the key sectors are: Agriculture; Metallurgy; Chemicals; Textiles; Food Products; Construction; Trade; Transportation (only for the year of 1985); and Services. In the North region (table 8.2) the key sectors are:

Agriculture; Machinery (for 1985 and 1990); Wood & Wood Products (for 1985 and 1990); Chemicals (for 1990 and 1995); Textiles; Food Products; Public Utilities; Construction; Trade; Transportation (only for the year of 1985); and Services. In the Northeast region (table 8.2) the key sectors are: Agriculture; Metallurgy; Paper Products & Printing; Chemicals; Textiles; Food Products; Public Utilities; Construction; Trade; and Services while for the Central West region (table 8.3) the key sectors are: Agriculture; Non-Metallic Minerals (only in 1985); Chemicals (in 1990 and 1995); Textiles; Food Products; Public Utilities (only in 1985); Construction; Trade; Transportation; and Services.

Table 8.2   Consolidated Key-Sectors, Hirschman/Rasmussen and Pure Linkages, for the Brazilian Economy and for the North and Northeast Regions, 1985, 1990, and 1995

Sectors	Brazil			North			Northeast		
	1985	1990	1995	1985	1990	1995	1985	1990	1995
1. Agriculture	0	0	0	0	0	0	0	0	0
2. Mining									
3. Non-Metallic Minerals									
4. Metallurgy	⊕	⊕	⊕				+	+	+
5. Machinery				+	+				
6. Electrical Equipment									
7. Transport Equipment									
8. Wood & Wood Prod.				0	0				
9. Paper Prod. & Printing							+	+	+
10. Rubber Industry									
11. Chemicals	0	⊕	⊕	0	0		⊕	⊕	⊕
12. Pharmaceutical									
13. Plastics									
14. Textiles	+	+	+	+	+	+	+	+	+
15. Clothing and Footwear									
16. Food Products	0	0	0	0	0	0	0	0	0
17. Miscellaneous Indust.									
18. Public Utilities				⊕	0	0	⊕	0	0
19. Construction	0	0	0	0	0	0	0	0	0
20. Trade	0	0	0	0	0	0	0	0	0
21. Transportation	0			0					
22. Services	0	0	0	0	0	0	0	0	0

+ Key sector by the Hirschman/Rasmussen approach (forward and backward linkages greater than 1.0)

0 Key sector by the pure linkage approach (normalized pure total linkage greater than 1.0)

⊕ Key sector by both approaches, Hirschman/Rasmussen and pure linkage

For the Southeast region (table 8.3), the key sectors are: Agriculture; Metallurgy; Machinery (in 1985 and 1990); Transport Equipment; Paper Products & Printing (only in 1990); Chemicals; Textiles; Food Products; Construction; Trade; Transportation; and Services and for the South region (table 8.3), the key sectors are: Agriculture; Metallurgy; Paper Products & Printing; Chemicals (in 1985 and 1990); Textiles; Clothing and Footwear (in 1985 and 1990); Food Products; Construction (in 1985 and 1990); Trade; Transportation; and Services.

Table 8.3 Consolidated Key-Sectors, Hirschman/Rasmussen and Pure Linkages, for the Central West, Southeast, and South Regions, 1985, 1990, and 1995

Sectors	Central West			Southeast			South		
	1985	1990	1995	1985	1990	1995	1985	1990	1995
1. Agriculture	⊕	0	⊕	0	0	0	0	0	0
2. Mining									
3. Non-Metallic Minerals	+								
4. Metallurgy				⊕	⊕	⊕	+	+	+
5. Machinery				+	+				
6. Electrical Equipment									
7. Transport Equipment				0	0	0			
8. Wood & Wood Prod.									
9. Paper Prod. & Printing					+		+	+	+
10. Rubber Industry									
11. Chemicals		0	0	0	0	0	0	0	
12. Pharmaceutical									
13. Plastics									
14. Textiles	+	+	+	+	+	+	+	+	+
15. Clothing and Footwear							0	0	
16. Food Products	0	0	0	0	0	0	0	0	⊕
17. Miscellaneous Indust.									
18. Public Utilities	+								
19. Construction	0	0	0	0	0	0		0	0
20. Trade	0	0	0	0	0	0	0	0	0
21. Transportation	0	0	0	0	0	0	0	0	0
22. Services	0	0	0	0	0	0	0	0	0

+ Key sector by the Hirschman/Rasmussen approach (forward and backward linkages greater than 1.0)

0 Key sector by the pure linkage approach (normalized pure total linkage greater than 1.0)

⊕ Key sector by both approaches, Hirschman/Rasmussen and pure linkage

From the above presentation of the key sectors in the economy, it is possible to explore some similarities and differences in the results. The following sectors are defined as key sectors exclusively by the Hirschman/Rasmussen criteria: Non-Metallic Minerals; Machinery; Paper Products & Printing; and Textiles, whereas according to the pure linkage criterion, the following sectors are considered key ones: Transport Equipment; Clothing and Footwear; Construction; Trade; Transportation; and Services. From the use of either approach in different regions and/or periods of time, the following sectors are considered key sectors: Agriculture; Metallurgy; Chemicals; Food Products; and Public Utilities.

Notwithstanding the similarities among the regions, there are some important differences. For example, one can note, as examples, the importance of the Paper Products & Printing sector in the Northeast and South regions, Transport Equipment in the Southeast region, Public Utilities in the North and Northeast regions, Agriculture sector under both approaches in the Central West region, Chemical sector also under both approaches for the Northeast region.

As revealed in the derivation of the above indices, there is a difference in one sector being a key sector in one or the other definitions. Defined as a key sector in the Hirschman/Rasmussen approach means being an important sector in terms of the productive *structure*, while designation as a key sector in the pure linkage approach means being a key sector in the process of generating *production*. As such, it may be claimed that a sector that is defined as key in both definitions is certainly a sector that is a very important one for the region. This may be the type of sector to which careful attention would need to be paid when considering any form of economic development policy.

Productive Structure in Space

Using the results of the Hirschman/Rasmussen and the pure linkage approaches for Brazil as a "numeraire," it is possible to examine how the results for the macro regions differ from the ones for the Brazilian economy. The general idea is that the closer the results for the regions are to the results for the Brazilian economy, the more similar the productive structures. Figures 8.2-8.5 provide the comparative analyses for 1985, 1990 and 1995 respectively.

These figures do resemble and are based on the idea of electroencephalograms used in medicine to measure the differences from a given standard; hence, these economic applications will be referred to as *Electroeconograms of the Productive Structure* (EPS). The higher the amplitude of the waves in the figures, the greater the differences in the productive structures. For 1985, the greatest amplitudes in the EPS are in the pure linkages, showing the difference in importance of the sectors in generating production value in the regions. Further, the forward linkages do reveal larger waves than the backward linkages. The same patterns repeat in 1990 and 1995.

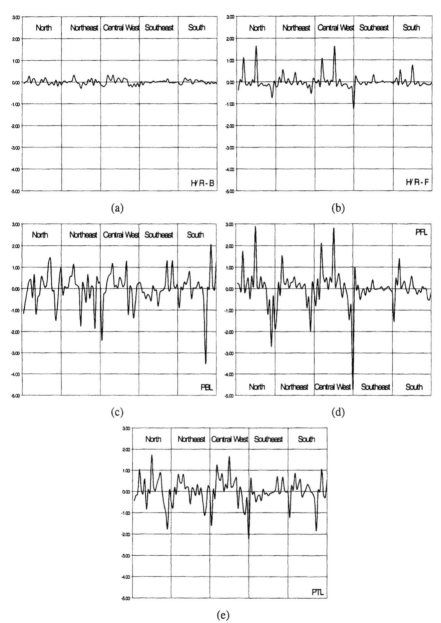

Figure 8.2   Electroeconogram of Linkages for the Brazilian Macro Regions – 1985

(a) Hirschman/Rasmussen Backward (b) Hirschman/Rasmussen Forward (c) Normalized Pure Backward Linkage (d) Normalized Pure Forward Linkage (e) Normalized Pure Total Linkage

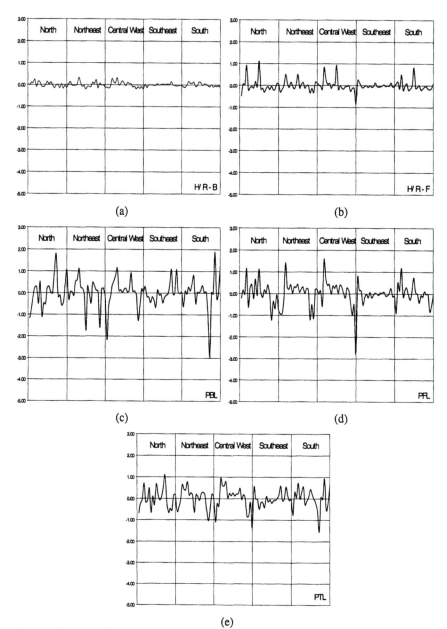

(a)   (b)

(c)   (d)

(e)

Figure 8.3   Electroeconogram of Linkages for the Brazilian Macro Regions – 1990

(a) Hirschman/Rasmussen Backward (b) Hirschman/Rasmussen Forward (c) Normalized Pure Backward Linkage (d) Normalized Pure Forward Linkage (e) Normalized Pure Total Linkage

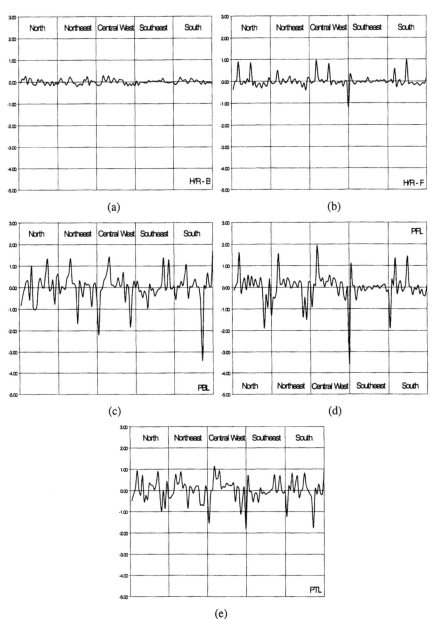

Figure 8.4   Electroeconogram of Linkages for the Brazilian Macro Regions – 1995

(a) Hirschman/Rasmussen Backward (b) Hirschman/Rasmussen Forward (c) Normalized Pure Backward Linkage (d) Normalized Pure Forward Linkage (e) Normalized Pure Total Linkage

For the Hirschman/Rasmussen indices, from the EPS for all the years of the analysis, it can be seen that for the backward linkages, the results show that the Southeast and the South regions are closer to the productive structure of the Brazilian economy, while the other regions present greater differences. For the forward linkages, the closest region to the productive structure of the Brazilian economy is the Southeast region, followed by the Northeast and the South regions, while the North and the Central West regions the more different.

Looking at the pure linkages approach, from the EPS, for all the years of the analysis one finds that the smallest waves are in the pure total linkages, implying that there is an averaging effect of the differences revealed in the backward and forward linkages. The closest productive structure to the Brazilian economy is the Southeast region, while the other four regions present differences from the Brazilian economy as a whole and the patterns of differences are not similar among region, indicating that every region has a particular pattern of production. The amplitude of the waves in the EPS show that, from 1985 to 1990, the differences of the regions to the Brazilian economy as a whole decreased, increasing again from 1990 to 1995. However, considering the whole period, from 1985 to 1995, the differences tended to decrease.

Guilhoto (1999), using the same interregional system for 1995 as the one used in this chapter, was able to estimate the *dependence* among the productive structure of the regions. The results showed that the North region has practically no relation with the Northeast region and vice-versa; while the South region has some impact on the production of the North region while the reverse is not true. Although the demands from the Central West region have some impact on the production of the other regions, the production in the Central West region has its relations concentrated with the Southeast and South regions. From this analysis, we can suggest that the South and Southeast regions are the most important regions in the system.

Productive Structure in Time

In similar fashion to the approach adopted in the previous section, using the results of the Hirschman/Rasmussen and the pure linkages approaches for the year of 1985 as a "numeraire," it is possible to explore how the results for the economies of Brazil and of its five macro regions have changed through time. The general idea is that the smaller the changes that did occur, the closer the results to those for the base year; the findings are summarized in figures 8.5 to 8.10, adopting the same convention as figures 8.2 to 8.4. However, the difference is that they now show changes through time and not across space but the interpretations are similar – larger differences in amplitude indicating more changes occurred in the productive structures through the time period of analysis.

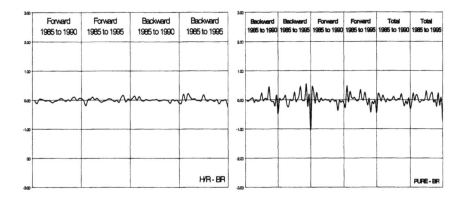

Figure 8.5   **Electroeconogram of the Changes in the Hirschman/Rasmussen and Normalized Pure Linkages for Brazil - 1985 to 1995**

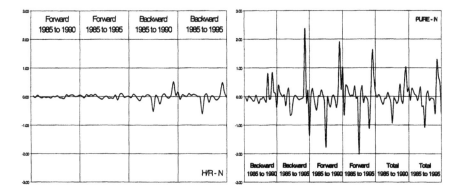

Figure 8.6   **Electroeconogram of the Changes in the Hirschman/Rasmussen and Normalized Pure Linkages for the North Region - 1985 to 1995**

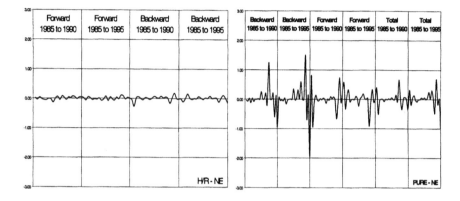

Figure 8.7   **Electroeconogram of the Changes in the Hirschman/Rasmussen and Normalized Pure Linkages for the Northeast Region - 1985 to 1995**

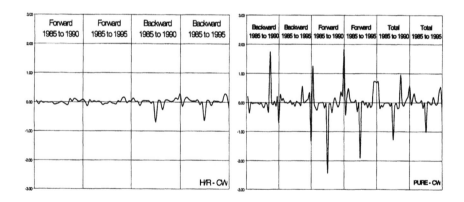

Figure 8.8   **Electroeconogram of the Changes in the Hirschman/Rasmussen Linkages and Normalized Pure for the Central West Region - 1985 to 1995**

In general, the changes reported in the Hirschman/Rasmussen approach are smaller than the changes that occurred in the pure linkages approach. Also, the waves in general are larger for the 1985 to 1995 period than from the 1985 to 1990 period, showing that changes are taking place in the economy through time.

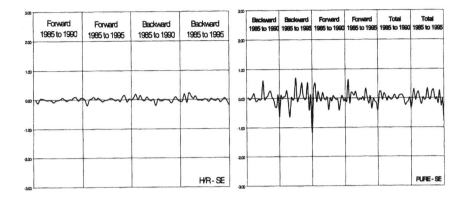

Figure 8.9   **Electroeconogram of the Changes in the Hirschman/Rasmussen and Normalized Pure Linkages for the Southeast Region - 1985 to 1995**

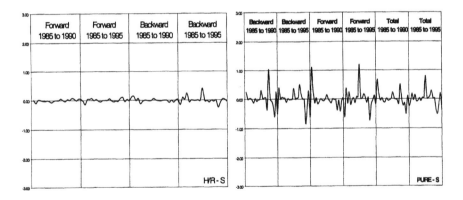

Figure 8.10   **Electroeconogram of the Changes in the Hirschman/Rasmussen Linkages and Normalized Pure for the South Region - 1985 to 1995**

For the Hirschman/Rasmussen indices, the larger waves are found in the forward linkages – indicating changes in the sales linkages. For the pure linkages indices, the larger waves are found either in the backward linkages (Brazil, Northeast and Southeast) or in the forward linkages (North, Central West, and South); as a general rule for all the regions being analyzed, the changes in the pure total linkages are smaller than the ones found in the backward and forward linkages.

The regions that show the largest waves, i.e., the economies that have undergone a lot of changes in the time period, are the North and Central

West regions. The Northeast occupies a middle position with modest change while the South regions are the ones with the smallest waves. The results for the Brazilian economy as a whole reveal the smallest waves of the whole system. Hence, while the economies of some regions experienced some evident change in their structure, this was not reflected in the national experience where the changes were modest. Also, there is a greater similarity in the patterns of change in the Brazilian economy with the ones found for the Southeast Region; this is not surprising given the dominant role that this region plays in the Brazilian economy.

Final Comments

The analysis began with an identification of the key sectors in the Brazilian economy and in five macro regions. Attention was then directed to a comparative analysis, first between the regions and the Brazilian economy as a whole and then in terms of change that had occurred over time. The key sector indices associated with Hirschman/Rasmussen and the pure linkage methodology was adopted and an innovation in presentation was proposed, the idea of an Electroeconogram that allows measurement of the differences in space and time of the productive structure of the economies.

The results in general show that the productive structure of the economies of the Brazilian regions are different one from another and also differ from the Brazilian economy as a whole. The patterns of change through time show that the evolution of the productive structure of the regions are also different one from another, however, maybe due to the greater share that the Southeast region has in the Brazilian economy, the patterns of changes in the Southeast region are very similar to the ones for Brazil as a whole.

While this analysis has suggested some new insights into ways of comparing the productive structure of the regions, there still some question that need to be answered. What are the causes for the differences in productive structure among regions? How do the economic relations (trading patterns) among the regions affect their productive structure? Are the differences in productive structure an indication merely of different sectoral mixes or do they reflect differences in the competitive advantage of different regions?

References

Baer W. (1996) *A Economia Brasileira*. São Paulo, Nobel.

Bonelli, R., and R.R. Gonçalves (1998) "Para Onde Vai a Estrutura Industrial Brasileira?" In *A Economia Brasileira em Perspectiva – 1998*. Rio de Janeiro:IPEA. Volume 2, capítulo 16, pp. 617-664.

Conjuntura Econômica (1997). "Indicadores Econômicos," 51, no. 8.

Guilhoto, J.J.M. (1999) "Decomposition & Sinergy: a Study of the Interactions and Dependence Among the 5 Brazilian Macro Regions". (Compact Disc). Dublin: Forfás. *39th Congress of the European Regional Science Association. Dublin, Ireland*.

Guilhoto, J.J.M., G.J.D. Hewings, and M. Sonis (1997) "Interdependence, Linkages and Multipliers in Asia: an International Input-Output Analysis," Urbana: University of Illinois. *Discussion Paper, 97-T-2* Regional Economics Applications Laboratory. 33p.

Guilhoto, J.J.M., M. Sonis, M., G.J.D. Hewings (1996). "Linkages and Multipliers in a Multiregional Framework: Integrations of Alternative Approaches." *Discussion Paper, 96-T-8* Regional Economics Applications Laboratory, University of Illinois, Urbana.

Hirschman, A.O. (1958) *The Strategy of Economic Development*. New Haven, Yale University Press.

IBGE (1997a) *Anuário Estatístico do Brasil 1996*, v. 56. Rio de Janeiro.

IBGE (1997b) *Contagem da População 1996*. Rio de Janeiro.

IBGE (1999) *Contas Regionais do Brasil: 1985-1997*. Rio de Janeiro.

McGilvray, J.(1977) "Linkages, Key Sectors and Development Strategy." In: W. Leontief (ed) *Structure, System and Economic Policy*. Cambridge, Cambridge University Press, pp.49-56.

Melo, H.P., F. Rocha, G Ferraz, G. di Sabbato, R. Dweck (1998) "O Setor Serviços no Brasil: uma Visão Global – 1985/95." In IPEA (1997). *A Economia Brasileira em Perspectiva*. Rio de Janeiro:IPEA. Vol. 2, Cap. 17, pp. 665-712.

Rasmussen, P. (1956) *Studies in Intersectoral Relations*. Amsterdam, North Holland.

9   An Econometric Input-Output Model for São Paulo State

CARLOS R. AZZONI and DÉCIO K. KADOTA

Introduction

The purpose of this chapter is to describe the econometric input-output model developed by the authors for the state of São Paulo, Brazil. The Brazilian economy is very concentrated spatially and the state of São Paulo is its most important economic area. With only 2.9% of the national territory, the state produces over 36% of national GDP and contains 26.2% of the total population. Together with the neighboring states of Paraná (south of SP) and Minas Gerais (north of SP), the region accounts for over half the national GDP. More importantly, the concentration is much higher in modern sectors, such as manufacturing (especially in technology intensive sectors), financial activities, etc. Although the economic importance of São Paulo state in the national economy is considerable, a decline has recently been observed, with neighboring states benefiting from the São Paulo metropolitan area diseconomies of agglomeration. In addition, new resource-oriented activities such as mining, agriculture and agribusiness have tended to settle in areas outside the state (Azzoni, 1993; Baer, 1995; Diniz, 1994; Willumsen *et al.*, 1996).

With the recent democratization of Brazil and the corresponding increase in the autonomy of states to establish their own economic policies, strong competition to attract new plants can be seen between states. At the same time, a massive fiscal crisis has affected the public sector, leaving the state and federal governments with few resources to pay even the operational costs of government, not to speak of resources for investment. This has created a generalized feeling that São Paulo state has been losing business to competing states and that the state government reaction needs to counteract the expected trend. As is common in these cases, a controversy centering on the meaning of recent facts has arisen (Is it a trend or just a set of episodic events?) and on their quantitative importance (How important are these events in terms of the state's economy? Does the state benefit in some way from the growth of neighboring states?).The state

171

secretary of planning decided to look for answers to these questions in order to guide the state's action (If they have to bargain to attract a new car assembly plant, how far should they go? Is it better to provide incentives for the growth of plants already located within the state or to attract new ones?).

The estimation of the impact of different events on the state's economy is thus a necessary condition. A static input-output model was produced in the past (Willumsen *et al.*, 1991) that led to the estimation of sectoral multipliers for the state economy, but the very static nature of the model limited the aims. Some of the problems with the former model were: (i) the use of 1980/85 input-output coefficients - with the increasing participation of Brazil in the global economy, some important modifications have been introduced into the structure of the state economy; (ii) no consideration of the economic relationships between the state of São Paulo and other states; (iii) impossibility of analysis of the time-related impact of different events. In order to overcome these limitations, the construction of the econometric input-output model described in this chapter was decided on.

The chapter is organized into four parts, in addition to the introduction and the conclusion. In the first section the model is briefly presented; the second section describes the procedures adopted for the estimation of regional economic time series; section three presents the equations and the basic case projections. Finally, in section four, the consistency of the results is analyzed and impacts are calculated for three different types of shocks.

The general structure of the model

The model developed is based on the methodology developed by Conway (1990) and further modified by the Regional Economics Application Laboratory of the University of Illinois, with successful experiences of applications for different areas within the US. The general structure of the model is shown in figure 9.1.

One main input into the model is what is shown as the "National economy" in figure 9.1, representing a set of nationally defined variables and relations that are exogenous to the model. These variables embrace different aspects of the Brazilian economy that are relevant for the economy of São Paulo state (national GDP, sectoral production values, interest rate, general and sectoral price indexes, factor income levels, public sector revenue and expenditure, the main monetary aggregates, working age population, employment and unemployment levels, population growth rates, birth and death rates) and constitute a point of reference for the estimation of the endogenous regional variables.[1] The source of values for the variables pertaining to the national economy block is an independent Brazilian econometric model that was adapted and up-dated by its author for the use in the São Paulo model (Fonseca, 1991). This adaptation guarantees not only the consistency between the regional and the national estimates but the consistency of the national estimates as such, for the econometric model that generates them is analytically and empirically consistent.

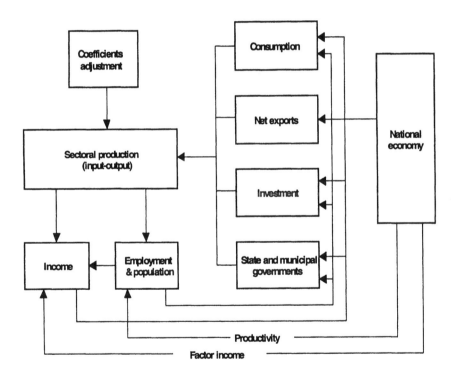

Figure 9.1 General Structure of the Model

The regional model considers 34 production sectors (agriculture, mining, construction, 22 manufacturing, 2 public utilities sectors, 5 services sectors, and public administration), three levels of government (national, state of São Paulo and the aggregate of municipal governments in the state); and four final demand components (consumption, investment, public expenditure and net exports of goods and services). The following set of variables were defined: value of production; factor income (wages and salaries and the payment to capital); sectoral employment of labor; state gross domestic product; consumption of families; investment in construction and in equipment; government operational and investment expenditure (state and the aggregate of municipalities); net exports of goods and services (federal government expenditure included); population; working age population; net migration rate and average family income.

As seen in figure 9.1, the final demand block includes the set of demands that directly affect the production levels of regional production sectors, as indicated by the arrow connecting them to the "Sectoral Production" block. The "Net Exports" component involves all net exports of goods and services for consumption or investment outside the region, whether from other Brazilian regions or other countries, and includes sales for consumption or investment by the federal government. These final demand components are exogenous to the region and constitute an important link to the "National Economy" block. The other components of final demand refer to the final consumption of goods and services by agents located within the region. They therefore affect and are indirectly affected by the levels of sectoral production in the region. This holds not only for the final consumption of families but also for investment and government expenditure, which makes it possible to estimate the impact on employment and income of autonomous increments in the demand for these items.[2]

The "Sectoral Production" block is the traditional input-output component, although in this case the coefficients are not treated as constant, as will be explained later. From this block, the "Income" and "Employment and Population" blocks are developed, in order to obtain the regional aggregate income, the family disposable income, employment, and population growth in the region. These variables depend directly on the sectoral production, but they also affect the demand for consumption of goods, investment and government expenditure, thus closing the chain of interdependence between the endogenous variables of the model. The modifications in the coefficients, which are introduced below, are based on the past evolution of labor productivity by sector, as econometrically related to ("explained by") national variables, providing another way of connecting the regional model to the national economy. The same holds true for the "Employment and Population" block, as one variable in the explanation of the regional population evolution is the demand for labor by production sectors.

Final demand equations[3]

In view of the absence of necessary information for the final demand components on a sector-by-sector basis, it was decided to define relations that reflect the behavior of demand respective to aggregated groups of goods and services. It was then supposed that the proportion of each sector in these aggregates is constant over time.[4] This supposition is of the same nature as that regarding the constancy of technical coefficients and will be treated equally, as will be shown below. On the other hand, there is no aggregate export (net) function in the model, for the net exports of the region are estimated sectorally.

Aggregate family consumption

$$SCP_t = F(SYD_t, RIR_t) \tag{9.1}$$

where: SCP_t is aggregate private consumption in the region in year t; SYD_t is aggregate disposable family income in the region; and RIR_t the real interest rate.

Private investment

$$SIPC_t = F(RIR_t, SIPC_{t-1}) \tag{9.2}$$

$$SIPE_t = F(RIR_t, SY_t, SY_{t-1}, SIPE_{t-1}) \tag{9.3}$$

where $SIPC_t$ is private investment in construction in the region; $SIPE_t$ is private investment in machinery and equipment in the region; and SY_t is regional gross domestic product.

Government expenditure (state and municipal aggregate)

$$SCG_t = F(SPOP_t) \tag{9.4}$$

$$SIGC_t = F(SPOP_t) \tag{9.5}$$

$$SIGE_t = F(SPOP_t, RIR_t) \tag{9.6}$$

where SCG_t is operational expenditure of state and municipal governments in the region; $SIGC_t$ is state and municipal government expenditure on construction in the region; $SIGE_t$ is state and municipal government expenditure on machinery and equipment in the region and $SPOP_t$ is regional population

Sectoral production and the adjustment of coefficients[5]

A very important feature of the model is the estimation of sectoral production equations from time series, allowing for the adjustment of technical input-output coefficients and aggregate final demand coefficients. This is done in two steps: initially, equations are specified for the "expected sectoral production" of each sector, obtained by utilizing base-year input-output and final demand coefficients; secondly, the time series estimated with the utilization of the base-year coefficients are compared with observed time series, leading to the change in the coefficients.

Let SZ_{it} be the expected production of sector i in the region in year t, defined as:

$$SZ_{it} = \sum_{j=1}^{n} a_{ij} SX_{jt} + \left[\alpha_i^{cp} SCP_t + \alpha_i^{cg} SCG_t + \alpha_i^{ipc} SIPC_t + \alpha_i^{ipe} SIPE_t + \right.$$
$$\left. + \alpha_i^{igc} SIGC_t + \alpha_i^{ige} SIGE_t + \beta_i VN_{it} \right] / \left(1 + T_{it}\right) \tag{9.7}$$

where:
SX_{it} is observed production of sector i in the region;
VN_{it} is the national exogenous variable associated with exports of sector i to outside the region;
T_{it} is the average indirect tax rate for products of sector i;
a_{ij} is an input-output technical coefficient, calculated for the base-year;
α_i^k is the proportion of final demand component k spent on products or services of sector i, ($k = cp, cg, ipc, ipe, igc, ige$);
β_i is the ratio of exports of sector i to the total exported by the region.

Thus, the series of values for sectoral expected production $[SZ_{i,t}]$ are estimated based on: (i) the regional input-output matrix technical coefficients $[a_{ij}]$; (ii) the final demand coefficients $[\alpha_i^k$ and $\beta_i]$ calculated for the base-year and (iii) the observed past series of sectoral production values, final demand components and national variables associated with sectoral net exports. These indicate the sectoral production that would be observed in each year in the region if the technical coefficients and the proportion of sectoral expenditure of each component of final demand were constant throughout the estimation period. Since this is not a valid supposition, the differences between these estimated series of sectoral production and the observed series throughout the estimation period are used to adjust the coefficients. Let SX_{it} be the observed values of production of sector i in year t; the adjustment of the coefficients is made by the following relationship:

$$Ln\left(\frac{SX_i}{SZ_i}\right)_t = F_{it}^{xz} \text{ (explanatory variables)} \tag{9.8}$$

The equation above shows the elasticity of the *observed* production with respect to the *expected* production of each sector. The function $F_{it}^{xz}()$ is estimated for each production sector, with explanatory variables that depend on the characteristics of each sector. The future sectoral production for the region is estimated initially with the forecast of X_{it} through time series analysis; the forecast values are then adjusted with the use of the elasticity provided by the respective sectoral function. It is supposed that the trend in the structural transformations in the regional economy captured by the functions $F_{it}^{xz}()$ will prevail in the future.

Income

This part of the model determines incomes generated by the production sectors, leading to the estimation of the aggregate disposable income of families. It is not supposed, as is common in models of this type, that value added per unit of output in each production sector is constant over time. Considering that the sectoral value added depends on the sectoral technical coefficients and on the sectoral labor productivity, on the one hand, and on the relationship between the price of the sectoral product, the price of sectoral inputs and the sectoral average wage, on the other, a set of equations is used to estimate the total value added of production sectors. The first part, addressed below, will show a block of equations that considers the relationship between sectoral production and employment; the second part deals with sectoral value added through equations such as

$$\left(\frac{SY_{i,t}}{SN_{i,t}}\right) = F_{it}^{yn} \text{ (explanatory variables)} \tag{9.9}$$

where SY_{it} is value added generated by sector i in the region and SN_{it} is total employed labor in sector i in the region.

The time series estimation of the above relationships allows for the evaluation of the observed trends in value added generated by a unit of labor in each production sector. As a general rule, a national variable is included in the set of explanatory variables, in order to relate this trend to the global (national) behavior of the sector. This provides a second connection between the regional endogenous variables and the national economy exogenous variables.

The disposable income of families is then given by:

$$SYD_t = SY_t(1 - SIT_t) + BYSS_t.SSSP_t \tag{9.10}$$

where:

$$SY_t = \sum_{i=1}^{34} SY_{i,t}$$

SYD_t is disposable income of families in the region;
SY_t is aggregate value added generated in the region;
SIT_t is the average indirect tax rate on income generated within the region;
$BYSS_t$ are global transfers of income from the national social service;
$SSSP_t$ is the proportion of global transfers of the national social service that enter the region.

Employment and population

The modifications in labor productivity over time are captured by equations such as

$$\left(\frac{SX_{it}}{SN_{it}} \right) = F_{it}^{xn} \left(\text{explanatory variables} \right) \tag{9.11}$$

The set of explanatory variables will vary between sectors, and, generally, national variables are utilized, allowing for a third link between the region and the national economy. It is admitted that the evolution of labor productivity is a national - as opposed to regional – phenomenon.
Let the employed working age population in the region in year t be given by:

$$SLFE_t = F(SNTOT_t) \tag{9.12}$$

where $SNTOT_t = \sum_{i=1}^{34} SN_{it}$, is the formal employment generated by production sectors and $SLFE_t$ is the employed working age population in the region.

The above equation considers the relationship between (SN) and total working age population ($SLFE$) in the region (the second includes *informal* employment). It is necessary then to establish the relationship between the evolution of the working age population and of the total population, as well as of the behavior of the unemployment rate in the region. This is done through the following relationships:

$$\left(\frac{SLF_t}{SPOP_t} \right) = F\left(\frac{BLF_t}{BPOP_t} \right) \tag{9.13}$$

$$SUNRT_t = F\left(SY_t, SY_{t-1}\right) \tag{9.14}$$

where SLF_t is the working age population in the region; $SPOP_t$ is the total population in the region; $SUNRT_t$ is the regional unemployment rate of the working age population and SY_t is aggregate income generated in the region Considering that, by definition, $(1-SUNRT_t) = \dfrac{SLFE_t}{SLF_t}$, the following

identity results

$$SPOP_t = \frac{SLFE_t}{\left(\dfrac{SLF_t}{SPOP_t} \right).(1-SUNRT_t)} \tag{9.15}$$

The economic rationale for the above relationship is the existence of equilibrium in the regional labor market. It implies that the labor supply expands (contracts) as the number of employed people grows (diminishes). The estimation of the three equations through time series assures that the obtained forecasts reflect historical trends and are consistent with projections of working age and total population at the national level. Since the region is "open," migration (considered as an adjustment residual) is included through the identity:

$$SMIGR_t = (SPOP_t - SPOP_{t-1}) - SBIRTH_t + SDEATH_t \tag{9.16}$$

where $SMIGR_t$ is net migration to the region; $SPOP_t$ is regional total population; $SBIRTH_t$ are the number of births and $SDEATH_t$ are the number of deaths in the region.

Relationship between the blocks

As mentioned before, the *SZ* equations establish the relationship between the expected sectoral production and the different components of final demand, both inside and outside the region. The expected and observed sectoral productions are then compared, leading to the following expression

$$SX_{it} = SZ_{it}.\exp\left(F_{it}^{xt}\right) \tag{9.17}$$

in which the functions $F_{it}^{xt}()$ capture modifications in input output coefficients and in the composition of the final demand.

The connection between observed sectoral production and employment is given by the equations that capture the modifications of labor productivity in time. This can be written as:

$$SN_{it} = \frac{F_{it}^{xn}}{SX_{it}} \tag{9.18}$$

The sectoral employment levels obtained determine the income generated by production sectors through the equations that capture the trend in value added by each unit of labor, or:

$$SY_{it} = SN_{it}.F_{it}^{yn} \tag{9.19}$$

Finally, the income generated by production sectors influence some of the components of the final demand for goods and services, thus closing one of the basic sequences of the model.

The other important sequence is related to regional population, for it is one of the explanatory variables in the final demand equations and is endogenously determined in the model. It is assumed that the regional population is determined by the demand for labor in the region, with migration acting as an adjustment factor.   When demand for labor increases, population will increase accordingly; if there is no supply of labor in the region, labor will migrate from other states to serve the demand.

Estimation of equations

The estimation period of the equations is 1970-1993 and the projection period is 1994-2004. The regional input-output matrix refers to 1980 and is composed of 34 production sectors. It was obtained by the application of the location quotient method to the national matrix. Due to the scarcity of data on a regional scale, a large part of the research effort concentrated on the building up historical regional series; in order to do this, a series of suppositions and simplifications had to be made.

Final demand equations

Considering the state of São Paulo as an isolated region, the basic macroeconomic relationship should be (superscript *SP* refers to the state of São Paulo)

$$Y^{sp} = C^{sp} + I^{sp} + G^{sp} + \left(X^{sp} - M^{sp} \right) \tag{9.20}$$

where *Y* is gross domestic product, market prices; *C* is aggregate consumption of families; *I* = private sector total gross investment; *G* is government total expenditure (all levels, operational and investment), *X* is the total export of goods and services (to other states and/or countries) and *M* are total imports of goods and services (from other states and/or countries).

For the sake of estimation, the private sector total gross investment (I) was obtained as a residual. Since the variable estimated as the residual incorporates the estimation errors of the other variables, it is advisable to choose as the residual the variable most difficult to estimate: private investment.

For the regional GDP, data are available for 1980-1993; earlier values were estimated applying sectoral growth rates in the region to the 1980 values. The proportion of market price values to cost of factors values observed nationally was applied to regional GDP data, as the regional series are expressed in cost of factors values.

The consumption function estimated was [*C/POP*]$_t$ = 34.5 + .516*[*GDP/POP*]$_t$, R^2 = 82% with statistically significant (>5%) coefficients. For government expenditure, only state and municipal expenditure were considered, due to lack of information on federal expenditure in São Paulo. Since the proportion of these expenditures in the regional product and the global expenditure of the federal government is small, this omission should not be of great importance. The regional balance of trade was composed of net exports to other countries and to other states. Since the series of net export to other states was not continuous, interpolations were necessary in some cases; this was done by regressing the regional balance against the national GDP.

Production, employment and wage equations

Series of values for production, employment and wage for each sector were constructed and utilized for the sectoral forecasts of these variables. Here a great deal of research effort was concentrated, for consistent regional data are only available in census years. Intermediate values for sectors were obtained by interpolation, following the equations below. Let:

$$v_{t+1} = [V_{t+5}/V_t]^{(1/5)} V_t \qquad\qquad (9.21)$$

with V indicating the census value and t the beginning of the inter census period. Then the sectoral index for each series (I) are computed:

$$i_{t+1} = I_{t+1}/\left[(I_{t+5}/I_t)^{(1/5)} I_t\right] \qquad\qquad (9.22)$$

The numerator in the second part of the equation above is the yearly observed sectoral index; the denominator indicates the expected value if the series grew every year by the geometrical yearly average. If $i>1$, the indicator has evolved above the geometrical average; if $i<1$, it evolved below the average. The values used in the estimations were $E_{t+1} = v_{t+1} i_{t+1}$. For the majority of cases, regional sectoral indexes were used; when these were not available, national indexes were used.

Results: the basic case

The equations described above were estimated by regression analysis. In most cases, OLS were used; in some, the Cochrane-Orcutt recursive method was employed. A total of 145 equations were estimated for (numbers in parentheses indicate number of equations of this type):

1. *Final demand* (6) - SCP- family consumption; SIPC- private investment-construction; SIPE-private investment-machinery and equipment; SCG-government expenditure-operational; SICG-government investment-construction; and SIGE-government investment-machinery and equipment

2. *Expected sectoral production SZ_i* (34)

3. *Adjustment of coefficients* (34) - $Ln\left(\dfrac{SX_i}{SZ_i}\right)_t = F_{it}^{xz}(\ )$

4. *Income generated by production sectors* (34) - $Ln\left(\dfrac{SY_i}{SN_i}\right)_t = F_{it}^{yn}(\ )$

5. *Employment* (34) - $Ln\left(\dfrac{SX_i}{SN_i}\right)_t = F_{it}^{xn}(\ )$

6. *Population* (3) - *SLF* - labor force; *SN* - formal employment; *SUNRT* - unemployment rate.

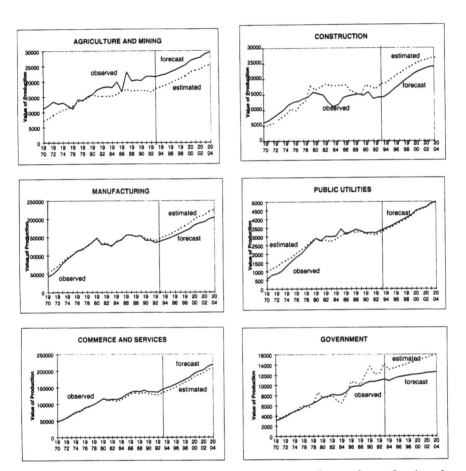

Figure 9.2   Observed, estimated and forecast values of production by groups of sectors

All regressions passed the appropriate statistical tests. For the sake of simplicity of exposition, only general results will be presented in this chapter.   Results for expected sectoral production, adjustment of coefficients and forecast sectoral production are given in figure 9.2, for groups of sectors. The solid lines indicate observed production values for the estimation period (1970-93) and forecasts for the period 1994-2004. The dotted lines indicate production values that would be observed if the technical coefficients and the structure of the final demand remained constant. The differences between the solid lines and the dotted lines throughout the observation period led to the estimation of functions incorporating the changes in coefficients and in the final demand structure; these functions were then used to calculate the forecast values. The dotted lines for the forecast period are only presented to indicate the effect of the introduction of the adjustment on the coefficients in relation to the constant coefficient alternative. It can be seen in the figure that the adjustment of coefficients improved the forecasts for most of the sectors.

Results from the scenarios produced by the national model

As for the final demand and population variables, figure 9.3 presents the ratio of the regional to the national values and figure 9.4 shows observed and forecast values for income, consumption and investment. As for figure 9.3, the ratios given for the observation period are the observed ones, based on which regressions were estimated; for the forecast period, they are the proportions between the values predicted by the regional model and the values predicted by the national model to which the regional model is attached.

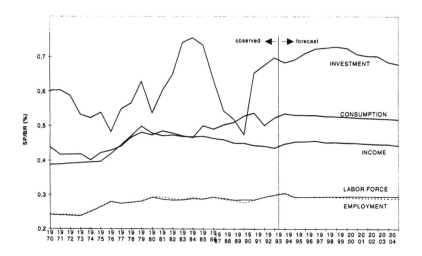

Figure 9.3   Consistency of Forecasts: São Paulo/Brazil

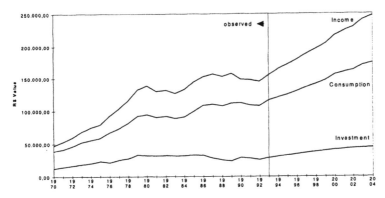

Figure 9.4   Final demand components

As can be seen in figure 9.3, there is nothing in the forecasts that indicates a sharp change in the trend observed in the estimation period. The only exception is private investment since in this case the forecasts led to a very low rate of investment for the state. Although this is the natural result of the application of the estimated regression, the available information on the regional economy suggests that it is better to make the assumption that the rate of investment in the region will remain constant at the 1993 level. The numbers displayed in figure 9.4 also indicate the same continuation of the past trend. In this case, the numbers are probably too optimistic, but they result from the scenarios produced by the national model.

Estimating the impacts of shocks on the regional economy

In this section the impacts of three different shocks on the regional economy will be simulated to illustrate the type of applications that can be made of the model. The shocks are: (a) a drastic drought that reduces agricultural production by 20% in one specific year; (b) the installation of a new automobile assembly plant; and (c) the stagnation of a traditional sector in the regional economy - textiles. The main aspects of the shocks are:

Agriculture - a severe drought takes place in the year 1996 and reduces the forecast production of the region by 20%.

Automobile - a new assembly plant is established in the region. Total investment is R$ 200 million (approximately USD 200 million), according to the sectoral distribution shown in table 9.1 below. The plant will start production in 1998, with sales of R$ 240 million per year.

Textiles - Starting in 1997, production will fall by half in the sector by the year 2004, as compared to expected production for that year. Production values are shown in table 9.2.

Table 9.1   Automobile impact scenario
Values (R$ million)

Sector	1996	1997	Total
Construction			
Material	20	20	40
Labor	15	15	30
Equipment			
Machinery	40	40	80
Electrical	10	10	20
Imports	15	15	30
Total	100	100	200

Table 9.2   Textile impact scenario
Values (R$ million)

Year	Basic forecast (A)	Production reduction (B)	(A)/(B)
1996	5,091.5	-	-
1997	5,250.0	444.2	.08
1998	5,406.0	869.7	.16
1999	5,559.9	1,278.1	.23
2000	5,859.3	1,817.8	.31
2001	5,977.1	2,162.3	.36
2002	6,047.9	2,447.1	.40
2003	6,312.9	2,914.1	.46
2004	6,416.2	3,208.1	.50

Table 9.3   Sectoral impacts on production of a new automobile plant in the region

Year	Agric & Mining	Construction	Manufng	Public Utilities	Commerce and Services	Govt	All Sectors
1994	0%	0%	0%	0%	0%	0%	0%
1995	0%	0%	0%	0%	0%	0%	0%
1996	0.02%	0.12%	0.07%	0.03%	0.02%	0.00%	0.04%
1997	0.00%	0.12%	0.07%	0.03%	0.02%	0.00%	0.04%
1998	0.00%	0.01%	0.32%	0.12%	0.07%	0.01%	0.16%
1999	0.08%	0.01%	0.31%	0.12%	0.07%	0.01%	0.16%
2000	0.08%	0.01%	0.29%	0.11%	0.06%	0.01%	0.15%
2001	0.08%	0.01%	0.29%	0.11%	0.06%	0.01%	0.14%
2002	0.07%	0.01%	0.28%	0.11%	0.06%	0.01%	0.14%
2003	0.07%	0.01%	0.27%	0.10%	0.06%	0.01%	0.13%
2004	0.07%	0.01%	0.26%	0.10%	0.05%	0.01%	0.13%

Table 9.4   Sectoral impacts on production of a decrease in textiles in the region

Year	Agric & Mining	Construction	Manufng	Public Utilities	Commerce and Services	Govt	All Sectors
1994	0%	0%	0%	0%	0%	0%	0%
1995	0%	0%	0%	0%	0%	0%	0%
1996	0%	0%	0%	0%	0%	0%	0%
1997	-0.26%	-0.01%	-0.64%	-0.23%	-0.13%	-0.02%	-0.31%
1998	-0.94%	-0.02%	-1.15%	-0.43%	-0.24%	-0.03%	-0.58%
1999	-0.49%	-0.03%	-1.63%	-0.61%	-0.34%	-0.05%	-0.83%
2000	-0.69%	-0.04%	-2.20%	-0.83%	-0.46%	-0.06%	-1.11%
2001	-1.10%	-0.05%	-2.55%	-0.97%	-0.53%	-0.07%	-1.29%
2002	-1.23%	-0.05%	-2.83%	-1.08%	-0.59%	-0.08%	-1.43%
2003	-1.41%	-0.06%	-3.24%	-1.25%	-0.68%	-0.10%	-1.64%
2004	-1.52%	-0.07%	-3.50%	-1.35%	-0.73%	-0.10%	-1.77%

Table 9.5   Sectoral impacts on production of a 20% decrease in agriculture in the region

Year	Agric & Mining	Construction	Manufng	Public Utilities	Commerce and Services	Govt	All Sectors
1994	0%	0%	0%	0%	0%	0%	0%
1995	0%	0%	0%	0%	0%	0%	0%
1996	-23.33%	-0.08%	-1.73%	-1.52%	-1.09%	-0.22%	-2.52%
1997	0%	0%	0%	0%	0%	0%	0%
1998	0%	0%	0%	0%	0%	0%	0%
1999	0%	0%	0%	0%	0%	0%	0%
2000	0%	0%	0%	0%	0%	0%	0%
2001	0%	0%	0%	0%	0%	0%	0%
2002	0%	0%	0%	0%	0%	0%	0%
2003	0%	0%	0%	0%	0%	0%	0%
2004	0%	0%	0%	0%	0%	0%	0%

Table 9.6   Sectoral impacts on employment of a new automobile plant in the region

Year	Agric & Mining	Construction	Manufng	Public Utilities	Commerce and Services	Govt	All Sectors
1994	0%	0%	0%	0%	0%	0%	0%
1995	0%	0%	0%	0%	0%	0%	0%
1996	0.02%	0.12%	0.13%	0.03%	0.03%	0.00%	0.05%
1997	0.00%	0.12%	0.12%	0.03%	0.03%	0.00%	0.05%
1998	0.00%	0.01%	0.33%	0.12%	0.08%	0.01%	0.13%
1999	0.08%	0.01%	0.31%	0.12%	0.08%	0.01%	0.13%
2000	0.08%	0.01%	0.30%	0.11%	0.07%	0.01%	0.12%
2001	0.08%	0.01%	0.29%	0.11%	0.07%	0.01%	0.12%
2002	0.07%	0.01%	0.28%	0.11%	0.07%	0.01%	0.12%
2003	0.07%	0.01%	0.27%	0.10%	0.06%	0.01%	0.11%
2004	0.07%	0.01%	0.27%	0.10%	0.06%	0.01%	0.11%

Table 9.7   Sectoral impacts on employment of a decrease in textiles in the region

Year	Agric & Mining	Construction	Manufng	Public Utilities	Commerce and Services	Govt	All Sectors
1994	0%	0%	0%	0%	0%	0%	0%
1995	0%	0%	0%	0%	0%	0%	0%
1996	0%	0%	0%	0%	0%	0%	0%
1997	0.00%	-0.01%	-0.98%	-0.23%	-0.14%	-0.02%	-0.36%
1998	0.00%	-0.02%	-1.85%	-0.43%	-0.27%	-0.03%	-0.68%
1999	-0.69%	-0.03%	-2.65%	-0.61%	-0.39%	-0.05%	-0.98%
2000	-0.94%	-0.04%	-3.61%	-0.83%	-0.52%	-0.06%	-1.34%
2001	-1.10%	-0.05%	-4.23%	-0.97%	-0.61%	-0.07%	-1.57%
2002	-1.22%	-0.05%	-4.73%	-1.08%	-0.68%	-0.08%	-1.75%
2003	-1.41%	-0.06%	-5.46%	-1.25%	-0.78%	-0.10%	-2.03%
2004	-1.52%	-0.07%	-5.93%	-1.35%	-0.84%	-0.10%	-2.21%

Table 9.8   Sectoral impacts on employment of a 20% decrease in agriculture in the region

Year	Agric & Mining	Construction	Manufng	Public Utilities	Commerce and Services	Govt	All Sectors
1994	0%	0%	0%	0%	0%	0%	0%
1995	0%	0%	0%	0%	0%	0%	0%
1996	-23.32%	-0.08%	-1.67%	-1.52%	-1.21%	-0.22%	-4.13%
1997	0%	0%	0%	0%	0%	0%	0%
1998	0%	0%	0%	0%	0%	0%	0%
1999	0%	0%	0%	0%	0%	0%	0%
2000	0%	0%	0%	0%	0%	0%	0%
2001	0%	0%	0%	0%	0%	0%	0%
2002	0%	0%	0%	0%	0%	0%	0%
2003	0%	0%	0%	0%	0%	0%	0%
2004	0%	0%	0%	0%	0%	0%	0%

Table 9.9   Aggregate impacts of a new automobile plant

Year	Production Direct	Indir.	Total	Multip.	Employment (formal) Direct	Indir.	Total	Multip.	Income Direct	Indir.	Total	Multip.
1996	70	107	177	2.52	2.217	2.666	4.884	2.20	50	59	108	2.18
1997	70	107	177	2.53	2.257	2.663	4.920	2.18	51	60	111	2.17
1998	240	449	689	2.87	3.401	9.777	13.177	3.87	148	252	400	2.71
1999	240	448	688	2.87	3.402	9.664	13.066	3.84	148	254	402	2.72
2000	240	447	687	2.86	3.404	9.529	12.933	3.80	148	255	403	2.73
2001	240	446	686	2.86	3.405	9.437	12.842	3.77	148	256	404	2.74
2002	240	445	685	2.85	3.405	9.368	12.773	3.75	147	258	405	2.75
2003	240	444	684	2.85	3.406	9.269	12.675	3.72	147	258	406	2.75
2004	240	443	683	2.85	3.406	9.206	12.613	3.70	147	259	407	2.76

Table 9.10   Aggregate impacts of a decrease in the textiles sector

	Production				Employment (formal)				Income			
Year	Direct	Indir.	Total	Multi	Direct	Indir.	Total	Multi	Direct	Indir.	Total	Multi
1997	-444	-818	-1262	2.8	-14103	-20293	-34396	2.4	-215	-412	-627	2.9
1998	-870	-1608	-2477	2.8	-27650	-39532	-67182	2.4	-430	-820	-1250	2.9
1999	-1278	-2370	-3648	2.9	-40893	-57918	-98810	2.4	-647	-1225	-1872	2.9
2000	-1818	-3396	-5214	2.9	-58487	-82333	-	2.4	-954	-1782	-2737	2.9
2001	-2162	-4050	-6212	2.9	-70356	-97892	-	2.4	-1163	-2150	-3313	2.8
2002	-2447	-4588	-7035	2.9	-79984	-	-	2.4	-1333	-2454	-3787	2.8
2003	-2914	-5501	-8415	2.9	-96074	-	-	2.4	-1641	-2977	-4618	2.8
2004	-3208	-6068	-9276	2.9	-	-	-	2.4	-1838	-3306	-5144	2.8
1997	-444	-818	-1262	2.8	-14103	-20293	-34396	2.4	-215	-412	-627	2.9

Table 9.11   Aggregate impacts of a 20% reduction in the agriculture sector

	Production				Employment (formal)				Income			
Year	Direct	Indir.	Total	Multi	Direct	Indir.	Total	Multi	Direct	Indir.	Total	Multi
1996	-4595	-5295	-9890	2.2	-247927	-133762	-381689	1.5	-2942	-2750	-5691	1.9
1997	0.00	0.02	0.02	0.0	-	0	0	0.4	-	0	0	0.0
1998	0.00	0.01	0.01	0.0	-	0	0	0.4	-	0	0	0.0
1999	0.00	0.01	0.01	0.0	-	0	0	0.4	-	0	0	0.0
2000	0.00	0.01	0.01	0.0	-	0	0	0.2	-	0	0	0.0
2001	0.00	0.01	0.01	0.0	-	0	0	0.1	-	0	0	0.0
2002	0.00	0.01	0.01	0.0	-	0	0	0.3	-	0	0	0.0
2003	0.00	0.00	0.00	0.0	-	0	0	0.2	-	0	0	0.0
2004	0.00	0.01	0.01	0.0	-	0	0	0.2	-	0	0	0.0

The agricultural shock is a once and for all natural shock; the other two exemplify policy alternatives for the state government: attracting new plants, accepting the so called "fiscal war" that takes place among neighboring states, or preserving the more vulnerable sectors already installed within the region. The detailed results by sector are presented in tables 9.3 to 9.8; the aggregate results are in tables 9.9 through 9.11.

As can be seen in tables 9.3 to 9.8, the impacts are differentiated temporally and sectorally. The agricultural shock has considerable impact in the shock year, reducing total production by 2.52% in that year; the final impact on agriculture is −23.33%, since indirect impacts are added to the original -20% shock simulated. A total of 381,689 jobs will be lost in that year, 247,927 directly and 133,762 indirectly.

The decrease in the textiles sector has the largest impact. Since the shock continues year after year, increasing its importance every year, the impact grows over time. In 2004, state total production will fall by 1.77%, and manufacturing production by 3.5%. Employment will fall by 5.93% in manufacturing and 2.21% in aggregate.

The new automobile plant, notwithstanding the political dividends that it may bring to politicians, has a moderate economic impact, with manufacturing production will grow by .26% and total production by .13% by the year 2004; employment figures are slightly lower. Of course, the sizes of the shocks are different, with the decline in textiles being sharp and the increase in automobile production small, compared to total regional production. The multipliers presented in tables 9.9 to 9.10 provide a better way of comparison. It can be seen that the employment multiplier for the automobile shock is 3.7 (in 2004) and the textiles sector is 2.4. Production and income multipliers are closer for textile and automobile shocks, but much lower for the agriculture shock.

Conclusions

In this chapter, an econometric input output model for the state of São Paulo, Brazil, was presented. The main features of the model are its connection to the national economy through three different links and the adjustment in the technical coefficients over time. For the estimation of the model a large part of the research time was devoted to the preparation of time series of data for the period 1970-1993 for the final demand components and sectoral production, employment and value added. Based on these series, the model was estimated and forecasts were derived for the period 1994-2004.

The results indicate that the forecasts are reasonable, with no disruption in observed trends. They were analyzed both individually, comparing the results for the observation period to the forecast period, and in relation to the national values of similar variables. The comparison of the results, including the adjustment of the coefficients to the results that would have been obtained without the adjustments, indicates a significant improvement. Finally, three different shocks on the regional economy were simulated and their results analyzed. Models of this kind have been completed for Minas Gerais, Ceará and the Northeast, offering the potential for comparative analysis of the structure of the regional economies of Brazil.

Notes

[1] For simplicity of exposition, the state of São Paulo will be referred as "the region".

[2] This is not equivalent to saying that investment and government expenditure are secondary factors in the promotion of the region's development. It only means that their impact on employment and income can be simulated in the same way as the impacts of increments in net exports.

[3] An "S" before the variable's symbol indicates São Paulo state (or the "region"); a "B" indicates Brazil; "t" refers to year.

[4] The sectoral structure of consumption was analyzed for three different years (1973, 1981 and 1991), in which family budget surveys produced to establish the weight of goods and services in the São Paulo City consumer price index were available. The results indicate no important structural changes at the sectoral aggregation level adopted in the model.

[5] Further details may be found in Israilevich *et al.*, (1997).

References

Azzoni, C. R. (1993) "Economia de São Paulo: ainda a locomotiva?" *São Paulo em Perspectiva*, 7, 2-13.

Baer, W. (1995) *The Brazilian Economy: Growth and Development*, New York, Praeger, 4th edition.

Conway, Jr. R. S. (1990) "The Washington projection and simulation model: a regional interindustry econometric model," *International Regional Science Review*, 13, 141-165.

Diniz, C. C. (1994) "Poligonized development in Brazil: neither decentralization nor continued polarization," *International Journal of Urban and Regional Research*, 18, 293-314.

Fonseca, M. A. R. (1991) "Um modelo macroeconométrico de simulação e previsão," *Anais do XIII Encontro Brasileiro de Econometria*, Curitiba.

Israilevich, P.R., G.J.D. Hewings, M. Sonis and G.R. Schindler, (1997) "Forecasting Structural Change with a Regional Econometric Input-Output Model," *Journal of Regional Science* 37, 565-90.

Willumsen, M. J. and Fonseca, E. G. ed. (1996) *The Brazilian economy: structure and performance*, Colorado, Lyne Riener.

Willumsen, M. J., A.E. Comune, and E.R. Pelin, (1991) "Construção da Matriz de Insumo-Produto para o Estado de São Paulo," *Relatório de Pesquisa*, Fundação Instituto de Pesquisas Econômicas, Fipe.

PART III: INFRASTRUCTURE ISSUES

10 Technical Efficiency and Returns to Scale in Local Public Spending in the Presence of Heterogeneous Data: The Brazilian Case

MARIA DA CONCEIÇÃO SAMPAIO DE SOUSA and
FRANCISCO S. RAMOS

Introduction

Measuring technical efficiency among decision-making units (DMUs) by using non-parametric approaches, such as Data Envelopment Analysis (DEA) and Free Disposal Hull (FDH), has been widely used in different economic situations. The huge popularity of those approaches comes from their flexibility as they impose no functional forms a priori on the underlying technology. They require only the production set to fulfill such properties as free disposal, convexity, and piece-wise linearity of the technology. Those methodologies, particularly DEA, have been expanded to address important economics issues such as the evaluation of returns to scale of the DMUs.

Yet, such measurements may be seriously misguided when the pattern of observations is highly dispersed. For example, a main concern with FDH lies on the fact that, by lack of comparability, this methodology tends to declare a great number of observations efficient *by default* thus providing limited discriminatory power. This problem seems to become critical when the DMUs are highly heterogeneous. Moreover, when this dispersion is combined with a relatively small sample size, the FDH method, nearly, collapses by declaring most of the DMUs efficient *by default*. Concerning the DEA variants, as their measurements are very sensitive to the presence of *outliers*, super-efficient observations, heterogeneity may aggravate this problem and underestimate, substantially, efficiency scores as in those methods, the frontier is constituted by a

195

surprisingly small number of municipalities. Therefore, to make efficiency indexes credible it is crucial to verify to what extent the impact of heterogeneity, on those scores and rankings, is significant.

In such a context, it becomes clear that the generalization of the use of non-parametric efficiency measurements such as DEA and FDH techniques requires a careful examination of the sensibility of the estimated indexes to the presence of data heterogeneity of the data set. Only in this case one can obtain truly representative estimators whose credibility may justify its use in process of decision-making.

In previous papers, Sampaio de Sousa and Ramos de Souza (1998, 1999), by using such techniques, estimated the efficiency levels of the Brazilian municipalities aggregated by states and regions. This first attempt to evaluate the performance of Brazilian municipalities provided a tool, based on economic theory and sufficiently flexible to be used as a permanent and systematic way to evaluate local governments. Nevertheless, is important to stress the exploratory nature of those studies. Efficiency scores should be used carefully as more detailed analysis is required to determine if the measured scores reflect genuine technical inefficiencies or if they are explained by the action of other factors such as heterogeneity and the particular set of chosen hypotheses.

The main objective of this chapter is, thus, twofold: firstly, we will compute DEA and FDH measures of technical efficiency and returns to scale, for public services provided by municipalities of the Brazilian Northeast and Southeast regions. Secondly, we will try to evaluate the sensibility of those computed efficiency scores when the DMUs are highly heterogeneous, as is the case with the Brazilian municipalities.

This chapter is organized as follows. Section 2 discusses the methodology used to compute the efficiency levels of Brazilian municipalities. Section 3 presents the data-base and discusses the physical indicators chosen as proxies for the supply of public services as well as the dispersion of the data set while section 4 discusses non-parametric efficiency calculations for FDH and DEA reference technologies. Section 5 covers the relationship between efficiency, heterogeneity of the data set and returns to scale. Finally, section 6 summarizes the main conclusions. Appendix A lists some summary statistics for the data set.

Data envelopment analysis and the free disposal reference hull measurements of technical inefficiencies

Non-parametric deterministic approaches to efficiency measurements are characterized by the use of very weak assumptions concerning the reference technology. Except for the usual regularity axioms such as the bounded-ness and closed-ness of the technology, those methods rely on very simple hypothesis such as convexity and strong free disposability in inputs and outputs. In particular, the linear programming based techniques, known as DEA (Data Envelopment Analysis), initiated a course of developments in which new applications, new models, new methods and concepts vigorously interacted in a great variety of ways.[1] More recently a new technique was developed known as FDH. Below we will briefly describe those methodologies.

Data Envelopment Analysis Reference Technology

For each decision making unit (DMU), the technology transforms nonnegative inputs $x^k = (x_{k1},...,x_{kN}) \in \mathfrak{R}^N_+$ into the non-negative outputs $y^k = (y_{k1},...,y_{kM}) \in \mathfrak{R}^M_+$. For the input-based measures of technical efficiency, the technology is represented by its production possibility set $T = \{(x,y): x \text{ can produce } y\}$, the set of all feasible input-output vectors. The input correspondence for the DEA reference technology, characterized by constant returns to scale, C, and strong disposability of inputs, S, defines a piecewise linear technology constructed on the basis of observed input-output combinations:[2]

$$L(y|C,S) = \{x: y \le zM, zN \le x, z \in \mathfrak{R}^K_+, y \in \mathfrak{R}^M_+\} \qquad (10.1)$$

The $k \times m$ matrix M contains the m observed outputs of each of the k observations in the data set, N is the $k \times n$ matrix of observed inputs and z is the $1 \times k$ vector of intensity parameters.[3] Now, for each activity, the technical efficiency on inputs, F_i, may be defined, as:

$$F_i(y^k, x^k | C, S) = \min\{\theta: \theta x \in L(y^k | C, S)\} \qquad (10.2)$$

This radial efficiency measure is always situated between zero and one. The efficient production on the isoquant is indicated by the unity. Thus, $1 - \theta$ represent the proportion at which the inputs could be reduced without changing the production. By using the technology specified in

(10.1), technical efficiency for the municipality k may be computed as the solution for the following linear program:

$$F_i\left(y^k, x^k \mid C, S\right) = \theta^{DEA-C} = \min_{\theta, z} \theta \tag{10.3}$$

subject to:

$$\theta x_{nk} - \sum_{k=1}^{K} z_k x_{nk} \geq 0 \quad n = 1, ..., N$$

$$\sum_{j=1}^{K} z_k y_{km} \geq y_{rk} \quad m = 1, ..., M$$

$$\theta, z_k \geq 0 \quad k = 1, ..., K$$

This first version of the DEA methodology – henceforth mentioned as DEA-C – implies strong restrictions concerning the production set. In particular, this methodology presupposes constant returns to scale. This hypothesis can be easily relaxed by modifying the restrictions on the intensity vector, z. Maintaining the hypothesis of strong disposability Färe, Grosskopf and Lovell (1985, 1994) extended this technique to include the existence of non increasing returns to scale, (N), by defining the reference technology as:

$$L\left(y \mid N, S\right) = \left\{ x : y \leq zM, zN \leq x, z \in \Re_+^K, \sum_{k=1}^{K} z_k \leq 1, y \in \Re_+^M \right\} \tag{10.4}$$

Here, the sum of the intensity variables can not exceed the unity implying that the different activities can be contracted but can not be expanded limitlessly. The computation of the efficiency levels is given by solving the following linear program:

$$F_i\left(y^k, x^k \mid N, S\right) = \theta^{DEA-N} = \min_{\theta, z} \theta \tag{10.5}$$

subject to:

$$\theta x_{nk} - \sum_{k=1}^{K} z_k x_{nk} \geq 0 \quad n = 1, ..., N$$

$$\sum_{j=1}^{K} z_k y_{km} \geq y_{rk} \quad m = 1, ..., M$$

$$\sum_{k=1}^{K} z_k \leq 1$$

$$\theta, z_k \geq 0 \quad k = 1, ..., K$$

Such efficiency levels are known as the FGL indexes or DEA-N. Adding the restriction that the sum of the intensity variables should be one imply that returns to scale are variable (V):

$$L\left(y|V,S\right)=\left\{x:y\le zM\,,zN\le x,\ z\in\mathfrak{R}_{+}^{K},\ \sum_{k=1}^{K}z_{k}\le1,y\in\mathfrak{R}_{+}^{M}\right\}\qquad(10.6)$$

Here, activities can not expanded or contracted radially without limits and radial contractions to the origin are also excluded. The feasible set of activities is formed by all convex combination of observed activities, located on the boundary of the productive set. We have, thus, increasing returns for low levels of production and decreasing returns for higher levels. The efficiency indexes associated with this technology - henceforth denominated DEA-V – are obtained by solving the following linear program:

$$F_{i}\left(y^{k},x^{k}|V,S\right)=\theta^{DEA-V}=\min_{\theta,z}\theta\qquad(10.7)$$

subject to:

$$\theta x_{nk}-\sum_{k=1}^{K}z_{k}x_{nk}\ge0\qquad n=1,...,N$$

$$\sum_{j=1}^{K}z_{k}y_{km}\ge y_{rk}\qquad m=1,...,M$$

$$\sum_{k=1}^{K}z_{k}\le1$$

$$\theta,z_{k}\ge0\qquad k=1,...,K$$

In the literature this model is referred as the BCC (Banker, Charnes and Cooper (1984)[4] model.

The Free Disposal Hull - FDH - Technology

Even though representing an alternative to parametric approaches, DEA techniques still rely on hypotheses very restrictive on the structure of the production set. Weaker assumptions have been proposed by Deprins, Simar and Tulkens (1984). They postulate that the frontier of the production set is simply the boundary of the Free Disposal Hull (FDH) of the data set. Strong disposability of inputs and outputs is maintained as well as variable returns to scale but no convexity hypothesis is required. In this method - henceforth referred to as FDH - the frontier is obtained by comparing inputs and outputs so as to establish the dominant points.

The FDH reference technology (equation (10.8)) assumes only strong input disposability. In this method, the frontier of the productive set is obtained by comparing inputs and outputs in order to establish the dominant points.

$$L(y|V - FDH, S) = \begin{cases} x : y \le zM, zN \le x, z \in \mathfrak{R}_+^K, \sum_{k=1}^{K} z_k \le 1, \\ z_k \in [0,1], y \in \mathfrak{R}_+^M \end{cases} \tag{10.8}$$

Consistent with variables returns to scale, the elements of the intensity vector z are restricted to sum to unity. The integrality restriction on the intensity variables imply that linear combinations of different observations are excluded and convexity is no longer imposed on the technology. In terms of DEA techniques this requires adding to program (10.7), the following restriction:[5]

$$z_k \in [0,1], \quad k = 1,..., K \tag{10.9}$$

Figures 10.1 and 10.2 (Tulkens (1990)) illustrate well this methodology for the one-input one-output case and allow its comparison with the DEA techniques (DEA-C, DEA-N and DEA-V). In figure 10.1, the points b e k f describe the typical staircase-shaped frontier of the production set. By construction, every inefficient observation is necessarily dominated by one or several observations. Thus, observation k is efficient as it dominates the observation a: comparing point k to point a, it can be seen the it is possible to produce more with a smaller quantity of input. On the other hand, the observation b neither dominates nor is dominated by any other point and, thus, is declared efficient by *default*.

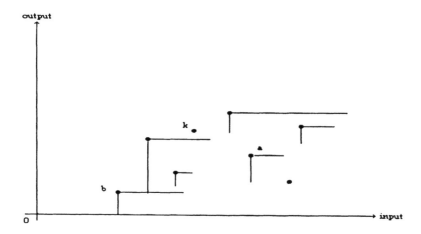

Figure 10.1   FDH Technique to Build up the Production Frontier

Figure 10.2 shows the FDH frontier as well as the DEA-C, DEA-N, DEA-V, and FDH frontiers. The implications of the convexity assumption are clearly perceived. The proportionality hypothesis in DEA-C frontier presupposes constant returns to scale. The frontier of the polyhedral production set is given by the segment OCG. For the DEA-N method, characterized by constant and decreasing returns of scale, the frontier takes the piecewise linear form represented by line OCEF. Excluding the origin, the frontier of the production set is given by the segment ABCEF corresponding to the variant DEA-V, which presents variable returns to scale. Finally, the FDH frontier is the staircase line ABCDEF.

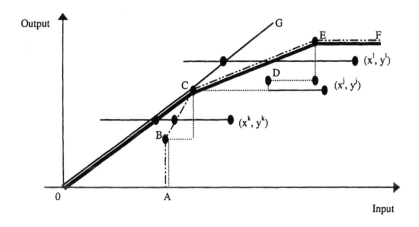

Figure 10.2 Alternative efficiency measures by using DEA-C, DEA-N, DEA-V, and FDH

Assessing returns to scale in DEA methodologies

The measurement of local returns to scale in DEA models was initiated by Banker (1984). It is based on summing the optimal activity vector z on a constant returns to scale technology.[6] This author proposed also a second method based on inspecting the sign of the shadow price of the convexity constraint. Yet, as pointed out by Chang and Guh (1991) both techniques do not hold in presence of multiple optimal solutions for this sum. Banker and Thrall (1992) generalized both methods to cope with such a problem.

The third method was first proposed by Färe, Grosskopf and Lovell (1985) by comparing the efficiency indexes for the different DEA variants. Indeed, since these methodologies are nested, the efficiency measures can be ordered as follows:

$$0 < F_i\left(y^k, x^k \mid C, S\right) \le F_i\left(y^k, x^k \mid N, S\right) \le$$
$$\le F_i\left(y^k, x^k \mid V, S\right) \le F_i\left(y^k, x^k \mid V - FDH, S\right) \le 1 \qquad (10.10)$$

This ordering, known as the FGL (Färe, *et al.*, 1994) Inequality, extended to include the FDH index, provides information on local returns to scale.[7] Clearly, the variants characterized by variable returns to scale envelop the data tightly. Thus, the efficiency measurements produced by the FDH technique are higher as this method use hypotheses less restrictive. On the other extreme, the method DEA-C presents lower indexes due to the use of proportionality hypothesis constant returns).

Defining the input-oriented scale efficiency measure, S_i, as:

$$S_i\left(y^k, x^k\right) = F_i\left(y^k, x^k \mid C, S\right) / F_i\left(y^k, x^k \mid V, S\right), \quad k = 1, 2, ..., K \qquad (10.11)$$

this ratio shows the lowest possible input combination that can produce the same output in the long run as a technically efficient combination on the variable returns to scale technology. In view of (10.10) and (10.11), we have:

$$0 < S\left(y^k, x^k\right) \le 1 \qquad (10.12)$$

If $S\left(y^k, x^k\right) = 1$, the technology exhibits constant returns to scale at the observation being evaluated.[8] When $S\left(y^k, x^k\right) < 1$, the point is to know if the inefficiency is due to the existence of low levels of production in a region characterized by increasing returns or if such inefficiency is caused by an excessively higher production in a region marked by decreasing returns. Figure 10.2 illustrates well this point; the inefficiency of activity $\left(y^j, x^j\right)$ results from increasing returns to scale whereas the inefficiency of activity $\left(y^i, x^i\right)$ comes from the existence of decreasing returns to scale. Therefore, the scale economies that characterize the different activities can be inferred by comparing the appropriate indexes. Thus, if $S\left(y^k, x^k\right) < 1$ and $F_i\left(y^j, x^j \mid C, S\right) = F_i\left(y^j, x^j \mid N, S\right)$, the inefficiencies result from the existence of increasing returns to scale; if $S\left(y^k, x^k\right) < 1$ and

$F_i\left(y^j, x^j \middle| C, S\right) < F_i\left(y^j, x^j \middle| N, S\right)$, then, scale inefficiency is due to the presence of decreasing returns to scale.[9]

Data

The implementation of the methodologies outlined above requires information about aggregate total costs (inputs) and the quantity of public services available to the population (outputs). In view of the large number of municipalities and the interregional income disparities typical of Brazil, as well as to obtain meaningful comparisons, the municipalities were aggregated by region.[10] Due to obvious space constraints, we will discuss only results for the Northeast and Southeast regions. The analysis can be applied, *mutatis mutandis,* to the other regions.[11]

Table 10.1   Input and Output Indicators and the Corresponding Municipal Services

Indicators	Code	Source	Municipal Services of which indicators serve as proxies
Input Indicator			
1. Current Spending	1.DSP92_C	STN[a]	1. Aggregate total costs
Output Indicators			
1.Total resident population	1. POP91_T	IBGE[b]	1. Administrative services
2. Domiciles with access to safe water	2. DOM91_A	IBGE	2. Public health services
3. Domiciles served by garbage collection	3. DOM91_L	IBGE	3. Public health services
4. Illiterate population	4. ANALF91	IBGE	4. Educational services
5. Enrollment in primary and secondary municipal schools	5. EDUC	MEC[c]	5. Educational services

Sources: [a]*STN - Secretaria do Tesouro Nacional (National Treasure Secretariat)*
            [b]*IBGE - Instituto Brasileiro de Estatística, Censo Demográfico de 1991*
            [c]*MEC - Ministério da Educação e Desportos*

Input and output indicators for the Brazilian municipalities

Aggregate total costs were computed as the value of municipal current spending (input).[12] As for output measurements, due to the impossibility of quantifying directly the supply of public services, they were approximated by a set of selected indicators, which are observable factors taken as proxies for the services supplied. After a careful choice, six output indicators were retained. A list of inputs and outputs are provided in Table 10.1.

Data for current spending were obtained from the Secretaria do Tesouro Nacional (STN). The data for output indicators Ns. 1 to 4, on Table 10.1, were obtained from the 1991 Population Census. Data on enrollment in primary and secondary municipal schools (indicator 5) refer to 1991 and were provided by the Coordenadoria Geral do SEEC/INEP of the Ministério da Educação e dos Desportos (MEC). Below, those indicators will be briefly discussed.

Current spending (DSP92_C) corresponds to the total amount of municipal current expenditure for 1992 as defined by Law 4320/64. It is expressed in cruzeiros, at prices of 1992.[13] Total population (POP91_T) refers to the population residing between August 31 and November 1, 1991. The variable Domiciles with safe water supply (DOM91_A) includes the number of those served by Rede Geral (potable water network). Domiciles served by garbage collection (DOM91_L) includes those where the garbage is collected directly or indirectly by public or private services. In the first case, the garbage is collected at the domicile whereas in the second case the garbage is dropped in garbage dumps and subsequently removed. Data on illiteracy (ANAL91) include people who are five years old or older and are unable to read and write a simple letter in their current idiom. Finally, student enrollment (EDUC) is the sum of students enrolled in the preprimary, primary, and secondary municipal schools.

Table 10.2   Data Heterogeneity in the Northeast and Southeast Regions: Pearson (CVP) Variation Coefficient - %

Population class size	Northeast Number of Municipal.	Northeast Spending per capita	Northeast CVP (%) Total data	Southeast Number of Municipal.	Southeast Spending per capita	Southeast CVP (%) Total data
0-9999	431	71.58	58.87	651	102.86	79.84
10000-19999	521	48.37	48.86	340	66.97	62.09
20000-29999	239	123.40	132.34	114	56.55	49.96
>30000	238	65.89	80.80	220	60.21	67.94
0-99999	1429	103.03	141.08	1325	121.58	146.5

The descriptive statistics of the sample of Brazilian municipalities are given in Table A-1 in the Appendix. Data heterogeneity was roughly estimated by calculating the Pearson Variation Coefficient for the data set. Two variants were calculated: the first one was computed based only on per capita spending and the other one computed the average variation coefficient for the whole set of inputs and outputs. They are shown in Table 10.2.

Notice that, as expected, the ungrouped data (0-99999) presents the highest coefficients for both regions. The Northeast cities, in the third population class (20000- 29999), also exhibit a substantial dispersion as the Pearson coefficients are as high as 123.4 and 132.3, respectively, for the pending per capita and total data. Finally, observe that the small municipalities of the Southeast are also characterized by high dispersion levels, probably, due to their intense dismembering in recent years.[14]

Data heterogeneity and efficiency measurements: summary of results

In order to examine the heterogeneity problem we have computed two different sets of efficiency indexes:

Ungrouped indexes: to serve as a benchmark, we calculated the efficiency indexes over the whole sample composed of 1,429 and 1,334 municipalities, respectively, for the Northeast and the Southeast regions. Afterwards, in order to establish relevant comparisons, efficiency scores were grouped into the same four classes of population as the grouped estimates.

Grouped indexes: to control for heterogeneity on the data set, the municipalities were grouped into a number of more homogeneous cohorts on the basis of size of the population.[15] Thus, the data were aggregated into four classes of population - 0-9999; 10000; 19999; 20000-29999; ≥ 30000. Then, efficiency scores were computed, separately, for each class of population.

The methodologies presented in Section 2 were used to measure technical efficiency for the Brazilian municipalities. Tables 10.3 to 10.4 summarize the results obtained. Tables 10.3 and 10.4 categorizes the municipalities of the Northeast and Southeast Regions into efficient and inefficient ones, according to three distinct methodologies: The CCR's method (DEA-C), the BCCs method (DEA-V), and the FDH technology.

Our results illustrate well the sensitivity of the efficiency measures to data heterogeneity. As a general rule, computing the efficiency indexes by grouping municipalities into more homogeneous classes of population considerably increases the number of efficient municipalities. Such a result is verified across regions and methodologies and applies, particularly, for the DEA techniques. For instance, for the northeast region, whereas the ungrouped DEA-V produces only 21 efficient municipalities out of the 1429 on the sample, the grouped estimates find 101 efficient ones, almost five times more than the ungrouped ones (table 10.3).

Notice also that FDH results strongly diverge from those obtained by using the DEA-C and DEA-V methods. Whereas the FDH methodology shows a larger proportion of efficient municipalities, on the other extreme, the hypothesis of constant returns incorporated in the variant DEA-C finds that only a few communes are efficient for all population class and regions; this proportion increases only slightly when the DEA-V method is used. Several reasons could be invoked to explain such divergence.

First, the frontier of cost efficiency computed by using FDH is based on a stricter concept of domination than the frontiers calculated by the DEA methods. A municipality is *FDH dominated* if and only if all his output indicators are inferior to the ones of an efficient municipality - effectively observed - with which it is compared, and its current spending is equal or superior to the expenses of this dominant municipality. On the other hand, a municipality is *DEA-dominated* by a fictitious observation defined as being a linear combination (convex if we use DEA-V) of a group of efficient municipalities. Therefore, FDH frontiers depend on the possibilities of factual comparison whereas DEA frontiers "fabricate" their own possibilities of comparison.

When, by lack of information, comparison is impossible, the FDH method declares the observation *efficient by default* leading to an increase in the number of efficient municipalities. Secondly, the convexity hypothesis incorporated in DEA frontiers puts an unnecessary restriction on the underlying technology for producing public services. In particular, the method DEA-C, that adjusts a cost-efficiency frontier characterized by constant returns, by ignoring local non-convexities, underestimates systematically the efficiency degree of the municipalities. Finally, recall from section 2, that the frontiers engendered by FDH, DEA-V, and DEA-C are "nested" in one another, with the FDH frontier staying more close to the data, and the DEA-C frontier being the farthest away. Such a close envelopment implies that the method FDH envelops the data tightly, thus having more municipalities being ranked as efficient.

Regions/ Classes of Population	Number of Municipalities	Efficient Municipalities - %						Inefficient Municipalities - %					
		DEA-C		DEA-V		FDH		DEA-C		DEA-V		FDH	
		U	G	U	G	U	G	U	G	U	G	U	G
Northeast													
0-9999	431	.23	3.2	.46	7.6	51.2	53.6	99.7	96.8	99.5	92.4	48.72	46.4
10000-19999	521	.00	1.7	.39	7.1	46.0	49.5	100	98.3	99.6	92.9	53.95	50.5
20000-29999	239	1.2	3.8	1.2	7.1	40.8	56.9	98.7	96.2	98.7	92.9	59.17	43.1
>30000	238	2.5	2.1	5.8	6.6	51.8	44.5	97.4	97.9	94.1	93.3	48.12	55.5
Total (#)	1429	10	31	21	101	682	731	1419	1398	1408	1328	747	709
Southeast													
0-9999	651	0.3	1.7	.92	4.4	44.8	46.4	99.6	98.3	99.0	95.6	55.1	53.6
10000-19999	340	0.6	2.4	.88	10.0	57.9	63.2	99.4	97.6	99.1	90.0	42.0	36.8
20000-29999	124	1.6	7.3	3.23	24.2	60.4	73.4	98.3	92.7	96.7	75.8	39.5	26.6
>30000	220	2.7	3.2	9.55	12.3	38.1	61.8	97.2	96.8	90.4	87.7	38.1	38.1
Total (#)	1335	12	35	34	120	648	744	1323	1300	1301	1215	635	591

Table 10.3 **Rating of the Municipalities by Methodology Northeast and Southeast Regions: Ungrouped (U) and Grouped (G) Estimations**

Notice that the degree of dispersion among cities not only affects the number of efficient communes but also, substantially, influences the magnitude of the computed scores (tables 10.4 – 10.6), particularly, when DEA techniques are used. Indeed, grouped efficiency estimates can lead to substantial increases in the mean scores, as is the case for the smallest cities of the northeast region (table 10.4 and 10.5). The DEA-C and DEA-V grouped efficiency scores for theses municipalities are 64 per cent greater than the ungrouped ones. Here, the size of the efficiency scores seems to be inversely related to the dispersion of the data set.

Table 10.4   Descriptive Statistics for DEA-C, Ungrouped (U) and Grouped (G) Efficiency Measures, Northeast and Southeast Regions

Population Classes	Number of Obs.	Mean		Standard Deviation		Skewness		Kurtosis		Minimum		Maximum	
Northeast		U	G	U	G	U	G	U	G	U	G	U	G
0- 9999	431	0.34	0.56	0.10	0.18	1.44	0.59	4.37	0.00	0.11	0.20	1.00	1.00
10000-19999	521	0.40	0.46	0.12	0.17	1.07	1.19	1.72	1.60	0.15	0.12	0.94	1.00
20000-29999	239	0.47	0.49	0.14	0.16	1.19	1.08	2.57	1.95	0.12	0.04	1.00	1.00
>30000	238	0.27	0.38	0.17	0.12	0.52	3.83	0.32	-21.83	0.13	0.00	1.00	1.00
Southeast													
0- 9999	651	0.39	0.52	0.13	0.17	0.70	0.58	1.26	0.38	0.12	0.15	1.00	1.00
10000-19999	340	0.48	0.63	0.15	0.16	0.55	0.03	0.70	0.06	0.11	0.14	1.00	1.00
20000-29999	124	0.53	0.67	0.17	0.18	0.89	0.18	0.82	-0.54	0.18	0.20	1.00	1.00
> 30000	220	0.57	0.60	0.20	0.19	0.18	-0.06	-0.22	-0.21	0.08	0.10	1.00	1.00

Table 10.5   Descriptive Statistics for DEA-V, Ungrouped (U) and Grouped (G) Efficiency Measures, Northeast and Southeast Regions

Population Classes	No. of Obs.	Mean		Standard Deviation		Skewness		Kurtosis		Minimum		Maximum	
Northeast		G	U	G	U	G	U	G	U	G	U	G	U
0- 9999	431	0.60	0.44	0.20	0.12	0.50	1.12	-0.47	2.77	0.20	0.15	1.00	1.00
10000-19999	521	0.54	0.46	0.21	0.13	0.82	0.99	-0.15	1.64	0.20	0.17	1.00	1.00
20000-29999	239	0.55	0.50	0.19	0.14	0.80	1.08	0.51	2.21	0.04	0.13	1.00	1.00
>30000	238	0.33	0.59	0.24	0.18	1.51	0.57	1.58	0.19	0.02	0.13	1.00	1.00
Southeast													
0- 9999	651	0.62	0.57	0.16	0.14	0.50	0.32	0.30	0.26	0.19	0.19	1.00	1.00
10000-19999	340	0.71	0.52	0.18	0.16	-0.13	0.42	-0.44	0.06	0.15	0.12	1.00	1.00
20000-29999	124	0.75	0.54	0.20	0.17	-0.22	0.85	-0.99	0.61	0.22	0.19	1.00	1.00
> 30000	220	0.67	0.61	0.21	0.22	-0.15	0.20	-0.61	-0.63	0.11	0.08	1.00	1.00

Skewness coefficients also help to detect the impact of heterogeneity on efficiency measures. Hence, the positive skewness for the DEA variants, indicating that the efficiency scores are biased downwards, are systematically higher for the ungrouped information where the problem of outliers - extremes values of the dimensional space of inputs and outputs that define non-parametric frontiers - is significant. Those atypical observations that differ significantly from the rest of the data, may considerably influence efficiency computations. By the same line of reasoning, the slightly negative skewness coefficients, for the Southeast municipalities, shown by the grouped DEA-V calculations, indicate a partial correction of the downwards bias presented by those estimations.

Once more, for the FDH calculations, such effects are clearly smaller. By grouping the information into more homogeneous classes of population, the FDH efficiency scores increases only slightly when compared with the ones calculated from the ungrouped set. The only exception is the class that includes the largest cities; in this case, grouping the data leads to a decrease on the average size of the estimated efficiencies. As will be seen in the next section, this result is explained by the problem of efficiency by default that artificially increases average scores. The distributions of the FDH indexes are negatively skewed, probably, reflecting the efficiency by default problem that tends to increases the average efficiency indexes. The positive kurtoses for the FDH measures - except for the Northeast largest municipalities - indicate that their distributions have fat tails relative to the normal distribution.

Table 10.6   **Descriptive Statistics, FDH Ungrouped (U) and Grouped (G) Efficiency Measures, Northeast and Southeast Regions**

Population Classes	No. of Obs.	Mean		Standard Deviation		Skewness		Kurtosis		Minimum		Maximum	
Northeast		G	U	G	U	G	U	G	U	G	U	G	U
0- 9999	431	0.89	0.89	0.15	0.15	-1.31	-1.21	0.59	0.32	0.38	0.38	1.00	1.00
10000-19999	521	0.87	0.87	0.18	0.16	-1.23	-0.99	0.72	-0.06	0.25	0.20	1.00	1.00
20000-29999	239	0.91	0.86	0.15	0.17	-2.03	-1.04	5.25	0.46	0.28	0.09	1.00	1.00
>30000	238	0.66	0.87	0.37	0.17	-0.45	-1.13	-1.58	0.04	0.17	0.08	1.00	1.00
Southeast													
0- 9999	651	0.89	0.39	0.14	0.13	-1.37	0.70	1.45	1.26	0.33	0.29	1.00	1.00
10000-19999	340	0.93	0.92	0.12	0.13	-2.13	-1.98	5.70	4.49	0.34	0.21	1.00	1.00
20000-29999	124	0.94	0.92	0.12	0.14	-2.16	-1.72	4.29	2.46	0.62	0.41	1.00	1.00
> 30000	220	0.91	0.91	0.17	0.17	-1.99	-1.99	3.56	3.56	0.42	0.17	1.00	1.00

To summarize, the distributions of the DEA indexes – particularly, DEA-C - are strongly shifted downwards as compared with the FDH results. This is due to the presence of non convexities and outliers that seriously distort the calculated efficiencies.   Clearly, the FDH-based efficiency scores are much less vulnerable to such observations, thus making this method more reliable.

Efficiency by default and data heterogeneity on FDH-based measurements

Recall that in the absence of a sufficient number of similar municipalities ("pairs") with which one given municipality can be compared, this municipality, instead of creating a relationship of the type dominant/dominated, is declared *efficient by default*. This ranking of efficiency does not result from any effective superiority but is due to the lack of information that would allow pertinent comparisons. In addition, by construction, the FDH concept of efficiency by default applies both to the municipality that presents the lowest level of spending and to those with the highest values for at least one output indicator. As the FDH method rests on the possibility of comparing observed municipalities, some large municipalities are declared efficient merely due to the impossibility of finding similar communes with which they could be compared. This does not mean that those municipalities are inefficient; it only means that if there were more municipalities in the relevant range, results could be different. This extreme form of the sparsity bias that characterizes the FDH technique certainly leads to a significant overestimation of the number of efficient municipalities and thus constitutes a serious shortcoming of the FDH approach.

Table 10.7 presents the information concerning this problem. Note that the phenomenon of efficiency by *default* is related to the degree of heterogeneity of the information as it depends not only on the totality of potential comparisons but also on the level of dispersion of the information. Thus, in the Northeast region, among the largest municipalities, the combined effect of a relatively small sample and a higher level of heterogeneity (see table 10.3) produces little discrimination as 69% of those cities are declared efficient by *default*. The number of such efficient municipalities is significantly lower for the more homogeneous Southeast cities of equivalent size.

Table 10.7   **Characterization of FDH Efficient Municipalities: Northeast and Southeast Regions**

	Total Grouped	Total Un-grouped	Efficient and Dominant Municipalities Grouped #	Grouped %	Ungrouped #	Ungrouped %	Municipalities Efficient by Default Grouped #	Grouped %	Ungrouped #	Ungrouped %
Northeast										
0-9999	231	221	129	55.9	120	54.3	102	44.2	101	45.7
10000-19999	258	239	191	74.0	162	67.8	67	26.0	77	32.2
20000-29999	136	98	83	61.0	59	60.2	53	39.0	29	29.8
>30000	124	106	38	30.6	25	23.6	86	69.4	81	76.4
Total	749	664	441	58.9	366	55.1	308	41.1	298	44.9
Southeast										
0-9999	302	292	219	72.5	211	72.3	83	27.5	81	27.7
10000-19999	215	197	122	56.7	126	64.0	93	43.3	71	36.1
20000-29999	91	75	56	61.5	43	57.3	35	38.5	32	42.7
>30000	136	84	63	46.3	38	45.2	73	53.7	46	54.8
Total	744	648	445	59.8	418	64.5	299	40.2	230	35.5

Note also that the influence of heterogeneity on the size of the efficiency estimates actuates through the phenomenon of efficiency by default. The decrease of heterogeneity reduces the number of municipalities efficient by default – whose scores are one - and thus may lead to a diminution of the average scores within the group considered as some of municipalities efficient by default turn out to be simply inefficient. This explain the decline on the efficiency scores of the largest northeast municipalities produced by the grouped estimates; their average scores is reduced to 66,4% against 87,3% for the ungrouped estimations (table 10.6). At the same time, efficiency by default, for this class of municipality, is reduced from 76,4% (ungrouped estimations) to 69,4% for the grouped estimations.

Efficiency, returns to scale and data heterogeneity

Up to now, we have analyzed the efficiency levels associated with the production of local public goods by the Brazilian municipalities. Next step is to determine whether the source of input scale inefficiency is due to the production of an output too small – in which case, we are on a region of increasing returns to scale - or if such inefficiency is provoked by the production of an excessively high output, thus being in a region of decreasing returns to scale. This question is particularly important for

Brazil since the proliferation of small communes resulting from the intense dismemberment of municipalities since 1985; serious doubts have arisen about the convenience of such dismembering in terms of economic viability.

Table 10.8   Returns to Scale and Data Heterogeneity in the Southeast Region: Ungrouped and Grouped Estimations

		Northeast										
		Constant Returns				Decreasing Returns				Increasing Returns			
Classes of	Total	Grouped		Ungrouped		Grouped		Ungrouped		Grouped		Ungrouped	
Population	Mun.	#	%	#	%	#	%	#	%	#	%	#	%
0-9999	431	17	3.9	1	0.2	64	14.8	4	0.9	351	81.3	426	98.9
10000-19999	519	9	1.7	0	0.0	80	15.4	0	0.0	430	82.9	519	100.0
20000-29999	240	5	2.1	4	1.7	47	19.9	4	1.7	184	78.0	232	96.6
> 30000	239	2	0.8	6	1.8	86	35.8	72	21.2	152	63.3	161	77.1
Total	1429	11	0.8	11	0.8	63	4.4	80	5.6	1355	94.8	1338	93.6

Table 10.9   Returns to Scale and Data Heterogeneity in the Southeast Region: Ungrouped and Grouped Estimations

		Southeast										
		Constant Returns				Decreasing Returns				Increasing Returns			
Classes of	Total	Grouped		Ungrouped		Grouped		Ungrouped		Grouped		Ungrouped	
Population	Mun.	#	%	#	%	#	%	#	%	#	%	#	%
0-9999	651	12	1.8	2	0.3	57	8.8	0	0.0	583	89.4	649	99.7
10000-19999	340	8	2.4	2	0.6	68	20.0	4	1.2	264	77.7	334	98.2
20000-29999	124	9	7.3	3	2.4	75	6.5	2	1.6	40	32.3	119	96.0
> 30000	220	8	3.6	19	8.6	143	65.0	87	39.5	69	31.4	114	51.8
Total	1335	19	1.4	26	2.0	88	6.6	93	7.0	1229	92.0	1216	91.1

In order to investigate this point, we estimated the returns of scale by using the methodology proposed by Färe, *et al.*, (1985,1994) previously described in earlier sections. Tables 10.8 and 10.9 show the grouped and ungrouped results for the Northeast and Southeast regions. In both regions, for the overwhelming majority of communes of less than 30000 inhabitants, local increasing returns to scale are prevalent. Hence, for those communes, a given proportional increase in all output indicators could be achieved with a proportionally inferior augmentation of current expenditures. This implies that it would be possible to increase the size of the typical Brazilian municipality and yet provide the required public services to these expanded communities without incurring in an equivalent increase in public expenditure.

Notice also that although it does not change their main implication, the grouping of observations make the results more credible as it reduces considerably the number of municipalities that presents increasing returns, particularly, for the cities in the Southeast Region. This suggests that heterogeneity also plays a role when evaluating economies of scale.

Those results help us to understand the poor adjustment of DEA frontiers – even when we consider the variable returns variant – DEA-V. The imposition of convexity of the data set imposed by those methodologies, clearly, transforms local (i.e., for the municipality under consideration) non-convexities into inefficiencies and thus underestimates substantially the efficiency scores of those communes.

Local non-convexities arise because cities too small are unable to exploit the economies of scale that characterizes the production of certain public services, hence do not use the available resources optimally. For instance, in the case of educational services, there is ample evidence that operating costs decrease with enrolment due to existence of high fixed costs.[16] Consequently, larger schools tend to be more cost-efficient because the fixed costs are diluted among a higher number of students. This fact, clearly, discriminates against small municipalities as their schools have, very probably, only a few students on average and thus tend to present excessively high average costs. Were those cities larger, they would be able to enroll a greater number of students and reduce the cost per student without significant loss of educational quality. A similar explanation applies to other local public services.[17] Hence, the dismembering of municipalities creates unnecessary administrative costs and pushes those communes to work on the decreasing portion of their average cost curves.[18]

Summing up, the convexity hypothesis, embedded in DEA techniques, is an unwarranted assumption for this case and attests the superiority of the FDH methodology that is free of such restriction.

Concluding remarks

In this chapter, we have attempted to appraise, quantitatively, the efficiency levels of the Brazilian municipalities. For that purpose, the chapter analyzed the relationship between aggregate municipal current spending and various indicators of the production of local public services by constructing non parametric cost-efficiency frontiers. Different techniques of efficiency analysis were used to determine this frontier: two DEA variants - DEA-C and DEA-V - and the FDH approach.

Our results show that diversity among the data set influences considerably efficiency measurements.   In particular, DEA-based efficiency estimates are quite sensitive to the dispersion in the data set. Indeed, in those methods, heterogeneity increases the number of outliers and artificially reduces the efficiency scores, thus, making DEA techniques unreliable when the degree of dispersion is relatively high as is the case with the Brazilian municipalities.

Moreover, the convexity of the data set that characterizes the DEA methods is, clearly, in our case, an unjustified assumption when analyzing the efficiency of the Brazilian municipalities as most of them tends to present local non convexities under the form of increasing returns to scale. Such a result suggests that the Brazilian recent municipal decentralization policy does not lead to an efficient use of public resources as the proliferation of small municipalities induced by this policy contributes to increase the average cost of public services.   Therefore, to prevent further losses in the overall efficiency of local public spending, this excessive dismembering of communes should be avoided.

Compared to the DEA techniques, FDH-based estimates, due to their more flexible hypothesis, are much less vulnerable to the impact of heterogeneity.   While reducing the dispersion tends to increase the efficiency scores, on the other hand, it also reduces the number of municipalities efficient by default and hence, to some extent, counterbalances the initial increases.   This gives the efficiency scores calculated by this method a greater stability.   Furthermore, instead of calculating an abstract frontier by referring to a fictitious combination of municipalities, as DEA methods do, this procedure build up its cost-efficiency frontier by contrasting actually observed municipalities.   That gives to the efficiency scores, mainly those applying to inefficient municipalities, a credibility that the DEA methods lack.

Notes

[1] See Charnes, Cooper and Rhodes (1978), Färe, Grosskpof e Lovell (1985, 1994), Seiford (1996). The expression DEA was introduced by Charnes, Cooper and

Rhodes (1978). In spite of the fact that all methods presented here envelop data, according to the tradition established in the literature, we will denote DEA only those techniques that suppose some form of convexity and compute the efficiency scores by using linear programs.

[2] Strong input disposability is defined as follows: inputs are strongly disposable if for x' > x $\in$ L(y) $\Rightarrow$ x' $\in$ L(y), where L(y) represents the set of all input vectors that can produce y $\in$ $\Re_+^M$.

[3] For a more detailed analysis of the technology see Färe, Grosskopf and Lovell (1985,1994).

[4] See Fare, Grosskopf and Lovell (1985,1994).

[5] Further details can be found in Deprins, Simar and Tulkens (1984) and Tulkens (1993).

[6] See Banker (1984).

[7] See Färe, Grosskopf and Lovell (1994).

[8] See Färe, Grosskopf and Lovell (1994), pp. 74.

[9] Alternatively, we may compute returns to scale keeping $S(y^k, x^k) < 1$ and comparing $F_i(y^j, x^j \mid N, S)$ with $F_i(y^j, x^j \mid V, S)$. In this case, if $S(y^k, x^k) < 1$ and $F_i(y^j, x^j \mid N, S) = F_i(y^j, x^j \mid V, S)$, inefficiencies result from the existence of decreasing returns to scale; if $S(y^k, x^k) < 1$ and $F_i(y^j, x^j \mid N, S) < F_i(y^j, x^j \mid V, S)$, thus, scale inefficiencies is due to the presence of increasing returns.

[10] See subsection 3.2, for details.

[11] Detailed results for all the Brazilian municipalities are shown in Sampaio de Sousa and Ramos de Souza (1999).

[12] We have dismissed investment expenditures as they are more erratic and would certainly jeopardize the comparison among municipalities. Such expenses will be considered when the study will be repeated for several years.

[13] This variable represented, in 1992, 75% of the total municipal expenditures.

[14] See section 5 for more details on this issue.

[15] Of course, this just a exploratory study. A more careful one should include common key characteristics other than size in order to increase the homogeneity degree.

[16] See Tan and Mingat (1992)) and Sampaio de Sousa (1998).

[17] For instance, the existence of important fixed costs involved in the production of administrative services (e.g. the creation and maintenance of a physical and human administrative infrastructure) explains why the per capita cost of those services are probably higher for smaller municipalities. A recent paper by Maia Gomes and MacDowell (1997) corroborate this point. Examining the Brazilian case, they show that municipal per capita expenses with personnel are substantially higher in small cities. For municipalities with 50,000 or less inhabitants, those authors show that the average cost curve for personnel expenses is clearly decreasing.

[18] For a good account of the dismembering of Brazilian municipalities, see Maia Gomes and MacDowell (1997).

References

Banker, R. (1984) "Estimating Most Productive Scale Size Using Data Envelopment Analysis," *European Journal of Operational Research,* 17, 35-44.

Banker, R. D., Charnes, A and Cooper, W.W. (1984) "Some Models for Estimating Technical and Scale Efficiencies in Data Envelopment Analysis," *Management Science,* 30, 1078-1092.

Banker, R. D. and Thrall., R. M. (1992) "Estimation of Returns to Scale Using Data Envelopment Analysis," *European Journal of Operational Research* 34, 513-521.

Chang, K. P. and Guh, Y.Y. (1991) "Linear Production Functions and the Data Envelopment Analysis," *European Journal of Operational Research,* 52, 215-223.

Charnes, A., Cooper, W.W. and Rhodes, E. (1978) "Measuring Efficiency of Decision Making Units," *European Journal of Operational Research,* 1, 429-44.

Deprins, D., Simar, L. and Tulkens, H. (1984) "Measuring Labor Efficiency in Post Offices." In Marchand, M., Pestiau, P. and Tulkens, H. eds., *The Performance of Public Enterprises : Concepts and Measurements.* Amsterdam: North Holland.

Färe, R., Grosskpof, S. and Lovell, C. K. (1985) *The Measurement of Efficiency of Production.* Boston: Kluwer-Nijhoff Publishing.

Färe, R., Grosskpof, S. and Lovell, C. K. (1994) *Production Frontiers.* Cambridge University Press.

Maia Gomes, G. e MacDowell, C. (1997) "Os Elos Frágeis da Descentralização: Observações sobre as Finanças dos Municípios Brasileiros, 1995." *Anais do XXV Encontro Nacional de Economia,* Recife, PE, pp. 645-660.

Sampaio de Sousa, M. C. (1998) "Efficiency and Equity Aspects of Social Spending in Selected Countries of Latin America and East Asia: A Comparative Approach." *Revista de Economia Aplicada* 2: 445-485.

Sampaio de Sousa, M. C. e Ramos de Souza, F. (1998) "Measuring the Efficiency of Public Spending in the Brazilian Municipalities: A Non Parametric Approach." Anais do XVI Encuentro Latinoamericano de la Sociedad Econometrica, Lima, Peru, 12 a 14 de Agosto de 1998. Trabalho completo publicado em CD-Room.

Sampaio de Sousa, M. C. and Ramos de Souza, F. (1999) "Eficiência Técnica e Retornos de Escala na Produção de Serviços Públicos Municipais: Uma Avaliação Não-Paramétrica dos Custos Associados à Descentralização Política no Brasil." *Revista Brasileira de Economia* 53, 433-461.

Seiford, L. (1996) "Data Envelopment Analysis: The Evolution of the State of the Arts (1978-1995)," *Journal of Productivity Analysis* 7, 99-137.

Tan, J. M. and Mingat, A. (1992) *Education in Asia: A Comparative Study of Cost and Financing*. Washington, DC: World Bank.

Tulkens, H. (1993) "Oh FDH Efficiency Analysis: Some Methodological Issues and Applications to Retail Banks, Courts, and Urban Transit," *Journal of Productivity Analysis*, 4, 183-210.

Vanden Eeckaut, Tulkens, H. and Jamar, M. A. (1991) "A Study of Cost-Efficiency and Returns of Scale for 235 Municipalities in Belgium." *Core Discussion Paper* n° 9158, CORE, Université Catholique de Louvain.

Appendix

Table A.1   Descriptive Statistics on the Sample of Brazilian Municipalities

Input and Output

Class.Pop/ Statistics	DESPC_92	POP91_TOT	DOM91_A	DOM91_L	ANALF91	EDUC
Northeast						
0-9999						
Mean	2208.3	6320.0	444.1	275.2	418.4	976.6
Stan.Deviation	779.4	2214.1	312.4	272.3	266.6	487.1
Minimum	445.1	1254.0	0.0	0.0	162.2	0.0
Maximum	6655.1	9982.0	1633.0	1384.0	2096.4	2780.0
10000-19999						
Mean	3608.2	14208.1	869.8	551.4	154.7	2035.0
Stan.Deviation	1569.4	2819.3	565.9	520.4	40.1	904.1
Minimum	893.0	10004.0	0.0	0.0	80.2	241.0
Maximum	25650.9	19997.0	2891.0	3293.0	314.3	6140.0
20000-99999						
Mean	5577.6	24254.9	1702.9	1220.4	136.9	3490.0
Stan.Deviation	3583.8	2770.0	1070.2	963.3	730.1	1517.6
Minimum	1543.5	20003.0	0.0	0.0	57.2	495.0
Maximum	53794.1	29718.0	5482.0	4635.0	11443.0	10315.0
< 300000						
Mean	10685.5	48356.2	4614.3	3270.9	53.2	6005.3
Stan.Deviation	22747.2	16420.2	3355.1	2790.1	15.2	3085.8
Minimum	1139.9	30052.0	0.0	0.0	22.3	1266.0
Maximum	352568.3	99407.0	15747.0	12789.0	130.8	25045.0
Southeast						
0-9999	DESPC_92	POP91_TOT	DOM91_A	DOM91_L	ANALF91	EDUC
Mean	3255.0	5194.7	732.0	544.4	586.6	544.4
Stan.Deviation	1462.0	2212.8	423.9	447.5	791.5	447.5
Minimum	958.5	751.0	0.0	0.0	25.5	0.0
Maximum	13401.6	9997.0	2204.0	2266.0	8849.6	2266.0
10000-19999						
Mean	6971.6	14234.7	2081.3	1755.2	220.2	1755.2
Stan.Deviation	3841.8	3059.3	918.9	1024.1	209.1	1024.1
Minimum	1961.2	10004.0	356.0	4.0	11.3	4.0
Maximum	28029.8	19969.0	4617.0	4777.0	727.8	4777.0
20000-99999						
Mean	10968.9	24271.0	4021.3	3381.0	138.5	3381.0
Stan.Deviation	4668.6	2935.3	1401.0	1687.8	120.7	1687.8
Minimum	3296.8	20048.0	663.0	242.0	6.3	242.0
Maximum	26509.8	29901.0	7021.0	6888.0	452.7	6888.0
< 300000						
Mean	10968.9	53010.5	10028.0	9058.3	91.7	9058.3
Stan.Deviation	4668.6	19207.7	5069.8	5222.2	73.4	5222.2
Minimum	3296.8	30148.0	983.0	392.0	3.2	392.0
Maximum	26509.8	99954.0	23533.0	23661.0	273.7	23661.0

11 Accounting for Education, Experience and Health as Investments in Human Capital

ANA LÚCIA KASSOUF

Introduction

Nowadays, the measurement of a country's human development is essential to evaluate its capacity to reach social welfare and to decrease poverty. The better the measures of human capital with respect to GNP, the better the perspectives for the country's development. This chapter intends to measure the contribution of health, education and on-the-job training to the productivity of Brazilian workers (see Mincer, 1962; Grossman, 1972; and Grossman and Benham, 1974). Although education and job training have often been considered as important factors affecting wages and labor force participation, rarely have studies of the Brazilian labor force accounted for health as an investment in human capital.

The analysis will consider separately formal and informal job markets. Differences are observed between formal and informal workers regarding education, experience, health and earnings. For example, formal workers have higher levels of education, health and salaries compared to informal workers. Also, there is a higher percentage of white workers in the formal sector, while blacks and mulattos concentrate in the informal sector. Moreover, formal workers concentrate in the Southeastern region as opposed to informal workers who concentrate in the Northeast, one of the poorer regions of Brazil.

Returns to education and experience, wage, gender, race discrimination, and market segmentation will be analyzed in this chapter, based on the coefficients derived from earnings' equations. However, traditional analyses estimating earnings equations may incur sample selectivity bias, since wages are observed only for those individuals employed in either formal or informal sectors. To solve this problem, a sample selectivity bias correction method proposed by Lee (1983) is used.

To this end, a detailed analysis using a multinomial logit model is developed, where the dependent variable takes the value zero if the person is not working, one if he or she is in the formal market place, and two if the individual is employed in the informal sector. Education, age, number of children, race, region and non-labor income are some of the factors assumed to affect the individual's job market participation. Based on the coefficients estimated in the polychotomus choice model, a lambda variable (the inverse of Mill's ratio) is calculated and used in the wage equation to obtain consistent estimates without sample selectivity bias.

Understanding the determinants of labor participation and earnings as well as the divergence between men and women in both the formal and informal sectors is essential to orient policy decisions to decrease discrimination and income inequalities in Brazil.

Methodology

Polychotomus-choice Model with Selectivity

The description of the Polychotomus-choice models with selectivity bias is based on Lee (1983) and Maddala (1990). Consider the following polychotomus-choice model with 3 categories represented by subscript s and N individuals represented by subscript i:

$$w_{si} = x_{si}\beta_s + u_{si} \qquad (s = 0,1,2) \tag{11.1}$$

$$I_{si}^* = z_{si}\gamma_s + \eta_{si} \qquad (i = 1,2,...,N) \tag{11.2}$$

where x_s and z_s are exogenous variables and $E(u_s | x_0, x_1, x_2, z_0, z_1, z_2) = 0$ and $E(\eta_s | x_0, x_1, x_2, z_0, z_1, z_2) = 0$. The three categories analyzed in this study are: not working, working in a formal job and working in an informal job. Each category is represented by an equation. The wage w_s is observed only if the sth category is chosen. In practice, I^* is not observed; what we observe is a polychotomus variable I taking values 0, 1 and 2. The sth category is chosen if $I=s$, which happens if and only if:

$$I_s^* > \mathrm{Max}\, I_j^* \quad (j = 0,1,2, j \neq s)$$

Let $\varepsilon_s = \mathrm{Max}\left(I_j^* - \eta_s\right) \quad (j = 0,1,2, j \neq s)$; it follows that $I = s$ iff $\varepsilon_s < z_s\gamma_s$

Suppose that η_j (j=0,1,2) has a cumulative distribution function:

$$F(\eta_i < c) = \exp\left[-\exp(-c)\right]$$

Then, it can be shown that:

$$\text{Prob}(\varepsilon_s < z_s\gamma_s) = \text{Prob}(I = s) = \frac{\exp(z_s\gamma_s)}{\sum_j \exp(z_j\gamma_j)} \tag{11.3}$$

Thus, the distribution function of ε_s is given by

$$F_s = \text{Pr}(\varepsilon_s < \varepsilon) = \text{Pr}\left[\left(\underset{j=0,1,2 j \neq s}{\text{Max }} I_j^* - \eta_s\right) < \varepsilon\right] = \frac{\exp(\varepsilon)}{\exp(\varepsilon) + \sum_{j=0,1,2 j \neq s} \exp(z_j\gamma_j)} \tag{11.4}$$

Therefore, for each choice, s, we have the model:

$$w_s = x_s\beta_s + u_s \tag{11.5}$$

where the dependent variable w_s is observed if and only if the category s is being chosen, i.e., $\varepsilon_s < z_s\gamma$. Consider the following transformation to normality:

$$\varepsilon_s^* = J_s(\varepsilon_s) = \Phi^{-1}[F_s(\varepsilon)] \tag{11.6}$$

where $\Phi(\cdot)$ is the standard normal distribution function.
The condition $\varepsilon_s < z_s\gamma_s \Leftrightarrow \varepsilon_s^* < J_s(z_s\gamma_s)$, and if u is normal distributed we have that,

$$E(w_s|w_s \text{ is observed}) = E(w_s|I = s) = E(w_s|\varepsilon_s < z_s\gamma_s) = E[w_s|\varepsilon_s^* < J_s(z_s\gamma_s)] =$$

$$= x_s\beta_s + E[u_s|\varepsilon_s^* < J_s(z_s\gamma_s)] = x_s\beta_s + \sigma_s\rho_s \frac{\phi[J_s(z_s\gamma_s)]}{\Phi[\Phi^{-1}[F_s(z_s\gamma_s)]]} \tag{11.7}$$

where ϕ is the density function of the standard normal, $\sigma_s^2 = Var(u_s)$, and ρ_s is the correlation coefficient between u_s and ε_s^*.
The following model can be estimated by two-stage methods.   The equation:

$$w_s = x_s\beta_s + \sigma_s\rho_s \frac{\phi[J_s(z_s\gamma_s)]}{F_s(z_s\gamma_s)} + v_s \tag{11.8}$$

where $\dfrac{\phi[J_s(Z_s\gamma_s)]}{F_s(Z_s\gamma_s)}$ is the inverse of Mill's ratio or lambda, can be estimated by ordinary least squares after substituting the estimated values of γ_s from the multinomial logit model, where I_s is regressed on z_s by maximum likelihood.

Data

The data set used to conduct this study is the 1989 National Health and Nutrition Survey, undertaken by the Brazilian Geographical and Statistical Institute (IBGE), Institute of Social Economic Planning (IPEA) and by the National Institute of Food and Nutrition (INAN). Approximately 63,000 individuals were interviewed from 17,920 households. It is possible to obtain information from specific regions of Brazil (North, Northeast, Central, South and Southeast) and sectors (rural and urban). However, data from the rural part of the Northern region were not collected. This survey is the more updated one with respect to health measures of the population, at the National level.

The data set provides information on monthly earnings (in US dollars) for individuals participating in the labor force a week before the interview, and any sort of payment in-kind received by the individual per month, which was already transformed into dollars. These variables were added to yield the monthly earnings. Information on the number of hours worked per week is also available. This variable was multiplied by 4 to obtain the number of hours worked per month. The monthly earnings were divided by the number of hours worked per month to get the hourly earnings.

The sample used in this study is composed of 14,611 men and 15,417 women, age 18 to 65, and includes those who do not participate in the labor market, as well as those participating in the formal or informal sector of the economy. Formal workers are defined as those who pay social security tax, while those who do not pay social security taxes are considered informal workers. The mean, standard deviation and the description of the variables for 6,139 men in the formal, 6,924 men in the informal, 3,192 women in the formal and 3,284 women in the informal sector are presented in table 11.1. There are approximately 13% more male workers in the informal than in the formal sector, and 3% more female workers. The women's earnings are 70% and 80% of the men's earnings, in the formal and informal sectors, respectively. Moreover, the earnings in the informal sector are about 50% of the earnings in the formal sector. One explanation for the lower earnings in this informal sector is that the formal sector requires a higher level of education and training.

Variables	Description of the Variables	MEN Formal Sector mean	s.d.	Informal Sector mean	s.d.	WOMEN Formal Sector mean	s.d.	Informal Sector mean	s.d.
WAGE	hourly wage rate	1.89	3.45	0.82	1.90	1.36	2.11	0.67	1.42
LNWAGE	logarithm of the hourly wage rate	0.09	0.58	-0.73	0.42	-0.23	0.49	-0.99	0.37
HOURS	number of hours working per week	46.59	12.85	46.41	12.99	39.83	12.10	34.02	17.45
LAMBDA	inverse of Mill's ratio	0.62	0.36	0.82	0.40	1.02	0.47	1.31	0.22
NORTH[1]	=1 if individual resides in the North	0.03	0.16	0.04	0.18	0.03	0.18	0.03	0.17
NORTHEAST	=1 if individual resides in the Northeast	0.16	0.34	0.42	0.30	0.19	0.38	0.34	0.33
CENTRAL	=1 if individual resides in the Central	0.06	0.24	0.08	0.28	0.07	0.25	0.07	0.25
SEAST	=1 if individual resides in the Southeast	0.60	0.49	0.34	0.47	0.56	0.50	0.42	0.49
SOUTH	=1 if individual resides in the South	0.18	0.38	0.16	0.37	0.18	0.38	0.17	0.38
URBAN	=1 if individual resides in the urban sector	0.90	0.31	0.53	0.50	0.94	0.23	0.73	0.45
WHITE	=1 if individual is white or Asian	0.64	0.48	0.43	0.50	0.66	0.48	0.48	0.50
MULATTO	=1 if individual is mulatto	0.30	0.46	0.51	0.50	0.29	0.45	0.44	0.50
BLACK	=1 if individual is black	0.06	0.19	0.06	0.22	0.05	0.19	0.08	0.22
HEAD	=1 if individual is the head of the household	0.77	0.41	0.69	0.46	0.23	0.42	0.18	0.38
WIFE	=1 if individual is a wife in the household	.				0.45	0.50	0.60	0.49
SON/DAUGT	=1 if individual is son or daughter in the hhold	0.19	0.37	0.27	0.44	0.25	0.42	0.15	0.37
HEALTH	body mass index (weigh/height²)	24.07	3.68	22.60	3.00	23.95	4.29	24.31	4.47
EXPERIENCE	individual's experience in years	23.17	13.42	26.36	14.41	19.35	12.80	25.21	14.26
EXPERIENCE2	individual's experience squared	716.5	748.43	902.2	864.3	540.22	630.9	848.76	820.1
EDUCATION	individual's number of years in school	6.67	4.47	3.40	3.27	8.21	4.54	4.65	3.77
EDUCEXP	individual's education times experience	122.6	95.95	64.76	68.15	123.7	94.53	79.86	72.57
NONLINC	nonlabor income (rent, pension, alimony, etc.)	22.99	168.38	12.14	75.44	14.52	70.31	8.01	57.10
AGE	individual's age in years	35.82	11.64	35.32	13.03	33.62	10.66	35.83	12.44

[1] Only the urban sector

Table 11.1   Description of the variables, means and standard deviations, for men and women in the formal and informal sectors

Note that the average number of years of education in the formal sector is almost twice the one observed in the informal sector, for men and women. Table 11.2 shows the percentage of workers in each sector, at different monthly earning ranges. While 63% of men working in the informal sector receive less than US$100.00 per month, only 23% receive this amount in the formal sector. On the other hand, the percentage of men workers receiving more than US$500.00 per month is 16% in the formal sector and only 4% in the informal sector. For women, 84% receive less than US$100.00 in the informal sector, against 49% in the formal sector.

Table 11.2   Percentage of workers at different monthly earnings range

	Men		Women	
Dollars	Formal	Informal	Formal	Informal
0-25	1.2	14.2	4.4	41.6
25-50	3.6	18.0	9.1	21.7
50-100	20.8	30.4	35.7	20.8
100-200	30.5	22.1	25.2	9.7
200-500	28.2	11.4	17.7	4.7
500-1000	9.9	2.7	5.1	1.0
>1000	5.8	1.1	2.6	0.5

The data set used in this study does not provide information on job training or experience. Therefore, a measure of experience was calculated as age minus years of schooling minus six. Table 11.1 shows that the average experience in the informal sector is greater than in the formal sector, which is a consequence of the method used to calculate experience. As discussed earlier, workers in the formal sector have significantly more years of schooling than those in the informal sector, but the age is almost the same in the two sectors of the economy.

Another interesting point to observe is that in the Southeastern and Southern regions as well as in the urban sector there are more workers in the formal than in the informal sector, for both men and women. However, in the Northeast and Central parts of Brazil, there are more informal than formal workers. Pastore (1981) observed that the richer the region, the larger is the participation in the protected labor market. Among races, differences are observable for white (including Asians) workers that, as opposed to mulattos and blacks, are in larger number in the formal sector.

This survey also provides individual's health measures, such as the body mass index, which is the ratio of weight (kg) to height squared (m^2);

in contrast to disease symptoms, anthropometric measures are more objective health indicators. Therefore, the body mass index (BMI), which according to James, *et al.* (1988) is a measure of energy deficiency in adults is used as health indicator in this study. The cut-off points were established following Coitinho *et al.* (1991), who cited Garrow (1981) from the World Health Organization. Hence, adults were classified as being underweight if the BMI was below 20; normal if the index was between 20 and 25; overweight if the index was between 25 and 30; and obese if it was larger than 30. From table 11.3 there is a larger percentage of men underweight in the informal sector compared to those in the formal sector. For women, however, the percentages are very similar in both sectors.

Table 11.3   **Percentage of workers at different body mass index range**

BMI (Kg/m^2)	Men		Women	
	Formal	Informal	Formal	Informal
underweight 0-20	11.5	17.6	16.1	15.9
normal weight 20-25	53.1	64.9	49.6	47.6
overweight 25-30	28.6	15.3	24.7	24.9
obesity > 30	6.8	2.2	9.6	11.7

Results

Participation in the Formal and Informal Sectors of the Economy

The coefficients of the multinomial logit model, estimated by maximum likelihood methods are presented in table 11.4, for men and women from age 18 to 65. This age range was chosen as a way to avoid large discrepancies, since very young workers receive a very low wage and very old persons can be retired or also receive low salaries. The dependent variable takes the value 0 if the individual is not working, 1 if he or she is working in the formal sector and 2 if he or she is working in the informal sector. As noted earlier, workers holding a formal job, as opposed to those with an informal job, pay taxes for social security purposes.

EDUCATION is an exogenous variable affecting labor force participation, measured by the highest degree of schooling completed in years. It has the expected positive coefficient, indicating that more years of schooling increases the possibility of being employed. Only the result for men in informal jobs is not significant. Tiefenthaler (1994a) found that education has stronger effects in increasing the participation of women in the formal sector than in the informal sector. In fact, her results show that additional education decreases the probability of women's participation in the informal sector.

Table 11.4   **Participation equations for men and women in the formal and informal sectors**

Variables	Men		Women	
	Formal	Informal	Formal	Informal
Constant	-2.460	1.760	-5.740	-1.900
	(-7.62) ***	(5.38) ***	(-20.62) ***	(-7.72) ***
Education	0.191	0.008	0.406	0.137
	(10.82) ***	(0.44)	(26.49) ***	(9.15) ***
Experience	0.132	0.081	0.256	0.106
	(9.46) ***	(5.73) ***	(20.18) ***	(9.34) ***
Experience2	-0.003	-0.002	-0.004	-0.002
	(-13.32)***	(-8.91)***	(-21.46)***	(-10.77)***
Expeduc	-0.005	-0.003	-0.010	-0.005
	(-7.00)***	(-4.82)***	(-15.63)***	(-8.17)***
Health	0.035	-0.031	-0.003	0.002
	(4.03)***	(-3.30)***	(-0.50)	(0.37)
Nonlinc	-0.002	-0.001	-0.002	-0.003
	(-9.36)***	(-4.87)***	(-5.79)***	(-4.74)***
Child ($\leq$2)[§]	-0.080	-0.003	-0.816	-0.535
	(-0.92)	(-0.04)	(-12.82)***	(-10.26)***
Child (3-5) [§]	0.261	0.254	-0.192	-0.0446
	(2.81)***	(2.73)***	(-3.58)***	(-0.98)
Child (6-12) [§]	0.120	0.161	-0.158	0.083
	(2.60)***	(3.48)***	(-5.05)***	(3.28)***
Childm ($\geq$13) [§]	-0.009	0.002	-0.202	-0.029
	(-0.21)	(0.04)	(-5.44)***	(-0.99)
Childf ($\geq$13) [§]	0.202	-0.004	0.053	0.072
	(3.84)***	(-0.07)	(1.27)	(2.08)**
Head	0.909	0.855	0.850	0.559
	(6.35)***	(5.79)***	(6.12)***	(4.19)***
Wife	-	-	-0.353	-0.256
			(-2.63)***	(-2.01)**
Son/Daughter	-0.680	-0.211	0.177	-0.0414
	(-4.97)***	(-1.49)	(1.31)	(-0.31)
Others	0.806	1.171	2.11	2.136
	(1.91)*	(2.80)***	(9.30)***	(9.82)***
White	0.0666	-0.0934	-0.246	-0.568
	(0.53)	(-0.73)	(-2.38)**	(-6.37)***
Mulatto	-0.0845	-0.0416	-0.191	-0.405
	(-0.66)	(-0.32)	(-1.77)*	(-4.47)***
North	0.360	0.496	0.425	0.0154
	(2.13)**	(3.02)***	(3.13)***	(0.12)
Central	0.656	0.429	0.250	-0.0573
	(5.07)***	(3.39)***	(2.46)**	(-0.64)

Table 11.4 (continued)

	Men		Women	
Southeast	0.996	0.0509	0.563	-0.0117
	(12.74)***	(0.66)	(8.38)***	(-0.21)
South	0.882	0.231	0.780	0.0534
	(8.45)***	(2.21)**	(9.29)***	(0.70)
Urban	0.278	-1.07	0.983	0.315
	(3.34)**	(-14.08)***	(11.82)***	(5.51)***
Variables	Formal	Informal	Formal	Informal
Education^h	-		-0.0364	-0.0327
			(-5.55)***	(-4.69)***
Experience^h	-		-0.00171	-0.000686
			(-1.17)	(-0.50)
Likelihood Ratio	5163.70***	5163.70***	4416.91***	4416.91***

Note: *The t-tests are given in parentheses below the coefficients*
*significant at the 10% level, **at the 5 level, and*** at the 1% level
§ *age of children*

The stock of on-the-job training human capital (EXPERIENCE) is hardly measured in survey questionnaires. Due to this fact, job experience is commonly estimated as the individual's age minus years of schooling minus 6. Thus, we are assuming that all workers begin elementary school at age six and that no time is spent outside the labor force or school (Berndt, 1991). Work experience, together with schooling, are activities through which human capital can be accumulated. However, human capital can also depreciate, following a parabolic curve reflecting increased job opportunities with experience until diminishing returns set in and thus participation in the labor force decreases. This is shown in table 11.4 by the positive coefficient for EXPERIENCE and the negative coefficient for EXPERIENCE2, respectively.[1]

An interaction term EDUCEXP represents years of education times years of experience. The negative sign shows that the effect of education (experience) decreases as the amount of experience (education) increases, i.e., the importance of a person's level of education (experience) to obtain a job is not so significant if he or she has substantial experience (education) in a specific area.

The HEALTH variable is not significant for women, but it is for men. However, while a positive effect between health and participation in the formal sector is observed, a negative one appears in the informal sector. This finding reflects the results derived by Thomas and Strauss (1993) who noted the possibility of healthier and, therefore, more productive workers, moving into sectors that reward health.

The non-labor income variable (NONLINC) represents income that does not come from salaries; rent, pensions, alimony, etc., were added to obtain the value of the family non-labor income per month. According to the results, the higher the income from non-labor sources, the less likely the person is to be employed, in both formal and informal sectors.

The number of children (son and daughters) with different age ranges reflects childcare costs (Tiefenthaler, 1994b). Hence, the variable representing the number of children from 0 to 2 years old is called CHILD2, from 3 to 5 years old CHILD3-5, from 6 to 12 CHILD6-12, the number of sons 13 years old or older CHILDM13, and the number of daughters 13 or older CHILDF13. Some of those variables can increase childcare costs (young kids) and others decrease child-care costs (teenagers).

While the presence of very young children practically did not have any effect or had a positive effect on the labor market participation of men, it had a strong negative effect on women's job market participation. The presence of children in the household increases the father's participation in the labor market, since it increases the need for household income. On the other hand, as the number of young children increases, the mother's reservation wage increases, i.e., the amount of extra earnings required by an individual, who is not working, to give up one unit of leisure. As a result, the mother's labor force participation decreases as the number of young children at home increases. Young children demand lots of care, increasing the mother's value of time. It is interesting to observe that teenager daughters presented a positive effect in both male and female job market participation. Older daughters act as substitutes for the mother's care of very young children, allowing them to work outside the house even in the presence of young kids. On the other hand, teenage sons had a negative effect on the mother's labor participation, acting as labor substitutes in the job market.

In previous analysis, fertility is seen as an exogenous decision. However, it is possible to have an endogenous fertility decision and, then, care has to be taken to interpret the results. If, for example, some mothers enjoy more than others to have children and stay at home taking care of them, then the negative correlation between number of children and labor force participation may be indicating not that children prevent mothers from participating in the job market, but that mothers who enjoy having children and staying home with them tend also to have more children.

Tiefenthaler (1994a) also found that Brazilian children under age five decrease women's participation in both sectors. However, she obtained a negative effect of teenage daughters on women's participation, indicating that they were not replacing their mother in childcare, as we found, but were instead replacing the mother in earning income.

Hill (1989), using a sample from Japan, concluded that young children reduce the women's propensity to work as employee or family workers. Tiefenthaler (1994b), studying Philippine women working in a piece-sector, formal and informal sectors, observed that the number of children younger than 6 decreases the probability of participation in both formal and piece sectors and is insignificant in determining informal-sector participation. Moreover, she concluded that the presence of daughters older than 13 increased the probability of the mothers to work in all of the three sectors, as they can reduce childcare costs or help their mothers with informal-sector work.

Variables representing the position of the individuals in the family (HEAD, WIFE, SON/DAUGHTER, OTHERS, relatives were omitted) showed that the head participates more in the job market than the son and also the female head works more outside the house than the wives, as we would expect. Women who are head usually are divorced, widowed or single and need to work to survive. On the other hand, wives may depend on their husbands as is very common in the Brazilian society.

The coefficients of the race variables (WHITE, MULATTO, black was omitted) were almost all not significant and, when significant, they were negative. It is interesting to observe in table 11.5 that blacks have the highest percentage of participation in the job market. Notice that 88% of the mulattos, 90% of the whites and 91% of the black men work. For women, 46% of the blacks, 43% of the whites and 40% of the mulattos are in the job market. Moreover, black and mulatto workers (men and women) concentrate in the informal market, while the proportion of white men working is higher in the formal market.

Table 11.5   Percentage of individuals working in the formal and informal markets

	Men			Women		
	Not working	Formal	Informal	Not working	Formal	Informal
White	10	49	41	57	24	19
Mulatto	12	35	53	60	17	23
Black	9	36	55	54	18	28

The results also showed positive and significant coefficients for regions (Central, Southeast and South) in the formal sector (the Northeast variable was omitted to avoid perfect collinearity). Job opportunities in the formal sector may increase as development and wealth in the regions increase. However, in the informal sector there was almost no statistical significance in the regions' coefficients. From table 11.1, there are more informal workers in the Northeastern region than in any other region. The lack of formal jobs in poor regions induces participation in informal activities.

Different results were also found between male workers in the formal and informal sectors living in the urban areas. While a significant positive coefficient was obtained in the formal sector, a negative one showed up in the informal sector. In the rural sector, most of the farmers do not pay social security tax[2]. Tiefenthaler (1994b) considered the urban dummy variable as a proxy for transportation costs and obtained results similar to the present one.

Variables representing the education of the household head (EDUCATIONH) and his job experience (EXPERIECEH) are included in the women's equations. The idea is that the wage of the head affects the women labor force participation. However, the wage rate is an endogenous variable and a better way to account for the head's influence over female labor force participation is to use the head's experience and education as exogenous variables. The result shows that the higher is the head's education, the lower is the women's job participation. A highly educated man has a greater chance to obtain a good job with a high salary, sparing a spouse from working.

Earnings Functions in the Formal and Informal Sectors of the Economy

Table 11.6 shows the earnings equations estimated by least squares, weighted by the sample expansion factors, for men and women in the formal and informal sectors. The dependent variable is the logarithm of the hourly earnings. The correction variable, LAMBDA, included as exogenous variable to avoid sample selectivity bias, presented a highly significant coefficient, indicating that its inclusion was necessary in the model. Its positive sign indicates that unmeasured factors that increase the probability of participation increase earnings.

As suggested by human capital theory, the earnings function is considered concave in experience, *i.e.*, a positive coefficient is expected for experience and negative one for experience square. Further, it is assumed that earnings are linear in education and that the effects of experience on earnings do not depend only on experience but also on education.   To capture this effect, an interaction term is added (see Berndt, 1991 and Willis, 1986). The estimated coefficients from table 11.6 confirm the concavity of the earnings function in experience.   Earnings follow a parabolic curve, peaking somewhere in mid-life. The decrease in earnings is due to a depreciation of the workers' human capital in the form of taking more time to perform tasks as a result of ageing.

Table 11.6   **Earnings equations for men and women in the formal and informal sectors. The dependent variable is log earnings**

Variables	Men		Women	
	Formal	Informal	Formal	Informal
Constant	-4.07	-2.82	-4.35	-4.29
	(-19.99)***	(-26.03)***	(-22.29)***	(-25.19)***
Lambda	0.235	0.911	0.393	0.585
	(3.42)***	(7.46)***	(7.84)***	(6.74)***
Experience	0.0920	0.0503	0.0806	0.0843
	(16.76)***	(12.03)***	(11.29)***	(12.80)***
Experience2	-0.001225	-0.000737	-0.00105	-0.00118
	(-15.15)***	(-12.25)***	(-9.62)***	(-12.36)***
Expeduc	-0.00158	-0.000503	-0.00174	-0.00126
	(-6.52)***	(-1.91)*	(-5.00)***	(-3.24)***
Education	0.182	0.0710	0.218	0.146
	(25.49)***	(7.67)***	(23.30)***	(15.20)***
Health	0.0373	0.0176	0.00180	0.0148
	(13.09)***	(4.00)***	(0.57)	(4.30)***
North	0.209	0.550	0.507	0.545
	(3.38) ***	(9.59)***	(6.80)***	(6.36)***
Central	0.320	0.373	0.404	0.382
	(6.98)***	(10.13)***	(6.97)***	(6.23)***
Southeast	0.331	-0.0198	0.483	0.326
	(8.73)***	(-0.52)	(11.84)***	(8.24)***
South	0.206	0.0706	0.418	0.240
	(5.06)***	(2.00)**	(8.39)***	(4.49)***
Urban	0.356	-0.154	0.488	0.183
	(7.77)***	(-2.57)***	(8.09)***	(4.51)***
White	0.351	0.133	0.315	0.195
	(8.54)***	(3.16)***	(5.50)***	(3.19)***
Mulatto	0.111	0.0844	0.182	0.0105
	(2.58)***	(2.05)**	(2.99)***	(0.18)
R^2	0.45	0.30	0.48	0.34
F - test	388.27***	227.06***	226.70***	130.52***
Observations	6,139	6,924	3,192	3,284

Note: *The t-tests are given in parentheses below the coefficients*
*significant at the 10% level; **at the 5 level; *** at the 1% level*

High significance is found for education; the greater the number of years in school, the higher the salaries for men and women in the formal and informal sectors. Observe that the coefficient values are higher and the tests more significant in the formal than informal sector. As noted also by Barros, *et al.* (1993), the degree of informality tends to be larger among less-educated workers.

As Mincer (1962) considered education and experience as investments in human capital, Grossman and Benham (1974) considered health also as investment in human capital, and as such, it is expected that better health will increase workers productivity and wages. The coefficients of health from table 11.6 were all positive and significant, except for women in the formal sector, whose coefficient besides being positive was not statistically significant. Kassouf (1998) estimated the earnings equations without including health. The education coefficients were smaller in the formal sector when including health, but had higher values in the informal sector. For experience, on the other hand, all coefficients were smaller when including health.

Men and women receive lower earnings in the Northeastern region (omitted variable) than working in the North, Central, Southeast and South of Brazil. The same phenomenon happens for workers in the urban areas, who receive higher earnings than those in the rural areas. These results can be observed in table 11.6 columns 1 and 3, where all the coefficients for regions and the urban areas are positive and significant. For men in the informal sector, however, the rural areas pay lower salaries for the workers than urban areas, as we can see by the negative coefficient in the second column of table 11.6 for the variable "urban." A large part of the workers in rural areas of Brazil are classified as informal workers because they work in agriculture or as craftsmen, where it is not mandatory to pay social security taxes. So, the earnings of those individuals in rural areas are better than informal workers in urban areas. Since characterizes job conditions for informal workers are precarious in the urban sector, they are chosen by them as a way to survive in the absence of anything better. The results for women in the informal sector (fourth column of table 11.6), on the other hand, follow those of the formal sector, indicating that women in the informal sector and urban areas might not have such precarious work conditions as men. The reason is that some women have jobs that are related to craftwork or hobby.

Savedoff (1990), based on household surveys data (PNAD) from 1976 to 1986 analyzed the wages influence by local and national factors. He concluded that regions in Brazil account for a significant part of the wage difference. However, he points out that the wages have also strong national components and it would be wrong to treat wage determination as either a purely national or an isolated regional process.

The results from the race variables show that blacks (variable omitted) receive lower salaries than whites and even mulattos, reflecting discrimination against blacks.

Returns to on the Job Training and Education

Consider the following equation:

$$\ln w = \alpha + \beta_1 exp + \beta_2 exp^2 + \beta_3 educ + \beta_4 exp \times educ + \varepsilon \qquad (11.9)$$

where w is hourly earnings, exp is experience and $educ$ is education.
To obtain the effect of experience on log earnings we compute the partial derivative:

$$\frac{\partial \ln w}{\partial exp} = \beta_1 + 2\beta_2 exp + \beta_4 educ \qquad (11.10)$$

Similarly, the effect of education on the log of earnings is:

$$\frac{\partial \ln w}{\partial educ} = \beta_3 + \beta_4 exp \qquad (11.11)$$

As an example, consider the earnings equation for men in the formal sector given in column 1 of table 11.6. The effect of experience on the log of earnings is:

$$\frac{\partial \ln w}{\partial exp} = 0.0920 - 2 \times 0.001225 \times exp - 0.00158 \times educ \qquad (11.12)$$

which is, considering 8 years of education, 6.96% at 4 years of experience, 5.98% at 8 years of experience, 5.00% at 12 years, and 3.04% at 20 years of experience.

Table 11.7 shows the returns to experience for men and women in the formal and informal sectors of the economy, based on the results of table 11.6.

Observe that the returns to experience in table 11.7 are positive and decline with increases in years of training and schooling. The values range from 1.47% to 7.59% for men and from 1.78% to 6.99% for women. Moreover, the returns to experience for men are higher in formal jobs than informal, while for women higher returns are observed in the informal jobs.

Looking at the formal sector, the returns are higher for men than for women, but the opposite is observed in the informal sector, where the returns to experience are greater for women than for men. The effect of schooling on log-earnings, also based on table 11.6, is presented in table 11.8.

Table 11.7   The effect of experience on log-earnings, in percentage

Experience	Formal			Informal	
	Men	Women		Men	Women
			Educ=4		
4	7.59	6.52		4.24	6.99
8	6.61	5.68		3.65	6.04
12	5.63	4.85		3.06	5.09
20	3.67	3.17		1.88	3.20
			Educ=8		
4	6.96	5.82		4.04	6.48
8	5.98	4.99		3.44	5.54
12	5.00	4.15		2.85	4.59
20	3.04	2.48		1.68	2.70
			Educ=12		
4	6.33	5.13		3.83	5.98
8	5.35	4.29		3.24	5.03
12	4.37	3.45		2.65	4.09
20	2.41	1.78		1.47	2.20

Table 11.8   The effect of education on log-earnings, in percentage

Experience	Formal		Informal	
	Men	Women	Men	Women
4	17.62	21.12	6.90	14.08
8	16.98	20.43	6.70	13.57
12	16.35	19.73	6.50	13.07
20	15.09	18.34	6.10	12.06

The returns to education presented in table 11.8 range from 6.10% for men in the informal sector to 17.62% for men in the formal sector and from 12.06% for women in the informal sector to 21.12% for women in the formal sector. Those returns are positive and decline with increases in years of experience. Observe that the returns to education are much higher than the returns to experience, and that the returns to education are larger in formal jobs than informal jobs. Moreover, returns to education for women are larger than for men in both formal and informal sectors.

Lam and Levison (1990), using Brazilian household data (PNAD) from 1985, observed that returns to education increased with age. They reached the same conclusion analyzing data from the United States. Moreover, they observed that the returns were higher in Brazil than in the United States. They found returns to education to be around 15%, close to the values observed in this present study.

Barros and Ramos (1992), analyzing the household surveys (PNAD) from 1976 to 1989, also obtained returns to education around 15%, when controlling for age and region, and even higher than 15% without variable controls. Psacharopoulos (1985) found a 14% return to education in Latin America, 11% in Asia, 8% in intermediate economies (Cyprus, Greece, Iran, Portugal), and 9% in advanced economies (Australia, Canada, France, Germany, Japan, Sweden, UK, USA).

Berndt (1991) presented results found by Psacharopoulos (1981) in the United States who observed rates of return to secondary education close to 12% from 1939 to 1976 and rates of return to college education near 11% from 1939 to 1969, falling to a value close to 5% in 1976. Berndt also reported the returns to experience found by Mincer (1974) who used 1959 data on white, nonfarm, nonstudent, American males up to age 65. As in our findings, the returns to experience decreased with an increase in educational attainment and in years of experience. The rates obtained ranged from 11% to 5%.

Discrimination by Gender and Race

To measure the male-female earnings differential, a hypothetical average hourly wage for women is obtained by using their own characteristics (means) and the men's structure (coefficients). After the adjustment, the increase in the women's wage is attributable to discrimination and the wage differential that remained between men and women is due to differences in characteristics. This approach was used by Brown, *et al.* (1980) and Barros *et al.* (1995). The bases for these studies, however, go back to Blinder (1973) and Oaxaca (1973), who argued that the coefficients (intercept and slopes) of the earnings regressions estimated separately for men and women, based on a set of personal characteristics, contain information about discrimination.

Table 11.9 displays the specific mean of log earnings for men and women in the formal and informal sectors and the average wage for women that would result if they faced the same wage structure as men. In the formal sector, the actual men's and women's average log earnings are 0.088 and -0.23 respectively, i.e., women receive 27% less than men[3]. However, the women's wage estimated by substituting the women's characteristics in the men's earnings equation is 0.34, which shows that women were supposed to receive 29% more than men, given their characteristics and the absence of discrimination. In the informal sector, the men's and women's average earnings are -0.73 and -0.99 respectively, i.e., women receive 23% less than men. In this case, the women's estimated wage is -0.48 or 28% more than the men's wage. Based on this analysis, it is possible to conclude that significant gender discrimination occurs in both the formal and informal sectors of the economy. Moreover, the magnitude of the gender discrimination is almost the same between the formal and informal sectors.

Table 11.9   Actual and estimated log earnings in the formal and informal sectors

	Average Men's Earnings	Average Women's Earnings	Estimated Women's Earnings
Formal sector	0.09	-0.23	0.34
Informal sector	-0.73	-0.99	-0.48

Barros, *et al.* (1997) observed that one third of the male-female wage differential for workers with the same age and education is attributable to the occupational attainment. They showed that female occupations are not only different than men's occupations but also inferior (in terms of skills), generating another form of discrimination.

As a way to understand the earnings differential among white (includes Asians), black and mulatto workers, the earnings equations for each race were estimated, correcting for sample selectivity bias, and the returns to education and experience were calculated. Table 11.10 shows the returns considering 8 years of education and experience, for men and women in the formal and informal sector, stratified by race. In the formal sector, it is very clear that the returns are higher for whites followed by mulattos and then blacks. However, in the informal sector the results are not so clear. The returns to experience and education for men were higher for blacks, while for women, the returns to experience were higher for mulattos and the returns to education were higher for whites.

Valle Silva (1980), using the 1960 Brazilian Census, concluded that white male workers had much higher returns to education and experience than non-white workers, i.e., blacks and mulattos. This result is similar to our finding in the formal sector, but the complexity of the informal market does not lead us to the same conclusion. Smith and Welch (1977) using the

1960 and 1970 U. S. census data, observed that returns to grade school for blacks were lower than for whites, while for post-secondary schooling, returns were higher for blacks.

Table 11.10   Returns to experience and education for different races at 8 years of experience and 8 years of education

	Men			Women		
	White	Black	Mulatto	White	Black	Mulatto
			Returns to Experience			
Formal	5.92	3.26	5.58	5.23	0	4.31
Informal	2.59	4.19	-5.89	5.88	5.19	11.26
			Returns to Education			
Formal	17.04	14.00	15.29	21.09	16.80	17.61
Informal	4.00	17.42	9.77	15.39	12.42	11.26

Table 11.11   Actual and estimated log earnings for different men's and women's race in the formal and informal sectors

	Average Men's Earnings			Estimated Men's Earnings		Average Women's Earnings			Estimated Women Earnings	
Sectors	White	Black	Mulatto	Black	Mulatto	White	Black	Mulatto	Black	Mulatto
Formal	0.29	-0.39	-0.25	-0.09	-0.08	-0.04	-0.69	-0.56	-0.41	-0.47
Informal	-0.51	-0.93	-0.90	-0.93	-0.83	-0.69	-1.25	-1.27	-1.05	-1.16

In attempting to measure wage race discrimination, the actual and estimated earnings were compared. Table 11.11 shows the average log earnings for men and women in the formal and informal sectors for white, black and mulatto. The estimated earnings were obtained using the means of the exogenous variables for the blacks and mulattos with the coefficients from the earnings equations estimated for the whites. The log wage differential among races is higher in the formal than informal sector, where blacks receive 40% less than whites and mulattos get 30% less than the whites' earnings. Based on the estimated and real average earnings between white and black and white and mulatto, the percentage of the difference in earnings is attributed to personal characteristics was distinguished from differences due to discrimination. The results are presented in table 11.12.

White men in the formal sector, for example, have average log earnings equal to 0.29, while for blacks average earnings are -0.39. The estimated log earnings for the blacks, however, is -0.087, i.e., keeping the black characteristics but the white structure, blacks would receive -0.087 as average log earnings. The difference between the white earnings and the black earnings is equal to 0.68 [0.29-(-0.39)], but 0.377 [0.29-(-0.087)] is due to differences in their characteristics or endowment, representing 55% of the difference. The remaining part is due to discrimination (45%). The other results in table 11.12 are obtained in an analogous manner.

Table 11.12   Percentage of the earnings differentials by race due to characteristics and discrimination

Sectors	Black Men Charactr.	Discrim.	Mulatto Men Charactr.	Discrim.	Black Women Charactr.	Discrim.	Mulatto Women Charactr.	Discrim.
Formal	55	45	68	32	57	43	83	17
Informal	100	0	82	18	64	36	81	19

Observe that blacks suffer more discrimination than mulattos. Also, race discrimination is higher in the formal than informal sector. In both sectors for either men or women, the highest percentage of the earnings differential between races is due to differences in characteristics. Valle Silva (1993) undertook a similar analysis using the 1988 national household survey PNAD, observing that the earnings differential between white and black heads of the households due to discrimination is close to 46%, while between white and mulatto it is 32%. Notice that these results are very close to ours for men in the formal sector. Corcoran and Duncan (1979) studied the race and sex wage gaps in the United States analyzing the relationship between wages and the following factors: on-the-job training, interrupted work experience, absenteeism due to one's illness and other family members, and self-imposed restrictions on job location and work hours. They concluded that even controlling for all those factors, there is still a large unexplained percentage in the wage gaps between men and women, and between blacks and whites. They found that discrimination accounted for 47% of the earnings differentials between black and white men.

Lovell (1992), comparing the Brazilian census from 1960 and 1980, concluded that discrimination between white and Afro-Brazilians increased significantly. It is good to point out that a great part of the difference in productivity from workers with different races comes from discrimination and unequal opportunities that occur even before entering into the job market (Barros and Mendonça, 1996).

Market Segmentation

The same analysis just performed is repeated as a way to measure the existence of market segmentation, i.e., that equally productive workers receive different wages depending on whether they are in the formal or informal sector. To this end, for men and women separately, wages were estimated by applying characteristics (means) in the informal market that were used in the formal sector structure (coefficients).

Table 11.13 displays the specific means of log earnings received in the formal and informal sectors, for men and women, and the average wage estimated in the informal sector if the wage structure was the same as in the formal sector. The earnings in the informal sector are almost half of the earnings in the formal sector. The percentage of the differential in log earnings, for men and women, due to differences in their characteristics is 84%, and therefore 16% of the wage differential is due to market segmentation.[4]

Table 11.13   Actual and estimated log earnings for men and women

	Average Formal Earnings	Average Informal Earnings	Estimated Informal Earnings
Men	0.09	-0.73	-0.60
Women	-0.23	-0.99	-0.87

Barros, Mello and Pero (1993)[5] using household surveys (PNAD) from 1981 to 1989 observed that workers with formal contracts earn twice the wages of workers without formal contracts and showed that "one half of this wage gap is explained by differences between workers with and without formal labor contracts with respect to education, age and region of residence." They found segmentation in the market, claiming that "if workers with same age and education who reside in the same metropolitan area were on average equally productive, then the metropolitan labor market of Brazil would be segmented with a randomly drawn worker in a job without formal labor contract experiencing a 50% wage increase if he/she could find a job with formal contract."

Labor supply equations

The weekly hours of work equations were estimated by two-stage least squares methods, including the estimates of log earnings from table 11.6 as a regressor in the hours of work equations. The results for men and women in the formal and informal sectors are presented in table 11.14. Following Heckman (1980), the labor supply function is also corrected for sample selectivity bias, including variable lambda, since only individuals employed in the labor market enter in the analysis. The lambda coefficients are highly significant.

Table 11.14 **Labor supply function estimated by two stage least squares. The dependent variable is the number of hours per week working in the labor market**

Variables	Men		Women	
	Formal	Informal	Formal	Informal
Constant	45.35	54.53	32.18	54.72
	(22.51)***	(17.27)***	(15.00)***	(10.73)***
Lambda	-0.662	-12.45	-5.80	-8.72
	(-0.47)	(-4.89)***	(-4.49)***	(-2.98)***
Logwage [a]	-2.99	5.67	- 7.64	1.36
	(-5.27)***	(4.04)***	(-9.36)***	(1.49)
Child2	-0.668	-0.628	-0.427	0.122
	(-1.92)*	(-1.73)*	(-0.62)	(0.14)
Child3-5	-0.00593	-0.124	0.160	1.401
	(-0.02)	(-0.34)	(0.33)	(2.13)**
Child6-12	0.514	-0.249	0.384	-0.784
	(2.80)***	(-1.19)	(1.35)	(-1.89)***
ChildM12	-0.196	0.155	0.225	-0.882
	(-0.81)	(0.61)	(0.58)	(-2.13)**
ChildF13	-0.225	0.534	-0.363	-0.141
	(-0.84)	(1.65)*	(-0.90)	(-0.29)
Head	3.39	1.162	-0.279	-0.096
	(4.03)***	(1.15)	(-0.22)	(-0.05)
Wife	-	-	0.753	-5.52
			(0.63)	(-2.98)***
Son/Daught	0.350	-0.487	-0.045	0.390
	(0.39)	(-0.48)	(-0.04)	(0.21)
Others	0.417	4.315	2.697	7.32
	(0.21)	(2.11)**	(1.69)*	(2.80)***
North	-0.743	-0.920	4.417	-1.663
	(-0.72)	(-0.67)	(3.62)**	(-0.89)
Central	1.858	3.54	6.546	-0.897
	(2.49)**	(4.03)***	(6.92)***	(-0.67)
Seast	0.645	5.46	7.527	-4.66
	(1.06)	(9.04)***	(12.05)***	(-5.32)***

Table 11.14 (continued)

Variables	Men		Women	
	Formal	Informal	Formal	Informal
South	0.823	4.33	6.40	-1.26
	(1.21)	(6.86)***	(8.27)***	(-1.11)
Urban	-1.792	2.89	4.053	0.257
	(-2.25) **	(3.00)***	(4.20)***	(0.28)
Nonlinc	0.000150	-0.00800	0.00674	-0.00093
	(0.12)	(-4.20)***	(2.19)**	(-0.13)
White	0.427	1.960	1.369	-3.166
	(0.61)	(2.48)***	(1.41)	(-2.31)**
Mulatto	-0.222	0.986	2.31	-4.064
	(-0.31)	(1.27)	(2.32)**	(-3.16)***
EducationH	-	-	0.0013	-0.127
			(0.02)	(-1.32)
ExperienceH	-	-	-0.00724	0.0618
			(-0.56)	(3.06)***
F test	12.45***	13.01***	22.31***	13.47***

Note: [a] - *endogenous variable*
The t-tests are given in parentheses below the coefficients
*significant at the 10% level; **at the 5 level; ***at the 1% level*

The discussion of the results will focus on the earnings variable (logwage), since the others are used as control variables, and they were already discussed in the participation equations. The coefficients of the logwage variable were significant and negative in the formal market sector and positive in the informal sector. The labor supply elasticities with respect to hourly wage rates at the sample means are: -0.064 and 0.12 for men and –0.19 and 0.04 for women in the formal and informal sectors, respectively. These results show that an increase in the wages would decrease the number of hours worked by men and women in the formal sector, but would increase them in the informal sector. It is interesting to notice that, in the formal sector, the effect of an increase in wages on hours of work is negative but much higher, in absolute value, for women than for men. This can be explained by the fact that women are more involved in household activities and child care than men, in the way that an increase in income would make them substitute time in the labor market by time spent in household activities in higher proportion than men. In the informal sector, an increase in wages increase the number of hours working. The schedule in the informal sector may be more flexible than in the formal sector. According to Hill (1989) "the presence of an informal sector of the labor market may allow women to engage in economic activity - by producing goods at home for market sale, working on a family farm, or working in a small family-run business - while simultaneously caring for children and performing other home-related duties".

Pencavel (1992) reported a number of wage elasticities estimates for men from U.S. nonexperimental data; the range was from -0.29 to 0.06. Heckman (1980) obtained, for white American wives from 35 to 44 years, elasticities ranging from 1.47 to 14.79 using different methods of estimation. Hill (1989) using a sample from Japan estimated labor supply elasticities with respect to wages of 0.26 for women employees and 0.25 for women as family workers. Martin and Robles (1997), using data from Peru, obtained an elasticity equal to 0.42 for adult men in the rural sector.

Conclusions

The labor force participation for men and women in the formal and informal sectors of the Brazilian economy was estimated by maximum likelihood using a multinomial logit model. The results show that the number of children, education, experience, and health, among other variables, affect the participation decision of men and women in the formal and informal markets. Some differences are present though; while young children have a negative impact on women's participation, they have a positive impact on men's participation. Moreover, teenage daughters increase the mother's participation in the job market, as they can act as substitutes for the mother's care of very young children. Connected to this fact is the result that the head of the household has a higher labor force participation than his spouse. Further, education has a very strong effect on participation for both men and women in the formal sector. However, in the informal sector, the effect is smaller for women and not even significant for men. The level of education required in informal jobs is lower than in formal jobs. Health positively affected male formal workers, but negatively affected informal male workers. There is a possibility that healthier and therefore more productive workers move to sectors that reward health. On women's participation, however, health did not show any effect.

The earnings functions were estimated by weighted least squares, correcting for selectivity bias. Education, experience and health positively affected earnings. Returns to education ranged from 6.10% to 21.12%, being much higher in the formal than informal sector.   Returns to experience were smaller than those to education, ranging from 1.47% to 7.59%. Brazil has one of the highest percentage of student absenteeism from primary school in the world. Illiteracy is very high and the quality of elementary school as well as the instructor's salaries very low. Moreover, the resources allocated to education are not well managed by the government, resulting in inefficiency and low quality public schools (see previous chapter).

According to the National Industry Confederation (CNI), the number of companies sponsoring medical assistance and education to their employees and family is increasing. Research shows that, in 1992, 3.3% of the collective agreements included health plans, while in 1995, the percentage had increased to 12%. Moreover, companies are financing childcare centers and they are participating in school tax payments.

Significant gender discrimination was found when comparing women's wages estimated by substituting their characteristics in the men's structure. While the actual average woman's earnings are approximately 30% below the men's wage, the estimated average women's earnings surpassed the average men's earnings. Wage race discrimination was observed in both sectors, but was higher in the formal job market. The results also showed that blacks suffered more discrimination than mulattos, except for men in informal jobs. Non-white men suffered more discrimination than women in the formal sector, but the opposite was observed in the informal sector. The percentage of wage differentials for black men due to discrimination was 45% and 0% in the formal and informal sectors, respectively, while for black women it was 43% and 36%.

Finally, the results showed that 16% of the wage differential between formal and informal sectors, for men and women, was due to market segmentation. This study detected race and gender discrimination as well as market segmentation in the Brazilian labor market. Those factors exacerbate the income inequality problem in Brazil, requiring the implementation of policies that will decrease unexplained wage gaps and consequently increase the welfare of the society.

Notes

[1] Heckman (1980) analyzed a possible endogeneity of labor market experience in the participation decision. According to the author, experience records previous work history and is highly correlated with unmeasured determinants of the current labor force.

[2] In the rural sector, the concept of an informal job does not apply very well. Based on that, the whole analysis was repeated considering only urban workers, but the results were practically the same.

[3] To obtain 27%, 1-exp(-0.23-0.088) was estimated since we are dealing with logarithms.
[4] To obtain 84% the following calculation was done: [0.088-(-0.60)]/[0.088-(-0.73)] and [-0.23-(0.99)]/[-0.23-(-0.87)].
[5] This study includes only male employees in the urban segment of nine metropolitan areas in the private sector with and without formal labor contract.

References

Barros, R. *et al.* (1995) "Técnicas Empíricas de Decomposição: Uma Abordagem Baseada em Simulações Contrafactuais." *Revista de Econometria*, 15, 33-63.

Barros, R., A. Machado and R. Mendonça. (1997) "A Desigualdade da Pobreza: Estratégias Ocupacionais e Diferenciais por Gênero." *Texto para Discussão 453*, IPEA.

Barros R., R. Mello and V. Pero. (1993) "Informal Labor Contracts: A Solution or a Problem?" *Texto para Discussão 291*, IPEA.

Barros R. and R. Mendonça. (1996) "Os Determinantes da Desigualdade no Brasil" in *A Economia Brasileira em Perspectiva*. IPEA, Rio de Janeiro, v. 2.

Barros, R. and L. Ramos. (1992) "A Note on the Temporal Evolution of the Relationship Between Wages and Education Among Brazilian Prime-Age Males: 1976-1989". *Texto para Discussão 279, IPEA*.

Berndt, Ernst R. (1991) *The Practice of Econometrics Classic and Contemporary*. New York, Addison Wesley.

Blinder, A. (1973) "Wage Discrimination: Reduced Form and Structural Estimates," *Journal of Human Resources*, 8, 436-455.

Brown, R., M. Moon and B. Zoloth. (1980) "Incorporating Occupational Attainment in Studies of Male-female Earnings Differentials," *Journal of Human Resources*, 15, 3-28.

Coitinho, D. C., M. Leão, E. Recine and R. Sichier. (1991) "Condições Nutricionais da População Brasileira: Adultos e Idosos", Ministério da Saúde e INAN.

Corcoran, M. and G. Duncan. (1979) "Work History, Labor Force Attachment, and Earnings Differences between the Races and Sexes," *Journal of Human Resources*, 14,1-20.

Garrow, J. S. (1981) *Treat Obesity Seriously - A Clinical Manual*, Edinburgh, Churchill Livingstone.

Greene, W. (1993) *Econometric Analysis*. London, Macmillan.

Grossman, M. (1972) "On the Concept of Health Capital and the Demand for Health," *Journal of Political Economy*, 80, 223-255.

Grossman, M. and L. Benham. (1974) "Health, Hours and Wages." In M. Perlman (ed.) *The Economic of Health and Medical Care*. London, Macmillan, pp. 205-233.

Heckman, J. (1980) "Sample Selection Bias as a Specification Error." In James P. Smith (ed.) *Female Labor Supply: Theory and Estimation*. Princeton, Princeton University Press.

Hill, M. A. (1989) "Female Labor Supply in Japan. Implications of the Informal Sector for Labor Force Participation and Hours of Work," *Journal of Human Resources*, 24, 143-161.

James, W., A. Ferro-Luzzi and J. Waterlow. (1988) "Definition of Chronic Energy Deficiency in Adults," *European Journal of Clinical Nutrition*, 42, 969-981.

Kassouf, A. L. (1998) "Wage Gender Discrimination and Market Segmentation in the Brazilian Labor Market," *Revista de Economia Aplicada*, 2, 243-269.

Lam, D. and D. Levison. (1990) "Idade, Experiência, Escolaridade e Diferenciais de Renda: Estados Unidos e Brasil," *Pesquisa e Planejamento Econômico*, 20, 219-256.

Lee, Lung-Fei. (1983) "Generalized Econometric Models with Selectivity," *Econometrica*, 51, 507-513.

Lovell, P. (1992) "Raça, Classe, Gênero e Discriminação Salarial no Brasil," *Estudos Afro-Asiáticos*, 22, 85-98.

Maddala, G. (1990) *Limited-Dependent and Qualitative Variables in Econometrics*. Cambridge, Cambridge University Press.

Martin, J. V. & M. Robles. (1997) Decisiones Laborales en las Economias Rurales del Peru. GRADE, Lima, Peru. (mimeo.)

Mincer, J. (1962) "On-the-job Training: Costs, Returns and some Implications," *Journal of Political Economy*, 70, S50-S79.

Mincer, J. (1974) *Schooling, Experience and Earnings*. New York, Columbia University Press for the National Bureau of Economic Research.

Oaxaca, R. (1973) "Male Female Wage Differentials in Urban Labor Markets," *International Economic Review*, 14, 693-709.

Pastore, J. (1981) "Mobilidade Social sob Condições de Segmentação do Mercado no Brasil," *Estudos Econômicos*, 11, 21-41.

Pencavel, J. (1992) "Labor Supply of Men: A Survey." In O. Ashenfelter and R, Layard (eds.) *Handbook of Labor Economics*, Amsterdam, Elsevier Science Publishers. pp. 3-102.

Psacharopoulos, G. (1981) "Returns to Education: An Updated International Comparison." *Comparative Education*, 17, 321-341.

Psacharopoulos, G. (1985) "Returns to Education: A Further International Update and Implications," *Journal of Human Resources*, 25, 583-597.

Savedoff, W. (1990) "Wages in Urban Brazil: Evidence of Regional Segmentation or National Markets?" *Texto para Discussão* n. 203, IPEA, Rio de Janeiro.

Smith, J. and F. Welch. (1977) "Black-White Male Wage Ratios: 1960-70," *American Economic Review*, 67, 323-338.

Thomas, D. and J. Strauss. (1993) "Health, wealth and wages of men and women in urban Brazil" mimeo, RAND, Santa Monica, California.

Tiefenthaler, J. (1994a) "Female Labor Force Participation and Wage Determination in Brazil, 1989." In G. Psacharopoulos and Z. Tzannatos (eds.) *Cases Studies on Women's Employment and Pay in Latin America.*

Tiefenthaler, J. (1994b) "A Multisector Model of Female Labor Force Participation: Empirical Evidence from Cebu Island, Philippines," *Economic Development and Cultural Change*, 42, 719-741.

Valle Silva, N. (1980). "O Preço da cor: Diferenciais Raciais na Distribuição da Renda no Brasil". *Pesquisa e Planejamento Econômico*, 10, 21-44.

Valle Silva, N. (1993). "Situação Social da População Negra." In João P. dos Reis Velloso and R. C. de Albuquerque (eds.) *Pobreza e Mobilidade Social.* São Paulo, Editora Nobel.

Willis, R. J. (1986) "Wage Determinants: A Survey and Reinterpretation of Human Capital Earnings Functions." In O. Ashenfelter and R, Layard (eds.) *Handbook of Labor Economics*, Amsterdam, Elsevier Science Publishers.

12 The Current Brazilian Transportation Structure

PAULO T.V. RESENDE

Introduction

The Brazilian transport system is currently characterized by highly concentrated flows of products and services in its highway network, whereas the railroad and inland waterway modes[1] are left aside to a secondary plan. No matter the high usage - more than 60% of the general freight is carried by heavy trucks - within the last two decades, there have been limited efforts directed towards continuous planning for maintenance, operation, and safety on the highway network. The other modes, such as railways, inland waterways, and coastal navigation, have shown much lower productivity levels. As an example, inland waterways account for just 1% of the general freight, despite the fact that the country has approximately 20,000 miles of navigable rivers. The railroad system, once considered to have a dominant role in territorial integration, has experienced significant deterioration in its equipment, personnel productivity, and operational network. Some hopes have been raised due to the recently completed process of privatization, since private funds have been made available for reconstruction and rehabilitation of the physical network.

Given this outlook of the Brazilian transportation system, there is an urgent need for a planning program with a detailed inventory of the critical links or bottlenecks, to provide strategic inputs into decisions about the spatial and temporal schedule of investments. If this program becomes a reality, then the transportation sector can be adjusted to enhance Brazil's competitiveness both in the internal and external markets. Nevertheless, it is important that the current short-run approach of Brazilian decision makers be changed to a more comprehensive view of the role played by infrastructure systems, so that investments are not made on inefficient transportation segments. Accordingly, in this chapter, analysis will be made of the level of service[2] of major highway segments, railroad networks, and river routes, so that the critical links can be identified as the prime candidates for immediate improvement.

To accomplish that, a set of simulations was conducted to examine the likely consequences of trade agreements, especially MERCOSUR,[3] on the efficiency, capacity, modal choice, and development of multimodal systems.[4] The main reason to consider MERCOSUR as the main source of trade impacts and changes in traffic volumes is exactly because this *free trade zone* is still the major factor in increasing demands for better and more competitive transportation facilities in Brazil. In this way, capacity problems, that cannot be solved in the short run, are evaluated in terms of their costs to the economy - i.e., lost output or increased transportation costs that reduce the competitiveness of the sectors. One of the major contributions of this analysis is the identification of bottlenecks, followed by suggestions for priorities in investment, so the existing facilities might be upgraded in terms of capacity levels. Naturally, due to the size limitations of this chapter, the link-by-link details of the original study are not shown, but the main findings of the impacts of MERCOSUR on the current Brazilian transportation systems are revealed.

Before any further detailed analysis of the transportation network, it is helpful to summarize the most important facts related to the historical developments of the transportation system in Brazil, so that its current status is better understood.

Historical Development

The Brazilian transportation system reflects, today, the historical absence of long-term-planning administrations. Since the colonization times, there has been a lack of rational and objective planning programs that could lead the country to more integrated and self-sustained transportation facilities. When it is said that in Brazil there has not existed a planning program able to cope with the economic transformations, it means that, over the years, most of the Brazilian transportation administrations have not paid *enough* attention to planning, designing, implementing and, above all, continuously evaluating the results of what has been built (see Resende, 1991).

The colonization premises dictated the evolution of the Brazilian transportation systems within each region. The occupation of the Brazilian territory was made gradually from the coast to the inland, and cyclically based on the production and exploitation of the natural resources. During the first two colonial centuries, the territorial occupation was restricted to a very narrow coastal strip that did not exceed 100 miles in width. Since the entire economy was focused on cyclical natural resources exploitation, that, by nature, were not renewable, the new production poles (i.e., exploitation areas) always led to disruptions in the growing process of the already settled poles. On that account, investment in transportation facilities was made in response to short-term and often transitory needs; as a result, the transportation networks were comprised of thousands of small routes, temporarily used, and then completed abandoned, most of them directed to the main maritime ports that connected the colony to the most important European centers (Resende, 1991).

With political independence, the colonialist eye was substituted by a more intensive trend of exploration and territorial expansion. At that time, the first governmental programs to implement a skeletal, planned transportation network were brought about, and the first highways were built, linking the most important cities, mainly those in the Minas Gerais, Rio de Janeiro and São Paulo States. It was also in that period when some railroad segments were constructed.

Despite the operational difficulties when the gold basis was changed to the federal bonus basis, together with the already incipient inflationary process, between 1890 and 1940 some very important railroads and highways were built. By 1950, the Brazilian federal highway system was approximately 35,000 miles in length, while the railroad network had around 20,000 miles of track. These numbers obviously account for an acceptable balance between the two most important transportation modes of that time, therefore showing promising perspectives as related to a future, well-developed multimodal network (Resende, 1991).

During the 1950's, the Brazilian government radically changed its polices toward the construction of an extensive highway network, with attention directed to expansion of this network by all levels of governmental. Accordingly, the Brazilian highway system reached, by 1982, approximately 75,000 miles of federally paved highways, within a total of one million and a half miles of federal, state, and county roads. With the arrival of the automobile industry, the Brazilian government agreed to invest in highways, so that the new vehicles would have a large transportation network on which to move. As a complement to the automobile industry, petroleum companies were created and expanded to supply the vehicles with the necessary fuels. This movement also resulted in a massive production of bituminous asphalt, thereby completing the highway-focused cycle during Brazil's golden period.

With the dominant focus on highway development, Brazilian decision makers ignored the most basic rules of planning, where any transportation system needs design, implementation, evaluation, and, most of all, maintenance (and not just construction). The maintenance issue of the planning process was just set aside, and, from the 1980s on, the entire highway system deteriorated, reaching levels of service much below the minimum standards of operation. Today, this deteriorated highway network is responsible for tremendous economic losses, extremely high accident figures and, obviously, negative effects on Brazil's international competitiveness.

With the incentives and federally centralized decisions toward the implementation of such a highway network, the other modes of transportation were relegated to secondary status, thereby leading to significant and potentially unrecoverable losses in their participation in the transportation matrix. As an example, the railroad system has not increased since the 1940s and the inland waterway mode practically does not exist. Despite the existence of approximately 20,000 miles of navigable rivers, the first notable inland waterway route, the Tietê-Paraná Project, mainly located in the state of São Paulo, became a reality only in the 1990s. As a result of several decades of unplanned policies, the Brazilian transportation share by mode is completely unbalanced, as it can be seen in table 12.1.

Table 12.1   Freight Transportation: Modal Distribution (1997)[5]

Transportation Mode	% Share
Highways	57.58
Railroads	21.22
Inland Waterways	1.00
Coastal and International Navigation	16.42
Pipeline	3.49
Air	0.29

Source: *GEIPOT (1996)*

Notwithstanding the historical disruptions and poorly planned decisions, the Brazilian transportation system still has unquestionable potential to achieve an efficient level of service, especially given the dimension of Brazilian natural resources and current levels of investment in the economy. What has been observed in Brazil today is a dynamic process of infrastructure privatization, that has already led to several planning programs directed towards intermodal systems, multimodal facilities, and private participation in decision making, among others. These initiatives tend to change the mentality of the transportation planner to a more comprehensive approach, where the level of service of the facilities will dictate the amount of investments within the macro regions of the country. These new perspectives for the role played by transportation facilities call for a more detailed understanding of the interface between economic trends and transportation systems, the subject of the next section.

Economic and Transportation Interface Modeling: Level of Service Analysis

Given the economic trends lately affecting the Brazilian economy, such as the globalization process and the implementation of MERCOSUR, the transportation infrastructure is supposed to undergo the direct impacts of the increases in traffic volume brought about by those trends. If there still exists operational capacity on the roads, then these impacts would lead to more profitable ways within which the Brazilian economy would expand its competitiveness. However, this does not happen. On the contrary, what has been observed is an elevated deterioration of the roads' capacity, thereby leading to negative effects in the efficiency level when it comes to the movement of goods within the most important regions. Therefore, the analysis undertaken here is directed to the identification of the main bottlenecks, where the magnitude of the economic losses due to higher operational costs will establish the level of investment needs.

Focusing on MERCOSUR as one of the primary sources of traffic volume increases, together with population growth and eventually the growth in income, the expected impacts of its implementation are investigated through the impact of changes in macro economic variables and their effects upon the volume-to-capacity ratio[6]. Accordingly, an analysis has been conducted on the increases in demand for transportation in six corridors, and how this demand will spread along the main routes of the highway network. The increases in demand are calculated and translated into coefficients that directly impact the level of service (i.e., volume-to-capacity ratios) of the most important highway segments of the Brazilian transportation network.

According to figure 12.1, the stepwise analysis of the MERCOSUR impacts upon the transportation systems is conducted as follows:

- There is a production/consumption activity level, which indicates the primary flows (origin-destination) within each corridor. The 1996 participation of each flow in the total freight movements in Brazil is adopted as the current one, considering that the main routes in 1996 are still the same in 1999;

- The main highway segments, given the unbalanced condition of the Brazilian transportation matrix (where, today, more than 60% of the total volume are transported by trucks), are taken as the primary transportation links;

- Within a certain region, each highway segment links a production pole area to a consumption center. Therefore, the goods and services are moved throughout existing routes, resulting in traffic volumes that can be easily quantified. Each segment, however, has a certain operational capacity that is limited to some mix of variables related to geometry, paving, design and traffic mix. In this way, it is not very difficult to come up with a ratio between that traffic volume and the operational capacity of each segment;

- The impact of MERCOSUR then leads to an increase, or even a decrease, in the traffic volumes of those segments;

- Finally, the level of service, quantified by the volume-to-capacity ratio, of each highway segment is negatively or positively altered, but eventually leading to bottlenecks in along some links. In other words, in 1996, each highway segment had a certain level of service, so defined by the relationship between the traffic volume and its operational capacity. Given the implementation of MERCOSUR, which generates trade coefficients, the traffic volume of each segment is affected, thereby changing the measure of the ratio between volume and capacity, resulting in changes in the level of service of the highway segments.

Origin-Destination Matrix

Data were collected on the origin-destination of 53 products, distributed all over the country. Actually, due to an absence of reliable data basis for all the products within all Brazilian regions, the main production/consumption areas were taken as the sources of the most significant traffic flows, so that a meaningful sampling of the Brazilian highway traffic volumes could be achieved. In the year 1996, a total of, approximately, 260 million tons were transported by railroads, 12 million tons by inland waterways, and 420 million tons by highways (FIPE, 1996; GEIPOT, 1996, IBGE, 1991-1992). Out of these 692 million tons, approximately 44% were surveyed and these are the data that form the basis of the investigation. Considering that a significant amount of the products included in the total volume is widely distributed along the regions, those 44%, which included only the products with high aggregate volumes, were taken as a statistically significant sample of the total traffic volume in the country.

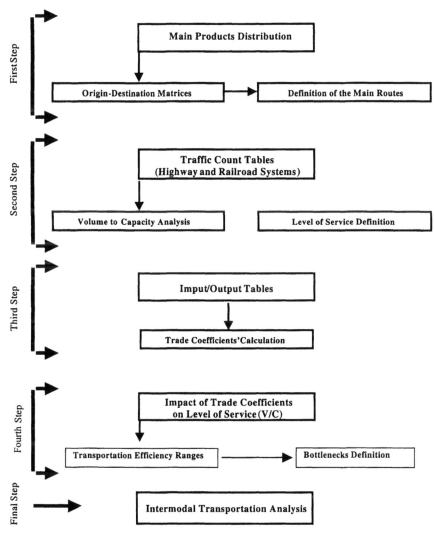

Figure 12.1   Stepwise Transportation Analysis

However, it is important to note that attention was paid to the regional representation of the sample size, so that a lack of equilibrium in the spatial distribution of the flows was avoided. That is why some regions with low production and consumption levels were also considered to have the potential to generate significant traffic volumes in the near future.

Definition of the Main Routes

From the origin-destination matrix, it was possible to define the main highway segments in each corridor. The basic approach was to select the most significant production and consumption areas not only within a certain corridor, but also from that corridor to the five others. To accomplish this, the origin-destination tonnage was transformed into percentages. Then, based on the internal and external distributions[7] of those percentage values, it was possible to identify the main flows upon which the impacts of MERCOSUR would surely fall.

For each corridor, a series of histograms was analyzed, where the volume in each origin-destination link was divided by the total volume of the corridor. In this way, it was possible to obtain the percent participation of each link in the total volume transported in that corridor. From this evaluation, it was determined that every link that had a percentage higher than 3% was considered as an important route. However, in some regions, where the distribution of production and consumption areas was very spread out, some small percentages were also considered, mostly because of the importance of those regions in the expansion of the Brazilian economy.

Once the primary links in each corridor were identified, another analysis was conducted to investigate the existence of highway segments that coincided with the origin-destination links. This analysis was very simple and based on two steps. First, in each corridor, there were groups of primary origin-destination routes, linking the most important production and consumption areas; and secondly, a mapping analysis was conducted to select the existing highway segments that serve the primary origin-destination routes, so that the origin-destination matrix was transformed into a highway network. After that, it was possible to calculate the level of service for each of the most significant highway segments, recalling that the level of service was given by the ratio between traffic volume and operational capacity.

Level of Service Estimation

The operational capacity of each highway segment is the result of geometric and traffic factors that affect the flowing quality of the segment National Research Council (1985). The Highway Capacity Manual, special report 209 - 1985,[8] was the source used to calculate the operational capacities of the segments, due to the absence of a manual that considers the real operational parameters of the Brazilian highways. In this analysis, all the segments were taken as from rural multilane highways with lateral access and two lanes per direction. The main reasons for such an assumption were that, in a very significant number of segments, the operational characteristics are similar to rural two-lane highways, however there are no data related to intersection parameters, travel time and traffic signal conditions. Moreover, most of the segments are located on the boundaries of the main cities, so that the suburban (not urban) characteristic is highly obvious. In addition, the unlimited access on all the segments does not allow them to be considered as freeway segments and thus, the linear coefficients applied to the traffic volumes and to the operational capacities are more valid to the densities in the ranges for rural multilane highways, when compared to other highway types.

Accordingly, the basic equation to calculate the operational capacity was taken as National Research Council (1985):

$$C_c = C_d \cdot N \cdot I_{hv} \cdot I_d \cdot I_g \cdot I_e \tag{12.1}$$

where,

C_c : operational capacity, in vehicles per day;

C_d : design capacity, equal to 1800 vehicles per hour per lane times 24 hours (the temporal distribution is considered similar for every hour of any day, which is typical of rural highways);

N : number of lanes;

I_{hv} : factor to adjust for the effects of heavy vehicles in the traffic stream, taken from Tables 7.3 to 7.6, 7.8, and 7.9 of the Highway Capacity Manual – 1985. The traffic equivalent is equal to 13, for 5% ramps and ramp lengths higher than 0.8 miles. The 5% ramp was used to partially compensate for the extremely high heavy vehicle traffic (the other compensation was made when a 0.29 coefficient was adopted to traffic mixes with heavy vehicle percentages higher than 20%), which is superior to the 20% maximum limit in the Highway Capacity Manual;

I_d : factor to adjust for the driver's population, which was considered as 1 for all the cases;

I_g : factor to adjust for the effects of restricted lane widths and/or lateral clearances, Table 7.2 of the Highway Capacity Manual – 1985. The choice was made to adopt one-side obstructions, lane width of 11 feet, two lanes per direction and shoulder width varying from 0 to 3.3 feet;

I_e : factor to adjust for the environmental development, when the segment was characterized as multilane highways, taken from table 7.10 of the Highway Capacity Manual - 1985.

According to the assumptions and parameters described above, the traffic coefficients assumed to adjust the design capacity in order to find the operational capacity are shown in table 12.2. Based on the above equation, a certain volume-to-capacity ratio was achieved for each of the main highway segments within each corridor.

In order to transform this ratio into a parameter that can be termed *level of service*, several ranges were identified and modified for Brazilian highway conditions (see table 12.3). The main reason to modify the original Highway Capacity Manual description is due to the operational differences between the Brazilian and the North American highway systems. This is because, in the United States, the pavement conditions, the conflict between vehicles and pedestrians, the lack of shoulders, as well as other variables do not represent negative barriers to the operational capacity estimation, mainly due to the planned (i.e., sustained and long range planning) maintenance programs.

Table 12.2 Traffic Coefficients to Operational Capacity Adjustments

Description of the Coefficient	Numerical Value
Design capacity	43,200 vpd
Factor to adjust for heavy vehicles	0.29 for heavy traffic higher than 20%
	0.32 for heavy traffic between 18% (exclusive) and 20%
	0.34 for heavy traffic between 16% and 18%
Factor to adjust for driver population	1.0
Factor to adjust for restricted lane widths and lateral clearances	Intermediary value of 0.82
Factor to adjust for the environmental development	Intermediary value of 0.89 (between rural and suburban)

Source: *AERI/CNT (1996)*

Table 12.3 Level of Service Based on the Volume-to-Capacity Ratio (V/C) for a Basic Design Speed of 65 mph and the American Conditions for Travel

Speed and Maximum Rate of Flow per Lane under Ideal Conditions

Level of Service	Ranges of Volume-to-Capacity Ratios	
	US Rural Multilane Highways	Brazilian Highways
A	0.01 - 0.33	0.01 - 0.09
B	0.37 - 0.50	0.10 - 0.19
C	0.51 - 0.65	0.20 - 0.45
D	0.66 - 0.80	0.46 - 0.79
E	0.81 - 1.00	0.80 - 0.85
F	> 1.00	> 0.86

Source: *AERI/CNT (1996)*

In Brazil, the highways are subjected to a level of deterioration so high that the direct translation of the North American level of service ranges would result in critical flaws, mainly in the A, B and C ranges. There are three main reasons for such differences in the level of service ranges. Most prominently, the paving conditions of the Brazilian roads are much more deteriorated than those in North American. Further, there are numerous instances where the highway geometry does not comply with the needs of 65 mph speeds. The final reasons stems from the fact that the conflict between heavy vehicles and passenger cars is much more intense in Brazil, as compared to the United States.

The Trade-Transportation Modeling Aggregation

The aggregation of the trade-transportation models was made through several steps, where the primary target was the spatial, or regional, standardization of the coefficients to be applied to the highway volumes. Figure 12.2 shows a schematic sequence of these steps. The spatial partitioning in the economic model was made for five macro-regions, i.e., North, South, Central, Southeast and Northeast. On the other hand, the transportation model grouped six corridors, based on the main routes of goods and services throughout the country. Accordingly, the first task was to manipulate the economic coefficients of the five macro-regions to regionally match with the six corridors, since one macro-region could be part of one or more corridors. This was accomplished by analyzing the origin-destination matrices containing the most important products. The economic model had 33 sectors, so there had to be a statistically significant sampling of products within each economic sector in the origin-destination matrix (Resende, 1997).

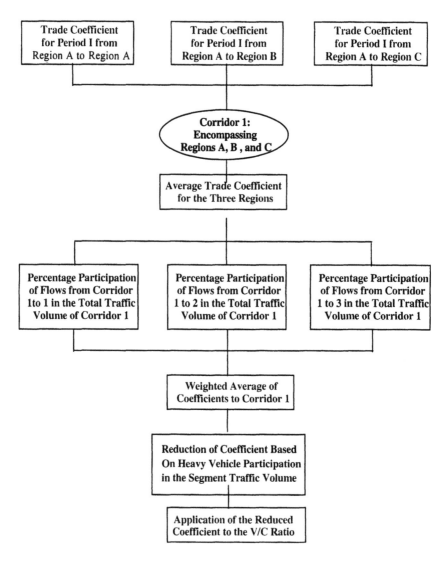

Figure 12.2   Stepwise analysis of the economic impacts of MERCOSUL: a three-region, three-corridor example

Taking into account the regional differences between the economic model and the transportation model, i.e., macro-regions and corridors, the stepwise analysis to standardize the trade coefficients to be applied to the highway traffic volumes had the following sequence:

1. Within a certain forecasting period, there exists one, and only one, trade coefficient from macro-region A to macro-region B, from macro-region A to macro-region C, and so on;
2. Since every corridor encompassed one or more macro-regions, a simple average was calculated to represent only one trade coefficient for each corridor. A macro-region can be part of more than one corridor; that is why an average of the coefficient had to be taken. However, it is important to emphasize that, since the regional differences between the two models (i.e., economic and transportation models) were not too critical, and since the nature of trade is naturally concentrated (gravity theory), the simple average did not result in significant distortions;
3. The flows among the corridors were identified by an origin-destination matrix (O-D matrix), as explained before. Since the O-D matrix was built upon micro-regional production/consumption areas, it was possible to aggregate all the areas into macro-regional groups within the corridors. Then, the percentage participation of each "corridor-to-corridor flow" as related to the total traffic volume of a certain corridor could be obtained;
4. By using these percentage participations as weights, a single weighted trade coefficient was generated for each corridor, within a certain forecasting period;
5. All the products considered in the O-D matrix are not subjected to significant transformations (i.e., meaningful value aggregation) from the origin to the destination. And since all the products were characterized by low aggregate values and high growth weights, it was feasible to assume that a certain percentage change in trade could be directly and linearly applied to the highway traffic volumes. However, this linear effect would be only valid for heavy traffic. In other words, one cannot assume that the changes in trade will linearly affect passenger cars. Since the operational capacity takes into account the heavy traffic factor as a result of the "truck-passenger car" equivalent values, the heavy traffic participation in the total traffic flow was taken as the "reduction factor" for the trade coefficients;
6. After reaching a reduced trade coefficient for each highway segment, the trade coefficients were applied to the volume-to-capacity ratios (V/C

ratios) to reflect the impacts of MERCOSUR on the highway transportation network of the six corridors.

Summarizing, based on this stepwise analysis, it was possible to identify one trade coefficient for each forecasting period, from 1997 to 2014 (since the base-year of the original study was 1996), within each corridor. The following equation shows an example of the mathematical standardization of the trade coefficients for each corridor AERI/CNT (1996):

$$I_{clr} = \left[(I_{11} x W_1 + I_{12} x W_2 + I_{13} x W_3)/100 \right] x \%_{hvl} \tag{12.2}$$

where:

I_{clr} - weighted trade coefficient for corridor 1 in the I period for a certain highway segment;

I_{11} - averaged trade coefficient resulting from the individual trade coefficients from macro-regions of corridor 1 to corridor 1;

W_1 - percent participation in total flows of corridor 1 to corridor 1;

I_{12} - averaged trade coefficient resulting from the individual trade coefficients from macro-regions of corridor 2 to corridor 1;

W_2 - percent participation in total flows of corridor 2 to corridor 1;

I_{13} - averaged trade coefficient resulting from the individual trade coefficients from macro-regions of corridor 3 to corridor 1;

W_3 - percent participation in total flows of corridor 3 to corridor 1;

$\%_{hvl}$ - reduction trade coefficient based on the heavy vehicle percentage for a certain highway segment.

With this stepwise analysis, it was possible to apply the trade coefficients to each V/C ratio from 1997 to 2014, so the deterioration in the level of service of each important highway segment was quantified, thereby identifying the main bottlenecks of the Brazilian highway system. The data from 1997 and 1998 were maintained in this chapter, despite the fact that they are now somehow outdated, because it is important to have a clearer idea of the deterioration process in the highway network over the years.

An Analysis of the Brazilian Transportation Systems by Corridor

After reaching a single trade coefficient for each corridor and for each projection period, it was possible to apply these coefficients to measure the impacts of MERCOSUR on the Brazilian highway transportation systems. According to table 12.4, the coefficients vary from 2.59% to 24.20%, with some periods made of 5-year ranges and some of 1-year ranges.

Based on these coefficients and their impacts in the Brazilian highways, an analysis is conducted for each corridor, where the production/consumption parameters change, according to the economic characteristics of each region. This analysis is shown here in summarized form; for more details, see AERI/CNT (1996).

Table 12.4   MERCOSUR Trade Coefficients by Corridor (%) per Projection Period

Projection Period	Rio Grande* Corridor	Paraná-Santa Catarina Corridor*	Santos Corridor*	Central-East Corridor	Northeast Corridor	Northern Corridor
1997	3.73	3.66	3.61	3.98	3.54	3.92
1998	6.57	6.30	6.71	5.97	5.97	6.01
1999	2.62	2.88	2.74	3.74	2.59	3.33
2000	5.75**	5.36	5.62	5.39	5.30	5.33
2005	23.30	23.69	23.07	24.18	22.68	23.77
2010	23.37	23.70	23.08	24.20	22.69	23.78
2014	18.28	18.53	18.11	18.98	17.73	18.66

Notes: **Rio Grande: southern region close to Argentina and Uruguay; Paraná-Sta Catarina: southern region close to Paraguay; Santos: São Paulo region, encompassing the biggest port in the Brazil (the Port of Santos).*
** As an example, in the year 2000, it is expected that the traffic volumes will grow 6% in the highways of the Rio Grande Corridor due to the impacts of MERCOSUR in the Brazilian economy.

Source: *AERI/CNT (1996)*

Rio Grande Corridor

The productive matrix of the Rio Grande Corridor is essentially built on agricultural products, such as soybean, wheat, corn, rice and meat. The Rio Grande Corridor incorporates the State of Rio Grande do Sul, in Brazil, and several regions of the Argentinean Northeast, and the North of Uruguay. The main production flows of the Rio Grande Corridor are in the direction of the Brazilian Southeast Region and the Santos and Paranaguá maritime ports, located, respectively, in the States of São Paulo and Paraná, both situated to the north of the Rio Grande Corridor.

According to the last census of the modal transportation distribution of the Brazilian Southern Regions, the highway system accounts for more than 45% of the total volume, with a relatively high participation of the coastal navigation, which takes approximately 46% of that total volume (FIPE, 1996). Based on this modal distribution, two findings stand out when analyzing the Rio Grande Corridor. Given the changes in the Brazilian legislation, where foreign companies can now operate in the coastal navigation system, allied to the high competitiveness of the Argentinean and Uruguayan agricultural products, the Rio Grande regions are negatively affected by the low prices of the products from those two countries in the Brazilian market. This fact leads to a decrease in the Rio Grande participation in the internal and external markets. Therefore, in order to reduce the transportation costs which highly affect the final prices, the most immediate action would be to increase the level of service of the highway and railroad systems of the Rio Grande Corridor, generating the second important finding. One of the most important highway segments serving the Rio Grande Corridor is a federal highway called BR 116. This highway crosses the entire State of Rio Grande do Sul State, linking the capital, Porto Alegre, to the main cities of the southern and southeastern regions, such as Curitiba, São Paulo, and, by some others connections, Rio de Janeiro and Belo Horizonte. However, according to figure 12.3, which shows just one example of a small segment of BR 116, the V/C ratio is already high, reaching a congestion level in the year 2000. Then, it turns out that, without an immediate program to invest in better services in the highway system, the Rio Grande Corridor will continue to be less competitive both in the internal and external markets. The multi-year plan of the current Federal Government, called "Brasil em Ação" takes into consideration a project to double the number of lanes, together with other operational improvements that, if completed, would solve the above mentioned bottlenecks.

It is important to note that the deterioration of the level of service in one highway segment has a ripple effect that spreads out the operational condition of that bottleneck to a large area along the main segment. In other words, once a highway segment deteriorates, the negative effects in the main operation are multiplied along other segments of the main and adjacent routes, leading to higher transportation costs, increases in travel time, less safety and, by all means, reductions in the competitiveness, given the increases in the final prices of the products.

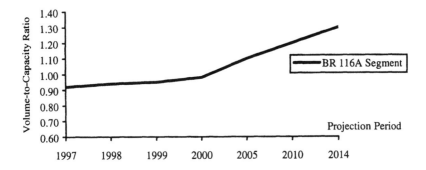

Figure 12.3   Impact of trade on a highway segment in the Rio Grande corridor

Source: *O impacto do Mercosul sobre os sistemas de Transportes do Brasil,*
                   CNT-AERI, 1996

While other transportation systems of the Rio Grande Corridor could be used to handle part of the highway traffic volume, their utilization would require the following actions: standardization of rail gauges; improvement of railway equipment and infrastructure; implementation of an efficient inland waterway system in the Jacuí River (State of Rio Grande do Sul); and expansion and specialization of the Port of Rio Grande to handle agricultural grains. Other improvements would be necessary to eliminate the bottlenecks in the primary segments, such as BR 101, 290 and 386, all in the direction of the Southern and Southeastern States, Argentina and Uruguay.

Paraná-Santa Catarina Corridor

The Paraná-Santa Catarina Corridor involves the other two Brazilian Southern States, Paraná and Santa Catarina, two Central States, Mato Grosso and Mato Grosso do Sul, and the Northeastern Region of Paraguay. This corridor is specialized in the transportation of general cargo, rice, soybean, meat, corn, wheat, fertilizer, and paper products. The Paraná-Santa Catarina Corridor also handles the agricultural flows from the central part of the country, mainly in the direction of the Paranaguá Port,[9] which specializes in the export of agricultural grains.

In terms of modal distribution, the Paraná-Santa Catarina Corridor is characterized by two different patterns. In the two Southern States, the highway system carries 45% of the total traffic; while in the two Central States, the highway system is responsible for 99% of the total volume (FIPE, 1996). These findings create different transportation planning needs. On one hand, the Southern States are well served by highways, with an overall level of service that is able to efficiently handle the traffic volumes. Figure 12.4 shows an example of a very important highway segment, BR 277, in the region.

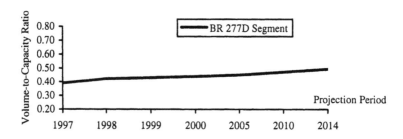

Figure 12.4   Impact of trade on a highway segment in the Paraná-Santa Catarina Corridor

Source: *CNT/AERI (1996)*

On the other hand, the highly concentrated flows on the highway system of the central regions are subjected to poor levels of service, as well as relatively few routes to transport the ever increasing agricultural production. Hence, investment in railroads would appear to be essential, such as the already planned rail tracks crossing the central regions in the direction of the Port of Santos, referred to as *Ferronorte* and *Ferroeste*. Also, the inland waterway system can be significantly improved through the navigation of the Araguaia River, which crosses the central regions in the direction of the northern ports of São Luís (State of Maranhão) and Belém (State of Pará). The use of this waterway system could lead to a lower concentration in the Paranaguá and Santos ports, especially during the peaks of grain exports.

The competition from the other member-countries of MERCOSUR, such as Argentina, Uruguay, and Paraguay, may turn out to be positive, if the maritime advantages of the Paraná-Santa Catarina Corridor are used in a different way. For example, from Paranaguá Port, in Paraná, it is possible to supply the MERCOSUR regions with fertilizers and other agricultural inputs, thereby changing the Paraná-Santa Catarina Corridor into the primary routes of agricultural commerce. Moreover, given the expansion of the agricultural lands in the Central States, if investments are directed to improving the railroad and waterway systems in the States of Mato Grosso and Mato Grosso do Sul, the Paraná-Santa Catarina Corridor can achieve important positions in enhancing Brazil's external competitiveness.

Other important actions in the Paraná-Santa Catarina Corridor are: the implementation of the inland waterway system in the Paraguay-Paraná rivers, in the direction of Paraguay and Argentina; the standardization of railroad gauges in the so called southern network; higher operational capacities in the federal highway routes BR 101, 280, 163, 463, and 267, mainly in the direction of the Southeastern States; and the specialization of the Santa Catarina ports to higher aggregate value products.

It is important to observe that the impacts of MERCOSUR in the highway transportation systems of the Paraná-Santa Catarina Corridor are the lowest among all the six corridors, mainly because the highway network in this corridor has shown levels of service much higher than the average of the other corridors. However, there still exists a need to improve the highway system, since the influence of the economic characteristics of the other member-countries of MERCOSUR is, by some means, negative and subjected to changes that can lead to reductions in the competitiveness of the States of the Paraná-Santa Catarina Corridor.

Santos Corridor

Among the six corridors, the Santos Corridor is the most important in traffic volume, since it crosses the most developed and industrialized State of Brazil, São Paulo. This corridor is basically represented by the State of São Paulo, responsible for approximately 40% of Brazilian Gross Domestic Product, and in which the port of Santos is located, the largest maritime port in South America. As part of the Southeastern Region, the highways in the Santos Corridor move approximately 40% of the total cargo within this corridor (FIPE 1996). The main products are vehicles, cellulose, paper products, metal-mechanics, steel, fertilizer, coffee, soybean, alcohol and sugar.

According to figure 12.5, there exist several highway segments that, once impacted by the trade coefficients, reach significant levels of deterioration as a result of congestion generated by forecasted levels of demands. The examples shown in figure 12.5 are state highway segments that carry the highest traffic volumes, where the V/C ratios, most of the time, achieve values higher than 0.80.

From the perspective of the whole Brazilian highway system, the São Paulo highway network is always an immense bottleneck, mainly because of the highly concentrated flows in that state. The majority of the main federal routes cross the region with products to be distributed to the Northeastern, Northern and Southern Regions, and the primary maritime ports. Throughout the years, the high costs of transportation due to the bottlenecks in São Paulo have generated significant losses in terms of Brazil's international competitiveness.

Another fact that contributes to the increasing number of bottlenecks in the Santos Corridor is the presence of different administrative highway systems in the State of São Paulo. On one hand, the state highway system functions under a more private perspective, which means that the state system is more able to collect taxes and reinvest these taxes directly to the highway network. On the other hand, the federal highway system is subjected to deficient and unplanned polices, leading the highway segments to an endless deterioration process. This explains the ripple effects of the very negative impacts of few bottlenecks in the competitiveness of the São Paulo economy.

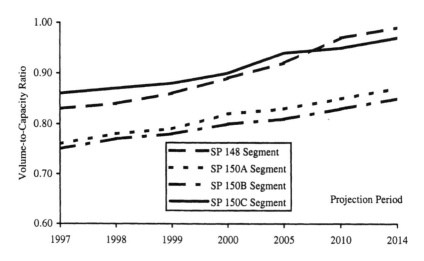

Figure 12.5   Impact of trade on a highway segment in the Santos Corridor

Source: *CNT/AERI, (1996)*

Among the main actions to the Santos Corridor are: acceleration of the highway privatization process; privatization of the railroad system, that already took place, however demanding very high investments; modernization and deregulation of the administrative and operational cargo handling in the Port of Santos; and increasing participation of the inland waterway system, Tietê-Paraná Rivers, in the modal transportation matrix of the Corridor.

Central-East Corridor

The second most important corridor in Brazil is the Central-East Corridor that lies in the States of Minas Gerais, Rio de Janeiro, Espírito Santo, Goiás and Tocantins, accounting for more than 30% of the Brazilian Gross Domestic Product. The impacts of MERCOSUR can be elevated commodity flows in the State of Minas Gerais, where more than 15% of the total freight of the country are moved. In this corridor, the steel industry, the metal-mechanic products, coffee, cellulose and paper products, vehicles, and many other products heavily influence the unbalanced Brazilian transportation matrix.

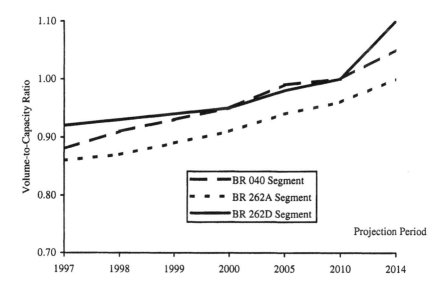

Figure 12.6   Impact of trade on a highway segment in the Central-East Corridor

Source: *CNT/AERI (1996)*

According to figure 12.6, there are several highway segments where the level of deterioration is clear, leading to significant losses in the internal and external competitiveness of the States that form the Central-East Corridor. All three segments exemplified in Figure 12.6 have shown a constant level of congestion due to the high values of the V/C ratios.

Most of the highway segments showing very low levels of service belong to the federal highway system. And the negative impacts of the trade coefficients are spread out to the main routes, in the direction of the ports of Rio de Janeiro and Espírito Santo. Moreover, the flow of agricultural products from the Central States, such as Goiás and Tocantins, is negatively affected by the lack of railroad and inland waterway routes, leading to highly concentrated flows for very long distances in the highway system.

If the participation of the inland waterway mode in the transportation matrix of the Central-East Corridor is considered, then this unbalanced situation becomes even more obvious; even with more than 3,000 miles of navigable rivers in the corridor, less than 1% of the total traffic is carried on the rivers.

Mostly importantly, the Central-East Corridor also contains a railroad network with more than 8,000 miles of track but with an average participation of less than 20% in the total cargo transported in the five states of that corridor. However, there is a spatial mismatch, with more than 70% of the total track mileage is concentrated in the Eastern States, while more than 70% of the agricultural lands are located in the Central States.

Considering this situation, the primary actions to help the expansion and higher competitiveness of the Central-East Corridor would include acceleration of privatization of the highway systems, modernization and deregulation of the administrative and operational cargo handling in the Rio de Janeiro and Vitória ports, standardization of railroad gauges and improvements of the railroad equipment and infrastructure facilities, improvements of the highway system in the Central Regions, mainly Goiás and Tocantins, and, primarily, implementation of an intermodal system where the railroad and inland waterway modes can have a higher participation in the transportation matrix of the Central-East Corridor.

Northeast and Northern Corridors

The two remaining corridors, the Northeast and Northern, are characterized by high levels of consumption, in contrast to their production potential.

For these two corridors, there are two facts that predominate throughout this analysis: these corridors do not exhibit traffic volumes that could lead to significant levels of congestion simply due to the impacts of trade coefficients; and secondly, there is a critical absence of highways, especially in the Northern Corridor. As a matter of fact, the Northern Corridor is more characterized by the presence of two extremes: a very productive railroad system, called Carajás, which is responsible for the transport of iron and metallurgic products in Pará State, in the Amazon Region; and the presence of a large inland waterway network that, with the exception of an embryonic soybean transport in the Madeira River, does not move significant freight volumes.

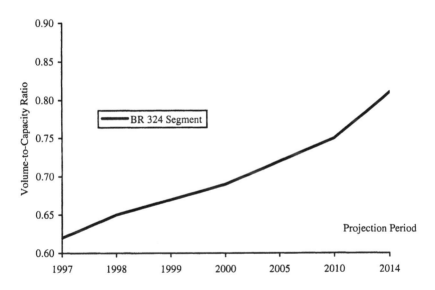

Figure 12.7   Impact of trade on a highway segment in the Northeast Corridor
Source: *CNT/AERI (1996)*

According to figure 12.7, most of the highway segments, as the example shows for the Northeast Corridor, do not present excessive V/C ratios such that they would require immediate investment with the sole purpose of increasing operational capacity. The primary demand of these two corridors is a transportation planning program to improve the quality of the pavement in most of the segments, where more than 60% of the roads are unpaved. In the Northeast Corridor, highways account for more than

84% of the total freight; this high modal concentration, even with relatively low volumes, does not offer prospects for efficiently handling current and future demands.

In the Northern Corridor, what has been observed is a very low participation of the highway system in the total traffic volume composition, where only 2% is moved by roads (FIPE, 1996). Of the total freight, 96% is handled by railroads, but this number is almost accounted for by the Carajás Railway System. Less than 1% moves by inland waterways, despite the fact that the Northern Corridor has more than 15,000 miles of navigable rivers. This finding is obviously the clearest consequence of a historical policy of neglecting the natural potential of this region in terms of inland waterway transportation.

With the spatial transfer of the most productive areas in Brazil from the Southern to the Central and Northern regions, the Brazilian Government must pay more attention to providing a better system to transport grain production. Today, there is a good perspective in the directions of the main flows, which can be directed not only to the Southeastern and Southern areas, but also to the international markets through the Northern ports. The inland waterway facilities would undoubtedly be the most efficient ways to move the grain production out of the region, with agricultural inputs providing back-haul possibilities.

It will be necessary to take advantage of the existing railroad system, provided improvements related to rail equipment and infrastructure are made. Accordingly, the Brazilian Government needs to understand that the natural transportation systems, as in the case of navigable rivers, together with the railroad tradition of the Northeast Corridor, may be the most efficient, economic, and profitable means to implement an intermodal system that will lead to higher competitiveness in both internal and external markets.

Overall Findings

Among the several findings that have resulted from the formal linkage between the trade and the transportation models, one has been of prime importance. It is the impact of enhanced trade on the number of bottlenecks in the main highway segments, given the already deteriorated conditions of the Brazilian highway system. According to figure 12.8, there is an emerging concentration in the number of bottlenecks. This result has highly negative consequences, mainly in those corridors where the primary segments cross largely industrialized regions, such as São Paulo, and Central-East, where the Rio de Janeiro and Belo Horizonte Metropolitan Areas are located. Most of Brazil's industrial plants, such as the automobile, steel, metallurgic, paper and cellulose, food processing and services industries are concentrated in these two corridors. Together, the three states of São Paulo, Minas Gerais and Rio de Janeiro account for approximately 55% of Brazilian Gross Domestic Product in 1997.

Figure 12.8 shows, for example, that the impact of MERCOSUR on the highway system of the São Paulo Corridor accounts for an increase of, approximately, 25% in the number of bottlenecks within the projection period. Moreover, in the Central-East Corridor, this increase reaches 60%, going from 10 critical links to 16 in the year 2014. The same pattern can be noticed for the other 4 corridors, where the main difference is only the smaller number of bottlenecks, while the patterns of change are similar to those observed in the São Paulo and Central-East Corridors.

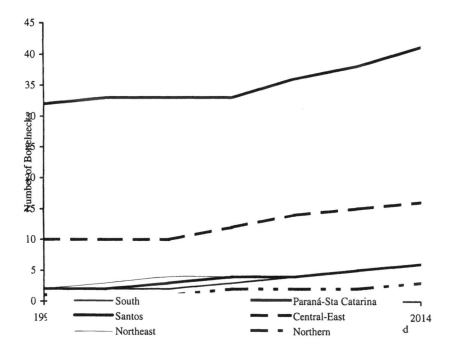

Figure 12.8   Number of highway bottlenecks by corridor, based on the impacts of trade coefficients on traffic volumes

Other findings could not be presented in detail, but the influence of the free trade agreements in the Brazilian highway systems reveals the potentially negative consequences of not being prepared to handle the increases in demands. It is important to note, once again, that the deterioration of the level of service in one highway segment has a ripple effect that spreads out from that bottleneck to a large area along the main route.

Therefore, this investigation has achieved its main objective, which is the quantification of the influence of the implementation of MERCOSUR on the main corridors of the Brazilian highway system. It has also shown that if there is not an immediate planning provision of investments in intermodal transportation, the negative effects are likely continue not only in response to MERCOSUR, but also because of the generally increasing globalization of the economy that will affect the volume of the internal flow of goods.

Conclusion

The impacts of MERCOSUR, together with the globalization and stabilization of the Brazilian economy, in the transportation systems must be analyzed under a regional perspective, where the trade characteristics of each area can be investigated and updated to the needs of a better transportation infrastructure. What has been observed in Brazil is an excessive participation of transportation costs in the final prices of products, mainly grains and low aggregate value cargo. This results in significant losses in competitiveness, both in the internal and international markets.

In the South, there is a negative impact of MERCOSUR on the southern states, mainly because of the competition between those states and Argentina, Paraguay and Uruguay. In the central part of the country, the findings reveal that greater competitiveness is limited by a transportation system with high levels of deterioration, with direct reflections on travel time, transportation costs, safety and so on. In the Northern States, the absence of key railroads and inland waterways results in an inability to take advantage of internal transfer to maritime ports, and the potential that this might have for reducing congestion in some of the inefficient ports of the Southern Regions.

Based on these findings, a number of actions could be taken to improve the Brazilian transportation system. These actions would include:

(1) expansion of intermodal systems, with an efficient consideration of the operational capacity of each mode; (2) massive investments in the recently privatized railroad system, mainly in cargo transfer points, so that a higher volume could be moved by the railway system; (3) regulation of the "Multimodal Operator's" role, that could facilitate the bureaucratic process of moving cargo; (4) higher participation of the railroad and inland waterway systems in the Brazilian transportation system; (5) acceleration of the privatization processes of highways, to generate more investment into the system; (6) capacity expansion of some highway segments, where competitiveness issue dictate the use of such a mode; and finally, (7) creation of the "Agência Nacional de Transportes" (Federal Transportation Agency) to control and regulate the myriad of actions, plans and projects related to transportation in Brazil.

Notes

[1] Mode: the same as systems, modal or type of transportation, indicating the system that carries the cargo, such as highways, railroads and inland waterways.

[2] Level of service: relationship between traffic volume and capacity.

[3] MERCOSUR: free trade area with Brazil, Argentina, Uruguay, and Paraguay as members.

[4] Mutimodal system: a transportation network with the presence of more than one mode.

[5] These figures for 1997 are still valid, since no significant changes have occurred since then.

[6] Volume-to-Capacity ratio: ratio between traffic volume and operational capacity, where the closer the result to the unity, the higher the congestion level of the highway segment.

[7] Internal and external distributions: internal distribution meaning within the corridor, and external distribution meaning among the corridors.

[8] This version was used, notwithstanding the existence of newer versions, mainly because of the absence of measures related to free flow speeds, densities and others.

[9] The Paranaguá Port is one of the most important ports in Brazil when it comes to agricultural grains, where, during some months of the year, the truck congestion in the port boundaries and access roads reaches extends for several miles.

References

AERI/CNT (1996) *O Impacto do MERCOSUR sobre os Sistemas de Transportes do Brasil* Brasília, D.F, Análise Econômica Regional e Internacional Ltda / Confederação Nacional dos Transportes.

FIPE, Fundação do Instituto de Pesquisas (1996) "Índice de Desenvolvimento Econômico do Transporte" - Universidade de São Paulo / Confederação Nacional dos Transportes - São Paulo, SP.

GEIPOT (1996) *Anuário Estatístico dos Transportes* Brasília, D.F., Empresa Brasileira de Planejamento de Transportes, Ministério dos Transportes.

IBGE (1991-1992) "Pesquisa Anual do Transporte Rodoviário" - Instituto Brasileiro de Geografia e Estatística - Volume 5 - Rio de Janeiro, RJ.

National Research Council (1985) *Highway Capacity Manual.* Washington, D.C., Transportation Research Board.

Resende, P. T. V (1991) "Comparative Analysis of the Transportation Systems in the United States and Brazil" Unpublished Master's thesis, University of Memphis Memphis, TN.

Resende, P. T. V. (1997) "MERCOSUR e os Sistemas de Transporte no Brasil: Problema ou Solução" - Análise Econômica do MERCOSUR - III Encontro das Américas em Belo Horizonte - pp. 76-87 - Belo Horizonte, MG.

PART IV: AGRICULTURE AND TRADE

13 The Structural Adjustment of Brazilian Agriculture in the 1980s and 1990s

JOAQUIM BENTO DE SOUZA FERREIRA FILHO

During the 1980s and the beginning of the 1990s, the Brazilian agricultural sector grew at a remarkable rate, considering the crisis faced by the country during this period. While industrial real GNP grew 3.84% in the period 1980-1990, real agricultural and services GNP grew 28.2% and 29.5% respectively, in the same period. This corresponds to an average growth rate in the 1980-1990 period of 2.5% for agriculture, 2.6% for the services sector, and only 0.38% for the industry sector. In addition, it is worth noting that this more rapid agricultural growth took place in an unfavorable economic environment. As noted by Ferreira Fo. (1994), the average contribution of the Brazilian agricultural sector to the GNP implicit deflator decreased in the period. This was due to the fall in the agricultural prices, since the real agricultural GNP was roughly constant in the 1980s.

The same process can be viewed in the analysis of the individual agricultural prices evolution, shown in table 13.1; the decreasing trend in agricultural prices is clearly revealed, beginning in the mid 1980s. Given these trends, how can one explain the almost continuous agricultural sector growth? Dealing with this question, it is necessary first to put the problem in perspective. Brazilian agricultural growth rate was, in fact, modest in the period, compared to what was observed in the 1970s when the agricultural sector grew at yearly average rates of 5.6% (Rezende *et al.*, 1994). What makes the agricultural growth in the 1980s surprising is its size compared to the industrial sector, whose real GNP was, at the end of the decade, only 3.84% greater than it was at the beginning.

Authors who have studied this question, such as Rezende (1986, 1988), Carvalho (1989), Rezende (1990,1992), Rezende and Buainain (1994), and Goldin and Rezende (1990) among others, have focused their discussion on the evolution of agricultural policy year by year, analyzing the domestic price and trade policies pursued, as well as the de-indexation periods faced by the Brazilian economy.

Table 13.1   Real Price Indexes of selected agricultural products

Year	Corn	Beans	Rice	Cotton	Coffee	Soya	Milk	Hogs	Chicken	Cattle
1980	100	100	100	100	100	100	100	100	100	100
1981	100	117	71	90	59	75	110	68	78	75
1982	75	54	85	79	62	71	89	80	66	64
1983	110	96	85	100	55	105	86	77	74	73
1984	103	112	76	115	61	108	77	91	83	83
1985	95	71	80	82	97	83	75	84	76	69
1986	94	73	67	85	86	72	71	97	91	94
1987	62	65	41	73	51	66	87	59	67	73
1988	74	55	49	64	41	83	68	54	61	52
1989	62	71	40	57	44	55	58	77	72	61
1990	52	41	40	43	61	36	54	52	51	69
1991	54	45	49	43	28	42	53	50	44	47
1992	53	38	37	38	23	46	53	45	42	45

Source: IEA data, author's elaboration

This chapter takes a different route, and brings to the analysis the discussion of two more aspects related to the theme. The central idea to be developed here is that the adjustment of Brazilian agriculture to the crisis of the 1980s generated the conditions that made it possible for Brazilian agriculture to growth faster than the industrial sector in large part because of a more adverse effect on the industrial demand. This phenomenon was caused by the type of aggregate demand contraction that the Brazilian economy has pursued as a way to generate foreign reserves. In addition, there was an important fall in the costs of agricultural production, caused by price declines in the main agricultural inputs. These two aspects will be analyzed separately.

The plan of this chapter is as follows. First, there will be a discussion of some aggregate indicators of the Brazilian economy since 1980, where we will focus on the evolution of the macroeconomics as well as some sectoral production indicators. It will be shown that the fall in absorption occurred mainly in the investment sectors. Then the evolution of agricultural costs will be analyzed. Finally, we will use an applied general equilibrium model to make some counterfactual analysis that will enhance our understanding about the Brazilian agricultural growth process in the near past.

Brazilian agricultural adjustment in the 1980s[1]

Since the foreign exchange crisis that began with the Mexican default in 1982, Brazil has initiated a period of more severe economic adjustment, based on the reduction of current account deficits. The mechanism chosen for that was a real devaluation of the exchange rate, together with policies of domestic absorption reduction. Thus, in February 1983, there was a maxi devaluation of the nominal exchange rate, made effective by pegging the nominal exchange rate to the general price index (IGP). As for the domestic absorption reduction, the fiscal and monetary adjustment implied a reduction of domestic credit that, for agriculture, meant a reduction in the production credits beginning in 1983 and the monetary indexation of agricultural credit contracts.

This was, in general, the focus of the Brazilian economic policy until 1986, when the Cruzado Plan began the era of the "heterodox" stabilization plans. The economic policy has assumed an almost random feature since then, especially with respect to agricultural policies. The main agricultural policy tools addressed short run objectives, losing their functions as mid to long term planning instruments. The resulting effects of those policies will now be analyzed, beginning with some important national accounts aggregates, presented in figure 13.1.

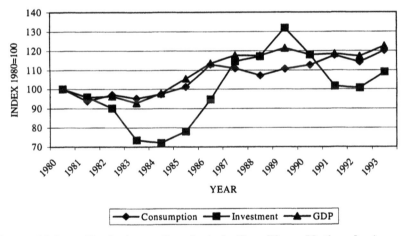

Figure 13.1   Evolution of selected Brazilian National Accounts aggregates

Figure 13.1 illustrates the point that aggregate consumption is far more stable than investment absorption in the economic cycle. As can be seen, the absorption reduction and the macroeconomic instability in the period affected more drastically aggregate investment than aggregate consumption. In fact, the crisis faced by the Brazilian economy in the 1980s can be characterized as an investment crisis, which began when the country was suddenly forced to modify its development financing model, based on foreign savings. The fall in the GNP growth rates (and, in some years, the fall in GNP) can be explained mainly by the fall in aggregate investment.

Table 13.2   Comparative evolution of Agricultural Real GNP and Real GNP of selected industrial sectors. 1980-1990

Year	Agric	Industrial consumption goods				Capital goods			
		Food	Paper	Beverage	Clothes	Constr.	Metall.	Machin.	Transpt.
1980	100	100	100	100	100	100	100	100	100
1981	108	103	93	92	99	94	83	80	77
1982	107	104	100	90	102	92	80	66	75
1983	107	107	102	86	89	79	78	58	70
1984	110	107	108	85	91	80	89	68	73
1985	121	107	116	95	97	85	95	75	82
1986	112	107	128	117	104	100	106	92	92
1987	128	115	132	113	94	101	107	96	83
1988	129	112	130	115	87	98	103	88	90
1989	133	113	137	132	89	102	109	92	88
1990	128	116	130	133	77	93	96	78	74
1991	130	-	-	-	-	83	-	-	-
1992	137	-	-	-	-	83	-	-	-
1993	145	-	-	-	-	86	-	-	-

Source: *IBGE*

However, capital formation in the economy is basically derived from industry sector output. According to the 1980 Brazilian Input-Output tables (IBGE, 1989), 61.37% of the capital formation demand in that year was for output of the civil construction sector, while 18.75% was for output of the machinery and electric industries. Thus, about 80% of the investment demand was concentrated in those industries' output. Table 13.2 provides some supporting detail.

As can be seen in table 13.2, the real output indexes of agriculture and some other consumption goods sectors (food industries, paper and apparel, beverages, clothes and shoes) show the same trends. There are, obviously, exceptions, like the clothing and shoe industries, but these trends probably reflect these sectors' consumption characteristics. It is clear that the industrial sectors that produce investment goods (civil construction, metallurgy, machinery and transport materials) show a contrary trend when compared to agriculture, and even when compared to other consumption output industries. Among the industrial sectors producing investment outputs, only the metallurgy sector showed, during the 1980s, four years where its output was greater than that observed in 1980; at the end of the decade, even this sector output index was smaller than at the beginning.

It is just natural, then, that industrial GNP has experienced a fall in the aggregate investment greater than the agricultural sector. The fall in aggregate income that followed affected the demand for all goods (normal goods, at least) in the economy through the income effect, but in a differentiated manner for each good. Since agricultural products have, in general, low aggregate price and income elasticities, the expectation would be that responses in the agricultural sector would be more muted. The halt in external financial flows, reducing Brazilian aggregate income, has reduced more drastically aggregate savings (and investment) than consumption in general, and consumption of agricultural products in particular.

These factors can help us to understand, at least in part, why the Brazilian agricultural sector showed a more favorable development compared to the industrial sector in the 1980s. We have argued that there was an important mechanism affecting differently the demand for agricultural and industrial products; however, one might expect that this mechanism should have just dampened the fall in agricultural output, since the scenario was one of falling agricultural prices whereas the sector continued to grow albeit at more moderate rates than in earlier periods. In what follows, we intend to show that there was an additional phenomenon that acted from the supply side, which may have have compensated in a non trivial manner for the fall in agricultural prices.

Agricultural production cost evolution

The explanation offered thus far for the agricultural growth in an adverse scenario in the 1980s has been centered on productivity growth. The evolution of productivity growth for some of the main agricultural products in Brazil can be seen in table 13.3. Whether the process has been driven by the adoption of new technologies or by the departure of less efficient producers or both, it is possible to argue that this forced the average cost curve down, keeping production stable or even growing.

As can be seen from this table, the annual rate of productivity growth in these agriculture products in Brazil has risen significantly, except for coffee.[2] This allowed agricultural GNP to keep growing, even after the decrease in the total harvested area observed from 1990, as shown in figure 13.2. In 1990, the adoption of the Collor Plan caused a deep fall in the cultivated area in Brazil, due to the liquidity constraints it imposed in the economy. As shown in table 13.2, agricultural GNP recovered its growth trend from 1991, though at moderate rates, after a fall in 1990.

Table 13.3   Productivity Index and Productivity Year Growth Rate for Selected Agricultural Products in Brazil. 1980-1993

	1980	1982	1984	1986	1988	1990	1992	1993	Average Annual Growth Rate
Coffee	100	116	130	92	105	115	119	130	-0.39
Sugarcane	100	106	107	106	110	108	113	111	0.31*
Rice	100	103	108	119	126	120	136	146	1.51*
Wheat	100	75	132	170	191	133	165	171	1.76**
Soybeans	100	91	95	84	99	100	118	123	0.47
Cotton	100	102	106	104	126	120	110	115	0.60*
Corn	100	97	99	93	106	105	128	142	0.80*

Notes: *OLS estimates. * Significant at 1%. ** Significant at 5%*

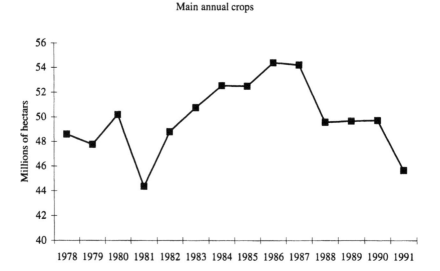

Main annual crops

Figure 13.2   Brazil Harvested Area

What is to be argued here is that there are other variables that can force the average cost curves down, generating the same result, contributing to the technical progress effect. These variables are the prices of the agricultural inputs. As noted by some authors (Melo, 1992; Rezende, 1989; Gasquez and Villa Verde, 1990), there was, in the period, a fall in the prices of some of the main agricultural inputs, dampening the fall in agricultural output prices. The fall is not limited to industrial inputs, but this process also occurred in the primary factors of production, generating a widespread reduction in agricultural production costs. This drop in costs seems to have had a more important effect in the Brazilian agricultural growth process in the last decade than has been attributed until now.

Table 13.4   Evolution of Agricultural Inputs Real Price Indexes in Brazil. 1980/1990

Year	Industrial Inputs				Labor		
	Machines	Fertilizers	Chemicals	Combust	Tractor ope.	Monthly	Daily
1980	100	100	100	100	100	100	100
1981	129	95	93	105	108	107	97
1982	141	93	89	99	111	114	101
1983	125	87	93	110	81	84	74
1984	116	92	98	110	84	84	71
1985	112	90	95	96	97	92	85
1986	100	68	84	82	123	115	145
1987	112	53	47	90	77	71	82
1988	151	50	37	75	62	59	54
1989	161	45	53	62	73	66	62
1990	173	46	46	62	67	59	69

Source: *Melo (1992) and IEA (1992)*

As revealed in table 13.4, the prices of fertilizers, agrochemicals and combustibles declined in the period. Interesting enough, this fall is not observed in agricultural tractors prices, a highly concentrated industrial sector. For labor, the tendency observed for wages of tractor operators, monthly and daily paid rural workers, are also decreasing, except for 1986, the Cruzado Plan year. A combination of productivity growth and fall in input prices can provide the major sources of explanation for the Brazilian agricultural growth phenomenon in the 1980s.

Another more illustrative and perhaps more fruitful way to deal with the problem is to analyze the evolution of the agricultural production costs in the period, since they embody both price and quantities (and quality) variations in factors use. The production costs are, then, a composite factor price index of all factors in the production process, weighted by each quantity used.

The Instituto de Economia Agrícola do Estado de São Paulo - IEA - has a long series of annual production costs of the main crops in São Paulo state. Although the data are for São Paulo, it does not seem to be unreasonable to consider them as a proxy for other regions in Brazil, especially center-south Brazil, where the bulk of agricultural production takes place. In addition, the technical coefficients in these cost spreadsheets are periodically revised, keeping track of technological changes.

The evolution of the production costs[3] for the chosen agriculture products can be seen in table 13.5, where data are presented in the form of real value indices of unitary production costs (cost per unit of product). As one can see, the evolution of agricultural production costs follows the tendency of falling input prices mentioned earlier.

Table 13.5   Unitary Production Costs Indexes

Years	Cotton	Rice	Beans	Corn	Manioc	Soybean	Wheat
1980	81	80	70	77	75	74	52
1981	100	100	100	100	100	100	100
1982	87	89	79	76	103	101	95
1983	118	82	95	81	66	127	110
1984	119	84	89	85	98	121	135
1985	76	61	162	67	67	101	89
1986	86	79	86	55	111	65	70
1987	95	83	46	97	153	79	77
1988	74	86	58	76	81	142	85
1989	135	95	50	77	152	126	95
1990	83	68	41	64	108	98	38
1991	78	57	27	47	139	72	34
1992	51	50	24	37	100	65	31
1993	30	29	14	24	53	45	-
1994	44	43	22	37	59	57	-

Source: *IEA data; author's elaboration*

It is clear, then, that Brazilian agriculture has experienced an important process of cost reduction since the mid of the 1980s. However, this fall in costs would have not been deep enough to sustain the increase in agricultural production in the period, given the fall in agricultural prices. To deal with this problem, we computed output price/unitary production cost ratios, the exchange relation between agricultural products and agricultural inputs, a parity index that represents a prices received/prices paid relation (PRPP). Adopting this approach also avoids possible distortions introduced into the price index used, as a result of successive heterodox plans (and price "freezes") implemented in Brazil since 1986.

This data transformation can be seen in table 13.6 and confirms, in general, the hypotheses that supply side factors acted to dampen the impact of the fall in agricultural prices in the 1980s. Beginning with cotton, one can see that the PRPP relation shows strong decreases between 1989 and 1991, increasing again since then. For rice, that relation begins to deteriorate earlier, in 1987, but rises again in 1991 also. Beans and maize did not show continuous periods of decline in the PRPP relation, though there are years when it declined rather significantly.

It is interesting to note that manioc presents a scenario far more unfavorable than the other crops chosen, illustrative of the lack of technological progress that still characterizes the activity, and the small economic importance it has for Brazilian South/Southeast regions. In the soybean case, the data show a scenario that is less favorable than the one observed for rice, with many years where the PRPP relation falls more deeply, the 1988/1991 period, resuming its growth since then.

Table 13.6   **Value Index of the relation Product Price/Unitary Cost of Production, and relation Price Received by Farmers/Price of Inputs from Outside the Farm (PRPOF)**
1980=100

Years	Cotton	Rice	Beans	Corn	Manioc	Soybean	PRPOF
1980	137	177	123	130	147	179	122
1981	100	100	100	100	100	100	100
1982	102	135	59	98	58	94	89
1983	94	147	86	136	72	110	116
1984	108	127	108	121	99	119	117
1985	119	186	37	141	101	110	123
1986	110	121	73	172	40	147	159
1987	86	71	122	64	22	111	79
1988	96	80	81	99	101	78	98
1989	47	59	122	81	56	59	66
1990	57	84	86	82	21	49	69
1991	61	122	144	114	19	78	66
1992	82	107	138	142	47	94	71
1993	148	172	252	204	75	125	85
1994	108	112	216	114	46	86	92

Source: *IEA data; author's elaboration*

Finally, table 13.6 shows another kind of exchange relation, Prices Received/Prices Paid for Inputs from Outside the Farm (PRPOF), calculated by IEA. As one can see, this indicator shows an upward trend until 1986, when it begins to fall; however, one should note that this indicator does not allow for productivity variations, while the PRPP relation does.

It is important to point out that the cost concept analyzed above does not embody all cost components, omitting important inputs such as the price of land and its value for rent. These are, however, important variables for the problem in focus, since they are related to land access facilities, both for farmers who want to increase their profits and for landless renters in general. The evolution of rental values for agricultural lands and pastures and their market prices (selling or buying prices for two agricultural land types, where 1 and 2 stand for better and worse quality, respectively, and pasture lands) are shown in table 13.7.

As can be seen in table 13.7, those values match the hypothesis that factors from the supply side were important explanatory variables; except for 1986 for all values and 1987 for first class agricultural prices, there is a marked tendency for both agricultural land rental prices and market prices to fall.   It can be noted that there was a decreasing trend in those values, interrupted by the Cruzado Plan in 1986[4], and resumed since then.

Table 13.7   Indexes of Rental Prices and Market Prices of Agricultural Lands and Pastures. 1980-1990

| | Rental values | | Market Prices | | |
Years	Agriculture	Pastures	Agriculture 1	Agriculture 2	Pastures
1980	100	100	100	100	100
1981	113	91	106	101	104
1982	98	81	96	86	85
1983	70	66	70	61	60
1984	87	88	74	72	74
1985	103	95	93	81	85
1986	136	158	155	175	177
1987	74	102	131	87	85
1988	66	66	66	55	56
1989	60	91	88	91	94
1990	72	76	76	70	72
1991	68	85	68	61	61
1992	64	-	55	51	51

Source: *IEA (1993) data; author's elaboration*

While the analysis to date contributes to our understanding of the changes in Brazilian agriculture, there were other important facts that simultaneously occurred towards the end of the 1980s, whose indirect effects upon agriculture are difficult to trace due to its broad influence on the economy. The most important change in the Brazilian economy since the beginning of the 1990s seems to be the external trade liberalization process initiated in the Collor Plan, in 1990. Quantitative restrictions were abolished then, and the average import tariffs were reduced by 50%. This process continued throughout the period. More recently, the introduction of the Real Plan in the economic sphere and the election of President Fernando Henrique Cardoso on the political side have caused a new surge of external capital flows to Brazil, a fact that (at least until early 1999) made it possible to maintain a valued currency. The agricultural policy instruments, on the other side, remained quite ineffective, due to the financial constraints faced by the government.

To gain a sense of the magnitude of these economy-wide impacts, we will, in the next sections, work with the aid of an applied general equilibrium (AGE) model developed for agricultural policy analysis in Brazil. We will first do a brief presentation of the model, with its main characteristics, and then explore some simulations, in order to analyze each of these effects separately.

The AGE model

The AGE model used in this study is based in the structure of the RUNS model (Burniaux and van der Mensbrugghe, 1990). A number of important modifications were made in the structure of that model, to make it suitable to match the Brazilian economy in the 1980s, as well as to deal with the problem at hand. To avoid confusion between them, the model presented here is named Megabrás; in what follows, an overview of the model is presented, with its main characteristics. The version presented is a static one, and for each year, the simulation is linked through exogenous growth rates attributed to factors and capital stocks.

The economy is divided in two distinct sectors: rural and urban. The rural sector has eleven activities, namely soybeans, sugarcane, corn, coffee, rice, cotton, wheat, other agricultural products, livestock, milk and poultry. Urban sector activities are separated into seven typically urban activities - transportation, machinery, fertilizers, chemicals, energy, services and others - and ten agroindustries: the industries of coffee, sugar (including alcohol), rice, wheat, fibers, vegetable oils, meat processing (excluding poultry), poultry processing, milk processing, and feed industries. Throughout, we will refer to these 17 non-agricultural activities or products as urban activities or products while, for all 28 productive activities, we assume that each produces one product only.

There are four institutions in the economy - rural and urban families, enterprises (investment) and the government - and three primary factors of production: labor, capital and land. Only the agricultural sector utilizes land. Due to its great degree of homogeneity, the domestic production of agricultural products is assumed to be a perfect substitute for imports, and for them the small country hypothesis is maintained. Thus, agricultural tradable prices are defined by the world exogenous prices and import or export tariffs, while agricultural non-tradable prices are defined by excess demand in each domestic market. There are only four raw agricultural tradables in the model, cotton, corn, soybeans and wheat; all other agricultural products, including coffee, are exported (and imported, in the case of wheat) by agroindustries. It is important to note that even soybean are mainly exported by the soybeans industry (vegetable oil processing industries), and not by the agricultural sector.

For non-agricultural products, on the other hand, as well for processed agricultural products, there is imperfect substitution between domestic production and imports, modeled through a CES formulation that defines a composite good for these activities. The prices of urban domestic production are defined by costs of production, while import prices depend on the external exogenous prices and tariffs. Urban export prices are defined internally, through domestic prices and taxes on exports. Thus, the demand for these goods is not perfectly elastic, though it can be high in some cases.

In the agricultural sector, the production structure is specific for the production of vegetables and animal products, both with decreasing returns relative to an aggregate input R, made up of urban and rural products, land and labor. The production function for each activity in the agricultural sector is a Cobb-Douglas type formulation:

$$X = a(R)^b (1+\alpha)t \quad \text{where} \quad 0<b<1; \tag{13.1}$$

and α is an exogenous technological parameter.

The supply function for each agricultural activity is then derived from these production functions and the profit maximization conditions. The same procedure generates the input demand equations for each activity. The aggregate input R is specific for each of the two types of agricultural activities, crops and animal products, and is an aggregation of each activity-derived demand in crop and animal production. Hence, it is not specific to each activity belonging to the subsectors crops and animal production; that is, the input used in corn production is the same as that used for soybean production, but both subsectors compete for the primary factors land and labor.

Once the aggregate input demand in each subsector is determined, producers must now minimize the cost of their purchases, through the choice of the optimal use of intermediate inputs and primary factors. Unlike urban intermediates, primary factors are in fixed amounts for each period. The model considers three primary factors in agriculture: labor, land and capital (machinery), all of them with perfect mobility between activities inside each agricultural subsector.

The model seeks to keep track of complementarity and substitution patterns in the way primary factors and intermediates combine in the production process. This is made through a CES-linked decision-tree structure, with two levels of linkages and two substitution elasticities. This kind of structure divides the cost minimization problem into two sub problems, separating decisions about the use of inputs in each level of the tree from input use in other levels.

For vegetable production, producers must decide how much to use of fertilizers, land and a composite of labor-tractor, in the first level of decision, and then decide about the quantities of labor and tractor in a second level, a process guided by relative prices and the elasticities of substitution. This formulation basically seeks to represent technology adoption consistent with factor scarcity, but it should be noted that aggregate input prices could be distorted by government, through the introduction of subsidies.

In the animal production sector, the choice is between land and feed, but just for livestock and milk production. Poultry production is entirely modeled through fixed coefficients. Production in the urban sector presents constant returns, through a Leontief formulation for intermediate inputs and a value added aggregate, that is a CES aggregation of capital and labor. The aggregation is for the urban sector as a whole, and implies that the capital/labor relation is the same for all activities inside the sector. The process of minimization of the cost of producing value added generates demand functions for urban capital and labor. The nominal urban labor wage is considered rigid, and was parameterized to reproduce the tendency of urban unemployment in the period under analysis. Agricultural wages are flexible and adjust to clear the rural labor market in each period.

The model presents a neoclassical closure, where total investment is given by saving. The nominal exchange rate is flexible, and the external capital flows are exogenous, providing closure for the external sector. Imports, however, may be submitted to quantitative restrictions, in proportion to the desired imports. This feature was used for the runs in the 1980s. The external sector closure is made with the model determining a nominal exchange rate that clears the balance of payments given the external capital flows and the level of import restrictions. This is a modified version of the closure used by Dervis and Robinson (1978), where import rationing is endogenous. The option we take here seems more appropriate for the problem at hand, since it is a retrospective application, and it was possible to find some estimates of import restrictions in the literature (Cavalcanti, 1988). However, this mechanism applies only to non-agricultural imports, since, in the time period we are considering, there was a great deal of public concern with the provision of agricultural products, due to inflation control and the characteristics of wage goods. Moreover, cereal imports (wheat is the import relevant for the model) have a relatively low value compared with urban imports.

Government consumption is exogenous and public tax revenues endogenous, making the government current account endogenous. The closure of the government sector is made by reducing aggregate savings. This is a variant of Dervis and Robinson's (1978) government sector closure. The equilibrium between government receipts and expenses is thus obtained through a kind of "seignorage," that is, a variable that ensures the equilibrium in the government current account. The government creates the money necessary to close the balance, and this extra receipt is extracted from the private sector aggregate savings. There is, thus, a share of savings that is not necessarily invested. Note that this is not a monetary variable, since the model contains no monetary sector that is explicitly modeled. It is just a mechanism of funds' transfer between institutions to simulate the effects of a monetary phenomenon.

Calibration and base run

Once the theoretical model has been defined, the next step was its calibration. This was made through the elaboration of a social account matrix (SAM) for Brazil in 1980. In Brazil's 1980 input-output matrix, however, the agricultural sector is presented as a single activity, although its production is disaggregated. It was necessary, then, to proceed to a disaggregation of that activity into the 11 activities used in this study. The resulting SAM for Brazil in 1980, evaluated at consumer prices.[5]

With the model reproducing satisfactorily the observed pattern of the variables in the base year (1980), it was then run for the period 1982-1994, in two-year intervals, solving for the endogenous variables given the exogenous (observed) ones, building the base case against which the counterfactual analysis will be made. The model was solved as a nonlinear optimization problem, using the General Algebraic Modeling System - GAMS - with MINOS5 (Brooke, Kendrik and Meeraus, 1988). The price of the urban value added is the *numéraire* of the model.

Simulation 1: The effects of quantitative imports restrictions reduction upon the Brazilian agriculture

The elimination of the quantitative imports restrictions in the beginning of the 1980s was thought to be one of the main changes in the Brazilian economy in the period. In this experiment, to evaluate the impact upon Brazilian agriculture, the model was solved again and the results were compared to those obtained in the base run, where the observed pattern of the exogenous variables were used. In this experiment, then, the quantitative import restrictions that existed in the 1980s and were eliminated in the 1990s were introduced again in the 1990s. This was made through the introduction of a 10% reduction in effective imports compared to the desired ones, thereby forcing importers from their existing import demand curves. The results of this experiment are now analyzed.

Table 13.8   **Nominal exchange rate in experiment 1**
Percent variations from the base run

Years	Nominal Exchange Rate
1990	-0.73
1992	-1.82
1994	-1.67

The first thing to note is that the imposition of quantitative restrictions would have allowed the exchange rate to fall compared to the base run. This can be seen in table 13.8. Due to the exchange rate definition in this study (domestic currency/foreign currency), a fall in the exchange rate means a revaluation of the domestic currency.

This is, of course, a standard result; with lower imports, the nominal exchange rate required for balance of payments equilibrium at given levels of foreign capital flows is smaller than it would be otherwise, lowering the effective prices of imported goods (note that we are supposing that a secondary market for import licenses is absent). This causes differential impacts on the cost structure of the economy, depending mainly on how much each sector relies on intermediate imported inputs, since consumption import goods became a significant share of imports only recently. The imposition of quantitative restraints on imports has been used traditionally by governments as an alternate way to achieve exchange rate devaluations, especially when inflation control programs are in operation. The Brazilian imports' liberalization program then caused an exchange rate pattern higher (that is to say, more devalued) than it would have been in the presence of import restrictions.

However, the fall in the exchange rate also tends to make the domestic export products more expensive in the external market, thereby reducing the external demand for such products. The resulting effect on export prices, then, is ambiguous, and specific to each sector. The results generated in this experiment can be seen in table 13.9.

As can be seen in table 13.9, the exchange rate revaluation has an effect upon export prices that vary between sectors, depending on each particular input structure. The relatively smaller exchange rate revaluation generated in the model for 1990 has caused the export prices of some sectors (fibers, vegetable oils, feedstuffs and other manufactures) to decrease in that year, increasing later when the exchange rate revaluation becomes greater. Some other urban sectors, like processed coffee, rice industry, meats, poultry, milk and sugar industry exhibited a fall in export prices for the entire period of the simulation, while the remaining sectors showed the standard export price increases due to an exchange rate revaluation.

Table 13.9   Industrial sectors export prices in experiment 1
Percent variations from the base run

Industrial Sectors	1990	1992	1994
Fiber	-0.27	0.89	0.71
Coffee	-1.43	-0.74	-0.58
Rice	-3.54	-1.66	-1.74
Wheat	0.33	1.12	1.00
Meat	-4.00	-2.26	-2.54
Poultry	-3.93	-2.27	-2.55
Milk	-3.10	-1.38	-1.66
Sugar	-2.40	-1.20	-1.39
Vegetable oils	-0.46	0.40	0.25
Mechanics	0.38	1.48	1.31
Chemicals	0.34	1.38	1.22
Energy	0.50	1.47	1.35
Fertilizers	0.37	1.30	1.16
Feedstuffs	-0.12	0.69	0.56
Services	0.34	1.50	1.33
Transportation	0.49	1.58	1.42
Manufactures	-0.09	1.13	0.95

The consequences of lower level of the exchange rate pattern in the simulation upon agriculture can be seen in table 13.10, where the percent variations in producer prices of agricultural products in experiment 1 are displayed. As one can see, the maintenance of a 10% quantitative import restriction would have caused a generalized fall in agricultural producer prices.

Table 13.10   Producer agricultural prices in experiment 1
Percent variations from the base run

Year	Coffee	Sugar	Rice	Wheat	Soybeans	Cotton	Corn	Others	Poultry	Meats	Milk
1990	-5.20	-6.90	-8.00	-0.73	-0.73	-0.73	-0.73	-12.97	-7.11	-7.98	-6.59
1992	-4.94	-8.04	-7.80	-1.82	-1.82	-1.82	-1.82	-12.40	-6.77	-7.72	-5.95
1994	-3.75	-7.50	-7.55	-1.67	-1.67	-1.67	-1.67	-11.78	-6.81	-7.68	-6.05

The exchange rate revaluation caused a generalized fall in prices in the economy, including the agricultural prices. The consumer price index fell

1.6% in 1990, and 1.3% in both 1992 and 1994, but the outcome of this change, shown in table 13.11, is not a fall in agricultural production, as one could expect in a partial equilibrium analysis. The fall in agricultural input prices that followed caused the agricultural producer prices/agricultural input prices relation to rise, generating a rise in agricultural production, as can be seen in table 13.12.

Table 13.11   Agricultural production in experiment 1
Percent variations from the base run

Year	Coffee	Sugarc	Rice	Wheat	Soybeans	Cotton	Corn	Others	Poultry	Meats	Milk
1990	0.500	0.695	0.406	4.632	4.449	5.363	2.468	-1.850	0.669	0.088	0.841
1992	0.462	0.156	0.290	3.743	3.596	4.331	1.998	-1.802	0.640	0.020	0.975
1994	0.571	0.233	0.268	3.646	3.504	4.219	1.947	-1.656	0.484	-.068	0.812

The fall in input prices caused a more favorable producer prices/input prices relation for agricultural production, generating a stimulus for agricultural supply, despite the fall in agricultural prices. It is interesting to note that this is the same kind of effect that we have argued was important for Brazilian agricultural development in the 1980s. One should note that the exchange rate has dropped continuously in Brazil since the mid 1980s. On the other hand, imports were under quantitative restrictions during the whole decade, being liberalized just at the beginning of the 1990s.

In the model, agricultural inputs are aggregate inputs, with particular compositions for agricultural activities and animal production activities. The fall in agricultural-type inputs in this experiment was about 8.5% on average, while for the animal production type, it was 7.5%. The fall in primary factors price was even greater; as can be seen in table 13.13, agricultural labor wages experienced a 16%-19% fall in the experiment, reducing significantly rural disposable income. This means that, despite the greater agricultural production in the experiment, the price reduction lowered agricultural income relative to urban income.

Table 13.12   Producer prices/input prices relation
Percent variations from the base run

Year	Coffee	Cane	Rice	Wheat	Soybeans	Cotton	Corn	Other	Poultry	Cattle	Milk
1990	4.24	2.33	1.10	9.09	9.09	9.09	9.09	-4.30	1.11	0.17	1.69
1992	3.91	0.52	0.78	7.32	7.32	7.32	7.32	-4.23	1.06	0.03	1.96
1994	4.86	0.77	0.72	7.13	7.13	7.13	7.13	-3.89	0.80	-0.13	1.63

Table 13.13   Aggregate Investment (Value), Aggregate Consumption (Value), Consumer Price Index (CPI), Rural Wages and Disposable Income in Experiment 1
Percent variations from the base run

	Investment	Consumption	CPI	Import Prices	Rural wages	Rural	Urban
1990	-10.0	-2.14	-1.6	-0.73	-16.5	-10.82	0.042
1992	-5.7	-1.64	-1.3	-1.23	-19.1	-11.24	0.049
1994	-5.6	-1.77	-1.3	-1.67	-16.4	-10.81	0.051

Simulation 2: The effects of import tariffs reduction upon the Brazilian agriculture

In this experiment, the import tariff level was adjusted to that observed in 1990. As noted before, in the beginning of the 1990s, the external trade liberalization that began in Brazil implied a sudden reduction in the import tariff structure. In the base run, this fact was represented by a 50% cut in import tariffs in years 1992 and 1994. In the present experiment, this tariff cut was eliminated, and the import tariff structure was returned to levels prior to 1990.

The rise in the external tariffs would raise the exchange rate in relation to the base run, as can be seen in table 13.14. This means that an exchange rate devaluation would be required to equilibrate the balance of payments, a movement contrary to what was observed in the first experiment. Here, the tariff increase was not matched by an equivalent import reduction, that created the need for the devaluation. Though small in size (a 0.10% devaluation in 1992 and 0.14% in 1994), this is important to illustrate the difference in the adjustment in both situations.

Table 13.14   Nominal exchange rate in experiment 2
Percent variations from the base run

Years	Nominal Exchange Rate
1992	0.10
1994	0.14

The impacts on the agricultural sector prices and production in this experiment can be seen in table 14.15. The effects of import tariff increases in this experiment were considerably smaller than those observed in experiment

1, when quantitative restrictions were introduced. As we have already seen, the exchange rate movement required to reach the new equilibrium is far smaller in this experiment than it was in the first one.

It should be noted that wheat, soybeans, cotton and corn would have had their prices increased in the experiment. As already noted, these are the agricultural products traded in raw form, and have their prices determined in the model by external prices, the tariff structure and the exchange rates. With the exchange rate increasing in the experiment, their prices have risen by the same amount of the exchange rate change, but all the other agricultural prices fell.

Table 13.15   Agricultural sector production and prices in experiment 2
Percent variations from the base run

	Production		Prices	
	1992	1994	1992	1994
Coffee	0.119	0.125	-0.211	-0.033
Sugarcane	0.068	0.079	-0.968	-0.805
Rice	-0.005	-0.008	-1.206	-1.086
Wheat	0.680	0.629	0.104	0.136
Soybeans	0.653	0.605	0.104	0.136
Cotton	0.785	0.727	0.104	0.136
Corn	0.365	0.338	0.104	0.136
Others	-0.183	-0.163	-1.621	-1.449
Poultry	-0.058	-0.079	-1.218	-1.154
Meats	-0.127	-0.133	-1.373	-1.286
Milk	-0.058	-0.081	-1.237	-1.183

Table 13.16   Producer prices/input prices relationships
Percent variations from the base run

Sectors	1992	1994
Coffee	0.992	1.043
Sugarcane	0.226	0.263
Rice	-0.015	-0.021
Wheat	1.311	1.214
Soybeans	1.311	1.214
Cotton	1.311	1.214
Corn	1.311	1.214
Others	-0.435	-0.388
Poultry	-0.097	-0.132
Meats	-0.253	-0.266
Milk	-0.116	-0.162

The impacts of these price changes on production are now more differentiated than in the previous experiment. Rice, other agricultural products, poultry, meats and milk, sectors that have experienced the greatest price falls, had their production diminished in the experiment, while coffee and sugarcane, although experiencing price declines, experienced increases in production.

This difference, of course, is due to the different evolution of the producer prices/input prices relation in each sector, as can be seen in table 13.16. The producer prices/input prices relation rises for coffee and sugarcane, since the price of the aggregate input in agriculture fell in greater proportion.

The effects of the import tariff increases on agricultural production are mixed, with some activities having their production increased and others reduced. The same is true for the agricultural prices evolution. The aggregate result in terms of rural income, wages, returns to land and disposable income can be seen in table 13.17.

Table 13.17   Experiment 2 results
Percent variations from the base run

	Wages		Returns to	Disposable income	
Years	Rural	Urban	Land	Rural	Urban
1992	-3.1	0.0	-2.9	-1.88	0.007
1994	-2.5	0.0	-2.4	-1.68	0.006

The effects of import tariffs increases on rural aggregates in experiment 2 are similar in nature to those in experiment 1, though different in size. The results reveal that, notwithstanding the increases in production of some agricultural activities, the sector would be better off in terms of disposable income, due to the decrease in rural factors income, like rural wages and returns to land.

Table 13.18   Experiment 3 results
Percent variations from the base run

					Savings	
Years	Consumption	Investment	CPI	Exchange rate	Rural	Urban
1992	-1.88	-4.72	-1.22	-1.73	2.02	-2.54
1994	-2.03	-4.69	-1.13	-1.54	-0.78	-2.44

Simulation 3: An analysis of the effects of trade liberalization in Brazil upon the Brazilian agriculture

In this experiment, we will put together the two events analyzed separately above, to infer about their joint effects. The model will be run simultaneously with the quantitative restrictions (experiment 1) as well as with the former import tariff structure (experiment 2). The results will be shown for the years 1992 and 1994 only since the results for 1990 are the same as for experiment 1, since the tariff structure has been changed in the model just from 1992 on. We begin the analysis with an overview of some macroeconomic effects in the simulation.

Table 13.18 provides some aggregate results arising from experiment 3. The exchange rate would have appreciated in the experiment, a result largely dictated by the imposition of quantitative restrictions in the model. As seen before, this result dominates the small exchange rate devaluation found in experiment 2. For the other aggregates, a more trade-restricted pattern of development would have required a smaller level of consumption (by households) and investment. Here, we can note again the effect already mentioned in the beginning of this chapter, that aggregate consumption is a more stable aggregate than aggregate investment. Yet it is interesting to note that this would have generated a fall in the consumer price index (CPI) in the model. Again, this is a result dictated by the quantitative restrictions in the model, since in experiment 2, the CPI rises. This is clear evidence of why developing countries with inflation problems choose so frequently to use this mechanism for restricting imports instead of relying on a tariff structure.

Table 13.19   Agricultural production and prices in experiment 3
Percent variations from the base run

	Production		Prices	
	1992	1994	1992	1994
Coffee	0.570	0.688	-5.132	-3.760
Sugarcane	0.205	0.296	-8.902	-8.209
Rice	0.279	0.255	-8.838	-8.480
Wheat	4.387	4.248	-1.733	-1.539
Soybeans	4.215	4.081	-1.733	-1.539
Cotton	5.079	4.917	-1.733	-1.539
Corn	2.339	2.265	-1.733	-1.539
Others	-1.989	-1.822	-13.747	-13.002
Poultry	0.576	0.402	-7.830	-7.812
Meats	-0.110	-0.203	-8.909	-8.798
Milk	0.905	0.719	-7.049	-7.104

In terms of the joint effects of these two experiments upon agriculture, one can see, in table 13.19, that the final result is near to the one found in the first experiment. The model shows an increase in agricultural production in general, except for other agricultural products and meats, and a general fall in prices. This is possible as a result of the fall in the agricultural producer prices/input prices relation that would follow.

The final result of this price fall and production increase would be a reduction in farm income (see table 13.20). The model generates a 12% reduction in rural disposable income, when compared to the base run. Urban income, on the other hand, remains approximately the same. The fall in disposable income in the rural sector is due to the fall in the wages of agricultural factors, like labor wages and returns to land.

Table 13.20   Experiment 3 results
Percent variations from the base run

Years	Labor Wages		Returns	Disposable income	
	Rural	Urban	Land	Rural	Urban
1992	-21.71	0.0	-21.9	-12.68	0.054
1994	-18.61	0.0	-17.0	-12.27	0.054

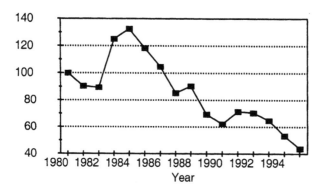

Figure 13.3   Real exchange rate, 1980-1995

Final remarks

On the basis of these results, what can then be inferred about the Brazilian agricultural sector's recent developments? The first point to note is that the trade liberalization process initiated at the beginning of the 1990s implied a more devalued pattern for the exchange rates than would have been required otherwise. This is an interesting point, since the Brazilian currency has showed a consistent pattern of revaluation since the mid 1980s, as one can see in figure 13.3. The results suggest that the exchange rate would have been even more revalued if trade liberalization had not happened.

According to model results, the elimination of the external trade quantitative restrictions was the key determinant of that effect. If the quantitative restrictions had been maintained, the modification in the import tariffs structure would have required a more devalued exchange rate than was observed.

For the agricultural sector, the general equilibrium effects arising from the model show that a more trade-restricted scenario would have allowed agriculture to grow with falling prices. This effect, possibly due to a more accentuated fall in input prices than in product prices, is the same kind of effect we showed in the first part of this chapter. It is important to note that this agricultural growth would make the agricultural sector better off in terms of income. The fall in input prices would affect relatively more the prices of primary inputs, like land and rural labor, than the prices of the inputs from the urban sectors.

The results further suggest that the pattern of structural adjustment in the Brazilian economy until 1994 generated general equilibrium effects that may have affected negatively the agricultural output of the sectors analyzed, when compared with the base run situation, one of trade liberalization. The salient point to be noted is that this would have happened in an apparently more favorable output prices scenario, since the model shows that the prices of these products would be lower than the actual pattern observed. The crucial variable for production decisions, the prices received/prices paid relationship, would have improved in the experiments, suggesting that the observed pattern of factor prices is more favorable to rural factors than otherwise would have been the case.

Finally, the similarity of facts of the more recent period with those analyzed here may prove interesting to note. The Real Plan, that began in 1994, generated a strong revaluation of the Brazilian currency, a situation that changed in the beginning of 1999, when Brazil decided to float its exchange rate to face the international financial instability of the period. The pattern of exchange rate revaluation observed through 1995 (see figure 13.3) continued throughout the period. As seen before, this is exactly the scenario related to the agricultural growth observed in the experiment. As noted in the first part of this chapter, the mechanism identified in the model as responsive to the agricultural growth, namely the increase in the agricultural product price/input price relation, is consistent with the facts observed in Brazilian agriculture. The effects of the exchange rate devaluation of January 1999 upon Brazilian agricultural growth will need to be monitored to explore the degree to which the prior pattern of behavior will be replicated in the future.

Notes

[1] This section is based in Ferreira Fo (1998).

[2] Table 13.3 shows data for selected years, but the year growth rate was calculated by Ordinary Least Squares for the entire period. Productivity growth rate for coffee is negative, though not significant statistically, due to the biannual production cycle of this culture, where years of good production are followed by years of bad production.

[3] The concept utilized is one of operational cost that encompasses variable costs plus depreciation. All the real values indexes utilized where constructed deflating the original series by the IGP-FGV.

[4] The edition of the Cruzado Plan in 1986 was followed by a huge speculation with inventories and real state.

[5] The disaggregated SAM can be obtained from the author upon request.

References

Brooke, A., D. Kendrick, A. Meeraus, (1988) *GAMS: A User's Guide*. The World Bank. The Scientific Press.

Burniaux, J. M., D. van der Mensbrugghe, (1990) "The RUNS model: A rural-urban north-south general equilibrium model for agricultural policy analysis," *Technical Paper* no. 33. Paris, OECD.

Carvalho, J.L. (1989) "Choques externos e a resposta interna: 'Semeando ventos e colhendo tempestades' na agricultura brasileira," *Revista Brasileira de Economia*, 43, 139-175.

Cavalcanti, C.B. (1988) "Transferência de recursos ao exterior e substituição de dívida externa por dívida interna," 12º Prêmio BNDES de Economia. Rio de Janeiro.

Dervis, K., Robinson, S. (1978) "The foreign exchange gap, growth and industrial strategy in Turkey: 1973-1983," *World Bank Staff Working Papers*, no. 306. Washington, D.C.

Ferreira Fo, J.B.S. (1994) "Notas a respeito do desempenho agregado da agricultura brasileira no período 1980-1991," *Revista de Economia e Sociologia Rural*, 32, 225-236.

Ferreira Fo, J.B.S., (1995) MEGABRÁS - *Um modelo de equilíbrio geral computável aplicado à análise da agricultura brasileira*. FEA/USP. Doutorado. São Paulo.

Ferreria Fo, J.B.S., (1998) "Ajustamento estrutural e crescimento agrícola na década dos oitenta: notas adicionais," *Revista de Economia Política*, 18, 84-95.

Gasquez, J.G., and C.M. Villa Verde (1990) "Crescimento da agricultura Brasileira e Politica Agricola nos anos 80." Texto para Discussão No. 204, Brasilia, IPEA.

Goldin, I., and G.C. Rezende, (1990) *Agriculture and economic crisis: lessons from Brazil*. OECD, Development Centre Studies. Paris.

Instituto De Economonia Agrícola (1992). "Estatísticas de salários agrícolas no estado de São Paulo." *Série Informações Estatísticas da Agricultura 01/92*. São Paulo, IEA.

Melo, F.B.H. (1992) "Tendência de queda nos preços reais de insumos agrícolas," *Revista de Economia Política*. 12, 141-146.

Rezende,G.C. (1986) "Crescimento econômico e oferta de alimentos no Brasil," *Revista de Economia Política*, 6, 64-81.

Rezende, G.C. (1988) "Ajuste externo e agricultura no Brasil, 1981-1986. *Revista Brasileira de Economia*, 42, 101-137.

Rezende, G.C. (1989a) "Agricultura e ajuste externo no Brasil: novas considerações," *Pesquisa e Planejamento Econômico*, 19, 553-578.

Rezende, G.C. (1989b) Política econômica e a agricultura na década de 80. *Anais do XXVII Congresso Brasileiro de Economia e Sociologia Rural*. Piracicaba, vol. II, 284-309.

Rezende, G.C and A.M. Buainain, (1994) "Structural adjustment and agriculture in Brazil: the experience of the 1980s," *Revista Brasileira de Economia*, 48, 491-503.

14 The Brazilian Trade Balance for Basic and Processed Agricultural Products from 1961 to 1995

CLÓVIS OLIVEIRA DE ALMEIDA and CARLOS JOSÉ CAETANO BACHA

Introduction

This chapter analyzes the role of the exchange rate on the determination of the Brazilian trade balance for basic and processed agricultural products (aggregated) from 1961 to 1995. Specifically, the study will first estimate an econometric model that explains the long and short-run variations in the trade balance of basic and processed agricultural products (total agricultural trade balance) and secondly, evaluate the effectiveness of an exchange policy compared to an income policy in terms of their effects on the total agricultural trade balance.

The chapter is organized into five sections. The first one analyzes the evolution of the Brazilian trade balance during the period from 1961 to 1995, showing the different performance of the aggregated basic and processed agricultural products sector in comparison to the other sectors of the economy. Section two presents a brief literature review on exchange rates and international trade of goods in order to stress that the specific objectives for this chapter have not been appropriately studied yet in Brazil. The focus of the third section is on cointegration analysis and the error correction mechanism, methods that are proposed as suitable econometric devices to determine the exchange rate's long and short-run effects on the total agricultural trade balance. The fourth section analyzes the research results and section five presents the conclusions emphasizing those most relevant to exchange rate policies.

Evolution of the Brazilian Trade Balance

Trade balance is the net result of commercial transactions of goods between one country and the rest of the world. When exports exceed imports a positive balance is obtained (surplus). On the contrary, when imports are larger than exports a negative balance results (deficit). Brazilian exports during the period 1961 to 1995 experienced many changes in composition and annual growth rates. The share of the processed and manufactured products in terms of value and quantities exported showed an increasing trend for that period. The 1970s and 1980s are noted as one of the periods with more changes in export components and high growth rates, mainly for manufactured products (see Homem de Melo and Zockun, 1976; Neves, 1984 and Bontempo, 1989). Basic and processed agricultural products accounted for 75% of total export value in 1970, 50% in 1980 and 34% in 1989 (see Homem de Melo and Zockun, 1976, and Guimarães and Oliveira, 1990).

The process of Brazilian industrialization and the promotion policy (in the form of fiscal and credit incentives) to enhance the export of processed products contributed to export growth of industrialized products. At the same time, according to several studies,[1] exports of agricultural products were harmed by the imposition of tariff and non-tariff barriers. During the 1980s, according to Pinheiro *et al.* (1993), agricultural exports continued to be discriminated against by broad export promotion policies, except for the credit incentives at the beginning of that decade.

Homem de Melo and Zockun (1976) found that, among the several policy instruments used to promote exports, only exchange mini-devaluations benefited agriculture because of the reduction of real exchange rate variations. Notwithstanding these findings, it should be noted that the subsidized credit policy benefited also the exportable agricultural products sector. More recently, in 1996, the government exempted exports of basic and semi-processed products from paying the tax on goods and services circulation (ICMS). This policy initiative should stimulate the exports of those products.

Although agriculture did not receive export promotion incentives to the same degree as other manufactured products, there is no doubting the agricultural sector's substantial contribution, jointly with the sector of processed agricultural products, to the process of Brazilian trade balance adjustment.

Figure 14.1 shows that the Brazilian total agricultural trade balance was in a surplus position throughout the period from 1961 to 1995.

Positive total trade balance results observed in some years of the period from 1961 to 1983 were generated by the positive results of the total agricultural trade balance;[2] this is also true for 1995. Therefore, over the 35 year period 1961 to 1995, aggregated non-agricultural sectors obtained a positive trade balance for just 11 years, during the period from 1984 to 1994. Nevertheless, even for those years, agriculture related trade balance was higher than that of the other sectors of the economy.

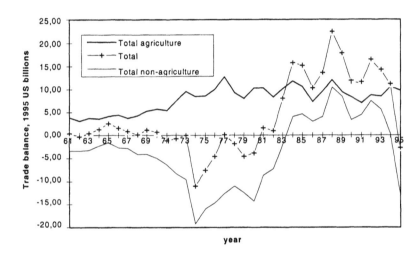

Figure 14.1   Brazilian   trade   balance   evolution: total,   total agricultural and non-agricultural, from 1961 to 1995

In addition, figure 14.1 shows that the biggest deficits in the trade balance occurred in 1974, 1975, 1976, 1979 and 1980[3] by the amounts of 10.95, 7.55, 4.60, 4.50 and 3.92 billions of US dollars, respectively. Subtracting from those figures the contribution of agricultural sectors to the process of trade balance adjustment, the deficits of the other sectors would be 19.36, 16.07, 14.65, 12.49 and 14.22 billions of US dollars.

Exchange Rate and Foreign Transactions of Goods in Brazil

The exchange rate is defined as the price of the domestic currency stated in terms of a reference foreign currency. An increase in the exchange rate represents a devaluation of the domestic currency; the reverse is true when a decrease in the exchange rate is enacted. A devaluation of the real exchange rate increases export profitability and, concomitantly, the cost of imports in domestic currency, tending to produce a surplus in the trade balance. Again, the reverse action would reduce exports and probably increase imports.

The devaluation of the exchange rate "is an implicit tax on exports whose impact in the domestic economy grows at the same proportion as the elasticity of foreign demand" (Schuh, 1983, p. 92). Brazilian participation in the international market might be considered marginal for most of the export products. As a result, the price elasticity of global demand should be high, implying in a high tax on the export sector due to the domestic currency revaluation (Schuh, 1977).

One of the few situations where an exchange rate revaluation is desirable occurs when the country is a price-maker in the international market of a certain product, as long as the price elasticity of demand for that product is smaller than one in absolute value. For example, this was the case for coffee during the period when Brazil was a price maker in the international market (see Schuh, 1977 and Almeida, 1993). In such a situation, an exchange rate revaluation causes a revenue increase due to the fact that the price increase in foreign currency is of a larger proportion than the reduction in the quantity exported.

In Brazil, the exchange policy began to be used, in a more generic way, with the purpose of promoting exports by August of 1968 when the country abandoned the maxi-devaluations system. The maxi-devaluations system generated uncertainties for export activities and stimulated financial speculation whenever a "maxi" was foreseen by economic agents. Beginning in August, 1968, Brazil adopted a system of exchange mini-devaluations where the differential between domestic and foreign inflation rates was a parameter to correct the nominal exchange rate. The system of exchange mini-devaluations functioned up to February 1990. In March 1990, the dirty flotation exchange rate system was adopted and used until June of 1994. Beginning in July 1994, Brazil implemented a limited, flexible exchange rate system.

Several analyses explored the dynamics of the exchange rate policies adopted in Brazil. For example, Senna (1974), Silva (1976), Suplicy (1976), Almonacid (1979) and Zini Jr. (1989 and 1993), among others, analyzed the bases for the exchange mini-devaluations policy. The latter two authors were able to distinguish the real from the monetary shocks, suggesting the inadequacy of the devaluation rule based on the purchasing parity power to balance the country's foreign accounts in situations where real shocks are present (oil shocks and world recession, for example).[4] The same conclusion was suggested in the studies by Pastore *et al* (1976 and 1978) investigating the exchange delay during the year of 1974.

The impact of exchange rates on the Brazilian foreign sector has been featured in many studies.[5] Prominently highlighted have been analyses that have attempted to verify the effects of exchange rate on the exports of manufactured products, basic products and on the trade balance. The exchange variable has been stated in different ways, with the concepts of real and effective rates being the most used. Exchange elasticities were found not to coincide on only one value, with estimated values varying according to the period of analysis, the degree of data aggregation and the estimation method.

Empirical evidence tends to confirm that the exchange rate is an important variable in the trade relations between Brazil and the rest of the world. For example, Suplicy (1976) and Viana (1993) estimated exchange elasticity values of 1.79 and 0.969 for the Brazilian exports of manufactured products, respectively. In the same way, Tyler (1982) indicates, based on studies for Brazilian exports of manufactured products, that the relevant exchange elasticities have varied from 1 to 1.5.

Braga and Markwald (1983) used equilibrium and disequilibrium models to study the effect of exchange rate devaluations on export revenues (in US dollars) for Brazilian manufactured products. They found that the long-run effects are larger than those in the short-run. Less optimistic estimates were obtained by Martner (1992) who suggests, simulating the effects of an exchange devaluation on the Brazilian economy, that the exchange variable has a limited impact on the generation of export exchange revenues. The importance of his simulation rests on the fact that the Marshall-Lerner hypothesis, commonly assumed in estimating the Brazilian foreign trade equations, was not considered in this case.

In relation to the effect of the exchange rate on the trade balance, Braga and Rossi (1986) estimated a long-run average elasticity coefficient of 2.5. In Zini's (1993) paper, the results show that the Brazilian trade balance presents a one year lagged response to variations in the real effective exchange rate.

The studies reviewed above made use of traditional econometric techniques to measure the effects of exchange rates on the exports of manufactured products and on the Brazilian trade balance. The problem with using these procedures is that the estimates obtained may reveal spurious relationships between the dependent variable and the regressor variables; this possibility always exists if the variables used in the estimation process are not stationary and linear combinations among them also produce a non stationary error term. The usual procedure to avoid the problem of spurious regression has been the one of estimating the regression in the first differences of the variables.[6] A criticism that is usually made of this procedure is that long-run information is lost in the process. Thus, the estimated coefficients would just be reflecting short-run adjustments. In case a long-run relationship exists among the variables being analyzed, such a procedure would lead to a model specification error because it leaves out the long-run effect.

During the 1980s, cointegration analysis was developed to allow for testing whether or not nonstationarity in the level series maintains a linear relationship of stable long-run equilibrium. If this were the case, then an error correction representation that shows the short-run dynamic behavior among the series considered would exist. The use of these devices allows for regression estimations using nonstationary variables - once some conditions are satisfied (as we will see in the next section of this chapter) - without taking the risk of developing spurious relationships.

The cointegrated systems and associated error correction representations came to be used mainly to study the relationships among macroeconomic variables. In this context, estimates of current account and trade balance equations were also included, with examples provided by Boucher (1991), who estimated an equation for the United States current account, and Rose (1991) who estimated equations for the trade balance of five countries: The United Kingdom, Canada, Germany, Japan and the United States. In both studies, the cointegration hypothesis among the dependent variable (current account or trade balance) and the independent variables (domestic income, foreign income and an index of price competitiveness), tested through Engle and Granger's method, was rejected.

Ferreira (1993) and Nunes (1994) used cointegration analysis with Engle and Granger's method to search for the existence of a stable relationship between the evolution of the Brazilian exchange rate and the trade balance. The periods analyzed were from 1982 to 1990 and from January of 1975 to March of 1991, respectively. Results found by those authors confirm the existence of a positive long-run relationship between domestic currency devaluations and trade balance. It should be stressed, however, that in Nunes' work that relationship was only verified when the real exchange rate concept was used (deflated by the United States IPA and the Brazilian ICV).

More refined equation estimates for Brazilian exports and imports were made recently by Castro and Cavalcanti (1997). They began testing for cointegrated relationships, using the method developed by Johansen for the case when the number of variables considered in the model is larger than two. Estimations were made taking into account exports as well as imports in aggregated and desegregated forms. From the export side, the following categories were considered: total exports, exports of manufactured products, exports of semi-manufactured products and exports of basic products; for the import side, total imports, imports of capital goods, imports of intermediate goods and imports of consumption goods were considered.

For all the export equations estimated by Castro and Cavalcanti (1997), it was verified that the exchange rate may be considered as an exogenous variable and that variations in the real exchange rate have positive short and long-run effects on export earnings by product category. Exceptions are made for the effects of exchange rate short-run variations on the value of total exports and on the value of basic products exports, which were statistically non significant. In relation to the import equations estimated by Castro and Cavalcanti (1997), it was concluded that the exchange rate may also be considered an exogenous variable and that its variations have negative short and long-run effects on import values for the analyzed categories.

Research on exchange rate and foreign agricultural goods transactions is seldom found in Brazil. According to Suplicy (1976), referring to Doellinger's (1971) estimates for the period 1963/68, the exchange elasticity calculated for exports of nontraditional basic products was 0.54.[7] Evaluating the effects of mini-devaluations on exports of basic products [8] for the period 1964/71, Suplicy found the same exchange elasticity as Doellinger's (1971). Both authors used export supply equations in the logarithmic form to determine elasticity coefficients. Almeida (1993), studying the period 1970/89, estimated an export supply equation for Brazilian coffee using a recursive system of equations. The exchange rate was included as one of the independent variables. The exchange elasticity coefficient obtained is similar to the one found by Doellinger and also to the one calculated by Suplicy.

Carvalho (1995) used the period from June to December of 1994 to study the variation of export revenues (in domestic currency) induced by variations in the exchange rate, foreign prices and quantities exported for coffee beans, soybean meal and orange juice. The results she found suggest that the variable exchange rate exercised a smaller impact than that of the other variables. Nevertheless, she indicates that in certain periods the exchange rate variations were one of the determinant factors for export revenues.

Although the empirical evidence cited above reveals a limited effect of exchange rates on the revenue from agricultural export products, it also shows that it should not be neglected, even more so if we consider that elasticities can change through time. Elasticities could change because of the period analyzed, the degree of data aggregation, the variable specification and the estimation method, among others factors. In addition, there will be differences between short and long-run effects.

Further, prior studies using traditional econometric techniques consider the effect of the exchange rate on agricultural products individually and grouped, but not on the trade balance of basic and processed agricultural products (total agricultural trade balance). It is known that the objective of the exchange policy is to affect the total trade balance. The importance of evaluating the impact on a product or a group of products decreases because of the fact that the orientation of such a policy is not a function of one product alone, unless it possesses a dominant share in the generation of exchange earnings for the country. This was the case for coffee in Brazil during the first three decades of this century. Thus, as previously stressed, the purpose of this chapter is to determine the effects of the exchange rate on the total agricultural trade balance for they represent the main source of trade surplus generated during the period under analysis (1961 to 1995).

Given the importance of the Brazilian processed agricultural products complex as a net exporter, its contribution to trade balance equilibrium should not be ignored, even more when it is known that the largest deficits in the balance of payments occurred in times of trade deficits. This observation had already been made by Homem de Melo and Zockun in 1976 and Veiga in 1977, but it continues to be valid today.

Currently, policy analysts in the Ministry of Finance also share that point of view. Data from the newspaper Gazeta Mercantil (January 13, 1997) reveal that the total agricultural trade balance was US$ 10.44 billions in 1996, compared to a deficit of US$ 5.53 billions in the trade balance. Therefore, it is confirmed that the trend verified in the period from 1961 to 1995 continues (see Figure 14.1), with agriculture and the processing industry generating trade balance surpluses and the other sectors of the economy contributing to the increasing trade balance deficit.

Methodology

Econometric procedures in order to estimate the model for the determination of the basic and processed agricultural products trade balance are presented in the next section. Thereafter, variable definitions and data sources are provided followed by a synthesis of the estimated model.

Econometric procedures

The estimation process used in this study involved three steps. Unit root tests to verify series stationarity were carried out as a first step in the estimation process. In the second step, the number of cointegration relationships are determined and the cointegration coefficient vectors are estimated in order to obtain the long-run effects of selected variables on Brazilian basic and processed agricultural products trade balance. Finally, once the cointegration hypothesis is accepted, short-run effects are measured using an error correction model.

Unit root tests Augmented Dickey Fuller test (ADF) was used to test for each time series integration order in this study because of its extensive use in the specialized literature. Accordingly, the unit root ADF test was applied to each individual data series following the sequential procedure suggested by Perron (see Harris, 1995) as the first step for data analysis in this study. Such a procedure is recommended because in applied research the true data generating process is unknown. Perron's sequential procedure to determine a time series integration order consists of estimating, through ordinary least squares, a reparametrized autoregressive process of order *p* using equations in table 14.1, for each data series.

Harris (1995) indicates that the null unit root hypothesis is tested by moving from the most general specification for the data generating process towards the most restricted specification. If the null hypothesis for the most general specification cannot be rejected, a model by model testing procedure continues up to the most restricted specification. Testing stops when the unit root null hypothesis cannot be rejected anymore (see the sequence in table 14.1). It should be pointed out that steps 14.2a and 14.4a in table 14.1 will only be performed if hypotheses 2 and 4 were jointly rejected.

Table 14.1   Unit root ADF test using Perron's sequential procedure

Step and model	Null hypothesis	Test statistic
$(14.1)\ \Delta y_t = \mu_c + \gamma_c t + \beta_0 y_{t-1} + \sum_{i=1}^{p-1} \beta_i\ \Delta y_{t-i} + \varepsilon_t$	$\beta_0 = 0$	τ_τ
$(14.2)\ \Delta y_t = \mu_c + \gamma_c t + \beta_0 y_{t-1} + \sum_{i=1}^{p-1} \beta_i\ \Delta y_{t-i} + \varepsilon_t$	$\beta_0 = \gamma_c = 0$	ϕ_3
$(14.2a)\ \Delta y_t = \mu_c + \gamma_c t + \beta_0 y_{t-1} + \sum_{i=1}^{p-1} \beta_i\ \Delta y_{t-i} + \varepsilon_t$	$\beta_0 = 0$	t
$(14.3)\ \Delta y_t = \mu_c + \beta_0 y_{t-1} + \sum_{i=1}^{p-1} \beta_i\ \Delta y_{t-i} + \varepsilon_t$	$\beta_0 = 0$	τ_μ
$(14.4)\ \Delta y_t = \mu_c + \beta_0 y_{t-1} + \sum_{i=1}^{p-1} \beta_i\ \Delta y_{t-i} + \varepsilon_t$	$\beta_0 = \mu_c = 0$	ϕ_1
$(14.4a)\ \Delta y_t = \mu_c + \beta_0 y_{t-1} + \sum_{i=1}^{p-1} \beta_i\ \Delta y_{t-i} + \varepsilon_t$	$\beta_0 = 0$	t
$(14.5)\ \Delta y_t = \beta_0 y_{t-1} + \sum_{i=1}^{p-1} \beta_i\ \Delta y_{t-i} + \varepsilon_t$	$\beta_0 = 0$	τ

Note: *The name of each test statistic is identical to its representation. For example, the τ_τ test is called tal tal*

Source: *Adapted from Harris (1995)*

The underlying hypothesis for the equations in table 14.1 is that the data generating process is a reparametrized autoregressive process of order *p*. The most general specification for the autoregressive process includes a constant term and a time trend while the most restricted one excludes all deterministic components of the data generation process.

In order to know whether or not the series analyzed is stationary the null hypothesis of an order one integrated series [I(1)] is tested. The ADF test is applied to the estimated β_0 coefficient associated with variable y_{t-1} in each model. If the null hypothesis $\beta_0 = 0$ cannot be rejected, there is evidence for the existence of a unit root in the data series, implying nonstationarity in levels. Conversely, if the null hypothesis is rejected, that is, if β_0 is statistically smaller than zero, then the series is stationary in levels.

The test statistics for testing joint hypothesis are versions of the *F* statistic. Those versions take different names because they do not present a standard distribution. The name of the statistic varies according to the null joint hypothesis being tested (see table 14.1). The statistic ϕ_3 tests the null joint hypothesis that the series analyzed may be represented by a unit root process and without a trend. The ϕ_1 statistic tests the null hypothesis that the data generating process has a unit root and an undetermined mean. The ϕ_1 and ϕ_3 table values are found in Dickey and Fuller (1981).

In practice, the procedure takes into account the possibility of there existing more than one unit root. In this study, up to two differences were considered due to the fact that the probability of economic series presenting integration order higher than two is very low. One of the difficulties for ADF use is the determination of the number of lagged differences for the variable in the equation. As a general rule, the number of lagged terms with differences should be established so that the error terms are serially uncorrelated. Many procedures can be used to help determine the autoregressive process lag order p. The Schwarz (SC) and the Akaike (AIC) criteria are the most commonly used procedures.

An additional difficulty in the selection of the criterion to be used arises because different criteria lead to different number of lagged terms. The Schwarz criterion was used in this study; it was selected because it is one of the most parsimonious and thus advantageous in this case because of the small sample size.

Cointegration test   After each series integration order was verified, it was determined whether or not they cointegrate. Cointegration relationships for an *n*-dimensional system are estimated in a systematic way departing from a reparametrized vector autoregressive process of order p as follows (see Johansen, 1988 and Johansen and Juselius, 1991 for a detailed discussion of the model used):

$$\Delta Z_t = \Pi Z_{t-1} + \sum_{j=1}^{p-1} \Gamma_j \Delta Z_{t-j} + \Psi D_t + \varepsilon_t \qquad t = 1,...,T \qquad (14.6)$$

where Z_t is an (n x 1) vector of nonstationary variables. In this study, it was assumed that all variables in Z_t are integrated of order one [I(1)]. Hence, ΔZ_t is a vector of stationary variables [I(0)].

The (n x n) Π matrix is associated with the vector of integrated lagged variables of order one (Z_{t-1}). The Π matrix is the product of the matrices α and β. The matrix α provides the average velocity measure of convergence toward long-run equilibrium (Hansen and Juselius, 1995).

For the purpose of this study, if it were possible to interpret one of the cointegration vectors as an equation for the total agricultural trade balance, then the α coefficient associated with it will represent the average velocity at which the total agricultural trade balance adjusts in response to a one-time shock on the equilibrium relationship (see Williams and Bewley, 1993).

Matrix β is formed by long-run coefficients in order for the $\beta' Z_{t-1}$ product to yield the cointegration relationships for the multivariate model (i.e. long-run relationships) that ensures that Z_t converges to its static long-run solution (Harris, 1995, p 79) in case cointegration relationships exist.

In synthesis, Π matrix reunites all coefficients associated with variables included in the cointegration space. The coefficients of the model's dynamic part are given by matrices Γj. The number of lags p used should be the one that makes the error term (ε_t) uncorrelated through time. The SC criterion was used to choose the lag order to estimate the system autoregressive vectors. Haug (1996, p. 95-96) cited by Reimers (1993), suggests that the SC test to select the lag order in cointegrated VAR systems is superior to Akaike's. In addition to the SC test, the residual diagnostic tests were also used (ε_t).

Finally, the non-restricted VAR Ψ vector (14.6) includes the coefficients that reveal the short-run system impacts such as intervention policies and impacts from external shocks. They are frequently stated in the form of dummy variables included in D_t (Harris, 1995). According to Hansen and Juselius (1995) vector D_t can also includes nonstationary weak exogenous variables that might be excluded from the cointegration space if certain conditions were satisfied (as we will see below).

In this study, the rank of Π matrix was jointly determined with the number of deterministic components to be included in model (14.6) (Johansen, 1992), using Pantula's criterion. Pantula's criterion consists of testing the no-cointegration null hypothesis for a set of models. Operationally, probable models are estimated and the number of cointegration relationships ($r = 0$, $r = 1$, $r = 2$, ..., $r = n - 1$, where n is the number of variables included in the cointegration space) is progressively tested model by model, from the most restricted model (with no deterministic component) up to the less restricted model (with a constant term and a time trend). Testing stops when the null no cointegration hypothesis cannot be rejected anymore. That is, the hypothesis $r = 0$ is first tested in every model; if the null hypothesis is rejected, testing continues with $r = 1$ and so on. When the null hypothesis cannot be rejected anymore, testing is completed and the model selected will be the one that has the null hypothesis accepted.

After having selected the model and determined the number of cointegration relationships, the next step is to estimate cointegrated vectors and test the null weak exogeneity hypothesis for the variables included in the cointegration relationships. In this study, the weak exogeneity test was performed assuming that one of the vectors can be interpreted as a total agricultural trade balance equation.

The weak exogeneity test is necessary because the cointegration relationships estimated by Johansen's method assume that all variables included in the cointegration space are endogenous. This fact does not allow for an accurate interpretation of the estimated parameters. Thus in the presence of weak exogeneity for a set of variables, the long-run relationships may be estimated (with no efficiency loss) from a VAR system in which only the equations for the endogenous variables are explicitly modeled.

Johansen's method was used following the interpretations and applications developed by Gonzalo (1994). The major objective of his research was to select the best method for estimating cointegrated vectors for empirical research. Gonzalo (1994) studied the asymptotic distribution of estimators for five alternative cointegrated vectors estimation methods - ordinary least squares, nonlinear least squares, maximum likelihood in an error correction model (Johansen's method), principal components and canonical correlation. He concluded that estimates obtained through Johansen's method have better properties than the ones produced through the other methods tested. Those results are also valid for finite samples.

In addition, Gonzalo (1994) points out that among the five methods analyzed, Johansen's was the only one to satisfy three desired requirements in the estimation of cointegration vectors, namely, (a) inclusion of *a priori* information in the determination of the presence of a unit root, (b) full system estimation and (c) identification of system dynamic effects.

Error correction model If accepts the cointegration hypothesis, the error correction model allows one to obtain short-run impacts of explanatory variables (weak exogenous variables) on the dependent variable (total agricultural trade balance) without loosing long-run information. In specifying the error correction model, the dependent variable (in the first differences) becomes a function of the error term of a one-lag form cointegration equation for the endogenous variable in first lagged differences and for the first current and lagged differences of explanatory variables.[9] The 5% critical limit was used to reject the null hypothesis in all tests performed.

Definition of variables

Variables used in the analysis are: trade balance of basic and processed agricultural products (*SAT*), exchange rate (*e-IPA*), terms of trade (*TT*), level of domestic activity (*RB*) and level of foreign activity (*RW*). An explanation of those variable calculations and use is given below.

Trade balance of basic and processed agricultural products Total agricultural trade balance (*SAT*) includes all basic agricultural products, live animals and forest products as well as manufactured products originating from them. Data from FAO publications on 397 products[10] were used. Fertilizer transactions were not included because no data for 1995 were available. Products with less than four years of trade transactions information were also excluded. Total agricultural trade balance values are expressed in constant 1995 US dollars. The United States wholesale price index was used as deflator.

Price competitiveness indices (1) Exchange rate (e-IPA) Stated according to the concept of real effective exchange rate, wholesale price indices (IPA) for Brazil and for the major Brazilian trade partners were used to deflate the effective exchange rate. The foreign IPAs were weighted by the relative participation of each partner in Brazilian foreign trade transactions.[11] These weights were changed every five years. The series base is 1985 since the Brazilian exchange markets were stable in that year (see Zini Jr., 1993). *(2) Terms of trade (TT)* As a proxy for the terms of trade, the ratio between exports and imports prices index was utilized. It is a Laspeyres type index with a base in 1961. An index increase means an improvement in the terms of trade.

Indicators for the domestic and foreign activity level (1) Domestic activity level (RB) The level of domestic activity was measured by Brazilian GDP, based on 1995 prices, using the implicit GDP deflator. *(2) Foreign activity level (RW)* The rest of the world import values for basic and processed agricultural products were used as a proxy for the share of foreign disposable income spent on basic and processed agricultural products. Values are in constant 1995 US dollars. The United States wholesale price index was used as a deflator.

Proxies to handle exogenous shocks[12] A dummy variable was used to measure the effect of the 1975 frost in Brazil on international market coffee prices and consequently on the total agricultural trade balance in 1976 and 1977. The dummy takes a value of 1 in 1976 and 1977 and zero otherwise, admitting a temporary effect of the 1975 frost, with potential impact on short-run relationships.

The estimated model

The model to be estimated is a non-restricted VAR [see model (14.6)] where:
$Z_t = [SAT_t, e\text{-}IPA_t, TT_t, RB_t, RW_t]$;
$D_t = 1$ for years 1976 and 1977, and zero otherwise;
$\Pi = \alpha\beta^1$; and,
α, β, Γ and Ψ are the parameters to be estimated.
The values of the variables are shown in table 2 and they correspond to the period 1961 to 1995, corresponding to 35 observations for each variable. All the series, except dummy variables, were used in logarithmic form.

The first step was the estimation of model (14.6) considering all variables (*SAT, e-IPA, TT RB* and *RW*) as being simultaneously endogenous. This is a non-restricted reparametrized VAR. Then, in the second step, the zero restrictions were imposed on model (14.6) α for the weak exogenous variables. Thus, this version becomes the restricted reparametrized VAR, also called the conditional model and the one used to make economic interpretations of relationships among the variables studied. Strictly speaking, the conditional model is the one with the weak exogenous variables appearing in the dynamic part of the model (short-run). However, that procedure requires the estimation of a large number of parameters diminishing the degrees of freedom. Due to the fact that the sample used in this study has only 35 observations, loosing degrees of freedom could harm the quality of estimations. Hence, weak exogenous variables were conditioned only in the error correction model (separately estimated). Short-run relationships are determined from that model.

Results and Discussion

Results obtained from the unit root tests (14.1), from the estimation of the cointegration vector (14.2) and from the error correction equation (14.3) are presented in this section. Based on the weak exogeneity tests, we assume that the cointegration vector can be interpreted as a reduced equation for the total agricultural trade balance.

Unit root tests

Table 14.2 shows the results of the unit root tests. Those results suggest that the data series on total agricultural trade balance, terms of trade, real effective exchange rate, domestic income and foreign income do not present two unit roots, *i.e.*, the series in the first differences are stationary.

Table 14.2   Augmented Dickey-Fuller unit root tests: dependent variable in the second differences ($\Delta^2 \ln y_t$)

Variables	N$^{\underline{o}}$ of lags	N$^{\underline{o}}$ of observations	Test statistics			
			τ_{μ}	ϕ_1	t	τ
ln *SAT*	1	32	-6.97^a	24.29^a	-6.97^a	-6.65^a
ln *TT*	0	33	-5.68^a	16.13^a	-5.68^a	-5.76^a
ln *e-IPA*	1	32	-5.47^a	14.95^a	-5.47^a	-5.52^a
ln *RB*	0	33	-3.18^b	5.07^{ns}	-3.18^a	-2.08^b
ln *RW*	0	33	-3.97^a	7.91^a	-3.97^a	-3.30^a

Note: *Superscripts "a" and "b" indicate significance at the 1% and 5% levels, respectively*

Table 14.3   Augmented Dickey-Fuller tests for unit root: dependent variable in the first differences ($\Delta \ln y_t$)

Variables	N$^{\underline{o}}$ of lags	N$^{\underline{o}}$ of observations	Test statistics				
			τ_τ	ϕ_3	τ_{μ}	ϕ_1	t	τ
ln *SAT*	2	32	-1.03	1.61	-1.83	2.95	-	1.45
ln *TT*	0	34	-2.79	3.91	-2.79	3.90	-	0.01
ln *e-IPA*	2	32	-0.55	4.10	-0.43	0.20	-	-0.50
ln *RB*	1	33	-0.90	1.25	-1.52	3.90	-	2.19
ln *RW*	1	33	-2.45	3.07	-1.18	2.69	-	1.94

The results in table 14.3 indicate that the null hypotheses of one unit root for all the series analyzed cannot be rejected. Thus, the hypotheses that all the series in level are I(1) is accepted implying that all data series are integrated of order one. In addition, the tests for the joint null hypotheses suggest that the series generating process (total agricultural trade balance, terms of trade, real effective exchange rate, domestic income and foreign income) presents a unit root and no time trend component.

Cointegration test

Cointegration relationships were estimated through the method proposed by Johansen. The estimated system included five variables I(1) in logarithmic form: total agricultural trade balance (*SAT*); real effective exchange rate (*e-IPA*); terms of trade (*TT*); domestic income (PIB); foreign income (*RW*); and, a one-time intervention dummy variable to take account for the effect of the 1975 frost on the 1976 and 1977 international coffee prices, and consequently, on the total agricultural trade balance.

The Schwarz criterion indicated that an order one VAR system should be estimated. Nevertheless, taking into account that more than one lag was necessary to ensure that the residuals were serially uncorrelated, an order two VAR system was estimated. The order two VAR system was used to perform the cointegration analysis.

Pantula's criterion showed the presence of a constant term in the cointegration space and only one stable long-run relationship (one cointegration vector).[13] Critical values from the Osterwald-Lenum (1992) tables were used as indicators[14] of true asymptotic values for λ_{max} and λ_{trace} statistics. The correction for small samples proposed by Reimers (1992) was not considered because it is arbitrary and conflicts with the existence of cointegration relationships (Nielsen, 1997).[15]

Reduced rank tests for the model selected through Pantula's criterion are presented in table 14.4. Based on a 5% significance level for the λ_{trace} statistic, it is possible to reject the null hypotheses that the number of cointegration relations equals zero (that is $r = 0$). Thus, the alternative hypotheses is accepted, namely that a cointegration vector among the *SAT*, *e-IPA*, *TT*, *RB* and *RW* variables exist. The λ_{max} statistic rejects the null hypotheses that the number of cointegration relations equals zero only when a 10% significance level is used.

The cointegration vector normalized for the natural logarithm of the *SAT* variable [ln(*SAT*)] is shown in table 14.5. The adjustment coefficients (α_{i1}) that show the equilibrium long-run error relationships and the student *t*-tests that identify the probable weak exogenous variables with respect to the long-run model are also presented in table 14.5. The values for the *t*-statistic suggest that the estimated cointegration relationships are significant just for the *SAT* equation. The adjustment coefficient for the *SAT* variable is larger than the ones for the other variables (see table 14.5). According to Hansen and Juselius (1995), this may be an indication that the estimated cointegration vector can have an economic interpretation.

Table 14.4   Cointegration reduced rank tests for the model selected, using data for the period 1961-1995

Null hypothesis (Ho: r)	Non stationary (n − r)	Estimated roots λ_i	λ_{trace}	λ_{max}
0	5	0.6207	78.44[b]	31.99[c]
1	4	0.5158	46.45	23.93
2	3	0.3165	22.52	12.56
3	2	0.2123	9.96	7.88
4	1	0.0612	2.09	2.08

Note: *superscripts "b" and "c" indicate null hypotheses rejection at the 5% and 10% levels, respectively*

Table 14.5   Cointegration vector, adjustment coefficients and student t statistic

Cointegration vector, normalized for the total agricultural trade balance (ln*SAT*)

ln(*SAT*)	ln(*e-IPA*)	ln(*TT*)	ln(*RB*)	ln(*RW*)	Constant
1.000	−1.081	0.319	−0.469	−0.428	5.957

Normalized adjustment vector α_{i1}

ln(*SAT*)	ln(*e-IPA*)	ln(*TT*)	ln(*RB*)	ln(*RW*)	
−0.758	0.221	0.068	0.073	0.047	-

Student t test values for the coefficients of the normalized adjustment vector

ln(*SAT*)	ln(*e-IPA*)	ln(*TT*)	ln(*RB*)	ln(*RW*)	
−4.780	1.812	0.275	1.423	0.596	-

Table 14.6   Weak exogeneity test for the logarithm of the variables (*e-IPA*), (*TT*), (*RB*) and (*RW*) in relation to the long-run parameters

Cointegration vector, normalized for the total agricultural trade balance (ln*SAT*)
(subject to a linear restriction on the adjustment parameters)

ln(*SAT*)	ln(*e-IPA*)	ln(*TT*)	ln(*RB*)	ln(*RW*)	Constant
1.000	−0.991	0.296	−0.498	−0.339	4.889

Normalized adjustment vector (subject to the restrictions zero on α_{i1}, with i = 2, 3, 4 e 5)

ln(*SAT*)	ln(*e-IPA*)	ln(*TT*)	ln(*RB*)	ln(*RW*)	
−0.914	0.000	0.000	0.000	0.000	-

LR test: X^2 (4) = 4.74 $p = 0.32$

The possibility of weak exogeneity for the logarithm of the *e-IPA*, *TT*, *RB* and *RW* variables, verified through the student t-test, suggests that the cointegration vector might be interpreted as a reduced form equation for the total agricultural trade balance (*SAT*). The likelihood ratio (LR) statistic, shown in table 14.6, leads to the same conclusion, namely that the null hypothesis that the variables noted above can be considered weakly exogenous in relation to the long-run parameters of the estimated model cannot be rejected.[16]

Table 14.7   Significance tests for the variables included in the cointegration space

Cointegration vector, normalized for the total agricultural trade balance (ln*SAT*)
(subject to restrictions zero on the estimated parameters α_{i1} and β^1 with i ≠ 1)

ln(*SAT*)	ln(*e-IPA*)	ln(*TT*)	ln(*RB*)	ln(*RW*)	Constant
1.000	0.000	0.115	−0.888	0.296	−1.820
LR test: X^2 (5) = 12.08		$p = 0.03$			
ln(*SAT*)	ln(*e-IPA*)	ln(*TT*)	ln(*RB*)	ln(*RW*)	Constant
1.000	−0.588	0.000	−0.508	−0.240	3.346
LR test: X^2 (5) = 8.86		$p = 0.11$			
ln(*SAT*)	ln(*e-IPA*)	ln(*TT*)	ln(*RB*)	ln(*RW*)	Constant
1.000	−1.386	0.366	0.000	−1.095	9.576
LR test: X^2 (5) = 9.60		$p = 0.09$			
ln(*SAT*)	ln(*e-IPA*)	ln(*TT*)	ln(*RB*)	ln(*RW*)	Constant
1.000	−0.828	0.294	−0.715	0.000	2.620
LR test: X^2 (5) =5.75		$p = 0.33$			
ln(*SAT*)	ln(*e-IPA*)	ln(*TT*)	ln(*RB*)	ln(*RW*)	Constant
1.000	−0.536	0.271	−0.864	0.260	0.000
LR test: X^2 (5) =8.02		$p = 0.16$			

Tests for the zero restriction on the estimated parameters β_i subject to the zero restrictions already imposed on the adjustment coefficients (see table 14.6) are presented in table 14.5 in order to determine the importance of the weak exogenous variables in the long-run model (cointegration space). Those tests suggest that only the real effective exchange rate (*e-IPA*) variable had a significant effect on the total agricultural trade balance (*SAT*) in the long-run. The 5% significance level LR tests for the zero restrictions on the coefficients associated with the other variables and to the constant term are not statistically significant (see the *p* values in table 14.7).

Error correction model

Table 14.8 presents the short-run dynamics for the total agricultural trade balance. The explanatory variables included in the estimated equation are: the endogenous variable stated in lagged differences; the one lag error correction term [corresponding to the cointegration vector in table 7]; and, the differences (current and lagged) of the variables real effective exchange rate (ln *e-IPA*), terms of trade (ln *TT*), domestic (ln *RB*) and foreign (ln *RW*) income.[17] An intervention dummy variable for the years of 1976 and 1977 was also included to capture the effect of the 1975 frost on international coffee prices and, consequently, on the Brazilian total agricultural trade balance.

The results in table 14.9 show that only three variables presented significant effects at the 5% level: the rate of growth of foreign income, in the current period of time; the one lag domestic income growth rate; and, the error correction term.   The effects of the dummy and the lagged endogenous variables were significant only at the 7% level.   The effect of the one-lag terms of trade growth rate on total agricultural trade balance was significant only at the 10% level.

The null hypothesis of no effect of the exchange rate in the current period, one lag terms of trade and the dummy variable on the total agricultural trade balance is rejected by the F test in the short-run model. Therefore, it was decided to maintain those three variables in the equation (see table 14.8); the other variables showed no significant effects.

Table 14.8   Estimate of the error correction equation for the Brazilian total agricultural trade balance, 1963-1995 with dependent variable: $\Delta(\ln SAT)$

Variable	Estimated	t test	Significance	Diagnostic tests	
$\Delta(\ln SAT_{t-1})$	0.287	1.900 [ns]	0.07	Observations (n)	33
$\Delta(\ln e\text{-}IPA_t)$	0.400	1.640 [ns]	0.12	Degrees of freedom	22
$\Delta(\ln e\text{-}IPA_{t-1})$	-0.013	-0.050 [ns]	0.96	Adjusted R^2	0.74
$\Delta(\ln TT_t)$	-0.149	-1.114 [ns]	0.28	DW	2.04
$\Delta(\ln TT_{t-1})$	0.176	1.727 [ns]	0.10	Q(8-0)	11.23 [ns]
$\Delta(\ln RB_t)$	0.268	0.465 [ns]	0.65		
$\Delta(\ln RB_{t-1})$	1.289	2.093	0.05		
$\Delta(\ln RW_t)$	0.953	2.416	0.03		
$\Delta(\ln RW_{t-1})$	-0.565	-1.194 [ns]	0.25		
D_t	0.226	1.951 [ns]	0.07		
u_{t-1}	-0.914	-5.311	0.01		

Tested null hypothesis: coefficients associated to the following variables are zero:
1^a $\Delta(\ln e\text{-}IPA_t)$, $\Delta(\ln e\text{-}IPA_{t-1})$, $\Delta(\ln TT_t)$, $\Delta(\ln RB_t)$ e $\Delta(\ln RW_{t-1})$ $\Rightarrow$ F(5.22) = 0.734 [ns] $p = 0.60$
2^a $\Delta(\ln e\text{-}IPA_t)$, $\Delta(\ln TT_{t-1})$ e Dt $\Rightarrow$ F(3.22) = 3.742 value-p = 0.03
3^a $\Delta(\ln e\text{-}IPA_t)$ e $\Delta(\ln TT_{t-1})$ $\Rightarrow$ F(2.22) = 3.184 value-p = 0.07

The low price elasticities for Brazilian agricultural export products as well as for the country's agricultural imports demand provide an explanation for the low statistically significant effect of an increase in the growth rate of real exchange devaluation on the growth rate of total agricultural trade balance.   From the export side, it is known that agricultural production (input for processed agricultural products) lags in response to price shocks. Thus, even if a residual increase of exports from the selling part of the stocks occurs, mainly in terms of processed agricultural products, it might not be significant in the short-run.

Table 14.9   Estimate of the error correction equation for the Brazilian total agricultural trade balance, 1963-1995 with dependent variable: $\Delta(\text{ln}SAT)$

Variable	Estimated	t test	Significance	Diagnostic tests	
$\Delta(\text{ln}SAT_{t-1})$	0.236	1.827	0.08	Observations (n)	33
$\Delta(\text{ln}e\text{-}IPA_t)$	0.295	1.411	0.17	Degrees of freedom	26
$\Delta(\text{ln}TT_{t-1})$	0.200	2.191	0.04	Adjusted R^2	0.72
$\Delta(\text{ln}RB_{t-1})$	1.253	2.940	0.01	DW	1.90
$\Delta(\text{ln}RW_t)$	0.785	2.350	0.03	Q(8-0)	8.46 [ns]
D_t	0.179	2.041	0.06		
u_{t-1}	-0.908	-6.897	0.01		

From the import side, it is known that the Brazilian agricultural import demand is of low price elasticity. For example, wheat, corn, rice, and malt are three important agricultural import products (because of their share of total agricultural import value). However, price variations in domestic currency have little effect, at least in the short-run, on the imported quantities of those products. For this reason, a major short-run effect of a real exchange devaluation on the agricultural export sector is to increase the unit value of exports in domestic currency, with a small effect on foreign sector competitiveness (defined as the sector capacity for increasing its trade balance). However, the cumulative revenue loss in domestic currency caused by a real exchange valuation will have a significant negative effect in the long-run, as was verified in this research.

A parsimonious version of the short-run total agricultural trade balance equation is presented in table 14.9. Non significant variables (identified through the *F* test) were excluded from that version [they are: $\Delta(\text{ln}e\text{-}IPA)$, $\Delta(\text{ln}TT_t)$, $\Delta(\text{ln}RB_t)$ and $\Delta(\text{ln}RW_{t-1})$]. The estimated coefficient for variable $[\Delta(\text{ln}e\text{-}IPA)]$ had a positive sign (similar to the finding for the long-run) but it was not statistically significant (see table 14.9). Estimated coefficients suggest that a 10% increase of the terms of trade growth rate $[\Delta(\text{ln } TT_{t-1})]$ and of the domestic income growth rate $[\Delta(\text{ln}RB_{t-1})]$ cause, in the next period, an increase of 2% and 12.53% in the total agricultural trade balance growth rate, respectively (see table 14.9).

If we consider that the supply of agricultural products is given in the short-run and that changes in alimentary habits occur in the medium- and long-runs, we may infer that the probable adverse long-run effects on the trade balance due to an increase in the country's terms of trade will not occur in the short-run. Even if the quantity exported from Brazil does not increase in the short-run, it is expected that an increase in the foreign prices of the exported products compared to import prices, will tend to improve the trade balance in the short-run.

It is also noted, in table 14.9, that a 10% increase in the foreign income growth rate $[\Delta(\ln RW_t)]$ causes, in the same period, a 7.85% increase in the total agricultural trade balance growth rate. The coefficient associated with the one-lag error correction term suggests that, after a shock, total agricultural trade balance converges towards the long-run equilibrium at an average velocity of 0.908 per year. That is, the annual correction of the total agricultural trade balance towards long-run equilibrium is about 91%. Finally, it can also verified that the 1975 frost shock had a positive and statistically significant (at the 6% level) effect on the growth rate of the total agricultural trade balance.

Final Considerations

The general objective of this research was to determine the short- and long-run effects of the real effective exchange rate on the Brazilian total agricultural trade balance. In addition, an attempt was made to identify the most influential variables in the foreign trade performance of the Brazilian basic and processed agricultural products' sectors from 1961 to 1995.

Results indicate that in the long-run, real effective exchange devaluations have positive and statistically significant effects on total agricultural trade balance. In the short-run, the relevant variables for explaining the total agricultural trade balance variations are (in order of importance) domestic and foreign income and, the terms of trade. The real effective exchange rate devaluations also showed a positive effect on total agricultural trade balance (as expected) but the effect was not statistically significant.

If the government was to depend only on the basic and processed agricultural products sectors, it would not be necessary to implement recessive policies to improve the total agricultural trade balance in the short-run. Frequently used policies pursuing the improvement of the trade balance through the reduction of the domestic income level should be followed by compensatory measures to stimulate the exporting sectors that are most competitive internationally. If the exporting sectors of the economy are affected by a non-selective policy, the effect of the policy may be contrary to the expected one. As a result of this finding, an income contracting policy should be followed by compensatory policies to stimulate production in the export sectors.

In terms of the effects of foreign income (represented by the import value of basic and processed agricultural products of the rest of the world), the relevant findings follow. It was only in the short-run that a statistically significant effect of the variations in the rest of the world imports on the Brazilian total agricultural trade balance was verified. The lack of such an effect in the long-run points out the passiveness of the Brazilian foreign trade policy. Thus, Brazil should implement a more aggressive foreign trade policy to make the country follow the long-run growth tendency observed for the rest of the world, in terms of the quantities of basic and processed agricultural products imported.

In relation to the terms of trade, it is worth to highlighting two relevant issues. Since foreign prices for exported and imported goods are exogenous, total agricultural trade balance becomes dependent on the short- and long-run paths of those prices. If this is the case, Brazilian agricultural and macroeconomic policy makers cannot interfere in the process. In addition, the terms of trade might vary greatly according to the quantities transacted in the market due to the low price elasticity of demand that the major part of the exported and imported basic and processed agricultural products exhibit. In other words, it is not possible to forecast with certainty the behavior of that relationship in a longer time horizon.

The small sample size used in this study might be pointed out as a limiting factor for the quality of econometric results. Essentially, this might imply that the asymptotic distribution of the rank statistics and the unit root tests may not be precise. If that were the case, policy considerations, especially for the long-run, should be interpreted carefully.[18] However, the economic policy variable (exchange rate) had a perceptible influence on total agricultural trade balance from 1961 to 1995, and evidence exists indicating that expected short- and long-run relationships were captured in our estimates. In addition, profound transformations occurred in the Brazilian economy during the period of study (1961-1995), especially in foreign trade activity. Those transformations are compatible, we believe, with a long-run situation.

Notes

[1] See, for example, Mendonça de Barros *et al*, 1975; Homem de Melo and Zockun, 1976; Schuh, 1977; Pastore *et al* and Coes cited by Pinheiro *et al*, 1993.

[2] It includes all basic and processed agricultural products, live animals and forest products in the FAO publications.

[3] Trade balance deficits in those years reflect the consequences of the two oil shocks that occurred in the 1970s.

[4] The first oil shock occurred in October of 1973, but its effect on the trade balance was only verified in the three subsequent years. The second shock took place in 1979, with effect on the trade balance in 1979 and 1980. From 1980 to 1982, the world economy entered into recession and the Brazilian trade balance suffered a new deterioration.

[5] See, for example, the studies by Pastore *et al* (1976 and 1978), Bacha (1977), Sayad (1979a and 1979b), Cardoso (1979 and 1981), Silva and Locatelli (1987) and Locatelli and Silva (1991).

[6] Two other procedures may be used to treat the problem of spurious regression. One of them implies the inclusion of lagged values of the dependent and the explanatory variables on the right hand side of the regression equation. The other one uses the Cochrane-Orcutt method to eliminate serial autocorrelation among residuals. See Hamilton (1994) for more details.

[7] It is an aggregate of all basic products except coffee, cereals, cotton, cocoa, banana and carnaúba wax.

[8] Among the products included in that group are cotton, cocoa, sugar and iron. Coffee was not included.

[9] The error correction model specification assumes that explanatory variables are exogenous in the short-run model.

[10] There are 357 basic and processed agricultural products, 12 are live animals and 28 are forest raw material and wood based processed products.

[11] The countries included in the basket of currencies were: The United States of America, Great Britain, Belgium, Denmark, France, Germany, Italy, The Netherlands, Norway, Sweeden, Switzerland, Canada, Japan, Spain, Argentina, Chile, Mexico, Paraguay and Venezuela.

[12] Because of the fact that the frost effect appears through a price effect there would not be, *a priori*, the need of an additional variable, since the model already includes the terms of trade. However, the inclusion of the dummy variable was necessary to make the estimates more stable.

[13] A VAR system with a constant term restricted to the cointegration space and, alternatively, a VAR system including a constant term in the dynamic part were considered as probable models when Pantula's criterion was applied. The selection of probable models was based on the unit root tests that suggested a series generating process with no time trend term. The model with no deterministic

component and the one with a quadratic trend were not considered because they barely appear in practice (see Hansen and Juselius, 1995, and Harris, 1995).

[14] Because those values are recommended only when the dummies are of the centered and seasonal type, due to the fact that they do not interfere in the asymptotic distribution of the rank statistics (Hansen and Juselius, 1995).

[15] Complementary information were given personally by Prof. Bent Nielsen, which confirms the citation.

[16] Likelihood tests (not presented here) individually applied to each adjustment parameter failed to reject the weak exogeneity null hypothesis for the e-IPA, TT, RB and RW variables.

[17] The only current variable with a significant effect in the error correction model was foreign income in the first difference. Taking into account that Brazil has just a marginal participation in the world import value, it was assumed that foreign income was an exogenous variable in the short-run model.

[18] Professor Bent Nielsen from Oxford University suggested performing an analysis of the economic implications when small samples are used to estimate cointegrated vectors (personal communication). See also Mark (1990).

References

Almeida, C.O. (1993) *Política cambial e receita de exportação de café do Brasil – 1970 a 1989*. Dissertação (Mestrado),Fortaleza, Universidade Federal do Ceará.

Almonacid, R.D. (1979) "Sugestões para uma nova política de minidesvalorizações cambiais," *Revista Brasileira de Economia*, 33, 287-299.

Bacha, E.L. (1977) "Sobre a taxa de câmbio: um adendo ao artigo de Pastore-Barros-Kadota," *Pesquisa e Planejamento Econômico*, 7, 237-244.

Bontempo, H.C. (1989) "Política cambial e superávit comerciais," *Pesquisa e Planejamento Econômico*, 19, 45-64.

Boucher, J. (1991) "The U.S. current account: a long and short-run empirical perspective," *Southern Economic Journal*, 58, 93-111.

Braga, H., and J.A. Rossi. (1986) "Dinâmica da balança comercial no Brasil, 1970/1984," *Anais. Encontro Brasileiro de Econometria*, 8, v. 2,145-160.

Braga, H.C., and R.A. Markwald. (1983) "Funções de oferta e demanda das exportações de manufaturados no Brasil: estimação de um modelo simultâneo," *Pesquisa e Planejamento Econômico*, 13, 707-744.

Cardoso, E.A. (1979) "Taxas cambiais fixas e flexíveis e a oferta de alimentos: um comentário," *Pesquisa e Planejamento Econômico*, 9, 885-894.

Cardoso, E.A. (1981) "Implicações de uma desvalorização cambial no Brasil," *Estudos Econômicos*, 11, 143-154.

Carvalho, M.A. de. (1995) "Taxa de câmbio e receita das exportações agrícolas," *Anais do Congresso Brasileiro de Economia e Sociologia Rural*, 33, 236-251.

Castro, A.S. de and M.A.F.H. Cavalcante (1997) "Estimação de equações de exportação e importação para o Brasil - 1955/95,"*Textos para Discussão*, no. 469, IPEA.

Dickey, D.A., and W.A. Fuller. (1981) "Likelihood ratio statistics for autoregressive time series with a unit root." *Ecomometrica*, 49, 1057-1072.

Doellinger, C.Von., H.B.B. Faria, J.E.C. Pereira and M.H.T.T. Horta. (1971) "Exportações dinâmicas brasileiras," Rio de Janeiro, IPEA.

FAO: http://apps.fao.org/cgi-bin/nph-db.pl. Consulted in March of 1997.

Ferreira, A.H.B. (1993) "Teste de cointegração e um modelo de correção de erros para a balança comercial brasileira," *Estudos Econômicos*, 23, 35-65.

FGV. Revista Conjuntura Econômica. (1997) Rio de Janeiro, nº 4.

Gazeta Mercantil (1997) "A alvancagem da agricultura," (editorial, 13 January).

Gonzalo, J. (1994) "Five alternative methods of estimating long-run equilibrium relationships," *Journal of Econometrics*, 60, 203-233.

Guimarães, C.V., and I.C. Oliveira. (1990) "Plano de estabilização e comércio exterior agrícola," *Anais.Congresso Brasileiro de Economia e Sociologia Rural*, 28, 329-341.

Hamilton, J.D. (1994) *Time Series Analysis*. Princeton, Princeton University Press.

Hansen, H. and K. Juselius. (1995) *Cats in Rats – Cointegration Analysis of Time Series*. Evanston, Illinois, Estima.

Harris, R.I.D. (1995) *Using Cointegration Analysis in Econometric Modeling*. New Jersey, Prentice Hall/Harvester Wheatsheaf.

Haug, A. A. (1996) "Tests for cointegration a Monte Carlo comparison," *Journal of Econometrics*, 71, 89-115.

Homen de Melo, F.B., and M.H. Zockun. (1976) "Exportações agrícolas, balanço de pagamentos e abastecimento do mercado interno," *Estudos Econômicos*, 7, 9-50.

Johansen, S. (1988) "Statistical analysis of cointegration vectors," *Journal of Economic Dynamics and Control*, 12, 231-254.

Johansen, S. (1992) "Determination of cointegration rank in the presence of a linear trend," *Oxford Bulletin of Economics and Statistics*, 54, 383-97.

Johansen, S., and L. Juselius. (1991) "Estimation and hypothesis testing of cointegration vectors in gaussian vector autoregressive models," *Econometrica*, 59, 1551-1580.

Locatelli, R.L., and J.A.B. Silva. (1991) "Câmbio real e competitividade das exportações brasileiras," *Revista Brasileira de Economia*, 45, 543-564.

Martner, R. (1992) "Efeitos macroeconômicos de uma desvalorização cambial: análise de simulação para o Brasil," *Pesquisa e Planejamento Econômico*, 22, 35-72.

Mendonça de Barros, J.R. *et al.* (1975) "Sistemas fiscais e incentivos às exportações," *Revista Brasileira de Economia*, 29, 3-24.

Neves, R.B. (1984) "Composição das exportações brasileiras e estabilidade da receita de exportações," *Pesquisa e Planejamento Econômico*, 14, 659-688.

Nielssen, B. (1997) "On the Distribution of Tests for Cointegration Rank," *Discussion Paper*, 133, Nuffield College Oxford.

Nunes, J.M.M. (1994) "Balança comercial e taxa de câmbio real: uma análise de cointegração," *Revista de Economia Política*, 14, 53-62.

Osterwald-Lenum, M. (1992) "A note with quantiles of asymptotic distribution of the ML cointegration rank test statistics," *Oxford Bulletin of Economics and Statistics*, 54, 461-472.

Pastore, A.C., J.R.M. Barros and D. Kadota. (1976) "A teoria da paridade do poder de compra, minidesvalorizações e o equilíbrio da balança comercial Brasileira," *Pesquisa e Planejamento Econômico*, 6, 287-312.

Pastore, A.C., J.R.M. Barros and D. Kadota. (1978) "Sobre a taxa de câmbio: resultados adicionais e uma réplica à análise de Bacha," *Pesquisa e Planejamento Econômico*, 8, 457-474.

Pinheiro, A.C. C.P. Borges, S. Zagury and M. Mesquita. (1993) "Composição setorial dos incentivos ás exportações brasileiras," *Revista Brasileira de Economia*, 47, 473-501.

Reimers, H.E. (1992) "Comparisons of tests for multivariate cointegration," *Statistical Papers*, 33, 335-359.

Reimers, H.E. (1993) "Lags order determination in cointegrated VAR systems with application to small German macromodels." Paper presented at the Econometric Society European Meeting, Uppsala, Sweden.

Rose, A. (1991) "The role of exchange rates in a popular model of international trade – Does the 'Marshall-Lerner' condition hold?" *Journal of International Economics*, 30, 301-316.

Sayad, J. (1979a) "Taxas cambiais fixas e flexíveis e a oferta de alimentos," *Pesquisa e Planejamento Econômico*, 9, 351-378.

Sayad, J. (1979b) "Taxas cambiais fixas e flexíveis e a oferta de alimentos: Réplica," *Pesquisa e Planejamento Econômico*, 9, 895-898.

Schuh, G.E. (1977) "A política cambial e o desenvolvimento da agricultura no Brasil," *Anais.Renunião Anual da Sociedade Brasileira de Economia Rural*, 14, T. 3, 3-24.

Schuh, G.E. (1983) "Taxa de câmbio e agricultura dos Estados Unidos." In: P. F. C. Araujo and G.E. Schuh (eds.) *Desenvolvimento da agricultura – Estudos de casos*. São Paulo, Pioneira, pp. 89-109.

Senna, J.J. (1974) "Notas sobre a origem do sistema de minidesvalorizações," *Revista Brasileira de Economia*, 28, 29-35.

Silva, A.M.da. (1976) "Bases da política de minidesvalorizações," *Estudos Econômicos*, 6, 97-112.

Silva, J.A.B., and R.L. Locatelli. (1987) "Câmbio e custo das exportações no Brasil," *Anais Encontro nacional de Economia*, 15, v. 1, 369-388.

Suplicy, E.M. (1976) *Os efeitos das minidesvalorizações na economia brasileira.* FGV, Rio de Janeiro.

Tyler, W.G.O (1982) "Viés antiexportador em políticas comerciais e o desempenho das exportações: alguns aspectos da recente experiência brasileira," *Revista Brasileira de Economia*, 36, 183-196.

Veiga, A.A (1977) "Agricultura e o balanço de pagamentos, 1946-75," *Anais.Renunião Anual da Sociedade Brasileira de Economia Rural*, 14, T. 3, 57-70.

Viana, G.C. (1993) "Tasa de câmbio real efectiva y exportaciones brasileñas de productos manufacturados," *Caderno de Economia*, 14, 84p.

Williams, C.H., and R.A. Bewley. (1993) "Price arbitrage between Queensland cattle auctions," *Australian Journal of Agricultural Economics*, 37, 33-55.

Zini Jr., A.A. (1989) "A política cambial em discussão," *Revista de Economia Política*, 9, 47-61.

Zini Jr., A.A. (1993) *Taxa de câmbio e política cambial no Brasil*. São Paulo: EDUSP, Editora da Universidade de São Paulo.

15 The World Meat Market and the Brazilian Economy: an Econometric Input-Output Analysis

FLÁVIA MARIA DE MELLO BLISKA AND JOAQUIM J.M. GUILHOTO

Introduction

The importance of the Brazilian meat sector to the Brazilian economy and the interconnection between this sector and the world meat market provides the focus for this chapter. Brazilian meat production in 1999 was estimated to be 12.8 million tons, with three main productive chains: beef (6.7 million tons or 49.9% of the total volume produced), poultry (5.0 million or 37.5% of the total volume produced) and pork (1.7 million tons or 12.6% of the total volume produced). Other meat production comprises horse, buffalo, sheep, goat and rabbit (USDA; ANUALPEC, 1996 / 1999).

Brazil is the world second largest beef producer (13.6% of the world's total volume); third largest poultry producer (12.5% of the world's total volume); and it is still the seventh largest pork producer (2.0% of the world's total volume) (USDA; ANUALPEC, 1996 / 1999). Brazil is also the world's third largest beef exporter (9.2% of the world's total volume); second largest poultry exporter (12.7% of the world's total volume); and tenth largest pork exporter (1.3% of the world total volume). Brazil's share in the world beef and pork market might increase since some Brazilian producer areas are becoming free of Malta fever, an important sanitary beef export barrier. Moreover Brazil has the world largest herd of commercial cattle (151 million head), and it has continually improved its production technology.

331

Cattle-raising's share in the Brazilian Gross Domestic Product (GDP) is above 3% (Números..., 1994) and beef is sold in more than 1.8 million commercial establishments; altogether, the beef chain employs around 8 million people (DBO Rural, 1995). Through the poultry chain, about US$ 6 billion flows yearly and it consumes a significant part of the Brazilian animal food. Pigs are raised on at least 2.7 million rural properties and through this chain flow about US$ 920 million yearly in farm production alone; the pork chain employs about 2.5 million people in the South and South-East region of the country and consumes a significant part of Brazilian production of corn and soy oil byproducts (ANUALPEC, 1996 / 1999).

There are two primary variables that can affect Brazilian meat exports and, consequently, change the levels of importance for different production sectors in the Brazilian economy. First, the domestic economic policies of the different countries that are currently importing or might possible import Brazilian meat; these effects will be felt mainly through changes in exchange rates, subsidies and customs duties, any one of which could change the domestic meat consumption in these countries. Secondly, changes in consumer behavior, with reference mainly to quality of life, food convenience, environmental problems, meat sanitation and animal well being, have increased poultry and pork consumption, and reduced beef consumption, especially in the industrialized countries.

In this chapter, we intend to analyze how the changes in domestic and foreign macroeconomic variables can affect Brazilian meat exports, and consequently the Brazilian economy, in particular its beef and poultry sectors. In the next section, we describe the economic model and the econometric analysis used to analyze the effects of changes in macroeconomic variables on the Brazilian meat exports and the impact of change in those exports on the Brazilian economy. The impacts on the Brazilian economy generated by meat exports will occupy the next section; thereafter, the data will be presented, the results, the impacts and finally some conclusions.

Theoretical Model and Econometric Analysis

This study is conducted in two stages; initially a vector auto-regression (VAR) model is used to evaluate the impact of changes in domestic and foreign macroeconomic variables on Brazilian meat exports. The results obtained in the VAR model are applied in an input-output model to evaluate the changes in the levels of importance of the different production sectors, and especially in the slaughter and meat preparation industry.

The impacts of domestic and foreign macroeconomic variables on Brazilian meat exports.

In this chapter, we used an approach similar to the one adopted by Liu, *et al.* (1993) to analyze the impacts of domestic and foreign macroeconomic variables on U.S. meat exports. These authors used a VAR approach to examine the resulting impacts on the U.S. beef, pork, turkey and chicken exports, in the context of an open economy, and they adopted the "error correction" method to account for co-integration effects that are usual in economic time series (Engler and Granger, 1987).

Economic Model Following Liu, *et al.* (1993), the macro sector in the open economy is composed of the goods market, the foreign-exchange market, and the money market. The goods market includes the demand, supply, and equilibrium condition of goods and services. The demand for goods and services of the home country is specified as consisting of domestic absorption and current account. For given levels of government expenditure (*G*) and taxes (*T*), domestic absorption (*da*) is specified as a function of real output (*y*) and the interest rate (*r*), as they affect consumption and investment. The current account (*ca*) measures the country's net exports of goods and services and is specified as a function of the relative price level (*ep**/*p*) and real outputs (*y* and *y**) of the domestic and foreign countries, given the tax levels (*T* and *T**). The exchange rate (*e*) is measured in terms of R\$/foreign currency. Thus:

$$da=da(y,r/G,T) \tag{15.1}$$

$$ca =ca \ (ep*/ \ p, \ y, \ y* \ / \ T, \ T*) \tag{15.2}$$

The nominal price (*p*) is expressed as a function of real output (*y*) and the nominal money supply (*m*). Real output captures the impact on price of the real sector, while the money supply captures the impact of the monetary sector:

$$p = p \ (y, \ m) \tag{15.3}$$

at equilibrium, supply equals demand:

$$y = da + ca \tag{15.4}$$

Given the exogenous variables (*G, T* and *T**) and foreign endogenous variables (*p** and *y**), equations (15.1) through (15.4) can be used to solve for the domestic price and the quantities of the variables *p, da, ca,* and *y,* if the exchange rate (*e*) and interest rate (*r*) can be also determined. Following Liu *et al.* (1993), this leads us to specification of the foreign-exchange market and money market.

The first market specification is the equilibrium in the foreign-exchange market when deposits of home and foreign currencies offer the same expected rate of return. The expected rate of return on home deposits is the sum of the foreign rate (*r**) and expected rate of home currency depreciation (as the foreign investments have to be repatriated eventually). The equilibrium condition can be written as:

$$r = r^* + (e^e - e) / e \qquad (15.5)$$

where *e* is the expected exchange rate and is proxied by a trade-weighted futures rate. To account for the simultaneous determination of the spot and future rates, the expected exchange rate is treated as endogenous and specified as a function of the spot rate:

$$e^e = e^e(e) \qquad (15.6)$$

The second market specification is the equilibrium in the money market when the money supply set by the central bank equals the aggregate money demand:

$$m / p = l (r, y) \qquad (15.7)$$

where *m/p* is the real money supply and *l* is the real money demand expressed as a function of interest rate and real output. According to Blanchard and Watson (1996), money supply is specified as a function of real output and price, as the monetary authority is assumed to target the levels of the two variables by adjusting its supply of money. Thus:

$$m = m (y, p) \qquad (15.8)$$

Equations (15.1) through (15.8) describe the domestic macro economy. The foreign variables (except *T**) appearing in the above equations are also treated as endogenous.

Vector Autoregression (VAR) Model   The VAR approach was developed by Sims (1980); in the current context, it has been used prominently in analyses of the dynamic relationship between macroeconomic and agricultural variables within an open economy. VAR analysis permits identification of the causality among more than two variables, the impact of forecasts of each variable on the other variables, and the determination of the intensity and duration of these impacts.

Usually, the parameters of a vector auto-regressive stochastic process are estimated and a moving-average representation is used to study the dynamic interrelationships among the variables in a VAR. In essence, the impulse response functions are determined by the coefficients of the moving-average representation and the forecast error variance decomposition *k*-steps ahead provides the percentage attributed to the impacts in each process of the model (Enders, 1996).

In this chapter, the effects of the shocks in macroeconomic variables on the Brazilian meat exports are the elasticities used later in the input-output model to analyze the impacts of changes in Brazilian meat exports on the Brazilian economy. Therefore, all variables were transformed to natural logs before estimation so that, in the impulse analysis, the effect on each variable divided by the standard deviation of the impacted variable is a percentage variation in that variable resulting from a variation of 1% in the impacted variable.

The Choleski decomposition is used to determine the effects of the shocks in each variable on the whole system and we can also obtain the forecast error variance decomposition, this identifies the proportion of the movements in a sequence due to its "own" shocks versus shocks in another variable. The Choleski decomposition presents some restrictions because there is a different restriction to each variable ordering and the effects observed depend on the ordering of the variables in the analyzed vector. To reduce the effects of these restrictions, the ordering of the variables was based on the results of previous studies, such as those of Liu *et al.* (1993).

Co-integration   Co-integration refers to a linear combination of non-stationary variables; following Enders (1996), it is possible that nonlinear long-run relationships exist among a set of integrated variables. All variables must be integrated by the same order; but this does not imply that all integrated variables are co-integrated. With the variables integrated by the same order, it is necessary to verify whether there is a linear combination of these variables, that is, to verify whether the series are co-integrated.

Following Engler and Granger (1987), Liu *et al.* (1993) and Enders (1996), when the variables are co-integrated, conventional VAR models result in either biased or inefficient estimates, because while capable of capturing the short-term dynamics of a system, the conventional VAR model ignores the long-term equilibrium relationship among variables implied by the co-integration.   If the co-integration hypothesis can be confirmed, the short-run effects should be determined by an "error correction" model (Engler and Granger, 1987; Enders, 1996).   In the present analysis, we applied the Dickey and Fuller unit root test for each individual data series to verify their order of integration.

In the Brazilian Meat Export model, the meat export volumes and prices are endogenous variables.   Based on the macroeconomic model described previously, we also introduce the following variables: domestic consumption (as a proxy for domestic absorption), domestic and foreign output and money supplies, and the exchange rate.   The VAR model still includes the Industrialized Countries Industrial Production Index (as a foreign economic activity indicator) and world meat imports (as a proxy for the world income level).

In the unit root tests, we initially considered six lags in each model estimated for each series.   Then, we performed successive adjustments and we considered as the better model the first one that presented significant coefficient lags (the rule to determine the number of lags to be included in each model can be found in Enders, 1996).   In the VAR model, we used Likelihood Ratio tests to determine the appropriate number of lags in the systems.   Following Enders, (1996), we estimated a system with seasonal dummies and another one without dummies, and we also conducted the Likelihood Ratio test to verify the necessity for the inclusion of seasonal dummies.

The ordering of the variables in the systems is very important, since the innovations in the first series affect contemporaneously all other variables; innovations in the second variables have no contemporaneous effects on the first variable, but affect the others, and innovations in the last variable have no contemporaneous effects on the other variables. Moreover, there is no economic reason to justify the effects of innovations in the Brazilian meat exports on the macroeconomic variables. As a result, the Brazilian poultry and beef exports were always classified in the last positions in the system. Thus, they are contemporaneously affected by all the other variables, but they have no contemporaneous effects on the others.

Impact of Changes in the Brazilian Meat Exports on the Brazilian Economy

The results obtained in the VAR model were applied in an input-output model to analyze the changes in the levels of the importance of the different production sectors. We used the Brazilian input-output matrix of 1995 (IBGE, 1997). Some sectors of the production and input tables were disaggregated into different segments to permit the study of the cattle and poultry-raising sectors and the meat industry sector. Then we made a final balance to redistribute the internal values of these matrices into row and column totals (Bacharach, 1970).

Input-Output Model   Intersectorial flows in a specific economy are determined by technological and economic factors, and these flows can be described by a system of simultaneous equations represented by:

$$X = A X + Y \qquad (15.9)$$

where X is a vector (n x 1) of total production by sector; Y (n x 1) contains the final demand values; and A is a (n x n) matrix of technical coefficients (Leontief, 1951, in Guilhoto *et al.*, 1994; Guilhoto, 1995; Guilhoto and Picerno, (1995); Miller and Blair, 1985). In (15.9), the final demand vector is usually considered exogenous to the system yielding the following system of equations:

$$X = B Y \qquad (15.10)$$

and

$$B = (I - A)^{-1} \qquad (15.11)$$

where B (n x n) is the Leontief inverse matrix.
    Starting from equation (15.10), we can evaluate the impact of different changes in the final demand on the total production, import volumes and total salaries. Thus,

$$\Delta X = B \, \Delta Y \qquad (15.12)$$

$$\Delta M = m \, \Delta X \qquad (15.13)$$

$$\Delta S = s \, \Delta X \qquad (15.14)$$

where ΔY, ΔX, ΔM and ΔS are (n x 1) vectors that show respectively the final demand increase, and the impacts on total production volume, on the import values and on the salary totals; m and s are diagonal (n x n) matrices in which the diagonal elements are the import and salary coefficients. Changes in meat exports correspond to changes in the ΔY vector; these changes are those obtained in the VAR model from the impulse analysis.

The effects of changes in Brazilian meat exports on the meat production level, import values and salary totals are obtained from equations (15.12), (15.13) and (15.14).

Of course, VAR analysis can measure impacts in the long run, but input-output analysis should be considered as providing short-run impacts. Thus, we assumed first that the technical coefficients were fixed during the period analyzed, and then we made simulations changing some technical coefficients. Starting from equation (15.11), and following Rasmussen (1956) and Hirschman (1958), we can determine which sectors present above average linkage power in a specific economy. That is, we can calculate how much a specific sector demands from the other sectors (backward linkage indices) and how much those other sectors demand of it (forward linkage indices).

Pure Inter-Industrial Linkages Index (GHS Approach)   The pure inter-industrial linkages index is an alternative procedure to separate the impacts of a certain sector from the other economic sectors. This index can also be used to separate the impacts of an individual region from the rest of the economy, or still to separate the impacts of certain country from the economic block in which it is inserted (Guilhoto, *et al.*, 1996; 1997).

The basic idea is to isolate a certain sector *j* from the rest of the economy and to define the effect of the total linkages of the sector *j* in the economy; that is, the difference between the total production of the economy and the production in the economy if sector *j* does not buy inputs from the rest of the economy and it does not sell its production to the rest of the economy. This situation is equivalent to estimating the impact on the economy that would arise should this sector disappear.

We can isolate the sector of focus, *j*, from the rest of the economy by partitioning the system as follows (see Guilhoto, *et al.*, 1997):

$$A = \begin{pmatrix} A_{jj} & A_{jr} \\ A_{rj} & A_{rr} \end{pmatrix} \tag{15.15}$$

where A_{jj} and A_{rr} are the quadrate matrices of direct inputs within the first and second sectors and A_{jr} and A_{rj} are the rectangular matrices showing the direct inputs purchased by the second sector and vice versa.

From (15.15), we can generate the following expression:

$$B = (I - A)^{-1} = \begin{pmatrix} B_{jj} & B_{jr} \\ B_{rj} & B_{rr} \end{pmatrix} =$$

$$= \begin{pmatrix} \Delta_{jj} & 0 \\ 0 & \Delta_{rr} \end{pmatrix} \begin{pmatrix} \Delta_{j} & 0 \\ 0 & \Delta_{r} \end{pmatrix} \begin{pmatrix} I & A_{jr}\Delta_{r} \\ A_{rj}\Delta_{j} & I \end{pmatrix}$$

$$(15.16)$$

where:

$$\Delta_{j} = (I - A_{jj})^{-1} \tag{15.17}$$

$$\Delta_{r} = (I - A_{rr})^{-1} \tag{15.18}$$

$$\Delta_{jj} = (I - \Delta_{j}A_{jr}\Delta_{r}A_{rj})^{-1} \tag{15.19}$$

$$\Delta_{rr} = (I - \Delta_{r}A_{rj}\Delta_{j}A_{jr})^{-1} \tag{15.20}$$

Through the equation (15.16) we can reveal the process of production in an economy as well as derive a set of multipliers/linkages. In the matrix:

$$\begin{pmatrix} I & A_{jr}\Delta_{r} \\ A_{rj}\Delta_{j} & I \end{pmatrix} \tag{15.21}$$

the first row separates final demand by its origin, distinguishing final demand that comes from inside the region (I) from that originating from outside the region ($A_{jr}\Delta_{r}$). The same idea is applied in the second row.

From the Leontief formulation:

$$X = (I - A)^{-1}Y \tag{15.22}$$

and using equations (15.16) to (15.21), we can obtain the formulations of the pure indices, which can be used to rank the sectors in terms of their importance in the economy and to see how the production process operates in the economy:

$$PBL = \Delta_{r}A_{rj}\Delta_{j}Y_{j} \qquad \text{and} \qquad PFL = \Delta_{j}A_{jr}\Delta_{r}Y_{r} \tag{15.23}$$

The PBL will give us the pure impact on the rest of the economy of the value of the total production in sector j, ($\Delta_{j}Y_{j}$). This impact is free from the demand inputs that sector j makes from sector j, and the feedbacks from the rest of the economy to sector j and vice-versa. The PFL will give us the pure impact on sector j of the total production in the rest of the economy ($\Delta_{r}Y_{r}$). We can obtain the total pure index by summing PBL and PFL.

The Data

In the estimations, we used annual data for the macroeconomic variables and meat variables for the period 1961 through 1995. All variables were transformed to natural logs before estimations. The annual volumes (tons) and values (US$) of Brazilian beef, poultry and pork exports (industrial and non-industrial), and of World Meat Imports were taken from the Food Agricultural Organization (FAO). The annual data for the Brazilian Gross Domestic Product (GDP) – US$, the Brazilian consumption (US$) and the exchange rate were taken from *Conjuntura Econômica* (FGV, 1986 to 1997). Finally, the annual Industrialized Countries Industrial Production Index, and the USA GDP and USA M1 were taken from the International Monetary Fund (IMF, Yearbook, 1992 to 1997). The GDP variables were deflated by an appropriate country-specific GDP deflator and the other variables measured in US$ were deflated by the USA Wholesale Price Index.

Results

Unit root tests

We conducted the Dickey and Fuller unit root test for each individual series. The statistical distributions used in those tests are from Dickey and Fuller (1979; 1981). Two primary problems with relations to unit root tests are emphasized in the literature. First, the tests for roots that approach one frequently point to the existence of a unit root and are not powerful enough to distinguish between a "difference stationary" process (DS) with "drift" and a "trend stationary." Secondly, tests to determine the number of the lags of the models used in unit root tests can point to different values according to different criteria.

The results of the unit root tests on the annual data show that the variables that can be considered stationary are: World Meat Imports (tons and US$), Industrialized Countries Industrial Production Index, the USA Gross Domestic Product (GDP), the USA Industrial Production Index, Total Brazilian Meat Exports (tons), Brazilian Poultry Exports (tons and US$) and Brazilian Beef Exports (tons and US$). Further, the variables that can be considered stationary after one differencing are: Brazilian GDP, Total Brazilian Meat Exports (US$), Brazilian Consumption and Real Exchange Rate Index.

Hence, we verified that we have stationary variables and non stationary variables. When there are stationary and integrated variables there is no consensus about the correct specification of a VAR model. Hence, we decided not to use the differentiated VAR model (the "error correction" method). We used all the variables in their level form, but we included in each estimated model stationary variables and just one integrated variable, to avoid the long-term equilibrium relationship among variables. Likelihood ratio tests indicated that the inclusion of seasonal dummies was not necessary and that two lags have to be included in each VAR model. We also estimated models with a trend variable and without it; we analyzed their statistical adjustments and we concluded that the trend should not be included.

Impulse response analysis and variance decompositions

In this section we provide and discuss the innovation accounting for VAR models with the best statistical adjustments estimated, that is, the impulse response analysis and the forecast error variance decomposition. We obtained the impulse responses and variance decomposition in 15-steps in each model estimated; then, we determined the average increase of the shocks on the determined variable.

Figures 15.1 and 15.2 show the responses to those shocks in percentages that result from a variation of 1% in the impacted variable to the models with the best statistical adjustments. Tables A1 to A6 in the Appendix show the decomposition of the variance for the Brazilian beef and poultry exports impacted series.

The innovation accounting shows that shocks in the beef and poultry export variables themselves explain the greater part of the variance decomposition. Shocks in the exchange rate affect beef and poultry exports and these shocks are important to explain variance decompositions for meat exports, but the effects of those shocks are more significant on beef exports. The small susceptibility of the poultry exports reflects the better competitive position of the poultry sector. Impacts from the exchange rate and the initial effects of these impacts on the meat exports are always in the same direction.

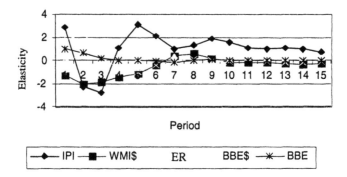

(a) variables industrial production index of the industrialized countries (IPI), world meat imports (WMI$), gross domestic product (BGDP), Brazilian beef price exports (BBE$) and Brazilian beef exports (BBE)

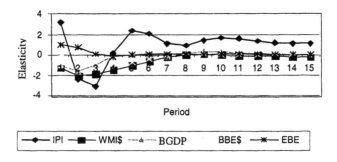

(b) variables (IPI), (WMI$), exchange rate (ER), (BBE$) and (BBE)

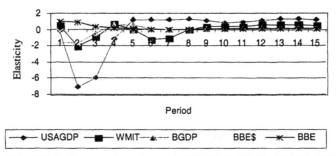

(c) variables USA foreign gross domestic product (USAGDP), (WMI), (BGDP), (BBE$) and (BBE)

Figure 15.1   Effects of shocks on Brazilian beef exports

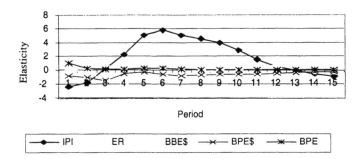

(a) variables industrial production index of the industrialized countries (IPI), exchange rates (ER), Brazilian beef price exports (BBE$), Brazilian poultry price exports (BPE$), and Brazilian poultry exports (BPE)

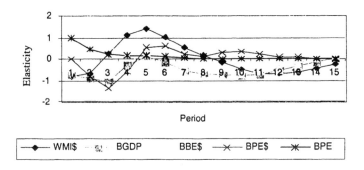

(b) variables world meat imports (WMI$), Brazilian gross domestic product (BGDP), Brazilian beef price exports (BBE$), (BPE$) and (BPE)

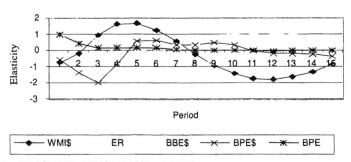

(c) variables (WMI$), (ER), (BBE$), (BPE$) and (BPE)

Figure 15.2   Effects of shocks on Brazilian poultry exports

World meat imports, as a proxy for the world income level, is very important in the variance decomposition for Brazilian meat exports, especially for beef exports, but on average the impact of a shock in the variable is more significant on poultry exports. The industrial production index (IPI) of the industrialized countries is also important in the variance decomposition for beef and poultry exports, but on average is more significant for poultry exports.

The initial impact of IPI on the beef exports is positive, while the initial impact on the poultry export is negative. In the IPI the ten main Brazilian beef importers are included (Germany, Canada, Spain, USA, France, Italy, Japan, Netherlands, United Kingdom and Switzerland), the indices of the main beef world producer (USA) and the three main beef world exporters (Australia, USA and Ireland). While the main world poultry producer and exporter (USA) are included in the IPI, it does not include the world's three main poultry producers and exporters (Brazil, China and Hong Kong). The IPI composition can explain the immediate impacts that are positive on beef exports and negative on poultry exports, but those results can also suggest that increases in the economic activity of an industrialized country can initially improve beef consumption.

Shocks in the beef export price affects poultry exports (an increase in the beef price causes a positive impact on the poultry exports), but shocks in the poultry exports price do not affect beef exports. The main Brazilian beef importers are also Brazilian poultry importers (Germany, Spain, Italy, Netherlands, United Kingdom and Switzerland). Hence, a positive change in the beef price, whose price level is higher than the poultry price, can improve poultry exports, although the high income level of many of the importing countries will tend to dampen the responses.

Table 15.1   Elasticities derived from the impulse responses

Initial average impact of a shock in the exchange rate on Brazilian beef exports	1.85
Maximum average impact of a shock on exchange rate on Brazilian beef exports	2.95
Initial average impact of a shock in domestic GDP on Brazilian beef exports	-1.31
Initial average impact of a shock in the industrial production index of industrialized countries on the Brazilian beef exports	3.33
Maximum average impact on the world meat imports on the Brazilian beef exports	1.30
Initial average impact of a shock on the exchange rate on the Brazilian poultry exports	0.33
Maximum average impact of a shock in the exchange rate on the Brazilian poultry exports	1.63
Maximum average impact of a shock on the world meat imports on the poultry exports	1.77
Initial av. impact of a shock on the Brazilian GDP on the Brazilian poultry exports	-1.21

Shocks in the Brazilian GDP are also important to beef and poultry exports and the participation of these shocks in the variance decomposition is almost constant over time, but shocks in the domestic GDP and the initial effect of these shocks on Brazilian meat exports have different impacts. Impacts of a shock in the foreign GDP tend to be delayed, but increase over time.

The effects of shocks in the domestic macroeconomic variables decline to zero over time, but effects of shocks in foreign macroeconomic variables tend to stabilize at a level different from zero. In general, foreign macroeconomic variables exert impacts on beef and poultry exports that are more significant than domestic macroeconomic variables in the first periods after the shocks, and the effects of shock in foreign variables are more persistent.

We determined the average impact in the first period after a shock in the determined variable and the maximum average impact in that variable for models with the best statistical adjustments (we obtained effects of shocks in a same variable in different models). These impacts are the elasticities used in the input-output analysis. The elasticities obtained in the impulse response analyses are shown in table 15.1.

Impact of changes in Brazilian meat exports on the Brazilian economy

Some of the highlights from the input-output analysis will be presented here. We emphasize that changes in the Brazilian meat exports represent different stimuli on final demand. We analyzed the Type 1 multipliers, the Rasmussen/Hirschman backward and forward linkage indices (table 15.2) and pure backward, forward and total linkage indices (table 15.3). The Type 1 multipliers indicate that changes in the final demands of the cattle slaughter industry and poultry slaughter industry can result in significant impacts on Brazilian economic production. Those sectors present, respectively, the highest multiplier and the third highest multiplier. The multipliers of the animal production sectors indicate that changes in their final demands, compared to the other sectors, do not generate significant impacts on the Brazilian economy.

Using the Rasmussen-Hirschman indices, we can consider that the beef, poultry and other animal-raising sectors, and the cattle, poultry and other animal slaughter and industrial sectors are key-sectors in the Brazilian economy (see table 15.2): the meat sectors present the highest backward linkages. The cattle and poultry slaughter and industrial sectors also present the highest and the third highest backward linkages and the small forward linkages index, indicating that those sectors demand products from the other several sectors, but they are not demanded by other sectors since most of their sales are to final demand. The poultry slaughter and industrial sector presents the smallest forward linkages index into Brazilian economy, therefore this sector should be more connected with the final demand.

Table 15.2   Type 1 Multipliers and Rasmussen/Hirschman backward and forward linkage indices

| Sectors | Multipliers | Order | Rasmussen/Hirschman linkage indices | | | |
| | | | Forward | | Backward | |
			Index	Rank	Index	Rank
1-Corn	1.6238	25	1.0060	11	0.8109	25
2-Cattle-raising	1.5625	29	0.9009	13	0.7803	30
3-Poultry-raising	2.0746	15	0.8188	14	1.0360	15
4-Other animals-raising	2.1585	12	0.6333	25	1.0779	12
5-Other farm products	1.5695	28	2.7366	2	0.7837	29
6-Mining	1.9552	19	1.1166	7	0.9764	19
7-Steel industry	2.3387	7	1.6713	5	1.1679	7
8-Machinery / vehicles	2.0361	16	1.0927	8	1.0167	16
9-Electric / electronic	1.9342	21	0.6608	22	0.9659	21
10-Wood / furnishings	2.0022	17	0.6536	23	0.9998	17
11-Paper / graphics	2.1552	13	0.9779	12	1.0763	13
12-Rubber industry	2.1526	14	0.8022	15	1.0749	14
13-Chemistry	1.9209	22	2.7639	1	0.9592	22
14-Pharmacy / veterinary	1.8384	23	0.5429	31	0.9181	23
15-Plastic goods	1.9584	18	0.7502	17	0.9780	18
16-Textile industry	2.2227	9	1.0318	10	1.1099	9
17-Shoes industry	2.2038	10	0.6123	27	1.1005	10
18-Coffee industry	2.3726	6	0.6762	20	1.1848	6
19-Vegetab. Prods. process	2.1967	11	0.6906	19	1.0970	11
20-Cattle slaughter	2.5524	1	0.6920	18	1.2746	1
21-Poultry slaughter	2.4566	3	0.5045	32	1.2268	3
22-Other animals slaughter	1.5165	31	0.5474	30	0.7573	31
23-Milk industry	2.4154	5	0.6372	24	1.2062	5
24-Sugar industry	2.4421	4	0.6731	21	1.2195	4
25-Vegetable oils industry	2.5043	2	0.7758	16	1.2505	2
26-Other food products	2.3070	8	1.0375	9	1.1520	8
27-Other industries	1.9432	20	0.6016	28	0.9704	20
28-Public Utilities	1.5990	27	1.1328	6	0.7985	27
29-Building	1.6257	24	0.5939	29	0.8118	24
30-Commerce / transport	1.6171	26	2.0746	3	0.8076	26
31-Communication	1.2533	32	0.6230	26	0.6258	32
32-Services	1.5718	30	1.9680	4	0.7849	28

The pure interindustrial indices (table 15.3) measure the monetary impacts (R$) of each Brazilian economic sector on the other economic sectors. As may be seen in table 15.3, changes in Brazilian beef and poultry exports generate impacts that are concentrated in other agricultural sectors as well as chemicals, services and food products. The results indicate that the disappearance of the animal raising sectors should not cause significant impacts on the Brazilian economy; in contrast, the disappearance of the cattle and poultry slaughter and industrial sectors would result in significant impacts. The pure indices confirm the results obtained in the Rasmussen/Hirschman analysis on the importance of the cattle and poultry slaughter and industrial sectors for the economy.

Table 15.3   Pure interindustrial linkage indices (R$-billions): Pure Forward Linkage - (PFL), Pure Backward Linkage (PBL) and Pure Total Linkage (PTL)

	Pure Indices					
Sectors	PFL		PBL		PTL	
	Index	Rank	Index	Rank	Index	Rank
1-Corn	3.564	22	0.058	32	3.620	30
2-Cattle-raising	5.173	16	1.720	25	6.890	22
3-Poultry-raising	2.633	23	1.474	27	4.110	29
4-Other animals-raising	1.976	25	1.646	26	3.620	31
5-Other farm products	34.655	4	9.846	9	44.500	5
6-Mining	19.730	6	2.882	22	22.610	9
7-Steel industry	34.785	3	6.128	13	40.910	7
8-Machinery / vehicles	15.752	8	27.376	4	43.130	6
9-Electric / electronic	5.317	15	15.462	6	20.780	10
10-Wood / furnishings	4.023	19	5.700	15	9.720	17
11-Paper / graphics	13.231	9	3.635	20	16.870	13
12-Rubber industry	5.463	14	0.589	31	6.050	24
13-Chemistry	49.544	2	5.595	16	55.140	3
14-Pharmacy / veterinary	0.980	28	7.337	11	8.320	18
15-Plastic goods	6.482	11	1.094	29	7.580	19
16-Textile industry / clothing	4.968	17	8.154	10	13.120	14
17-Shoes industry	0.383	31	4.230	18	4.610	27
18-Coffee industry	0.603	30	3.651	19	4.250	28
19-Vegetab. prod. Process.	4.245	18	14.702	7	18.950	11
20-Cattle slaughter	1.947	26	9.984	8	11.930	15
21-Poultry slaughter	0.296	32	5.522	17	5.820	25
22-Other animals slaughter	0.657	29	0.852	30	1.510	32
23-Milk industry	1.082	27	6.056	14	7.140	20
24-Sugar industry	1.985	24	3.156	21	5.140	26
25-Vegetable oils	3.764	20	7.232	12	11.000	16
26-Other food products	7.058	10	19.564	5	26.620	8
27-Other industries	3.586	21	2.526	23	6.110	23
28-Public Utilities	15.856	7	2.322	24	18.180	12
29-Building	5.521	13	48.012	2	53.530	4
30-Commerce / transport	44.232	1	35.540	3	79.770	2
31-Communication	5.832	12	1.195	28	7.030	21
32-Services	34.082	5	78.002	1	112.080	1

Table 15.4   Changes in the production level of the Brazilian economic sectors resulting from shocks in the Brazilian meat exports (R$)

Sectors	Changes in the production level (R$-million)							
	DX1	DX2	DX3	DX4	DX5	DX6	DX7	DX8
1-Corn grain	3.44	-2.43	6.19	-2.42	8.93	9.70	-6.63	5.25
2-Cattle-raising	44.27	-31.35	79.68	-31.20	0.13	0.14	-0.10	44.30
3-Poultry-raising	0.06	-0.05	0.12	-0.05	48.91	53.11	-36.31	9.97
4-Other animals-raising	12.50	-8.85	22.50	-8.81	0.20	0.22	-0.15	12.54
5-Other farm products	7.44	-5.27	13.40	-5.25	8.72	9.47	-6.47	9.21
6-Mining	1.22	-0.86	2.19	-0.86	1.78	1.93	-1.32	1.58
7-Steel industry	2.10	-1.49	3.78	-1.48	2.91	3.16	-2.16	2.69
8-Machinery / vehicles	1.47	-1.04	2.65	-1.04	1.97	2.13	-1.46	1.87
9-Electric / electronic	0.16	-0.11	0.29	-0.11	0.28	0.30	-0.21	0.22
10-Wood / furnishings	0.16	-0.11	0.28	-0.11	0.29	0.31	-0.22	0.22
11-Paper / graphics	0.68	-0.48	1.22	-0.48	1.32	1.43	-0.98	0.95
12-Rubber industry	0.25	-0.18	0.46	-0.18	0.34	0.37	-0.25	0.32
13-Chemistry	6.94	-4.91	12.49	-4.89	10.00	10.86	-7.43	8.97
14-Pharmacy / veterinary	0.95	-0.67	1.70	-0.67	0.37	0.40	-0.27	1.02
15-Plastic goods	0.38	-0.27	0.69	-0.27	4.16	4.51	-3.09	1.22
16-Textile / clothing	0.37	-0.27	0.67	-0.26	0.85	0.92	-0.63	0.55
17-Shoes industry	0.18	-0.13	0.33	-0.13	0.07	0.07	-0.05	0.20
18-Coffee industry	0.01	-0.01	0.03	-0.01	0.03	0.03	-0.02	0.02
19-Vegetab. prods process.	0.78	-0.55	1.41	-0.55	3.04	3.31	-2.26	1.40
20-Cattle slaughter	87.82	-62.19	158.07	-61.90	0.23	0.25	-0.17	87.87
21-Poultry slaughter	0.02	-0.02	0.04	-0.02	93.97	102.04	-69.76	19.05
22-Other animal slaughter	2.47	-1.75	4.44	-1.74	0.06	0.06	-0.04	2.48
23-Milk industry	0.11	-0.08	0.19	-0.08	0.15	0.16	-0.11	0.14
24-Sugar industry	0.25	-0.18	0.46	-0.18	0.64	0.69	-0.47	0.38
25-Vegetable oils industry	0.61	-0.43	1.10	-0.43	1.36	1.47	-1.01	0.89
26-Other food products	5.33	-3.77	9.59	-3.76	15.53	16.87	-11.53	8.47
27-Other industries	0.14	-0.10	0.24	-0.10	0.45	0.49	-0.34	0.23
28-Public Utilities	2.00	-1.42	3.60	-1.41	2.64	2.87	-1.96	2.53
29-Building	0.31	-0.22	0.56	-0.22	0.40	0.44	-0.30	0.39
30-Commerce / transport	10.19	-7.22	18.35	-7.18	12.39	13.46	-9.20	12.70
31-Communication	0.54	-0.38	0.98	-0.38	0.73	0.79	-0.54	0.69
32-Services	5.73	-4.06	10.31	-4.04	7.40	8.03	-5.49	7.22
Total impact	198.89	-140.84	358.01	-140.20	230.22	249.99	-170.90	245.51

*: DX1 results from changes minimum of 18.5% in the Brazilian beef exports caused by a shock of 10% in the exchange rate; DX2 = results from changes of 13.1% in the Brazilian beef exports caused by a shock of 10.0% in the Brazilian GDP; DX3 = results from changes of 33.3% in the Brazilian beef exports caused by a shock of 10.0% in the foreign industrial production; DX4 = results from changes of 13.0% in the Brazilian beef exports caused by a shock of 10.0% in the world income level.; DX5 = results from changes of 16.3% in the Brazilian poultry exports caused by a shock of 10% in the exchange rate; DX6 = results from changes of 17.7% in the Brazilian poultry exports caused by a shock of 10% in the world income level.; DX7 = results from changes of de 12.1% in the Brazilian poultry exports caused by a shock of 10.0% in the Brazilian GDP; DX8 = results from changes of 18.5% in the Brazilian beef exports and 3.3% in the Brazilian poultry exports caused by a shock of 10.0% in the exchange rate.

Table 15.5   Changes in the import levels of the Brazilian economic sectors resulting from shocks in the Brazilian meat exports (R$)

Sectors	Changes in the total imports (R$ - thousand)							
	DX1	DX2	DX3	DX4	DX5	DX6	DX7	DX8
1-Corn grain	19.00	-13.50	34.20	-13.40	49.40	53.60	-36.60	29.00
2-Cattle-raising	20.30	-14.40	36.60	-14.30	0.10	0.10	0.00	20.30
3-Poultry-raising	0.00	-0.00	0.10	0.00	34.50	37.50	-25.60	7.00
4-Other animals-raising	14.60	-10.30	26.20	-10.30	0.20	0.30	-0.20	14.60
5-Other farm products	106.30	-75.30	191.30	-74.90	124.50	135.20	-92.40	131.50
6-Mining	22.20	-15.70	39.90	-15.60	32.50	35.20	-24.10	28.70
7-Steel industry	114.20	-80.90	205.50	-80.50	158.20	171.70	-117.40	146.20
8-Machinery / vehicles	101.40	-71.80	182.60	-71.50	135.70	147.30	-100.70	128.90
9-Electric / electronic	21.30	-15.10	38.30	-15.00	37.20	40.40	-27.60	28.80
10-Wood / furnishings	2.20	-1.60	4.00	-1.60	4.00	4.40	-3.00	3.00
11-Paper / graphics	40.10	-28.40	72.20	-28.30	77.70	84.40	-57.70	55.90
12-Rubber industry	20.10	-14.20	36.20	-14.20	26.60	28.90	-19.70	25.50
13-Chemistry	758.60	-537.20	1365.50	-534.70	1093.40	1187.30	-811.70	980.00
14-Pharmacy / veterinary	95.80	-67.80	172.50	-67.50	37.10	40.30	-27.60	103.30
15-Plastic goods	21.30	-15.10	38.30	-15.00	231.80	251.80	-172.10	68.20
16-Textile industry	26.70	-18.90	48.00	-18.80	60.70	65.90	-45.00	38.90
17-Shoes industry	9.40	-6.60	16.80	-6.60	3.40	3.70	-2.50	10.00
18-Coffee industry	0.00	-0.00	0.00	0.00	0.00	0.00	0.00	0.00
19-Veget. Prod. Process.	32.50	-23.00	58.40	-22.90	126.20	137.00	-93.70	58.00
20-Cattle slaughter	492.20	-348.50	885.90	-346.90	1.30	1.40	-1.00	492.40
21-Poultry slaughter	0.10	-0.10	0.30	-0.10	576.80	626.30	-428.10	116.90
22-Other animal slaughter	13.00	-9.20	23.40	-9.20	0.30	0.30	-0.20	13.10
23-Milk industry	1.70	-1.20	3.10	-1.20	2.40	2.60	-1.80	2.20
24-Sugar industry	4.10	-2.90	7.40	-2.90	10.30	11.20	-7.70	6.20
25-Vegetable oils industry	43.80	-31.00	78.90	-30.90	97.20	105.60	-72.20	63.50
26-Other food products	492.80	-349.00	887.10	-347.40	1436.60	1560.00	-1066.50	783.70
27-Other industries	1.20	-0.80	2.10	-0.80	3.90	4.20	-2.90	1.90
28-Public Utilities	318.00	-225.20	572.50	-224.20	419.60	455.70	-311.50	403.00
29-Building	12.50	-8.80	22.40	-8.80	16.10	17.40	-11.90	15.70
30-Commerce / transport	469.30	-332.30	844.70	-330.80	570.60	619.60	-423.60	584.80
31-Communication	0.90	-0.60	1.50	-0.60	1.10	1.20	-0.80	1.10
32-Services	2150.70	-1522.90	3871.30	-1516.00	2777.00	3015.50	-2061.50	2712.90
Total impact	5426.30	-3842.30	9767.20	-3824.90	8146.40	8846.00	-6047.30	7075.20

Notes: See table 15.4

Tables 15.4 to 15.6 show, respectively, the impacts on the total production, imports and salary levels of the Brazilian economy. The main impact of changes in the beef and poultry exports on the total production level of the economy is concentrated in the animal production and slaughter sectors, followed by corn grain, commerce and transport, other farm products, chemicals, services and other food products. The main impacts on the total import and salary levels would also affect the public utilities, plastic goods and the steel industry. Changes in factors such as the exchange rate, Brazilian GDP, world income level, industrial production indices of the industrialized countries and in their own meat exports that initially affect the Brazilian beef and poultry exports, also affect these dependent sectors more prominently than other sectors of the economy.

Table 15.6   Changes in the salary levels resulting from shocks in Brazilian meat exports

Sectors	Changes in the total salary (R$ - thousand)							
	DX1	DX2	DX3	DX4	DX5	DX6	DX7	DX8
1-Corn grain	580.90	-411.30	1046.00	-409.50	1.509.00	1.638.60	-1.120.20	886.40
2-Cattle-raising	7098.40	-5026.40	12777.0	-5003.40	20.80	22.60	-15.50	7102.6
3-Poultry-raising	7.10	-5.00	13.00	-5.00	5.429.80	5.896.10	-4.030.80	1106.4
4-Other animals-raising	1267.30	-897.40	2281.00	-893.30	20.60	22.40	-15.30	1271.5
5-Other farm products	427.60	-302.80	770.00	-301.40	500.80	543.80	-371.70	529.00
6-Mining	114.30	-80.90	206.00	-80.60	167.50	181.90	-124.30	148.20
7-Steel industry	168.30	-119.20	303.00	-118.60	233.10	253.10	-173.00	215.50
8-Machinery / vehicles	167.20	-118.40	301.00	-117.80	223.60	242.80	-166.00	212.50
9-Electric / electronic	12.80	-9.10	23.00	-9.10	22.50	24.40	-16.70	17.40
10-Wood / furnishings	22.30	-15.80	40.00	-15.70	40.90	44.40	-30.30	30.60
11-Paper / graphics	82.30	-58.30	148.00	-58.00	159.40	173.10	-118.40	114.60
12-Rubber industry	16.80	-11.90	30.00	-11.80	22.20	24.10	-16.50	21.30
13-Chemistry	323.30	-228.90	582.00	-227.90	466.00	506.00	-345.90	417.70
14-Pharmacy / veterinary	106.50	-75.40	192.00	-75.10	41.30	44.80	-30.60	114.80
15-Plastic goods	43.50	-30.80	78.00	-30.70	474.30	515.10	-352.10	139.50
16-Textile industry/clothing	34.50	-24.40	62.00	-24.30	78.50	85.30	-58.30	50.40
17-Shoes industry	27.20	-19.30	49.00	-19.20	9.90	10.70	-7.30	29.20
18-Coffee industry	0.60	-0.40	1.00	-0.40	1.10	1.20	-0.90	0.90
19-Veget. prod. Process.	44.10	-31.20	79.00	-31.10	171.40	186.10	-127.20	78.80
20-Cattle slaughter	4569.10	-3235.40	8224.00	-3220.60	12.00	13.00	-8.90	4571.5
21-Poultry slaughter	1.40	-1.00	2.00	-1.00	5.339.60	5.798.10	-3.963.80	1082.4
22-Other animal slaughter	121.10	-85.80	218.00	-85.40	2.80	3.10	-2.10	121.70
23-Milk industry	4.10	-2.90	7.00	-2.90	5.60	6.10	-4.20	5.30
24-Sugar industry	19.90	-14.10	36.00	-14.00	50.10	54.40	-37.20	30.10
25-Vegetable oils industry	12.20	-8.70	22.00	-8.60	27.10	29.50	-20.10	17.70
26-Other food products	459.60	-325.50	827.00	-324.00	1.339.80	1.454.90	-994.60	730.90
27-Other industries	18.70	-13.30	34.00	-13.20	62.70	68.10	-46.50	31.40
28-Public Utilities	441.50	-312.60	795.00	-311.20	582.50	632.50	-432.40	559.40
29-Building	20.10	-14.30	36.00	-14.20	25.90	28.20	-19.30	25.40
30-Commerce / transport	2031.50	-1438.50	3657.00	-1431.90	2.470.20	2.682.30	-1.833.70	2531.6
31-Communication	121.00	-85.70	218.00	-85.30	162.20	176.10	-120.40	153.80
32-Services	1728.00	-1223.60	3110.00	-1218.00	2.231.20	2.422.90	-1.656.30	2179.8
Total impact	20093.2	-14228.3	36167.0	-14163.2	21.904.4	23.785.7	-16.260.5	24528.3

Notes: See table 15.4

Conclusions

This chapter has analyzed how changes in domestic and foreign macroeconomic variables can affect Brazilian meat exports and consequently the Brazilian economy. The main results indicate that changes in macroeconomic variables can cause significant impacts on Brazilian meat exports, that, in turn, affect a large number of other agriculture sectors together with a select number of other sectors such as services, chemicals and food production that are strongly linked with agriculture in general.

The main aspect to emphasize is that foreign macroeconomic variables exert more significant and persistent effects on the Brazilian meat exports than domestic macroeconomic variables. The industrialized countries industrial production index (as proxy for the foreign economic activity level) is the foreign variable that affects the Brazilian beef and poultry exports more significantly. While the foreign industrial production index and the exchange rate affect beef exports more significantly, world meat imports (as a proxy for the foreign income level) exerts more impact on poultry exports. Changes in those variables cause impacts on all the Brazilian meat exports in the same direction as the initial change. On the other hand, the impacts caused by changes in gross domestic product on the Brazilian meat exports present the contrary direction of the initial change and suggest that an increase in domestic economic activity improves the domestic meat consumption and reduces meat exports.

Thereafter, the impacts of the macroeconomic variables on the meat exports affect mainly the following sectors: corn farming, cattle, poultry and other animal-raising sectors, other farm products, chemistry, pharmacy and veterinary, plastic goods, beef, poultry and other meat process industries, other food products, commerce and transport, public utilities and services. Additionally, the strong backward linkages exhibited by the meat sectors suggest that they are clearly key sectors in the Brazilian economy.

References

ANUALPEC (1996/99). Anuário da Pecuária Paulista. São Paulo: FNP Consultoria and Comércio.

Bacharach, M. (1970) *Biproportional Matrices and Input-output Change.* Cambridge, University Press.

Blanchard, O. and M.W. Watson. (1996) "Are business cycles all alike?" In R. Gordon, (ed.) *The American Business Cycle-Continuity and Change*, Chicago, University of Chicago pp. 123-179.

Bliska, F. M. M. and J. J. M. Guilhoto. (1996) "Abate de animais e preparação de carnes no Brasil: importância e comportamento do setor - 1970/75/80," *Coletânea ITAL*, 26, 55-70.

Conjuntura Econômica (1986-1997). Conjuntura Estatística. Rio de Janeiro: FGV - Fundação Getúlio Vargas.

DBO Rural. (1995) "Sistema bovino lidera faturamento na economia rural."

Dickey, D. A. and W.A. Fuller. (1979) "Distribution of the estimator for auto-regressive time series with a unit root," *Journal of the American Statistical Association*, 74, 427-31.

Dickey, D. A. and W.A. Fuller. (1981) "Likelihood ratio statistics for autorregressive time series with a unit root," *Econometrica*, 49, 1057-1072.

Enders, W. (1996) *RATS Handbook For Econometric Time Series*. Ames, Iowa, Iowa State University.

Engle, R. F. and C.W.J. Granger. (1987) "Co-integration and error correction: representation, estimation, and testing," *Econometrica*, 55, 251-276.

FAO (nd) FAOSTAT – Statistics data base: agricultural trade data.

Guilhoto, J.J.M. (1992) "Mudanças estruturais e setores chaves na economia brasileira, 1960-1990," *Anais Encontro Brasileiro de Econometria*, 14, v.1, 293-310.

Guilhoto, J. J. M. (1995) *Um modelo computável de equilíbrio geral para planejamento e análise de políticos agrícolas (PAPA) na economia brasileira.* Tese (Livre Docência) - Escola Superior de Agricultura "Luiz de Queiroz," Piracicaba, Universidade de São Paulo.

Guilhoto, J. J. M., P.H.Z. Conceição and F.C. Crocomo. (1996) "Estruturas de produção, consumo e distribuição de renda na economia brasileira: 1975 e 1980 comparados," *Economia and Empresa*, 3, 33-64.

Guilhoto, J. J. M., G.J.D. Hewings, M. Sonis, and J. Guo. (1997) "Economic structural change over time: Brazil and United States compared," *Economia Aplicada*, 1, 35-57.

Guilhoto, J. J. M., M. Sonis, and G.J.D. Hewings. (1996) "Linkages and multipliers in a multiregional framework: integration of alternative approaches," *Discussion Paper 95-T-7*, Regional Economics Applications Laboratory, University of Illinois, Urbana.

Guilhoto, J. J. M. G.J.D. Hewings, and M. Sonis. (1997) "Interdependence, linkages and multipliers in Asia: an international input-output analysis," *Discussion Paper 97-T-2*. Regional Economics Applications Laboratory, University of Illinois, Urbana.

Guilhoto, J.J.M., M. Sonis, G.J.D. Hewings, and E.B. Martins. (1994) "Índices de ligações e setores-chave na economia brasileira: 1959/90," *Pesquisa e Planejamento Econômico*, 24, 287-314.

Guilhoto, J.J.M. and A.E. Picerno. (1995) "Estrutura produtiva, setores-chave e multilplicadores setoriais: Brasil e Uruguai comparados," *Revista Brasileira de Economia*, 49, 35-61.

Hewings, G. J. D., M.A.R. Fonseca, J.J.M. Guilhoto, and M. Sonis. (1989) "Key sectors and structural change in the Brazilian economy: a comparison of alternative approaches and their policy implications," *Journal of Policy Modeling* 11, 67-90.

Hirschman, A.O. (1958) *The Strategy of Economic Development.* New Haven, Yale University Press.

IBGE (1995) *Produção da Pecuária Municipal – Brasil.* Rio de Janeiro, IBGE.

IBGE (1997) *Matriz de insumo produto - Brasil - 1995.* Rio de Janeiro, IBGE.

IFM (1992-1997) *International Financial Statistics Yearbook.* Washington, D.C., International Monetary Fund.

Liu, J. D., P.J. Chung and W.H. Meyers. (1993) "The impact of domestic and foreign macroeconomic variables on U.S. meat exports," *Agricultural and Resource Economics Review,* 22, 210-224.

Miller, R. E. and P.D. Blair. (1985) *Input-output analysis: foundations and extensions.* Englewood Cliffs, NJ, Prentice-Hall.

NÚMEROS e metas para a pecuária bovina de corte. *Revista Nacional da Carne,* 19, 213, p.113, nov. 1994.

Picerno Pongibove, A. E. (1996) *Políticas macroeconômicas, agricultura e comércio de produtos agrícolas: o caso do Brasil e Uruguai.* Tese (Doutorado) Escola Superior de Agricultura "Luiz de Queiroz," Piracicaba, Universidade de São Paulo.

Rasmussen, P. (1956) *Studies in Inter-sectoral Relations.* Amsterdam, North Holland.

Sims, C. (1972) "Money, income and causality," *American Economic Review,* 62, 540-552.

Sims, C. (1980) "Macroeconomics and reality," *Econometrica,* 48, 1-48.

Appendix

Table A1   Decomposition of variance for Brazilian beef exports I

	Decomposition of the variance for Brazilian beef exports (%)				
Step	IPI	WMI$	BGDP	BBE$	BBET
1	9.34	11.45	11.87	0.31	67.03
2	6.94	18.81	19.66	5.05	49.54
3	9.09	24.86	19.86	5.53	40.67
4	8.44	28.03	18.53	6.71	38.29
5	9.43	28.33	17.04	9.97	35.22
6	10.30	28.28	16.59	10.66	34.17
7	10.57	28.20	16.54	10.59	34.10
8	10.78	28.07	16.55	10.62	33.98
9	11.22	27.81	16.76	10.53	33.67
10	11.86	27.51	16.85	10.42	33.36
11	12.42	27.31	16.79	10.34	33.14
12	12.82	27.18	16.71	10.29	32.99
13	13.14	27.10	16.65	10.25	32.87
14	13.41	27.07	16.58	10.20	32.74
15	13.65	27.06	16.50	10.16	32.62
Average	10.89	25.81	16.90	8.78	37.63

Table A2   Decomposition of variance for Brazilian beef exports II

	Decomposition of the variance for Brazilian beef exports (%)				
Step	IPI	WMI$	BER	BBE$	BBET
1	7.84	12.15	21.73	0.21	58.07
2	6.37	20.38	29.33	2.43	41.50
3	8.41	27.25	26.55	2.57	35.23
4	8.03	30.64	24.17	5.31	31.84
5	10.21	30.38	21.41	9.82	28.18
6	11.14	29.57	21.50	10.48	27.32
7	11.28	29.61	21.47	10.35	27.28
8	11.65	29.90	21.30	10.24	26.91
9	12.52	29.54	21.14	10.11	26.69
10	13.14	29.35	20.98	10.04	26.49
11	13.41	29.26	20.97	9.99	26.37
12	13.62	29.20	20.92	9.99	26.26
13	13.86	29.18	20.83	10.04	26.10
14	14.03	29.19	20.78	10.08	25.93
15	14.12	29.19	20.78	10.09	25.81
Average	11.31	27.65	22.26	8.12	30.66

Table A3   **Decomposition of variance for Brazilian beef exports III**

		Decomposition of the variance for Brazilian beef exports (%)			
Step	USAGDP	WMIT	BGDP	BBE$	BBET
1	0.01	0.21	15.54	0.55	83.68
2	7.80	2.39	16.98	1.47	71.37
3	11.90	2.56	15.80	1.33	68.40
4	11.69	2.70	16.17	2.87	66.58
5	11.65	2.65	16.63	3.40	65.67
6	11.71	3.34	16.48	3.53	64.94
7	11.73	3.75	16.28	3.91	64.32
8	11.90	3.74	16.25	3.96	64.16
9	11.99	3.79	16.18	3.94	64.10
10	12.00	3.83	16.11	3.94	64.13
11	12.03	3.89	16.10	3.96	64.02
12	12.13	4.00	16.13	3.97	63.77
13	12.26	4.12	16.16	3.97	63.49
14	12.39	4.22	16.16	3.99	63.24
15	12.51	4.31	16.15	4.01	63.02
Average	10.91	3.30	16.21	3.25	66.33

Table A4 Decomposition of variance for Brazilian poultry exports I

		Decomposition of the variance for Brazilian poultry exports (%)			
Step	IPI	BER	BBE$	BPE$	BPET
1	30.64	0.78	0.43	9.57	58.58
2	29.68	2.75	11.95	15.20	40.42
3	14.98	22.04	23.99	18.45	20.54
4	14.63	39.65	20.28	12.24	13.20
5	28.71	37.49	16.00	8.41	9.39
6	39.30	32.61	14.11	6.69	7.29
7	45.05	29.72	12.56	6.41	6.26
8	49.39	27.17	11.41	6.33	5.70
9	52.12	25.48	10.89	6.19	5.33
10	52.84	25.20	10.64	6.20	5.12
11	52.16	25.80	10.73	6.33	4.98
12	50.79	26.84	11.19	6.34	4.84
13	49.38	28.05	11.62	6.25	4.71
14	48.43	29.03	11.76	6.17	4.61
15	47.98	29.57	11.80	6.11	4.54
Average	40.41	25.48	12.62	8.46	13.03

Table A5 Decomposition of variance for Brazilian poultry exports II

	Decomposition of the variance for Brazilian poultry exports (%)				
Step	WMI$	BGDP	BBE$	BPE$	BPET
1	9.57	30.46	10.86	0.00	49.11
2	7.63	37.49	22.26	3.37	29.24
3	5.15	41.48	25.86	8.24	19.28
4	9.51	39.06	24.98	8.53	17.92
5	15.24	34.96	25.15	8.37	16.28
6	16.54	30.74	30.25	8.18	14.29
7	14.93	29.29	36.47	7.08	12.22
8	12.61	28.84	42.33	5.97	10.26
9	10.76	28.75	46.57	5.21	8.72
10	9.84	29.37	48.41	4.71	7.67
11	9.75	30.12	48.73	4.36	7.04
12	10.06	30.49	48.55	4.17	6.73
13	10.42	30.60	48.27	4.11	6.61
14	10.67	30.59	48.08	4.09	6.58
15	10.74	30.53	48.09	4.08	6.57
Average	10.89	32.18	36.99	5.36	14.57

Table A6 Decomposition of variance for Brazilian poultry exports III

	Decomposition of the variance for Brazilian poultry exports (%)				
Step	WMI$	BER	BBE$	BPE$	BPET
1	8.83	21.17	5.07	2.73	62.21
2	5.25	20.88	20.68	11.73	41.47
3	7.99	17.79	25.80	21.48	26.95
4	18.06	15.08	24.96	19.61	22.28
5	26.25	15.44	21.32	17.48	19.51
6	29.82	14.52	20.05	17.14	18.47
7	29.69	14.43	21.42	16.67	17.80
8	27.26	14.75	26.30	15.44	16.25
9	25.57	15.98	30.97	13.60	13.89
10	25.86	18.77	32.22	11.52	11.63
11	27.29	21.45	31.57	9.80	9.89
12	29.07	22.91	30.62	8.67	8.73
13	30.65	23.68	29.61	8.02	8.04
14	31.70	24.20	28.67	7.74	7.69
15	32.17	24.42	28.15	7.71	7.55
Average	23.70	19.03	25.16	12.62	19.49

16 The Insertion of the Brazilian Economy in MERCOSUR: an Approach by Value Added

MARCO ANTONIO MONTOYA

Introduction

The MERCOSUR process, as well as the other schemes for integration of the American Continent, is currently directed towards a different philosophy than the one that boosted various integration projects in the past. From an integrationist concept of autarkic characteristics, based on a strong protection against third-party countries and with a slow and difficult elimination of reciprocal tariffs, a scheme of accelerated integration has been chosen that aims at the eventual implementation of a common market.

Given these dynamics, one might suspect that MERCOSUR economic integration is a process that will favor the economic development of Brazil, and, concomitantly, create potential regional imbalances and strong inequalities in the production and consumer structures across member countries. The reason is that, based on the population of 1990, one suspects that, initially, the opportunities related to demand seem substantially larger to the other economies than to Brazil since the amplification of market potential was of the order of 5 times for Argentina; 14 times for Chile, 63 times for Uruguay while only 33% for Brazil.

Prior analysis by Montoya (1998), exploring sectoral interdependence among the MERCOSUR member countries using a variety of measures (Rasmusen (1956) and Hirschman (1958) indices, the field of influence developed by Sonis and Hewings, 1989, 1994 and the pure index from Guilhoto *et al.* 1995), found strong interindustrial linkage patterns in Brazil but relatively weaker patterns in Argentina, Chile and Uruguay. This finding provides evidence that Brazilian industrial diversification is more advanced centered in raw-material production and manufacturing and, therefore, with a greater opportunity to promote growth in the region.

357

Hence, there would appear to be a development potential that would enhance the markets (mainly in Brazil) for producers in Argentina, Chile and Uruguay while Brazilian producers stand to benefit from supplying greater volumes of intermediate inputs. Which of these two dimensions will dominate remains to be seen. In this chapter, an initial exploration will be conducted using input-output analysis. The theory of input-output meets the analytical need, and its simplified picture, presenting systemic properties, such as dependence and independence, hierarchy and circulation among sectors, constitutes the empirical fundamental base to identify the most important links for the economical development of the member countries. Thus, using the international input-output matrix of MERCOSUR for 1990 (Montoya, 1998) with a focus on value added, the objective of this chapter is to evaluate in a comparative way the insertion of the Brazilian economy in MERCOSUR, establishing, through the identification of the degree of industrial development existing among the partner countries, the perspectives for business opportunities in the region.

In the next section, the input-output structure will be presented. The following section examines in a comparative way the value added induced by the final demand of each country, facilitating development potential to be assessed through enhanced commercial interdependence in the region. The chapter concludes with some summary evaluations.

Structure of the Input-Output Model of MERCOSUR

The analysis adopted in this research uses an international input-output model developed for MERCOSUR by Montoya (1998), and is based on the interregional model of Isard (1951). In view of the spatial integration of the economies in the model, the production coefficients do not only depend on the utilized technology and on the structure of relative prices, but also on inputs from sectors in other countries. Consequently, in order for the structures of national and intercountry provision to be part of an integrated economic system, the exchange rates, the prices and production costs of the countries are assumed to remain constant during the period of analysis.

In this context, the international input-output model of MERCOSUR for the year 1990 represents a world economic system that specifies four countries (Argentina, Brazil, Chile and Uruguay), the other countries being specified as *rest of the world*.[1] The summary structure of the international input-output flows is shown in table 16.1.

The demand sectors located in the columns are internationally divided into sectors of intermediate demands (A), final demand sectors (F), rest of the world sector or sector of exports to the rest of the world (E) and one sector for changes in the transit inventory (W). The intermediate and final demand sectors are subdivided into Argentina (α), Brazil (β), Chile (γ), and Uruguay (λ). In turn, the supply sectors include insurance, international freight (S), rest of the world imports (M), import taxes (T) and one sector of value added (V). Each one is divided into the four countries under study.

Table 16.1   Simplified picture of the international input-output model of MERCOSUR

Countries and Sector		Intermediate demand (A)				Final demand (F)				Export Rest of the world (E)	Inventory transit (W)	Total Products (X)
		Argentina (α)	Brazil (β)	Chile 0(γ)	Uruguay (λ)	Argentina (α)	Brazil (β)	Chile (γ)	Uruguay (λ)			
Production	Argentina (α)	$A^{\alpha\alpha}$	$A^{\alpha\beta}$	$A^{\alpha\gamma}$	$A^{\alpha\lambda}$	$F^{\alpha\alpha}$	$F^{\alpha\beta}$	$F^{\alpha\gamma}$	$F^{\alpha\lambda}$	E^{α}	W^{α}	X^{α}
	Brazil (β)	$A^{\beta\alpha}$	$A^{\beta\beta}$	$A^{\beta\gamma}$	$A^{\beta\lambda}$	$F^{\beta\alpha}$	$F^{\beta\beta}$	$F^{\beta\gamma}$	$F^{\beta\lambda}$	E^{β}	W^{β}	X^{β}
	Chile (γ)	$A^{\gamma\alpha}$	$A^{\gamma\beta}$	$A^{\gamma\gamma}$	$A^{\gamma\lambda}$	$F^{\gamma\alpha}$	$F^{\gamma\beta}$	$F^{\gamma\gamma}$	$F^{\gamma\lambda}$	E^{γ}	W^{γ}	X^{γ}
	Uruguay (λ)	$A^{\lambda\alpha}$	$A^{\lambda\beta}$	$A^{\lambda\gamma}$	$A^{\lambda\lambda}$	$F^{\lambda\alpha}$	$F^{\lambda\beta}$	$F^{\lambda\gamma}$	$F^{\lambda\lambda}$	E^{λ}	W^{λ}	X^{λ}
Insurance of international freights (S)		$S^{A\alpha}$	$S^{A\beta}$	$S^{A\gamma}$	$S^{A\lambda}$	$S^{F\alpha}$	$S^{F\beta}$	$S^{F\gamma}$	$S^{F\lambda}$	0	0	0
Imports from the rest of the world (M)		$M^{A\alpha}$	$M^{A\beta}$	$M^{A\gamma}$	$M^{A\lambda}$	$M^{F\alpha}$	$M^{F\beta}$	$M^{F\gamma}$	$M^{F\lambda}$	0	0	0
Import tax (T)		$T^{A\alpha}$	$T^{A\beta}$	$T^{A\gamma}$	$T^{A\lambda}$	$T^{F\alpha}$	$T^{F\beta}$	$T^{F\gamma}$	$T^{F\lambda}$	0	0	0
Value added (V)		$V^{A\alpha}$	$V^{A\beta}$	$V^{A\gamma}$	$V^{A\lambda}$	0	0	0	0	0	0	0
Total inputs (X)		X^{α}	X^{β}	X^{γ}	X^{λ}	0	0	0	0	0	0	0

Notice that the summary table does not show the number of industrial sectors of each country. Each country contains 31 comparable sectors, yielding a matrix of total intermediate demand of dimension 124 x 124 sectors. For instance, the input structure of the industrial sector of Argentina, in the transaction bloc $A^{\alpha\beta}$, shows how much the Brazilian industries buy from the Argentine industries, which can be represented as $\sum_i \sum_j A_{ij}^{\alpha\beta}$ ($i, j = 1, 2, 3, \dots, 31$). Here, i stands for the Argentine industries and *j*, the Brazilian industries. Similarly, the amount of products that the Argentine industry (*j*) purchases from Chilean industry (*i*) is represented as $A_{ij}^{\gamma\alpha}$. Thus, the input structure for the Argentine industry (*j*) can be expressed through the following accounting relationship:

$$X_j^\alpha = \sum_i A_{ij}^{\alpha\alpha} + \sum_i A_{ij}^{\beta\alpha} + ... + \sum_i A_{ij}^{\lambda\alpha} + S_j^{A\alpha} + \sum_i M_{ij}^{A\alpha} + T_j^{A\alpha} + \sum_n V_{hj}^{A\alpha} \qquad (16.1)$$

where:

$S_j^{A\alpha}$ is the freight and international insurance;

$M_{ij}^{A\alpha}$ are the imports by the jth Argentine industry from the ith sector of the rest of the world.

$T_j^{A\alpha}$ is the import tax paid by the jth Argentine industry;

$V_j^{A\alpha}$ is the hth component of value added generated by the jth Argentine industry.

The input structures of the industries of the other countries can also be expressed in a similar way.

Similarly, the demand structure for the products of the Argentine industry (*i*) can be expressed through the following accounting relationship:

$$X_i^\alpha = \sum_j A_{ij}^{\alpha\alpha} + \sum_j A_{ij}^{\alpha\beta} + ... + \sum_j A_{ij}^{\alpha\lambda} + \sum_K F_{iK}^{\alpha\alpha} + \sum_K F_{iK}^{\alpha\beta} + ... + \sum_K F_{iK}^{\alpha\lambda} + E_i^\alpha + W_i^\alpha \qquad (16.2)$$

where:

$F_{iK}^{\alpha\beta}$ is the final demand for the ith sector of Argentine products through the Kth sector (family consumption, government consumption, capital formation and stock variation) of the Brazilian final demand;

E_i^α are the exports of the Argentine i^{th} sector to the rest of the world;

W_i^α represents the transit inventory of the ith Argentine sector.

Generalizing the input structure for the jth industry of the qth country ($q = \alpha, \beta, \gamma, \lambda$), equation (16.1) can be expressed in the following way:

$$X_j^q = \sum_r \sum_i A_{ij}^{rq} + S_j^{Aq} + \sum_i M_{ij}^{Aq} + T_j^{Aq} + \sum_h V_{hj}^{Aq} \qquad q \neq r; \qquad (16.3)$$

where $r = \alpha, \beta, \gamma, \lambda$ represents r^{th} country under study.

Simultaneously, generalizing the demand structure of the ith sector, equation (16.2) can be expressed in this way:

$$X_i^r = \sum_q \sum_i A_{ij}^{rq} + \sum_q \sum_K F_{iK}^{rq} + E_i^r + W_i^r \tag{16.4}$$

As long as the total value of the utilized inputs is equal to the value of the total production ($X_j^q = X_i^r$), table 16.1 of the international input-output model will be consistent.

The technique used by the author to estimate the technical coefficients for each country utilizes the import matrices, as well as the structures of the export vectors by origin and destination. The usual input-output technical coefficients can be defined, with appropriate spatial designation for the source of inputs, with a typical element:

$$a_{ij}^{\alpha\beta} = \frac{A_{ij}^{\alpha\beta}}{X_j^{\beta}} \tag{16.5}$$

that reveals, for example, the use of input i, produced in Argentina (α), by sector j in Brazil (β). Together, these coefficients form matrix A:

$$A = \begin{bmatrix} a_{ij}^{\alpha\alpha} & a_{ij}^{\alpha\beta} & a_{ij}^{\alpha\gamma} & a_{ij}^{\alpha\lambda} \\ a_{ij}^{\beta\alpha} & a_{ij}^{\beta\beta} & a_{ij}^{\beta\gamma} & a_{ij}^{\beta\lambda} \\ a_{ij}^{\gamma\alpha} & a_{ij}^{\gamma\beta} & a_{ij}^{\gamma\gamma} & a_{ij}^{\gamma\lambda} \\ a_{ij}^{\lambda\alpha} & a_{ij}^{\lambda\beta} & a_{ij}^{\lambda\gamma} & a_{ij}^{\lambda\lambda} \end{bmatrix} \qquad i,j = 1,...,31 \tag{16.6}$$

This matrix shows, simultaneously, the technological structure within each country as well as the interdependence among countries. Thus, using matrix A and the MERCOSUR simplified picture (table 16.1), in an analogous way to the Leontief basic model, one can represent the various trade flows as a system of simultaneous equations:

$$\sum \sum a_{ij}^{rq} X_j^q + F_i^r = X_i^r \quad \begin{cases} i,j = 1,2,...,31 \\ r,q = \alpha,\beta,...\lambda \end{cases} \tag{16.7}$$

In this model, the final demand vector is usually considered as exogenous to the system, so that the total production vector is determined exclusively by the final demand vector. One can then express equation (16.7) in terms of final demand components:

$$X_i^r = \left(I - \sum \sum a_{ij}^{rq}\right)^{-1} \cdot F_j^q \quad \begin{cases} i,j = 1,2,...,31 \\ r,q = \alpha,\beta,...\lambda \end{cases} \tag{16.8}$$

or

$$X_i^r = \sum_q \sum_j b_{ij}^{rq} \cdot F_j^q \qquad (16.9)$$

where b_{ij}^{rq} is an element of the Leontief inverse matrix $\left(I - \sum\sum a_{ij}^{rq}\right)^{-1}$ and indicates the direct and indirect requirements from sector i in country q by final demand unit j in country r. The flow information is in 1990 U.S. million dollars, and the concept of model construction assumes that each sector produces an homogeneous adopting the standard assumptions of the Leontief industry x industry system.

Value Added, Industrial Development and Structural Trends in MERCOSUR

In the evaluation to be conducted, attention will be focused on value added to avoid double-counting problems. In each stage of production of a commodity, only the value that each sector adds to the commodity is considered, so that, if this process is followed up to the end for all sectors, the amount of value added will be equal to the GDP value of the country. (see Dornbusch and Fischer, 1991; Mochon and Troster ,1994; Viceconti and Neves, 1996; and Rossetti, 1997).

The volume of value added will indicate the impact from changes originating within the country or elsewhere, reflecting to some extent the degree of economic development. Following Souza (1998), as the economic development increases, the industrial product/total product relation should increase. Thus, the input-output framework provides the basis for comparison of structures, the degree of industrial development, and the nature and level of the spatial insertion of different economies into the creation of valued added. By using valued added, it will be possible to reveal the impact of Brazil's entry into MERCOSUR in terms of the impact on the Brazilian economy as well as the other members of the economic union.

Effects of the final demand on the value added

In order to answer this question, one must first establish in a comparative way the amount of the value added induced by the final demand of each country. Using equation (16.1), the impacts derived from domestic and inter-country trade can be estimated from the following equation:

$$V_i^* = \hat{V}_j \left(I - \sum\sum a_{ij}^{rq} \right)^{-1} \cdot F_j^q \qquad (16.10)$$

where:

V_i^* is the vector of the induced value added;

$\hat{V}_j$ is the diagonalized matrix of the proportions of the value added for the total of inputs ($\hat{V}_j = V_j / X_j$);

$\sum\sum a_{ij}^{rq}$ is the matrix of MERCOSUR technical coefficients

F_j^q is the vector of the final demand of each country.

Thus, the induced value added can be obtained by the multiplication of the proportion of value added ($\hat{V}$) by the induced production $\left(I - \sum\sum a_{ij}^{rq} \right)^{-1} \cdot F_j^q$.

Table 16.2   Total value added induced by the final demand of each country and of the rest of the world

(current million dollars in 1990)

	Argentina	Brazil	Chile	Uruguay	Rest of World	Total
Argentina	103680	868	237	152	6571	111508
Brazil	1436	397515	570	272	30400	430193
Chile	109	201	13226	11	4319	17866
Uruguay	116	273	16	3863	824	5092
Total	105340	398857	14049	4298	42114	564658
Final demand	109615	426187	18027	4980	46433	605242

Table 16.3   Dependence of value added induced by the final demand of each country and the rest of the world in percentages

	Argentina	Brazil	Chile	Uruguay	Rest of world	Total
Argentina	92.98	0.78	0.21	0.14	5.89	100.00
Brazil	0.33	92.40	0.13	0.06	7.07	100.00
Chile	0.61	1.12	74.03	0.06	24.17	100.00
Uruguay	2.27	5.36	0.31	75.87	16.19	100.00

Table 16.2 summarizes the amounts of value added induced by the final demands of each country and by exports to the rest of the world: the columns show how much value added the final demands of a given country generated in each partner country. In relation to Brazil, induced value added in 1990 comprises for Argentina, Chile and Uruguay respectively 25.92%, 4.15% and 1.18%. In concert with the patterns of strong

interindustrial links and industrial diversification which the Brazilian economy presents (Montoya and Guilhoto 1998), this signifies Brazil as the country that holds the greatest industrial development potential in the region on the basis of its capacity to generate value added.

Defining the dependence levels of value added ($Dv^{rs} = V^{*rs} / V^{*r}$) of the rth country on the final demands of the sth country, where r denotes the recipient country and s is the generating country; V^{*rs} is the total induced value added in r by the final demand of s, and V^{*r} is the total induced value added in r, it is possible to explore the nature of dependence (table 16.3 and figure 16.1). In this context, the contribution of the countries in inducing value added reveals high dependence on *domestic* final demands in Argentina (92.98%) and Brazil (92.40%), and relatively lower demands in Chile (74.03%) and Uruguay (75.87%).

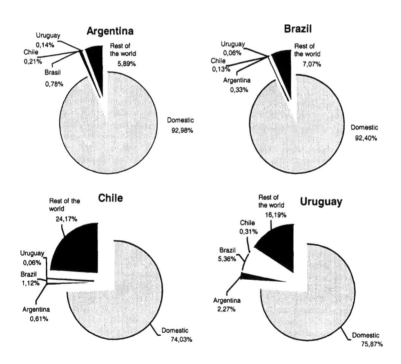

Figure 16.1   Participation of value added induced by final demands and exports to the rest of the world on the total induced value added of each country

This low intercountry input interdependence in the region can be explained by ascribed to the impacts of policies such as those directed to import substitution and the promotion domestic production, (CEPAL, 1951). Secondly, as a partial result of this process, there has been a lack of international competitiveness exhibited by domestic industry. Thirdly, the exports among the countries of the region were often regionally oriented in view of their limited receptivity in the international market (see Tussie, 1981 and Sandroni, 1994). Finally, there is relatively little need for many imported intermediate inputs because of the low industrialization levels of Uruguay and Chile and, to a lesser extent, Argentina. One might also venture that many exports from these countries (including Brazil) are natural resources and processed farm products that often overlap, thereby providing limited regional trade possibilities.

In figure 16.2, the total per capita domestic production and the domestic dependence of the value added are shown (participation of the induced domestic value added of a certain country in the total added value that the country generated with its final demand derived from table 16.2). Following Furukawa (1989), this analysis may allow characterization of the level of industrial development and the expected trend of interregional commerce. This trend may arise because changes in the structure of domestic dependence on the value added of a country imply changes in their production processes in either national and or international intersectoral relations and, finally, in their total per capita production. Certainly, depending on the level of economic development, the relationship between domestic dependence and per capita product, which can be directly or inversely proportional, will indicate the trends of the region's trade.

In this context, three additional traits are noticed: first, among the smaller, less industrialized countries (Chile and Uruguay), the total per capita domestic production of each country and the domestic dependence of value added are inversely related; at the other end of the economic spectrum (Argentina and Brazil), the opposite is true, *i.e.*, the total per capita domestic production and the domestic dependence of the value added are positively correlated; thirdly, the levels of total per capita domestic production are higher in the second group of countries (Argentina and Brazil) than in the first group (Chile and Uruguay).

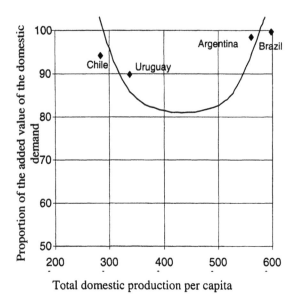

Figure 16.2   **Dependence standard and domestic production of the MERCOSUR countries**

The trend line shown in figure 16.2, suggest that economies such as Chile and Uruguay, due to the limited industrial intermediation that they present in the sectors of basic industrial materials, normally import capital goods and intermediate materials to stimulate the production of their industries that are ultimately directed to export. Certainly, as this process is intensified, one would expect a decrease in the domestic dependence of the value added since the imports of these types of goods will grow. However, if, simultaneously, the Chileans and Uruguayans are reaching, thanks to the imports of capital goods and intermediate materials, a certain level of industrial development that increases the total per capita production, (*e.g.* in Argentina) the economic structure becomes more connected and the demand for basic industry increases.   In these circumstances, programs of import substitution, as the one that was applied in Brazil, can increase the network of domestic suppliers; as a result, the economy becomes more oriented to service activities (the relative participation of the service sector in the value of national production will have a tendency to increase), the relative weight of the international market decreases (the domestic dependence of value added increases) and the domestic interindustrial links will strengthen.

If the patterns of figure 16.2 were used to anticipate the trends of the MERCOSUR economies, the external dependence of Chile and Uruguay in the next years, in relative terms, would probably increase much more than the external dependencies of Argentina and Brazil. So the perspectives of a larger trade complementarity in the region, are promising, unless the structure and the trade levels change drastically.

Coefficient of value added induced by final demand

Still based on table 16.2, one can establish the coefficient of value added induced by final demand ($CVI^{Fr} = V^{*rs} / F^{s}$), where r denotes the recipient country and s, the generating country; V^{*rs} is defined as before and F^{s} is the final demand of country s. The value added coefficients of table 16.4 allow analysis of how much value added is induced by an additional unit of final demand for each country. In this table, the columns show the amount of induced value added in each country by unit change in final demand in each country. For instance, an additional unit in the final demand of Uruguay will induce an increase of 0.78 units in its own economy, 0.03 in Argentina, 0.05 in Brazil and 0.002 in Chile, summing to 0.8631 units in the four countries, with the remainder supplied by the rest of the world.

Table 16.4   Value added coefficient induced by final demand for each country

	Argentina	Brazil	Chile	Uruguay	Rest of the	Total
Argentina	0.9459	0.0020	0.0131	0.0305	0.1415	0.1842
Brazil	0.0131	0.9327	0.0316	0.0546	0.6547	0.7108
Chile	0.0010	0.0005	0.7337	0.0022	0.0930	0.0295
Uruguay	0.0011	0.0006	0.0009	0.7757	0.0178	0.0084
Total	0.9610	0.9359	0.7793	0.8631	0.9070	0.9329
Final demand	1.0000	1.0000	1.0000	1.0000	1.0000	1.0000

If there were not any trade with the rest of the world, the value added for the four countries would be equal to their respective final demands, and thus sum to 1. This does not happen in the MERCOSUR matrix because the rest of the world countries are treated as *exogenous* in the model. Notice, from table 16.4, that the highest total coefficient is that of Argentina (0.96); of this proportion, the domestic coefficient is 0.95 and all the coefficients of the partner countries are equal to 0.015. As for the Brazilian total coefficient, it is the second highest (0.9359), of which the domestic coefficient is 0.9327 and the coefficients of the remaining countries sum to 0.003. In both cases the proportions of induced value added generated by the partner countries are small, especially in Brazil where it is five times smaller than in Argentina.

On the other hand, Chile has a total coefficient of only 0.7793, with a domestic coefficient of 0.7337 and the sum of the remaining MERCOSUR coefficients equals to 0.046 some three to four times larger than the impacts noted for Argentina and Brazil, respectively. In the case of Uruguay, the total coefficient presents an intermediate level between Argentina and Chile, but its capacity to induce value added in the region is relatively superior if compared to all the partner countries.

In this context, a common trait of Argentina, Chile and Uruguay is that the coefficients of induced value added in relation to Brazil are the highest. This fact, associated with the levels of industrialization reached by Brazil, shows the relative importance of the Brazilian economy as a supplier of finished products, of basic industrial materials and of capital goods to the MERCOSUR countries. It becomes clear that as the development process is fostered in the region, associated with greater industrial interdependence, the level of value added in Brazil will increase.

Sectoral structure of the induced value added

Attention will now be directed to sectoral impacts, using equation (16.8). The industries were separated into eight aggregated sectors, the results of the calculations being presented in tables 16.5 to 16.8.

Argentina As table 16.5 shows, from the total value added of Argentina (US$ 111.5 billion), 92.98%, or US$ 103.7 billion, is induced by domestic final demand. Within this, the induced value added in industries, such as services, is large, comprising 29% of the total value added. Next, in order of relative importance, come manufacturing (23.6%), commerce (20.6%) and farming and cattle raising (9.6%).

In this context, one notices that the exports to the rest of the world in relation to the region have contributed significantly to the creation of value added. This occurs because the exports of farm and livestock products and manufactured goods to the rest of the world provide US$ 3.2 billion (2.8%) and US$ 2.0 billion (1.84%) of the total induced value added (US$ 111.5 billion), which is equivalent to, respectively, 48.2% and 31.2% of the value added generated by the total of exports to the rest of the world (US$ 6.6 billion). In the region, Argentina's links to the MERCOSUR economies are very weak, Brazil being the partner that induces more value added in its economy. Notice, however, that the *structure* of interregional contributions is similar to the one of the rest of the world.

Table 16.5   Contribution of final demands and off exports to the rest of the world in the induced sectoral value added of Argentina
(current million dollars in 1990)

	Sectors	Argentina	Brazil	Chile	Uruguay	Rest of the world	Total
1	Farming and livestock	6971	479	48	19	3165	10682
2	Mineral extraction	6036	43	31	27	412	6549
3	Manufactures	23748	277	131	88	2048	26291
4	Public industrial service	3120	9	4	2	85	3220
5	Civil construction	5033	0	0	0	0	5033
6	Commerce	22968	0	0	0	0	22968
7	Transportaton	2986	17	5	3	503	3514
8	Services	32818	43	18	12	359	33250
	Total	103680	868	237	152	6571	111508

In general, the value added induced by foreign demands is important to the Argentine farm and livestock industries as well as to manufacturing. However, a still more detailed analysis, at the 31-sectors level based on table A1 (Appendix), focusing on industries with a larger amount of induced value added, shows that most value added is concentrated in terms of raw materials involving simple processing.

Brazil   According to table 16.6, more than 92% (US$ 397.5 billion) of the total value added in Brazil is induced by domestic final demands; consequently, the dependence on foreign demands is very low (8%). Basic industries, however, account for a little more that 10% of the total induced value added, which means that this proportion has relatively little weight in the Brazilian economy if compared to the Argentine dependence on exports that oscillates around 16%.

The highest values of the value added induced by foreign demands are concentrated basically in the manufacturing sector although the size of these proportions varies from country to country. Thus, from the total induced value added that Argentina generates in Brazil (US$ 1.4 billion), the manufacturing sector accounts for 65.74% (US$ 944 million). Comparable proportions are 70.35% (US$ 401 million) in Chile; 67.28% (US$ 183 million) in Uruguay, and only 48.75% (US$ 14.8 billion) in the rest of the world. These relatively high participations in the generation of value added in the Brazilian manufacturing sector are due, in part, to the fact that in Argentina, Chile and Uruguay, the imports of capital goods and of various materials for the working of their industries are a structural need of their economies, reflecting the modest levels of intermediation evident in these economies.

Table 16.6   Contribution of final demands and exports to the rest of the world in the induced sectoral value added in Brazil
(current million dollars in 1990)

	Sectors	Argentina	Brazil	Chile	Uruguay	Rest of the world	Total
1	Farming and livestock	104	30996	27	2b3	3109	34259
2	Mineral extraction	100	9551	28	12	2220	11910
3	Manufactures	944	90470	401	183	14819	106818
4	Public industrial	45	10946	18	8	837	11854
5	Civil construction	5	38516	2	1	123	38647
6	Commerce	79	43710	32	15	2293	46130
7	Transportation	47	14494	19	9	3313	17881
8	Services	112	158832	43	20	3686	162693
	Total	1436	397515	570	272	30400	430193

Table A1 (Appendix), that shows the most disaggregated manufacturing sectors, makes this point clear, since the industries with a relatively high degree of external dependence are oil refinery, machinery, transportation materials, vegetable processing, textile industry, pharmaceutical chemicals and perfumes.

Chile   As may be seen from table 16.7, approximately 74% (US$ 13.2 billion) of the total Chilean value added (US$ 17.8 billion) is induced by the domestic final demand, *i.e.*, the dependence on exports is high since it corresponds approximately to 26% (US$ 4.6 billion) of the total induced value added.

In the structure of induced value added that depends on domestic final demand, mineral extraction presents the smallest domestic dependence (20.81% or US$ 465 millions); on the other hand, for manufacturing, a little more than three-quarters (US$ 2.1 billion) of the value added depends on the domestic demand. Notice that the degree of domestic dependence of the mining sector associated with the contributions of the rest of the world in the same sector (37.86% or US$ 1.6 billion of the total value added induced by exports to the rest of the world, US$ 4.3 billion), amplifies the Chilean economy's dependence on mining activities.

Table 16.7   Contribution of final demands and exports to the rest of the world in the sectoral induced value added of Chile
(current million dollars in 1990)

	Sectors	Argentina	Brazil	Chile	Uruguay	Rest of the world	Total
1	Farming and livestock	14	20	1215	1	476	1726
2	Mineral extraction	33	99	465	3	1635	2234
3	Manufactures	36	30	2074	4	557	2702
4	Public industrial	4	9	387	0	155	555
5	Civil construction	1	2	1040	0	35	1079
6	Commerce	7	14	2248	1	499	2768
7	Transportation	6	10	732	1	432	1180
8	Services	8	17	5066	1	530	5622
	Total	109	201	13226	11	4319	17866

In turn, the set of Chilean exports to the partner countries is 1.80% (US$ 4.6 billion) of the total induced value added (US$ 17.9 billion), that means that its links in the region are weak, Brazil being the biggest partner of the region in the generation of value added. In this perspective, the mining, manufactures and farming and livestock sectors are the ones that stand out the most and, among them, (table A1, Appendix), the most relevant industries in the generation of value added are the food products, public industrial services, cellulose and printing paper, oil and gas, and plastics.

Uruguay   As can be seen in table 16.8, Uruguay, in similar fashion to Chile, presents a domestic dependence of 75.86% (US$ 3.8 billion). The participation of the farming and livestock sector, however, is 15.34% (US$ 781 million) of the total induced value added (US$ 5.1 billion), revealing a weight similar to the one of Argentina.

The Uruguayan manufacturing sector presents a participation of 28.16% (US$ 1.4 billion) in the total induced value added. The most remarkable trait in this sector is that the industries are typical processors of raw materials from farming and livestock origin (see table A1, Appendix). One still notices that 34.02% (US$ 164 million) of the sector's total exports (US$ 1.4 billion) have their destination in Brazil or Argentina.

Finally, the participation of the basic sector (farming and livestock, and mineral extraction) on the total value added of each country synthesizes the nature of the induced value added in MERCOSUR, since from it there emerge two different patterns of behavior. One group has a high participation (Chile, 22.2%; Uruguay, 17.3% and Argentina, 15.4%) while Brazil has a relatively small participation (10.7%). Therefore, it becomes evident, in the generation of value added, that the relative importance of the activities of basic production is more relevant in the first group of countries, even though the levels of industrialization of their economies are lower than for Brazil. Yet, one must stress that for the economies of Argentina, Chile and Uruguay, the largest partner in the generation of value added is Brazil.

Table 16.8 **Contribution of final demands and exports to the rest of the world in the induced sectoral value added of Uruguay**
(current million dollars in 1990)

	Sectors	Argentina	Brazil	Chile	Uruguay	Rest of the world	Total
1	Farming and livestock	18	91	4	462	205	781
2	Mineral extraction	2	2	0	89	5	98
3	Manufactures	56	108	7	953	311	1434
4	Public industrial	2	4	0	167	15	189
5	Civil construction	1	1	0	242	5	249
6	Commerce	19	39	2	385	102	546
7	Transportation	6	10	1	202	56	275
8	Services	12	18	1	1362	126	1519
	Total	116	273	16	3863	824	5092

Conclusions

The purpose of this chapter was to evaluate through value added how the Brazilian economy is inserted in the MERCOSUR. The impacts resulting from the interindustrial links of production in the generation of value added indicate, in the intercountry trade, that the final demands of the countries generate larger volumes of value added in Brazil, followed, at some distance, by Argentina. The confrontation of total domestic production per capita and the relative participation of the domestic induced value added suggest, in MERCOSUR, that the external dependence of Chile and Uruguay, in relative terms, will increase much more in the next years than the external dependence of Argentina and Brazil. The reason is because the Chilean and Uruguayan economies, due to the evolving structure of the sectors of basic industrial materials, normally import capital goods and intermediate materials to stimulate the production of their industries that are directed to export. This process will most likely intensify with the opening of the regional market, and thus their domestic dependence will decrease, since imports will rise. Therefore, the MERCOSUR countries may enjoy the benefits of greater trade complementary and the perspectives of a larger commercial interdependence in the region are promising, unless the structure and the trade level change drastically in favor to the rest of the world.

The coefficients of value added induced in Brazil by the demands of Argentina, Chile and Uruguay are the highest in the region. This finding, associated with the industrialization levels reached by Brazil, reveals the relative importance of the Brazilian economy as a supplier of finished products of basic industrial materials and capital goods to the MERCOSUR countries. Hence, as the development process advances in the region, accompanied by higher industrial interdependence, value added in Brazil will probably increase; in Argentina, on the other hand, this process will not be so prominent because the industrialization of its economy is not so consolidated. The detailed analyses of the sectoral structures of the value added induced by the final demand supports these interpretations, since in Argentina, Chile and Uruguay the relative participation of the value added of the basic sectors is high and, in Brazil, it is low. However, it also became evident that, for the economies of Argentina, Chile and Uruguay, the largest partner in the generation of value added is Brazil.

In synthesis, the data suggest that the markets in the region are potentially complementary, so MERCOSUR will effectively come to represent to Brazil and its partner countries a permanent option for amplification of production space and circulation of goods.

Note

[1] In the world system, the economies of Bolivia and Paraguay were not specified, because the information necessary was either not available or had not been assembled. However, as these two countries together represent only 1.72% of the total product of the MERCOSUR economy, the results were probably not affected (Montoya, 1998).

References

CEPAL. (1951) *Estudio Econômico de América Latina*. Santiago do Chile: Nações Unidas (E/CN 12/164 rev. 1).

Dornbusch, R., and S. Fischer. (1991) *Macroeconomia*. São Paulo, Makron, McGraw-Hill.

Furukawa, S. (1986) *International input-output analysis: compilation and case studies of interaction between ASEAN, Korea, Japan, and the United States, 1975.* Tokyo, Institute of Developing Economies.

Guilhoto, J.J.M., M. Sonis, and G.J.D. Hewings. (1995) "Linkages and multipliers in a multiregional framework: integration of alternative approaches," *Disccussion Paper*, 95-T-7, Regional Economics Applications Laboratory, University of Illinois, Urbana.

Hirschman, A. (1958) *The Strategy of Economic Development.* New Haven, Yale University Press.

Isard, W. (1951) "Interregional and regional input-output analysis: a model of a space-economy," *Review of Economics and Statistics*, 33, 319-328.

Mochon, F., and R. Troster. (1994) *Introdução à Economia.* São Paulo, Makron Books, 1994.

Montoya, M. A. (1998) *Matriz Insumo-produtoInternacional do Mercosul em 1990: A Desigualdade Regional e o Impacto Intersetorial do Comércio Inter-regional.* Tese de Doutorado, São Paulo, ESALQ-USP.

Montoya, M. A., and J.J.M. Guilhoto. (1998) "The interregional and intersectoral structure of MERCOSUR. an application, of input-output analysis," *Australasian Journal of Regional Studies*, 4, 93-112.

Rasmussen, P. N. (1956) *Studies in Inter-sectorial Relations.* Amsterdam, North-Holland.

Rosetti, J. (1997) *Introdução a Economia.* São Paulo, Atlas, (17th ed).

Sandroni, P. (1994) *Novo Dicionário deEeconomia.* São Paulo, Ed. Best Seller.

Sonis, M., and G.J.D. Hewings. (1989) "Error and sensitivity input-output analysis: a new approach." In, R.E. Miller, K.R. Polenske and A.Z., Rose (eds.) *Frontiers of Input-output Analysis.* New York, Oxford University Press.

Souza, N. (1998) "Evolução da estrutura econômica do Brazil e dos estados da região Sul entre 1985 e 1995." In, M.A. Montoya (ed.) *Relações Intersetoriais do Mercosul e da Economia Brasileira: uma Abordagem Insumo-produto.* Passo Fundo, Ediupf.

Tussie, D. (1981) "Nuevas rutas de la integración latino-americana, de la substituición de importaciones y la eficiencia mercantil," *Revista de Comércio Exterior* (Mexico), 1, 1397-1403.

Viceconti, P., and S. Neves. (1996) *Introdução à Economia.* São Paulo, Frase Editora, (2nd ed.).

Appendix

Table A1 Value of interregional imports induced by final demand of each MERCOSUR-member country
(value in million dollars)

	SECTORS	Argentina	Brazil	Chile	Uruguay	Rest of world
1	Farming and livestock	3	418	11	7	78
2	Mineral extraction	0	1	0	1	1
3	Oil and Gas	0	0	0	0	0
4	Non Metallic Mining	0	2	1	1	1
5	Basic Metallic industry	0	7	7	4	5
6	Mechanical equipment	0	20	8	3	9
7	Electric material	0	5	0	3	1
8	Electronic equipment	0	1	0	0	0
9	Transportation material	2	58	6	7	13
10	Timber and furniture	0	0	0	0	0
11	Paper products	1	6	3	4	3
12	Rubber Industry	0	2	2	1	2
13	Basic Chemicals	1	48	18	10	15
14	Oil Refining	1	11	29	21	24
15	Chemical, Iron and Perf.	1	20	9	14	8
16	Plastic Industry	0	6	5	2	3
17	Textile Industry	1	18	10	5	6
18	Clothes Manufacture	0	0	0	0	0
19	Leather Industry	1	33	2	6	21
20	Vegetable Processing	0	5	6	0	1
21	Animal Slaughtering	0	7	1	0	1
22	Dairy Industry	0	1	0	0	0
23	Sugar Refining Plant	0	1	11	1	3
24	Vegetable and animal oil	0	32	34	4	13
25	Other Food Factories	0	4	1	0	1
26	Manufacture Industry	0	0	0	0	0
27	Public Ind. Service	0	0	0	0	0
28	Civil Construction	0	0	0	0	0
29	Commerce	0	0	0	0	0
30	Transportation	0	4	1	1	2
31	Services	0	0	0	0	0
	Total Argentina	**13**	**709**	**167**	**96**	**211**
32	Farming and livestock	28	1	1	5	5
33	Mineral extraction	81	2	3	6	17
34	Oil and Gas	0	0	0	0	0
35	Non Metallic Mining	23	0	6	2	3
36	Basic Metallic industry	233	8	106	47	79
37	Mechanical equipment	58	1	12	5	10
38	Electric material	58	1	8	6	4
39	Electronic equipment	4	0	4	0	1
40	Transportation material	372	7	82	33	45
41	Timber and furniture	6	0	0	3	0
42	Paper products	80	2	19	12	13

Table A1 (continued)

	SECTORS	Argentina	Brazil	Chile	Uruguay	Rest of world
43	Rubber Industry	48	1	9	4	9
44	Basic Chemicals	57	2	8	4	10
45	Oil Refining	28	1	16	1	14
46	Chemical, Iron and Perf.	47	3	14	16	13
47	Plastic Industry	15	1	5	3	4
48	Textile Industry	60	2	31	9	13
49	Clothes Manufacture	2	0	0	0	0
50	Leather Industry	1	0	1	2	3
51	Vegetable Processing	16	0	8	0	2
52	Animal Slaughtering	0	0	0	0	0
53	Dairy Industry	0	0	0	0	0
54	Sugar Refining Plant	0	0	2	0	1
55	Vegetable and animal oil	10	0	7	2	3
56	Other Food Factories	2	0	1	0	0
57	Manufacture Industry	1	0	2	1	1
58	Public Ind. Service	0	0	0	0	0
59	Civil Construction	0	0	0	0	0
60	Commerce	0	0	0	0	0
61	Transportation	2	0	1	0	1
62	Services	0	0	0	0	0
	Total Brazil	**1232**	**34**	**349**	**161**	**253**
63	Farming and livestock	8	19	0	1	4
64	Mineral extraction	45	156	2	4	51
65	Oil and Gas	0	0	0	0	0
66	Non Metallic Mining	0	0	0	0	0
67	Basic Metallic industry	19	1	0	1	2
68	Mechanical equipment	2	1	0	0	0
69	Electric material	1	0	0	0	0
70	Electronic equipment	0	0	0	0	0
71	Transportation material	0	0	0	0	0
72	Timber and furniture	2	0	0	0	0
73	Paper products	26	21	0	4	5
74	Rubber Industry	0	0	0	0	0
75	Basic Chemicals	1	2	0	0	0
76	Oil Refining	0	0	0	0	0
77	Chemical, Iron and Perf.	1	3	0	0	0
78	Plastic Industry	0	0	0	0	0
79	Textile Industry	2	0	0	0	0
80	Clothes Manufacture	0	0	0	0	0
81	Leather Industry	0	0	0	0	0
82	Vegetable Processing	0	1	0	0	0
83	Animal Slaughtering	0	0	0	0	0
84	Dairy Industry	0	0	0	0	0
85	Sugar Refining Plant	0	0	0	0	0
86	Vegetable and animal oil	0	0	0	0	0
87	Other Food Factories	4	9	0	0	1
88	Manufacture Industry	0	0	0	0	0
89	Public Ind. Service	0	0	0	0	0

Table A1 (continued)

	SECTORS	Argentina	Brazil	Chile	Uruguay	Rest of world
90	Civil Construction	0	0	0	0	0
91	Commerce	0	5	0	0	1
92	Transportation	1	4	0	0	1
93	Services	0	2	0	0	0
	Total Chile	**114**	**226**	**2**	**11**	**68**
94	Farming and Livestock	3	68	1	0	13
95	Mineral Extraction	1	0	0	0	0
96	Oil and Gas	0	0	0	0	0
97	Non Metallic Mining	2	1	0	0	0
98	Basic Metallic Industry	3	2	0	0	1
99	Mechanic equipment	1	1	0	0	0
100	Electric Material	2	1	0	0	0
101	Electronic equipment	0	0	0	0	0
102	Transportation material	13	0	0	0	0
103	Timber and furniture	0	0	0	0	0
104	Paper products	14	0	0	0	1
105	Rubber Industry	2	2	0	0	1
106	Basic Chemicals	2	2	0	0	1
107	Oil Refining	0	10	0	0	2
108	Chemical, Iron and Perf.	9	16	1	0	2
109	Plastic Industry	0	1	0	0	0
110	Textile Industry	11	13	2	0	2
111	Clothes Manufacture	7	0	0	0	0
112	Leather Industry	1	4	1	0	2
113	Vegetable Processing	1	12	0	0	1
114	Animal Slaughtering	0	10	8	0	1
115	Dairy Industry	6	5	0	0	0
116	Sugar Refining Plant	0	0	0	0	0
117	Vegetable and animal oil	0	2	0	0	0
118	Other Food Factories	0	2	0	0	0
119	Manufacture Industry	0	0	0	0	0
120	Public Ind. Service	0	0	0	0	0
121	Civil Construction	0	0	0	0	0
122	Commerce	0	0	0	0	0
123	Transportation	3	4	1	0	2
124	Services	0	2	0	0	0
	Total Uruguay	**78**	**160**	**14**	**0**	**30**

Index